THE IMMERSER

Studying the Historical Jesus

It was once fashionable to claim that Jesus could not be known as a figure of history and that even if he could be known in that way the result would not be of interest for faith. Both contentions have been laid to rest over the past twenty years.

Scholarship has seen archaeological discoveries, advances in the study of Jewish and Hellenistic literature, a renewed interest in the social milieu of Judaism and Christianity, and critical investigation of the systematic relationship between those two religions (and others in the ancient world). In the midst of these discussions — and many others — Jesus has appeared again and again as a person who can be understood historically and who must be assessed before we can give any complete explanation of the history of the period in which he lived. As he and his movement are better understood, the nature of the faith that they pioneered has been more clearly defined.

Of course, the Jesus who is under investigation cannot simply be equated with whatever the Gospels say of him. The Gospels, composed in Greek a generation after Jesus' death, reflect the faith of early Christians who came to believe in him. Their belief included reference to historical data, but also included the interpretation of Jesus as it had developed after his time.

The critical tasks of coming to grips with the development of the New Testament, the nature of primitive Christian faith, and the historical profile of Jesus are all interrelated. The purpose of this series is to explore key questions concerning Jesus in recent discussion. Each author has already made an important contribution to the study of Jesus and writes for the series on the basis of expertise in the area addressed by his or her particular volume.

Of the many studies of Jesus that are available today, some are suspect in their treatment of primary sources and some do not engage the secondary literature appropriately. **Studying the Historical Jesus** is a series of contributions that are no less sound for being creative. Jesus is a figure of history as well as the focus of Christian theology: discussion of him should be accessible, rigorous, and interesting.

BRUCE CHILTON
Bard College

CRAIG A. EVANS
Trinity Western University

The Immerser

John the Baptist within Second Temple Judaism

Joan E. Taylor

William B. Eerdmans Publishing Company
Grand Rapids, Michigan / Cambridge, U.K.

255 Jefferson Ave. S.E., Grand Rapids, Michigan 49503 /
P.O. Box 163, Cambridge CB3 9PU U.K.

Printed in the United States of America

02 01 00 99 98 97 7 6 5 4 3 2 1

Library of Congress Cataloging-in-Publication Data

Taylor, Joan E.
The immerser : John the Baptist within Second Temple Judaism /
Joan E. Taylor.
p. cm. — (Studying the historical Jesus)
Includes bibliographical references.
ISBN 0-8028-4236-4 (paper : alk, paper)
1. John, the Baptist, Saint. I. Title. II. Series.
BS2456.T38 1997
232.9′4 — dc21 97-6258
CIP

For Paul,

and our little children,

Emily and Robert

Contents

Abbreviations

AB	Anchor Bible
ABD	D. N. Freedman, ed., *Anchor Bible Dictionary*
'Abot R. Nat.	*'Abot de Rabbi Nathan*
ABRL	Anchor Bible Reference Library
Adv. Haer.	Irenaeus, *Against Heresies*
Adv. Pelag.	Jerome, *Against Pelagius*
Ag. Ap.	Josephus, *Against Apion*
AJA	*American Journal of Archaeology*
ALGHJ	Arbeiten zur Literatur und Geschichte des hellenistischen Judentums
Ant.	Josephus, *Antiquities of the Jews*
ANTJ	Arbeiten zum Neuen Testament und Judentum
ANRW	*Aufstieg und Niedergang der römischen Welt*
2 Apoc. Bar.	Syriac *Apocalypse of Baruch*
Apost. Trad.	Hippolytus, *Apostolic Tradition*
ArBib	Aramaic Bible
As. Mos.	*Assumption of Moses*
ATANT	Abhandlungen zur Theologie des Alten und Neuen Testaments
AUSS	*Andrews University Seminary Studies*
b.	Babylonian Talmud tractate
BA	*Biblical Archaeologist*
BAFCS	The Book of Acts in Its First Century Setting
BAIAS	*Bulletin of the Anglo-Israel Archaeological Society*
BAR	*Biblical Archaeology Review*

Barn.	*Barnabas*
BBR	*Bulletin for Biblical Research*
BCE	Before the Common Era
BCR	Biblioteca di Cultura Religiosa
BDB	F. Brown, S. R. Driver, and C. A. Briggs, *A Hebrew and English Lexicon of the Old Testament*
Ber.	*Berakot*
Bib	*Biblica*
BibS(N)	Biblische Studien (Neukirchen)
BJS	Brown Judaic Studies
BR	*Bible Review*
BWANT	Beiträge zur Wissenschaft vom Alten und Neuen Testament
BZ	*Biblische Zeitschrift*
BZAW	Beihefte zur Zeitschrift für die alttestamentliche Wissenschaft
BZNW	Beihefte zur Zeitschrift für die neutestamentliche Wissenschaft
B. Qam.	*Baba Qamma*
CBQ	*Catholic Biblical Quarterly*
CD	Cairo Genizah text of the *Damascus Document*
CE	Common Era
ConJud	*Conservative Judaism*
Dem.	*Demai*
Dial.	Justin Martyr, *Dialogue with Trypho*
Did.	*Didache*
DJD	Discoveries in the Judaean Desert
DSS	Dead Sea Scrolls
Eccl. Rab.	*Ecclesiastes Rabbah*
'Ed.	*'Eduyyot*
EKKNT	Evangelisch-katholischer Kommentar zum Neuen Testament
EncJud	C. Roth, ed., *Encyclopaedia Judaica*
ExpTim	*Expository Times*
FolOr	*Folia Orientalia*
FRLANT	Forschungen zur Religion und Literatur des Alten und Neuen Testaments
Gen. Rab.	*Genesis Rabbah*
Giṭ.	*Giṭṭin*

GNS	Good News Studies
Haer.	Epiphanius, *Haereses*
Ḥag.	*Ḥagiga*
HeyJ	*Heythrop Journal*
Hist. Eccl.	Eusebius of Caesarea, *Ecclesiastical History*
HJ	*Historisches Jahrbuch*
HR	*History of Religions*
HTKNT	Herders theologischer Kommentar zum Neuen Testament
HTR	*Harvard Theological Review*
HUCA	*Hebrew Union College Annual*
Ḥul.	*Ḥullin*
IBS	*Irish Biblical Studies*
IEJ	*Israel Exploration Journal*
Ign. *Eph.*	Ignatius of Antioch, *Letter to the Ephesians*
Ign. *Smyrn.*	Ignatius of Antioch, *Letter to the Smyrnaeans*
IMJ	*Israel Museum Journal*
Int	*Interpretation*
JBL	*Journal of Biblical Literature*
Jdt.	Judith
JJS	*Journal of Jewish Studies*
JNES	*Journal of Near Eastern Studies*
JQR	*Jewish Quarterly Review*
JSJ	*Journal for the Study of Judaism*
JSNT	*Journal for the Study of the New Testament*
JSNTSup	Journal for the Study of the New Testament — Supplement Series
JSOT	*Journal for the Study of the Old Testament*
JSOTSup	Journal for the Study of the Old Testament — Supplement Series
JSP	*Journal for the Study of the Pseudepigrapha*
JSPSup	Journal for the Study of the Pseudepigrapha — Supplement Series
JTS	*Journal of Theological Studies*
Jud	*Judaica*
Kel.	*Kelim*
Ker.	*Keritot*
Ketub.	*Ketubot*
4 Kgdms.	4 Kingdoms (Greek version of 2 Kings)

Kil.	*Kil'ayim*
Lam. Rab.	*Lamentations Rabbah*
LCL	Loeb Classical Library
LEC	Library of Early Christianity
LSJ	H. G. Liddell and R. Scott, *A Greek-English Lexicon with a Supplement*, 9th ed., rev. and ed. H. S. Jones and R. McKenzie
LXX	Septuagint
m.	Mishnah tractate
1 Macc.	1 Maccabees
2 Macc.	2 Maccabees
3 Macc.	3 Maccabees
4 Macc.	4 Maccabees
Mak.	*Makkot*
Ma'aś. Š.	*Ma'aśer Šeni*
MB	*Le Monde de la Bible*
Meg.	*Megilla*
Menaḥ.	*Menaḥot*
Mid.	*Middot*
Miqw.	*Miqwa'ot*
MT	Masoretic Text
Naz.	*Nazir*
Neg.	*Nega'im*
Neot	*Neotestamentica*
Nid.	*Niddah*
NIGTC	New International Greek Testament Commentary
NJB	New Jerusalem Bible
NovT	*Novum Testamentum*
NRSV	New Revised Standard Version
NRT	*La nouvelle revue théologique*
NT	New Testament
NTAbh	Neutestamentliche Abhandlungen
NTOA	Novum Testamentum et Orbis Antiquus
NTS	*New Testament Studies*
NTTS	New Testament Tools and Studies
OCT	Oxford Centre Textbooks
Ohol.	*Oholot*
OT	Old Testament

OTP	J. H. Charlesworth, ed., *The Old Testament Pseudepigrapha*
OxBib	Oxford Bible Series
PAPS	*Proceedings of the American Philosophical Society*
par(r).	parallel(s) in the Gospels
PEQ	*Palestine Exploration Quarterly*
Pesaḥ.	*Pesaḥim*
Pesiq. R.	*Pesiqta Rabbati*
Pss. Sol.	*Psalms of Solomon*
Q	Quelle (sayings source used by Matthew and Luke)
1Q, 2Q, 3Q, etc.	Numbered caves of Qumran
1QH	*Thanksgiving Hymns* from Qumran Cave 1
1QPHab	Commentary *(pesher)* on Habakkuk from Qumran Cave 1
1QS	*Community Rule* from Qumran Cave 1
1QSa	Appendix A *(Rule of the Congregation)* to 1QS
4QJer^{b}	Second copy of Jeremiah from Qumran Cave 4
4QS^{b}	Second copy of *Community Rule* from Qumran Cave 4
4QS^{d}	Fourth copy of *Community Rule* from Qumran Cave 4
4QS^{e}	Fifth copy of *Community Rule* from Qumran Cave 4
Qidd.	*Qiddušin*
RB	*Revue biblique*
RSV	Revised Standard Version
RevQ	*Revue de Qumran*
Sanh.	*Sanhedrin*
SBL	Society for Biblical Literature
SBLDS	SBL Dissertation Series
SBLMS	SBL Monograph Series
SBLSP	SBL Seminar Papers
SBT	Studies in Biblical Theology
Šabb.	*Šabbat*
Šeb.	*Šebiʿit*
Šebu.	*Šebuʿot*
Šeqal.	*Šeqalim*
Sir.	Sirach, Wisdom of Jesus Son of
SJLA	Studies in Judaism in Late Antiquity
SJT	*Scottish Journal of Theology*
SSN	Studia Semitica Neerlandica

SNTSMS	Society for New Testament Studies Monograph Series
SR	*Studies in Religion/Sciences religieuses*
STDJ	Studies on the Texts of the Desert of Judah
Str-B	H. Strack and P. Billerbeck, *Kommentar zum Neuen Testament aus Talmud und Midrasch*
StudLit	*Studia Liturgica*
StudPost-Bib	Studia Post-Biblica
StudTheo	*Studia Theologica*
t.	Tosephta tractate
Ta'an	*Ta'anit*
T. 12 Patr.	*Testaments of the Twelve Patriarchs*
T. Levi	*Testament of Levi*
TDNT	G. Kittel and G. Friedrich, eds., *Theological Dictionary of the New Testament*
Ter.	*Terumot*
Tg. Ps.-J.	*Targum Pseudo-Jonathan*
Theo	*Theology*
Ṭohar.	*Ṭoharot*
TS	*Theological Studies*
TynBul	*Tyndale Bulletin*
USQR	*Union Seminary Quarterly Review*
v(v).	verse(s)
VC	*Vigiliae Christianae*
War	Josephus, *The Jewish War*
WMANT	Wissenschaftliche Monographien zum Alten und Neuen Testament
WUNT	Wissenschaftliche Untersuchungen zum Neuen Testament
y.	Jerusalem Talmud tractate
Yad.	*Yadayim*
Yebam.	*Yebamot*
Zebaḥ.	*Zebaḥim*
ZNW	*Zeitschrift für die neutestamentliche Wissenschaft*
ZTK	*Zeitschrift für Theologie und Kirche*

Acknowledgments

I would like to acknowledge first with great thanks the help of the editors, Bruce Chilton and Craig Evans, for their important comments on my typescript and for their acceptance of this work in their series on the historical Jesus.

I am especially grateful to Jacob Neusner, who made astute and important corrections to a draft version of Chapter 2 and who has generously sent advice, books, and articles that have been invaluable. My thanks also to Graham Stanton, who read through the entire first draft of this study and made extremely helpful suggestions on how it might be improved. I am indebted to Steve Mason, who meticulously read through Chapter 4 and provided a very helpful critique. Obviously, the views expressed in these pages are my own, but my work would have been much worse had it not been for the important assistance of these three.

Scholarship always builds on the work of others, and I am indebted to many people who have not only written on subjects useful to this study but also made comments that have been helpful, both to me personally and in the electronic discussion group IOUDAIOS. I am also indebted to a number of people who have helped in small or large ways with bibliographic material and corrections, including Herman Lichtenberger, Robert Webb, Geza Vermes, Paul Morris, and Philip Davies. My thanks to Hero Granger-Taylor of the British Museum for discussing in detail what John's attire may have been and for alerting me to the leather loincloths in the Museum's collection. My colleague at Waikato University, Dennis Green, has been helpful throughout. I am very grateful to Norman Franke for his invaluable German translations. Comments from the participants at the New Testament seminar at Harvard Divinity School in September 1996 on a paper that was substantially the basis for Chapter 2, were very important. I am grateful to all those who have noted my errors and omissions, especially Dr. Daniel C. Harlow of Eerdmans; any that remain are, of course, entirely my responsibility.

I am indebted to Waikato University for providing me with a Post-Doctoral Teaching and Research Fellowship in the Humanities from 1992 to 1993, especially to Doug Pratt, convener of the Religious Studies programme, and the Dean of Humanities, Peter Oettli. This position enabled me to begin the project. I am grateful also to the Federation of University Women for a Harriette Jenkins Award in 1994–95; to the interlibrary loan personnel of the Waikato University library, who have been patient and diligent at all times and very helpful in my searches; and also to Faye Schmidt, the Religious Studies secretary.

My great thanks go to my husband Paul, who discusses Second Temple Judaism with interest and who is becoming quite knowledgeable, even though this is far from his own specialty. I am lucky also to have had, through Paul's work, the experience of living in the Gambia, in a traditional culture so different from the Western cultures with which I am familiar. To discover a contemporary society perhaps closer in some ways to the societies of the ancient world has helped me very much in removing a few cultural blocks. Paul has been a source of great encouragement and support from the very beginning of this project. I could not have completed it so quickly without his doing all the things he does to ensure that I have time, space, and energy to work.

I would like to thank the other women at Waikato and elsewhere who are combining motherhood and scholarship and who have provided friendship and support in this difficult but rewarding undertaking. In particular, I am grateful to Dorothy Spiller, Aroha Yates-Smith, Anne McKim, and Kathryn Pelissier. Finally, I thank my little children, Emily and Robert, for helping me to keep everything in perspective and for grounding me in what is truly important in life.

Ἄφετε τὰ παιδία ἔρχεσθαι πρός με, μὴ κωλύετε αὐτά, τῶν γὰρ τοιούτων ἐστὶν ἡ βασιλεία τοῦ θεοῦ (Mark 10:14).

Joan E. Taylor,
Hamilton, New Zealand

Introduction

For several decades scholars have made a clear distinction between the Jesus of history and the Christ of faith. Jesus is understood primarily as a Jewish man active in a Jewish environment; he has become "Jesus the Jew," to use Geza Vermes's apt phrase.[1] What kind of Jewish man may yet be debated, but the importance of his historical identity and context is no longer disputed. Alongside this century's quest for the historical Jesus has been an interest in the historical John the Baptist.[2] Generally, attempts to place him in the context of Second Temple Judaism have been undertaken with a view to understanding Jesus or the early Church.[3] Indeed, it seems impossible not to consider John in

1. See G. Vermes, *The Gospel of Jesus the Jew* (London: SCM, 1981); idem, *Jesus the Jew: A Historian's Reading of the Gospels,* 2d ed. (London: SCM, 1983); idem, *The Religion of Jesus the Jew* (London: SCM, 1993). For a survey of research on the historical Jesus during the 1980's, see chapter one of J. H. Charlesworth, *Jesus within Judaism: New Light from Exciting Archaeological Discoveries* (New York: Doubleday, 1988). For a survey of major trends and interpretative issues in the study of Jesus, see W. R. Telford, "Major Trends and Interpretative Issues in the Study of Jesus," in *Studying the Historical Jesus: Evaluations of the State of Current Research,* ed. B. D. Chilton and C. A. Evans (Leiden: Brill, 1994) 33-74.

2. See J. Reumann, "The Quest for the Historical Baptist," in *Understanding the Sacred Text: Essays in Honor of Morton S. Enslin on the Hebrew Bible and Christian Beginnings,* ed. J. Reumann (Valley Forge, PA: Judson, 1972) 181-99.

3. See M. Dibelius, *Die urchristliche Überlieferung von Johannes dem Täufer* (Göttingen: Vandenhoeck & Ruprecht, 1911); M. Goguel, *Au seuil de l'évangile: Jean-Baptiste* (Paris: Payot, 1928); E. Lohmeyer, *Das Urchristentum 1: Johannes der Täufer* (Göttingen: Vandenhoeck & Ruprecht, 1932); C. H. Kraeling, *John the Baptist* (New

the light of subsequent events. The emergence of Christianity stands as one of the most influential phenomena of history. As Robert Webb notes in his recent study of John as prophet and baptizer, if John had not been recorded in the Gospels in relationship to Jesus, he would have been "the subject of a footnote or two in academic writing."[4]

Of course, it is one thing to state that John would not be very significant historically if he had not had some contact with Jesus, but it is another thing to accept the Gospels' presentation of John, in which he is a kind of proto-Christian pointing the way to Jesus as Messiah. The Gospel writers wish us to believe that John really had no importance whatsoever in his own right and that his importance was entirely the result of his witnessing to the arrival of the Messiah. This is stated most explicitly in the Fourth Gospel,[5] which illustrates precisely how the Church wished John to be remembered. John says of himself, "I am the voice of one crying in the wilderness, 'Make straight the way of the Lord'" (John 1:23). Of his baptism, John says, "I baptize with water, but among you stands one whom you do not know, he who comes after me. I am not worthy to untie the thong of his sandal" (John 1:26). John sees Jesus coming towards him and declares to everyone:

> See the lamb of God who takes away the sin of the world. This is he of whom I said, "After me comes a man who ranks ahead of me, because he was before me." I myself did not know him, but I came baptizing with water for this reason, that he might be revealed to Israel.
>
> And John bore witness saying, "I saw the Spirit descending from heaven like a dove, and it remained upon him. I myself did not know

York: Scribner, 1951); J. Steinmann, *Saint John the Baptist and the Desert Tradition* (New York: Harper, 1958); C. H. H. Scobie, *John the Baptist* (London: SCM, 1964); J. Schütz, *Johannes der Täufer* (Zürich: Zwingli, 1967); J. Becker, *Johannes der Täufer und Jesus von Nazareth* (Neukirchen-Vluyn: Neukirchener Verlag, 1972); E. Lupieri, *Giovanni Battista fra Storia e Leggenda* (Brescia: Paideia, 1988); J. Ernst, *Johannes der Täufer: Interpretation, Geschichte, Wirkungsgeschichte* (Berlin: de Gruyter, 1989); R. L. Webb, *John the Baptizer and Prophet: A Socio-Historical Study* (Sheffield: JSOT Press, 1991); J. P. Meier, *A Marginal Jew: Rethinking the Historical Jesus. Volume Two: Mentor, Message, and Miracles* (New York: Doubleday, 1994) 19-233. See also W. B. Tatum, *John the Baptist and Jesus: A Report of the Jesus Seminar* (Sonoma, CA: Polebridge, 1994).

4. Webb, *John the Baptizer and Prophet,* 19.

5. To avoid confusion, the Gospel of John will be referred to as "the Fourth Gospel."

> him, but the one who sent me to baptize with water said to me, 'The one on whom you see the Spirit descend and remain is the one who baptizes with the Holy Spirit.' And I myself have seen and have borne witness that this is the Son of God." (John 1:29-34)

John himself directs two of his disciples — Andrew and Peter — to Jesus by saying, "See. Here is the lamb of God" (John 1:35). Later, John states without any competitive undercurrent that Jesus must increase and he must decrease (John 3:30). He is simply the friend of the bridegroom (Jesus), who rejoices very much at hearing the bridegroom's voice (John 3:29).

The reasons that the writer of the Fourth Gospel portrayed John in the way that he did need not delay us at this early stage. It will suffice to say in these introductory remarks that this tradition is fairly well-known to be the culmination of a process that we can see beginning in the earliest complete gospel, the Gospel of Mark.[6] All the gospel writers seek to present John as a true prophet and baptizer, but in a narrowly defined way. His prophecy is understood to involve predictions of Jesus' imminent arrival as Messiah. His baptism of people in water is preparation for later Christian baptism in the Holy Spirit, resulting from the resurrection of Jesus as the Son of God.

Redaction-critical studies of the New Testament have helped us to distinguish how the Gospels manage to deal with John by making him more prone to consider Jesus the Messiah — by far his superior — with each edition of the material.[7] These studies have led to a general consensus about the way in which the Baptist material was shaped. In summary, the three synoptic Gospels — Mark, Matthew, and Luke — begin the account of Jesus' activity with his baptism in the river Jordan (Matt. 3:13-17; Mark 1:9-11; Luke 3:21-22), and according to Acts 1:21-22 the replacement of the deceased Judas Iscariot among the Twelve

6. I follow the scholarly consensus concerning the two-document hypothesis to explain the formation of the synoptic Gospels; see B. H. Streeter, *The Four Gospels: A Study of Origins* (London: Macmillan, 1924) 150-331. For Q, see J. S. Kloppenborg, *The Formation of Q: Trajectories in Ancient Wisdom Collections* (Philadelphia: Fortress, 1987) esp. 317-28; D. R. Catchpole, "The Beginning of Q: A Proposal," *NTS* 38 (1992) 205-21.

7. See E. Bammel, "The Baptist in Early Christian Tradition," *NTS* 18 (1971-72) 95-128; J. P. Meier, "John the Baptist in Matthew's Gospel," *JBL* 99/3 (1980) 383-405; W. Trilling, "Die Täufertradition bei Matthäus," *BZ* 3 (1959) 271-89; and esp. W. Wink, *John the Baptist in the Gospel Tradition* (Cambridge: Cambridge University Press, 1968).

Apostles had to be someone who had been with Jesus "from the baptism of John until the day when he [Jesus] was taken up from us." However, having admitted John's (and his baptism's) importance at the genesis of Christianity, the synoptic Gospels proceed, in various ways, to explain him away. In Mark 1:7-8 John predicts the coming of "one who is mightier than I," but does not specifically identify the coming one with the Messiah, let alone with Jesus. Matthew — that is, the writer of the Gospel of Matthew[8] — develops the Marcan story and has John demur before baptizing Jesus, so that Jesus has to convince him that it is necessary to "fulfill all righteousness" (Matt. 3:13-14). Luke minimizes any reference to the actual baptizing of Jesus by John, and the baptism of Jesus is referred to as having taken place "when all the people were baptized"; the baptism of Jesus is therefore assimilated to that of the throng. The vision experienced by Jesus, which Mark and Matthew place at the time of his baptism, becomes associated in Luke's Gospel with a prayer afterwards (Luke 3:21-22). In the didactic schema of the Fourth Gospel, John gladly identifies Jesus as the one he has expected (John 1:6-8; 19:37; cf. 3:22-30; 4:1-3).

Although all the implications have not been fully teased out, most recent studies conclude that John definitely baptized Jesus.[9] Ed Sanders, for instance, lists John's baptism as one of the surest facts we know about Jesus.[10] It is sure because it was so embarrassing to the early Church; by the second century, there were people in the Church who could argue that Jesus would have resisted any suggestion that he needed to be baptized. For example, in the *Gospel of the Nazareans,* dated to the second century, Jesus' mother and brothers urge Jesus to come to John's

8. In this study, the names "Matthew," "Luke," and "Mark" are meant to refer to the authors of the Gospels of Matthew, Luke, and Mark respectively, not to actual individuals with these names.

9. Even Rudolf Bultmann, who was wary of stating that many historical facts about Jesus could be known, noted that Jesus must have been baptized by John; see R. Bultmann, *The History of the Synoptic Tradition* (Oxford: Blackwell, 1963) 47. The view that John and Jesus never met, argued by E. Haenchen, *Der Weg Jesu: Eine Erklärung des Markus-Evangeliums und der kanonischen Parallelen* (Berlin: de Gruyter, 1968) 60-63 and M. S. Enslin, "John and Jesus," *ZNW* 66 (1975) 1-18, has generally failed to convince; see R. L. Webb, "John the Baptist and his Relationship to Jesus," in *Studying the Historical Jesus: Evaluations of the State of Current Research,* ed. B. D. Chilton and C. A. Evans (Leiden: Brill, 1994) 214-99.

10. E. P. Sanders, *Jesus and Judaism* (Philadelphia: Fortress, 1985) 11; idem, *The Historical Figure of Jesus* (London: Penguin, 1993) 92-94.

baptism, and he replies: "How have I sinned, that I would need to be baptized by him?"[11] Indeed, there was an awkward awareness in the early Church that John's baptism had something to do with the remission of sins; so, if Jesus was baptized, did that mean he needed to have his sins remitted? In view of this difficulty, Jesus' baptism by John has come to be understood as one of the key problems that the early Church needed to "explain" in the Gospels. It was this problem that gave rise to the apologetic modifications of the Baptist story.[12] No one would have invented something so painfully hard to justify.

Since mention of John the Baptist in the New Testament is obviously overlaid with a developing Christian insistence on Jesus' superiority, we can suppose that the issue of John himself was a problem for the early Church. Clearly, John was not a nobody in his time, and the Gospels accord him respect. However, John was not permitted too much respect; people had to know his place. As John Meier states, most often "the interpretation aims at neutralizing the Baptist's independence to make him safe for Christianity."[13]

Significantly, however, we do have one independent document that informs us about John and that presents a striking picture at once very similar to the Gospels' portrayals and yet very different from them in various ways. John is described in glowing terms by the Jewish historian Josephus in his work *The Antiquities of the Jews*, which was written in 93-94 CE. In the context of Josephus' narrative, the report is a flashback. In 37 CE, Herod Antipas had gone to war with the Nabatean king Aretas and suffered a crushing defeat. Josephus, who was no great supporter of the Herodian dynasty, records what he must have heard as a reason to account for the destruction of Antipas' army. At a time when people believed that divine beings organized history, what heinous deed had Antipas done that could explain such a terrible military annihilation? The passage reads as follows:

> To some of the Jews it seemed that Herod's army was very justly destroyed by God, who was punishing him to avenge John, called

11. See the *Gospel of the Nazareans*, in *New Testament Apocrypha I: Gospels and Related Writings*, ed. W. Schneemelcher; English trans. ed. R. McL. Wilson (Cambridge: Clarke, 1991) 160, frag. 2 (Jerome, *Adv. Pelag.* III 2).

12. So Wink, *Gospel Tradition*, 107; Kraeling, *John the Baptist*, 161-63.

13. Meier, "Matthew's Gospel," 384.

"Immerser." For Herod killed him, although he was a good man who was exhorting the Jews to practice virtue and righteousness towards each other and to act with piety towards God, and [thereafter] to come together for immersion. Because then indeed the immersion would now appear acceptable to Him, if it was not about pleading forgiveness for certain sins they had done, but for a purification of the body, now that the soul had been cleansed already by righteousness.

And when the others [i.e., "some of the Jews"] gathered together, because they were indeed excited to the highest degree by hearing his teaching, Herod feared that such great persuasiveness over the people might lead to some kind of conflict, for they looked as if they would do everything by his advice. [He thought it] much better to get rid [of John] before some innovation from him took place, striking first to remove [the possibility of any] change coming about, so as not to regret getting into complicated affairs.

Therefore, on account of the suspicion of Herod, John was sent in chains to Machaerus . . . and there he was killed.

But for the Jews, the belief came about that with the destruction of the army God was wishing to harm Herod as vengeance for [the death of] that man.

Josephus, *Antiquities* 18.116-19[14]

It is clear from this that some Jews thought very highly of John and considered him to be divinely approved. Herod Antipas acted in direct contradiction of the will of God in having John killed and therefore suffered divine vengeance. Josephus himself states that John was a good man, and he appears to agree with his sources that Herod Antipas was rightly punished. We will consider Josephus' statement at numerous times in the present study.

Despite the current scholarly recognition that John must have been a significant and respected man at the time of Jesus, the Gospels' picture of John as essentially a preparatory and rather severe figure remains. John is viewed as a preacher of apocalyptic doom who baptized Jews in expectation of judgment by a stern God. As the theologian Edward Schillebeeckx states, "John is the penitential preacher prophetically announcing the imminent judgement of God. The future here

14. For the authenticity of the passage see Meier, *Marginal Jew,* vol. 2, 19-20.

is God's wrath, his inexorable sentence."[15] The salvation of those accepted by God is not considered to be a key element of John's prophecy, and yet, given the apocalyptic milieu of Judaism in which John is surely to be understood, doom is necessarily balanced by salvation. God destroys the wicked in fire and lovingly admits the (resurrected) righteous into a life of perfect happiness. To many Christian scholars, John's God is an angry judge, while Jesus' God is a loving father. This dichotomy seems to derive ultimately from deep-seated Christian preconceptions about the nature of the "Old Testament God," whom the "New Testament God" apparently supersedes. But the two are in fact one. In the eschatological schema shared by John and Jesus, God metes out punishment for the wicked and reward for the righteous; the one does not exist without the other. Indeed, against the multilayered complexity of the Gospels' depiction of Jesus, John can come across in the literature as one-dimensional and severe. He is not allowed to show much compassion. Almost all the references to John in the New Testament are designed to ensure that the readers and hearers of the Gospels know where to put John in the scheme of things, and nothing about his presentation is allowed to indicate that he was in any way a match for Jesus. On this view, John is seen, at best, to represent how Judaism should have been, as far as the Church saw it — primed and ready to be eclipsed by Christianity. This presentation is, of course, extremely limiting and gives us no real indication of the historical John; yet the ancient Christian view of John continues to influence how he is seen today. Despite the recognition that the Gospel writers were engaged in extensive damage control as regards Jesus' relationship with John, an exploration of what exactly was so potentially damaging has not been fully undertaken, and John's character remains established as grim.

A central issue for Christian theologians has been not the implication of Jesus' baptism by John and Jesus' acceptance of John's teaching, but the general problem of Jesus' subordination to John — at least during some period of Jesus' life. The Gospel writers were certainly at pains to reverse this subordination. Historically, however, we may conjecture that the reasons for reconstructing John in a harmless way may have had something to do with the substance of John's predictions as

15. E. Schillebeeckx, *Jesus: An Experiment in Christology* (New York: Seabury, 1979) 127.

well, and also with the nature of his baptism.[16] Jesus and his first disciples may have accepted John's teaching and baptism, but with the new consciousness arising from the perception of Jesus as resurrected Lord, the early Church as a whole may not have done so. John's views may not have been popular in the increasingly Gentile Christian community as it spread out to encompass the world.

My purpose in this study is to provide a concise and accessible argument that redefines John as a Jewish immerser and teacher of righteousness who was accepted by many Jews as an exceptionally good and faithful man and regarded by some — including Jesus — as a prophet. As I hope to show, John may be seen as a building block on which the Church would be constructed, but he was also very much a Jew of his time and place. John could never have imagined that the Church would subsume his message. Rather, as will be argued in this study, he wished to point people towards a renewed commitment to Torah and total obedience of the heart to God in the light of eschatological events soon to unfold.

In terms of the scope of this study, I will not repeat the systematic examinations of John the Baptist in the literature (New Testament, Josephus, apocryphal and Gnostic writings, Mandaean material, and patristic texts); these have been undertaken by Josef Ernst, Walter Wink, Ernst Bammel, Robert Webb, and Edmondo Lupieri.[17] The basic conclusion of these excellent studies of the Baptist tradition-history suggests that only the New Testament material and the evidence of Josephus (excluding the Slavonic version) are historically valuable. Although traditions found in later literature may be important and should not be completely ignored, examinations of the Baptist material have shown

16. That John's baptism had to do with bodily purification from ritual uncleanness following repentance has been proposed by B. D. Chilton, *Judaic Approaches to the Gospels* (Atlanta: Scholars Press, 1994) 1-37 and will be argued in detail below.

17. Ernst, *Johannes der Täufer;* Wink, *Gospel Tradition;* Bammel, "The Baptist in Early Christian Tradition"; Webb, *John the Baptizer and Prophet;* Lupieri, *Giovanni Battista.* Lupieri in particular examines the evidence of later Mandaean literature. See also Tatum, *John the Baptist and Jesus,* 84-104, who notes, "The fragmentary gospels of the Ebionites, the Nazoreans, and the Hebrews, the Infancy Gospel of James, and the Mandaean writings contain nothing of value for understanding JB (John the Baptist)" (p. 104). See also P. W. Hollenbach, "The Conversion of Jesus: From Jesus the Baptizer to Jesus the Healer," *ANRW* II.25.1, 888-90.The theory that parts of the book of Revelation originate with John's tradition will also not be considered. For this theory see J. Massyngberde Ford, *Revelation: Introduction, Translation, Commentary,* AB 38 (Garden City, NY: Doubleday, 1975) 28-37.

how later groups molded John to fit their own particular purposes and have demonstrated that later traditions were, in the main, very heavily dependent on the canonical New Testament.

This study is not a "life of John." We can know very little about John as a person. The most biographical section of the New Testament as far as John is concerned — the infancy narrative of Luke (1:5-80) — is generally held to be a literary construct intent on teaching Christians that John was inferior to Jesus at the very start, as Raymond Brown has convincingly argued.[18] Even John the Baptist's conception "prepares the way" for that of Jesus, but it remains inferior. Jesus' conception without a male parent is more miraculous than John's conception by aged, barren parents. Elizabeth praises Mary as the "mother of my Lord" and declares her unworthiness to be visited by her (in this story) cousin; John jumps with happiness in Elizabeth's womb when the fetal Jesus draws close; the angel Gabriel announces both conceptions, indicating that both John and Jesus are part of a unified plan of salvation. The very familial relationship between Jesus and John (Luke 1:36) testifies to their closeness and serves to make John either an "incipient Christian," as Brown calls him, or a figure situated "firmly within the Christian sphere."[19] To what extent any historical material concerning John is contained in the Lucan infancy narrative may be questioned. Given the purpose of the story as a whole, it is probably best to adopt a highly cautious approach to the material. Details of the infancy story will be looked at in this study where relevant, but the story as such will not be the subject of a detailed discussion.

18. See R. E. Brown, *The Birth of the Messiah: A Commentary on the Infancy Narratives in Matthew and Luke* (London: Chapman, 1977) esp. 256-85, 330-92. It has been suggested that the infancy story of John is based on written material from the Baptist movement; so P. Winter, "The Cultural Background for the Narratives in Luke I–II," *JQR* 45 (1954) 159-67, 230-42, 287; idem, "The Proto-Source of Luke 1," *NovT* 1 (1956) 184-99; cf. J. A. Fitzmyer, *The Gospel According to Luke I–IX: Introduction, Translation, and Notes* (Garden City, NY: Doubleday, 1981) 303-30; Scobie, *John the Baptist;* and Kraeling, *John the Baptist.* This notion, however, is problematic; see S. Ferris, *The Hymns of Luke's Infancy Narratives: Their Origin, Meaning and Significance* (Sheffield: JSOT Press, 1985) 86-98, and Bammel, "The Baptist in Early Christian Tradition," 96. Even if some material derives from the oral tradition of John's disciples — so Wink, *Gospel Tradition,* 58-81 — it has been so heavily worked over by a Christian author that it is hard to claim any historical value for the story at all. For a brief summary of the problem, see Tatum, *John the Baptist and Jesus,* 22-23, 112-14.

19. Brown, *Birth of the Messiah,* 284-85.

Of key importance throughout this study is where John might fit within the framework of Second Temple Judaism. In the fractured universe of first-century Jewish ideas and lifestyles, where can John be placed? Especially since the discovery of the Dead Sea Scrolls, it has been suggested that John might have been an Essene. This suggestion will be considered in Chapter 1. It will be argued that there is no strong evidence that John and the Essenes were ever linked in any way.

We will then explore why John was called "the Immerser" or "the Baptist" and consider the specific characteristics of his immersion that made it both unique and yet also understandable in the light of other Jewish immersions and purification rituals. John's immersion is not explicated in the Gospel accounts; it did not need to be for the evangelists' purposes. At any rate, it was, in the Christian view, completely superseded by Christian baptism, which involved the gift of the Holy Spirit. It had historical significance, especially in regard to the authenticating vision of Jesus and the origins of his mission, but we need not dwell on this. The immersion of John was irrelevant in a Gentile Christian community. If Christians like Philip and Apollos continued to immerse, as John had, in line with Jewish concepts of ritual purity, they were soon followed by others who completed true Christian baptism with the imparting of the Spirit.

In Chapter 3 we will consider John as a teacher and explore the essential components of his teaching. In the Gospels, John is not presented as a teacher, but rather more nebulously as a prophet. Mark, Matthew, and the Fourth Gospel provide no serious indications that John taught anything very much. But this impression is not maintained by Luke, who alone includes traditions of John's specific teaching (Luke 3:10-14; cf. 11:1).[20] The only other clue we have to the perception of John as a teacher is that the Gospels continually refer to "disciples" (μαθηταί) of John (Mark 2:18; 6:28; Matt. 9:14; 11:2; 14:12; Luke 5:33; 7:18; John 1:22, 32, 35, 37; 3:25, 27). If a man has disciples then he is a teacher. Strictly speaking, μαθητής (masc.) or μαθήτρια (fem.) means "learner, student," deriving from the verb μανθάνω, "learn, study."[21] John is fittingly addressed as "teacher" (διδάσκαλε, Luke 3:12) or, in

20. For the authenticity of this section, see Webb, *John the Baptizer and Prophet,* 358-59, n. 16.

21. For a detailed discussion of μαθητής in Hellenistic, Jewish, and Christian literature, see K. H. Rengstorf, "μαθητής," *TDNT* 4 (1967) 415-61.

Aramaic and Hebrew, "rabbi" (John 3:26).[22] Yet John's identity as a teacher seems to have been very substantially downplayed in the New Testament material, where the view that he was a prophet who directed people to Jesus as the salvific Messiah obliterates nearly all other dimensions of the historical John. The predictive or "prophetic" elements of his teaching will also be discussed in this chapter.

We will then consider John's relationship with another "sect" or philosophical school of Second Temple Judaism: the Pharisees. In Christian discourse on John, John and the Pharisees are generally considered to have been conceptually opposed. It will be argued that there are no sound reasons to place the Pharisees in opposition to John and that there are, in fact, good reasons to suppose that John's relationship with the Pharisees was positive. The notion that the Pharisees were in charge of judicial processes in the land of Israel and in league with the chief priests in opposing both John and Jesus will be directly challenged.

In this study, the notion that John was considered a prophet by people of his age will be accepted, but there will be no attempt to categorize him in accordance with any current scholarly typology, for reasons that will be explained in Chapter 5. Rather, we will question whether the term "prophet" is self-evident and explore what people of the age might have understood John to be by calling him a prophet.

Finally, we will briefly and tentatively explore the relationship between John and Jesus. It is a basic presupposition of this study that we can understand Jesus better if we understand John. It will be argued that Jesus greatly esteemed John and probably identified him as Elijah the prophet *redivivus.* There may have been an understanding that Elijah would suffer at the hands of wicked men, identified by Jesus as being the chief priests and Herod Antipas. We cannot know for sure why Jesus came to John for immersion; but if Jesus did place himself among the unrighteous in need of repentance and immersion, this may not have been uncharacteristic of his self-assessment. According to the tradition of Mark's Gospel, Jesus snapped to a man who addressed him as "good teacher," "Why do you call me good? No one is good but God alone!" (Mark 10:18 = Luke 18:19; cf. Matt. 19:17). Jesus was without a doubt deeply impressed by John and sought to follow his example and his

22. See Vermes, *Jesus the Jew,* 115 for the meaning of "rabbi" in the first centuries. Rengstorf notes, "There is . . . no μαθητής without a διδάσκαλος. The process involves a corresponding personal relation" (Rengstorf, "μαθητής," 416).

teaching, bringing the same message of the coming of the kingdom of God and the urgency of repentance. Jesus himself may have been an "Immerser," and he appears to have greatly expanded on John's essential teaching, accepting both John's immersion and teaching as authoritative. Yet it cannot be argued that Jesus simply continued John's message as a disciple; Jesus was a "prophet" in his own right, legitimated by God (in his own experience) at his immersion by John.

A principal aim of this discussion is to provide John with a context, so that he may become a less isolated figure. That John had a social context is a reality overlooked by most of the primary literary material about him. In the Lucan narrative, he appears in the wilderness completely alone — untaught, unmarried, his old father and mother surely dead, without connection to any place, relatives, or sects. At the start of Mark's Gospel, he is both adopted by the Church and separated from his Jewish context. He stands "at the beginning of the good news of Jesus the Messiah, the Son of God" (Mark 1:1), as the messenger who will prepare his way (Mark 1:2; cf. Mal. 3:1; Isa. 40:3). John has no background; he simply appears (cf. Matt. 3:1).

In the same way, John appears abruptly as a witness at the beginning of the Fourth Gospel. The beautiful prologue to the Fourth Gospel is designed to culminate in a relativizing appraisal of John the Baptist: "There came a man sent from God whose name was John. He came as a witness to the light so that everyone might believe through him. He was not the light, but he came to bear witness to the light" (John 1:6-8). By seeing John in isolation, Gentile Christians could partially detach him from the rest of Judaism and include him in an honorary way as part of the Church even though, strictly speaking, they recognized that he preceded Jesus and did not live to see the salvific events of Jesus' crucifixion and resurrection. Considering him a prophet, they understood him to have known by means of his divinely inspired foresight all about what would take place.

The Gospels' depiction of John was designed to sever him from the Jewish world around him so that his characterization as the precursor and pointer to Jesus would not be blurred by distractions. In terms of history, however, John's context cannot have been simply the desert. He cannot have come into existence in some magical way as a voice in the wilderness calling people to look towards Jesus. This is the stuff of myth. The real John was probably far more a man of his age. We can assume that he operated with an awareness of society and with purposes that took into account the events of his time. His execution by Herod Antipas suggests that the world beyond the wilderness considered his activity deeply relevant.

The material at our disposal on John is not extensive, and much will never be known. This modest study can only propose a few historical suggestions and amendments. All historical reconstruction remains at best good guesswork based on the data at our disposal, and throughout this examination the provisional nature of the conclusions must always be borne in mind. I hope that this work will lead to new studies, critiques, and evaluations. It is designed to provoke further discussion rather than to provide definitive solutions concerning the elusive figure who appeared at the genesis of Christianity.

CHAPTER 1

John and the Essenes

Ever since the discovery of the first of the Dead Sea Scrolls (DSS) in 1947 and their subsequent piecemeal publication, scholars have pondered the possible relationship between John the Baptist and the people — often called "the Qumran community" — who wrote the sectarian documents among the Scrolls. It has sometimes been suggested that there are intriguing parallels between John and this community, usually identified as Essene in character.[1] As James VanderKam has recently noted in regard to the image of John we can form from the New Testament, a "great deal of this picture is reminiscent of the Qumran community."[2] In other words, in placing John within the context of

1. This is not to say that the sectarian documents or communities that produced them were homogeneous in all respects. See, for the classic exposition, A. Dupont-Sommer, *The Jewish Sect of Qumran and the Essenes: New Studies on the Dead Sea Scrolls* (London: Vallentine, 1954) and, more recently, T. Beall, *Josephus' Description of the Essenes Illustrated by the Dead Sea Scrolls* (Cambridge: Cambridge University Press, 1988); also E. P. Sanders, *Judaism: Practice and Belief 63 BCE–66 CE* (London: SCM, 1992) 24-25, 341-79; G. Vermes, *The Dead Sea Scrolls in English*, 4th ed. (Harmondsworth: Penguin, 1995) xxix-xxxii, 20-22, and for a concise statement, J. C. VanderKam, "The Dead Sea Scrolls and Christianity," in *Understanding the Dead Sea Scrolls: A Reader from the Biblical Archaeology Review*, ed. H. Shanks (New York: Random House, 1992) 181-202.

2. VanderKam, "The Dead Sea Scrolls and Christianity," 190. The literature comparing John and Qumran is huge, but for a list of noteworthy examples see R. L. Webb, *John the Baptizer and Prophet: A Socio-Historical Study* (Sheffield: JSOT Press, 1991) 213 n. 137. In summing up the results of the Jesus Seminar on John, W. B. Tatum states, "At one time John himself may have been an Essene, even if not a member, or former

Second Temple Judaism, it is to the Essenes that scholars have generally looked.

However, it is worth asking whether interesting parallels are really enough to form a basis for linking John and the Essenes. Even if parallels between John and the Essenes can be traced, they may not necessarily mean that we can trace influence from one group to another. Moreover, we would have to prove not only that parallels exist between John and the Essenes, but also that these parallels are neither found in regard to other groups within Second Temple Judaism nor traceable to common source material. The parallels between John and the Essenes would have to be unique and explicable only in terms of direct relationship.

In this chapter we will look at a few of the more important parallels that have been identified between John and the Essenes and judge whether these withstand scrutiny. Are these really areas of unique correlation between John and the Essenes? As I hope to show, the evidence is far from persuasive. Before proceeding, however, a brief overview of the Essenes in our sources may help with our study.

The Essenes

The Essenes are fairly well described in ancient sources, all dating from the first century.[3] The earliest evidence comes from Philo of Alexandria, who writes about them in two different places (ca. 35-45 CE). In his *Hypothetica* (11.1-18) he describes them as living in many cities and villages of Judea. They reside together in communes in which there is no private property (houses, slaves, cattle, etc.); even clothing is group owned. They eat communally. They work at horticulture, animal

member, of the community of Essenes at Qumran. At the time of his initial appearing and subsequent ministry, however, John was . . . neither an Essene nor a lone sage and holy man like Bannus — mentioned by Josephus — who also withdrew into the wilderness to live an ascetic style of life" (W. B. Tatum, *John the Baptist and Jesus: A Report of the Jesus Seminar* [Sonoma, CA: Polebridge, 1994] 20).

3. See for a detailed account G. Vermes and M. Goodman, *The Essenes according to the Classical Sources* (Sheffield: JSOT Press, 1989). For a comparison between Josephus and 1QS, see Beall, *Josephus' Description of the Essenes.*

husbandry, or crafts, and their income is put into a common fund administered by a treasurer. They are celibate old men. The very old and infirm are looked after by the others as if they were fathers. In *Every Good Man Is Free* (75–91), Philo notes that there are over 4,000 Essenes in Palestinian Syria. Here he states that they live in villages and avoid cities. They live together in communes in which there is no private property. They do not own slaves. They eat communally. They work on the land or on crafts. They do not make weapons, engage in business, or amass wealth. They do not offer sacrifices at the Temple. They study Scripture, especially on the Sabbath, when they assemble in orderly rows, youngest to eldest. They interpret Scripture allegorically. They maintain a constant state of ritual purity. They do not swear oaths. They welcome visitors of their own sect. Elder men are respected as fathers. They are treated by the authorities as self-governing.

Writing in ca. 77 CE, some years after the quashing of the Jewish revolt against Rome and the destruction of the Temple, Pliny the Elder (*Natural History* 5.15.73) notes simply that Essenes live on the western shore of the Dead Sea above Engeddi. They are celibate males, living communally, with no private property. It may be noted at this stage that the Essenes mentioned by Pliny are not located at the site of Qumran adjacent to caves where some of the DSS were discovered, for two reasons: first, Engeddi is described as being physically below the place where the Essenes lived; second, the site of Qumran was abandoned in ca. 70 CE, and Pliny's reference is clearly to a situation after this date (Engeddi is "now like Jerusalem a heap of ashes" [*Natural History* 70]).

In his work *The Jewish War* the first-century Jewish historian Josephus, writing in ca. 75 CE, mentions a certain Essene named John in the revolt against Rome (*War* 2.567) and gives us a detailed description of the Essenes (*War* 2.119-161), apparently deriving from someone who was closely involved in the sect or from his own investigative experience with it. He states that there are many Essenes in every town. They are celibate and very self-controlled males who live in communes, with communal ownership. They live to a great age. They despise wealth. They are all brothers with a single father. They keep their skin unoiled, regard the body as base and transient, and think that our immortal souls get entangled with it. In death, they believe their souls will go to a lovely place, but the souls of others will go to a dark dungeon of never ending punishment. They dress in white and never get a new garment or pair of shoes till one is worn out. They welcome visitors of their own sect and therefore travel with nothing but weapons (in case of highway robbery). They elect community officers, including one for visitors. They have four grades; a senior member will bathe if touched by a less pure junior member. They do nothing without orders from their superiors, except charitable acts, and presents to relatives are allowed only with permission.

They pray before dawn (to the east/sun). They work at crafts till the fifth hour and then assemble, wearing linen loincloths. They immerse in cold water and then put on their white garments, assemble in a special room, and eat communally a meal (of loaves). A priest says grace before and after the meal. Then they take off their white garments and go to work. In the evening they do the same, along with visitors. At meals they speak in turn and are generally rather quiet; no one will speak if most want silence. They will not spit in an assembly or to the right. They do not swear oaths. They study the Scriptures and also medicinal roots and minerals. They are very careful not to work on the Sabbath, and on that day they will not pick up any container or relieve themselves. On other days, when they need to relieve themselves, they go out to some uncultivated area and dig a hole and do it there, very modestly. They always wash afterwards.

A new member of Josephus' Essenes has to be on probation for a year and is given only a hatchet (for digging a toilet hole), a linen loincloth (for immersion and work), and a white garment. After a year he can immerse in their special purification water, but he cannot join in communal meals for another two years, and then only after taking great vows of morality, obedience, self-control, and secrecy. Those guilty of serious crimes are expelled, which is tantamount to death by starvation, but sometimes they are taken back out of compassion. The Essenes have their own court of no less than 100 men to decide verdicts. Anyone blaspheming God or Moses is punished with death. Josephus notes that many of them were tortured to death by the Romans but showed great courage. Some of those well-versed in sacred books, purification, and the sayings of the prophets claim to predict the future and seldom err. Josephus also notes here that there is another order of Essenes who marry for the sake of procreation but who are otherwise the same as those he has described.

In his later historical work, *The Antiquities of the Jews* (written in ca. 93-94 CE), Josephus notes that Essenes could interpret dreams (*Ant.*

17.346-47, on Simon's interpretation of Archelaus' dream) and predict the future (*Ant.* 13.311-13, on Judas' prophecy concerning Antigonus; cf. *Ant.* 15.370-79, on Manaēmus' predictions about Herod). They are fatalistic, believing that everything is determined by God (*Ant.* 13.171-73). There are 4,000 Essenes (celibate men) who live communally with group ownership of property supervised by officers. They do not want slaves, do not sacrifice in the Temple, are excluded from the common court there, and believe in the immortality of souls.

The picture we get from these three independent sources is remarkably consistent. It also coheres with the evidence of the sectarian DSS in many pertinent ways, especially as regards one of the two major documents: the *Community Rule* (1QS), though it may be noted that currently in scholarship there is an ultra-skeptical reaction against a previous scholarly consensus that 1QS is an Essene document.[4] It is impossible here to do justice to the similarities between 1QS and the descriptions of Essenes in the classical sources, but one may note that in the *Community Rule* we appear to have a celibate group of males (women and children are not mentioned) who live together with shared property (1QS 1:11-12; 5:1-22; 6:16-23), have a special communal meal of great purity (1QS 3:4-5; 5:13-14; 6:2, 25; 7:2-3; cf. CD 10:10-13), engage in sectarian rites of purification, and follow strict procedures for

4. The most serious challenge to the Essene identification has come from Norman Golb, who argues that the documents come from a Jerusalem library and that the nearby settlement of Qumran is not an Essene "monastery" but a fortress. See N. Golb, "The Problem of Origin and Identification of the Dead Sea Scrolls," *Proceedings of the American Philosophical Society* 124 (1980) 1-24; idem, "Who Hid the Dead Sea Scrolls?" *BA* 48 (1985) 68-82; idem, "Khirbet Qumran and the Manuscripts of the Judaean Wilderness: Observations on the Logic of their Investigation," *JNES* 49 (1990) 103-14; idem, *Who Wrote the Dead Sea Scrolls? The Search for the Secret of Qumran* (New York: Scribner, 1995). Pertinent reasons to doubt the Essene identification have also been explored by A. D. Crown and L. Cansdale, "Qumran: Was it an Essene Settlement?" *BAR* 20/5 (1994) 24-35, 73-78. However, these and other objections to the Essene hypothesis may better address the issue of a narrowness of thinking in regard to Essenes, in that they have been seen too much as forming a monolithic movement modeled on Christian monasticism of a later time. Moreover, the DSS comprise a library, and there is no reason to suppose that every document among them is Essene, even if the main sectarian documents are to be identified as such. In addition, these rival hypotheses do not take adequate account of the idiosyncratic literary purposes of our classical authors, and they overlook the striking correspondences in favor of a few apparent anomalies. For a critique of Golb, see T. H. Lim, "The Qumran Scrolls: Two Hypotheses," *SR* 21/4 (1992) 455-66.

new entrants (1QS 6:13-23). They find substitutes for the Temple rites and reject the cultus. They are very self-controlled, modest, and deferential to the elders; they are bound by rigorous rules of conduct and sit in order (1QS 6:10-13). Even the rule not to spit in an assembly is found here (1QS 7:13).

The *Community Rule* exists in ten copies.[5] There is in addition another rule book, the *Damascus Document* (CD), extant in nine copies, that differs in numerous ways from the *Community Rule* but that nevertheless seems to relate to a group of similarly minded men; in this case the members do marry, keep slaves, and even sacrifice sometimes in the Temple. Josephus describes, albeit cursorily, another group of marrying Essenes. The Essene group he was (more) familiar with was a celibate male commune probably somewhere in a town (possibly Jerusalem); it was not that of Qumran. The other sectarian documents of the DSS indicate considerable diversity of thought and practice in different groups, but given the comparable model of early Christianity, this may be expected. Essene groups may have differed in numerous respects in different places at different times, but there is no reason to doubt that the DSS contain alongside the many biblical and other writings some key Essene documents.[6]

Before beginning the discussion proper concerning John's relationship with the Essenes, we should highlight a key characteristic of John that would be completely out of place if he were (or had been at one time) part of the Essene movement. Our sources describe the Essenes as comprised of groups of men who had self-consciously separated from other Jews and bound themselves together by a complex set of rules focused on communal living and shared resources, purification, and a pure meal. The rules ensured that each member lived a pious and pure life. By keeping to the rules and by truly worshipping God correctly, each member (and his family, if married) had the assurance of salvation. As for John, he apparently did not live at an Essene settlement (let alone at Qumran). He was a loner, whereas the Essenes appear to have been concerned with living in community. In fact, nothing suggests that John wished to found a sect, quasi-Essene

5. See Vermes, *The Dead Sea Scrolls in English,* 4th ed., xxxi.

6. They may also contain Zadokite or Sadducee texts; see L. Schiffman, *Reclaiming the Dead Sea Scrolls: The History of Judaism, the Background of Christianity, the Lost Library of Qumran* (Philadelphia/Jerusalem: Jewish Publication Society, 1994).

or otherwise.[7] Even allowing for considerable diversity within the Essene movement as evidenced by material as different as the *Damascus Document* and the *Community Rule,* the very fact that these sources define a distinctive set of community norms sets them in striking contrast to what we find in the independent presentation of John in Josephus' account and in the Gospels.

Scholars who think that John was an Essene (or former Essene) sometimes stress the similarities and attribute any differences to his supposed status as a "non-orthodox" member of the sect.[8] There is a widespread tendency to identify the Qumran community as the definitive Essene community, when in fact we have no way of knowing whether the Qumran group was mainstream or marginal in relation to the larger Essene movement. Otto Betz has suggested that John may once have been a member of the Qumran community but later separated from it to pursue an independent career.[9] Daniel Schwartz has stated that whether or not John spent any time at Qumran, "it is clear that this ascetic community by the Dead Sea shows us the setting according to which he is to be understood."[10] Schwartz usefully sum-

7. Contra Webb, *John the Baptizer and Prophet,* 197-202; J. Steinmann, *Saint John the Baptist and the Desert Tradition* (New York: Harper, 1958) 5; cf. W. Wink, *John the Baptist in the Gospel Tradition* (Cambridge: Cambridge University Press, 1968) 107.

8. D. Flusser, "The Baptism of John and the Dead Sea Sect," in *Essays on the Dead Sea Scrolls: In Memory of E. L. Sukenik,* ed. C. Rabin and Y. Yadin (Jerusalem: Hekhal Ha-Sefer, 1961) 209-38 (Hebrew); idem, *Judaism and the Origins of Christianity* (Jerusalem: Magnes, 1988) 713.

9. O. Betz, "Was John the Baptist an Essene?" in *Understanding the Dead Sea Scrolls: A Reader from the Biblical Archaeology Review,* ed. H. Shanks (New York: Random House, 1992) 205-14, following W. H. Brownlee, "John the Baptist in the New Light of Ancient Scrolls," in *The Scrolls and the New Testament,* ed. K. Stendahl (New York: Harper, 1957) 71-90; and J. A. T. Robinson, "The Baptism of John and the Qumran Community: Testing a Hypothesis," in his *Twelve New Testament Studies* (London: SCM, 1962) 11-27. See also A. S. Geyser, "The Youth of John the Baptist: A Deduction from the Break in the Parallel Account of the Lucan Infancy Story," *NovT* 1 (1956) 70-75; H. Lichtenberger, "Johannes der Täufer und die Texte von Qumran," in *Mogilany 1989: Papers on the Dead Sea Scrolls Offered in Memory of Jean Carmignac,* ed. Z. J. Kapera, 2 vols. (Krakow: Enigma, 1991-93).

10. D. R. Schwartz, *Studies in the Jewish Background of Christianity* (Tübingen: Mohr-Siebeck, 1992) 3; see also Steinmann, *Saint John the Baptist,* 5-61. Even before the discovery of the DSS, R. Eisler suggested that both John and Jesus were Essenes; see R. Eisler, *The Messiah Jesus and John the Baptist according to Flavius Josephus' Recently Rediscovered 'Capture of Jerusalem' and the Other Jewish and Christian Sources* (London:

marizes what some scholars would see as the key parallels between John and the Essenes: John the Baptist and Qumran "shared the same desert"; had a special interest in Isa. 40:3; practiced asceticism; were concerned with ritual purity and immersion; had a priestly background (Luke 1:5; cf. 1QS 6:1-3, 21-22; 8:1; 9:7); called for the sharing of property (Luke 3:11; cf. 1QS 3:2; 5:2; 6:19-22); and had a special sensitivity to incest (Mark 6:17-18; cf. CD 4:17-18).[11]

A few of these points do not need extensive discussion. For example, it is hard to see how a priestly background means anything as far as affiliation with sectarian groupings, since priests and Levites were found in all the major Jewish sects. Chief priests may have had a special affinity with Sadducean views (Acts 4:1; 5:17; cf. *b. Pesaḥ.* 57a), but there were no hard-and-fast rules.

John's baptism in water may very well have shared common concerns with Essene immersion. His baptism does seem to have been concerned with the removal of ritual impurity, as we shall see in the next chapter. However, such a concern does not link him exclusively with the Essenes, whose characteristic purification ritual was, according

---

Methuen, 1931). The points made by B. Thiering will not be discussed here, since they involve reading the relevant Qumran material as *pesharim,* which seems a fundamental error in assigning their literary genre. Thiering's fanciful argument that the Teacher of Righteousness of the scrolls is John (the "pope") is probably best countered by calling into question her dating of the material. See B. Thiering, *Re-dating the Teacher of Righteousness* (Sydney: Theological Explorations, 1979); eadem, *The Teacher of Righteousness, the Gospels and Qumran* (Sydney: Theological Explorations, 1981); eadem, *Jesus the Man* (Sydney: Theological Explorations, 1992).

11. Those who contest any connection between John and the Essenes of Qumran include H. H. Rowley, "The Baptism of John and the Qumran Sect," in *New Testament Essays: Studies in Memory of Thomas Walter Manson, 1893-1958,* ed. A. J. B. Higgins (Manchester: Manchester University Press, 1959) 218-29; E. F. Sutcliffe, "Baptism and Baptismal Rites at Qumran," *HeyJ* 1 (1960) 179-88; J. Ernst, *Johannes der Täufer: Interpretation, Geschichte, Wirkungsgeschichte,* BZNW 53 (Berlin: de Gruyter, 1989) 325-30; B. D. Chilton, *Judaic Approaches to the Gospels* (Atlanta: Scholars Press, 1994) 17-22; and J. P. Meier, *A Marginal Jew: Rethinking the Historical Jesus. Volume Two: Mentor, Message, and Miracles* (New York: Doubleday, 1994) 25-27. Webb substantially agrees with the argument presented here when he states that "similarities do not establish a connection. It is better to trace these similarities to the common milieu of sectarian Judaism in the late Second Temple period. . . . But common milieu is not the same as connection or dependence" (Webb, *John the Baptizer and Prophet,* 351 n. 4). A detailed refutation is needed in view of the persistence of the notion that similarities do indeed mean there was a connection.

to our sources, of a particular type and ultimately connected with the communal eating of a pure meal. Concern with ritual purity and immersion is very strongly attested in later rabbinic tradition; nearly twenty-five percent of Mishnaic law concerns purity.[12] Jacob Neusner has conclusively shown that this rabbinic concern with purity can be traced back to Pharisaic circles of the first century.[13] The Essenes may have gone further than the Pharisees and later rabbis in this regard. Josephus notes that senior members of the Essene sect bathed (immersed?) after physical contact with a junior member (*War* 2.150). But concern with ritual purity and immersion was not monopolized by the Essenes. Immersion baths *(miqva'ot)* for the purposes of removing ritual impurity, which have been found in so many archaeological sites from the first century, testify to the widespread belief that this impurity needed to be removed.[14] A concern with ritual purity seems to have been characteristic of Second Temple Judaism in general. Nearly two hundred years later, the Mishnah would record discussions apparently between Pharisees and Sadducees in which issues of purity were of fundamental concern.[15]

The sharing of property as outlined by John in the tradition recorded in Luke 3:11 is not necessarily connected with an Essene or sectarian community; the practice of sharing appears to be general and based on the ethical teaching found in prophetic literature. John advises those who come to him that "the one who has two tunics should share with the one who has none, and the one who has food should do likewise." It is not at all implied that this sharing is to be done only within some group of John's disciples or in a wider Essene movement. The root of this teaching may be traced to Ezek. 18:5-9, where it is written:

> If someone is righteous and does justice and righteousness . . . if one does not oppress anyone, but restores to the debtor his pledge, and does not commit robbery, gives his bread to the hungry, and covers

12. J. Neusner, *The Idea of Purity in Ancient Judaism. With a Critique and a Commentary by Mary Douglas* (Leiden: Brill, 1973) 8.

13. J. Neusner, *A History of the Mishnaic Law of Purities*, 14 vols. (Leiden: Brill, 1974-77).

14. E. P. Sanders, *Judaism: Practice and Belief 63* BCE*–66* CE (London: SCM, 1992) 222-30, esp. 229-30.

15. See J. M. Baumgarten, "The Pharisaic-Sadducean Controversies about Purity and the Qumran Texts," *JJS* 31 (1980) 157-70.

> the naked with clothing . . . if he walks in my statutes and observes my ordinances, acting faithfully, then he is righteous and will surely live, says the Lord YHWH.[16]

That one should give one's extra clothing and food to those in need is certainly part of the moral law. John advised a more radical charity and disbursement of possessions than was commonly the case in almsgiving — his definition of "extra" appears to have been drastic — but one could still possess very basic clothing and food for oneself. There is no indication that he advised people to live communally with entirely shared resources, as we find in the *Community Rule* (1QS 6:19-23), or to give two days' wages per month to a charitable fund administered by group leaders, as we find in the *Damascus Document* (CD 14:12-16). Moreover, if genuine, the specific advice John gives to toll collectors and soldiers in Luke 3:12-13 would not have been considered adequate by the Essenes as a prescription for righteousness. We shall look at this specific teaching in detail in Chapter 3. John apparently did not ask toll collectors or soldiers to leave their occupations and join a commune.

John's sensitivity to incest is, again, not reflective of a sectarian mentality but is based on Lev. 18:16. Furthermore, in Lev. 20:21, it is explicitly stated, "If a man takes his brother's wife, it is impurity; he has uncovered the nakedness of his brother. They shall be childless." Illicit bodily connection between people resulted in ritual bodily impurity and the curse of childlessness. John did not attack Antipas because he had technically married his niece. Marriage of uncles and nieces is forbidden in the *Damascus Document* (CD 6:17-18), but for John that was not the point. His case rested on biblical law.

The use made of Isa. 40:3a in the Gospels in regard to John and in the *Community Rule* needs to be explored more extensively. We shall then consider the view that John participated in a heterodox anti-Temple "Baptist movement." The significance of his asceticism and the placement of his activities close to Qumran will also be discussed. These points seem to constitute the most significant potential evidence for any connection between John and the Essenes.

16. See also Isa. 58:7, 10; Job 31:52. The masculine language of the Hebrew is followed in this translation, to avoid awkwardness, but it should be remembered that masculine language often functions inclusively in Hebrew.

Isaiah 40:3a

W. H. Brownlee was the first to suggest that the employment of Isa. 40:3 in 1QS 8:13-16 and 9:19-20 demonstrates that John "must have been familiar with Essene thoughts regarding the coming of the Messianic age."[17] However, as noted above, parallels do not themselves justify assuming any direct influence between groups within Second Temple Judaism. Use of a scriptural text in itself cannot be seen as meaningful. It is the similarities and differences in interpretation that will mark out individuals and groups as related or distinct, not the mere use of the same scriptural texts. The Hebrew Scriptures were the property of all groups, and each made use of this resource in varying ways. Moreover, we may expect similarities in the use of Scripture, but, as Samuel Sandmel has stated, "In the variety of Judaisms, as represented by terms such as Pharisees, Sadducees, Qumran . . . it is a restricted area which makes each of these groups distinctive within the totality of Judaisms; it is the distinctive which is significant for identifying the particular, and not the broad areas in common with other Judaisms."[18]

Therefore, when we consider the issue of Isa. 40:3a, used in regard to John by the Gospel writers and by certain Essenes in regard to their own purposes, we need to look closely at any differences in interpretation that may mark out the two as being distinct. Only if the interpretation is precisely the same can we suppose that the two may have been linked. For the moment, we will consider the issues with a presupposition that the Gospels accurately reflect the fact that John made special mention of the verse in regard to his own purpose.

Isa. 40:3a is used by all four Gospel authors to sum up what John wanted to achieve. The Masoretic Text (MT) reads: קול קורא במדבר פנו דרך יהוה, "A voice is calling in the wilderness prepare (the) way of YHWH." How do we punctuate this

Perhaps the most natural way of punctuating the statement is to consider the quotation marks as coming after the participle "is calling," קורא. Furthermore, 40:3b goes on to read, "straighten a highway in the desert for our God." This punctuation would most naturally result from an interpretation that the way of YHWH should be prepared in the wilderness. Therefore, in translation the verse may read, "A voice is

17. Brownlee, "John the Baptist," 73; cf. Steinmann, *Saint John the Baptist,* 59.

18. S. Sandmel, "Parallelomania," *JBL* 81 (1962) 3.

calling, 'In the wilderness prepare the way of the LORD.'" The translation, "A voice of one calling," may make better English sense, but the Hebrew noun קול is not found in its construct state, to read "a voice of." It is the agent. The voice itself is calling. The *Targum Pseudo-Jonathan* has "people of YHWH" where we find "YHWH" in the MT, but the *Targum* also has the same vagueness of language, allowing for alternative punctuations. In the Septuagint (LXX), this alternative punctuation is made explicit: the disembodied — perhaps heavenly — voice is not doing the actual calling. There is a person calling in the wilderness, and it is his voice that is heard. We find a "voice of one calling in the wilderness, 'Prepare the way of the LORD.'" This may be considered a valid interpretation of the vague wording of the Hebrew, apart from the fact that the voice is "of one calling," even though it seems to disregard the parallel statement of 40:3b.

As noted above, in 1QS use is made of Isa. 40:3a on two occasions, 8:13-16 and 9:19-20. In the Isaiah scrolls from the DSS collection, the form is identical to what is found in the later MT. In 1QS 8:13-16 and 9:19-20 it is understood that the disembodied voice is calling, "Prepare in the wilderness the way of YHWH."[19] In other words, it is not the reading reflected in the LXX, where the voice is of someone in the wilderness. In the *Community Rule,* the voice is not itself calling in the wilderness, but it exhorts people to prepare in the wilderness the way of the Lord. 1QS 8:15-16 explains that the path is the study of the Law, in order that they may do all that has been revealed from age to age. The "children of righteousness," the members of the community, are to "walk perfectly together in all that has been revealed to them. This is the time for preparing the way into the wilderness . . ." (1QS 9:19-20). In other words, the placement of the voice is different in the LXX and 1QS. For clarity, the difference may be summarized as follows:

1QS Voice somewhere calls for preparation of the way in the wilderness

LXX Voice of someone in the wilderness calls for preparation of the way

19. Isa. 40:3 is absent from 4QS[d], which also omits the earlier Bible quotations, but it is present in 4QS[e] (3:4-6). I am grateful to Prof. Geza Vermes for this observation. For the different versions of the Community Rule, see Vermes, *The Dead Sea Scrolls in English,* 4th ed., 69-94.

The synoptic Gospels follow the LXX exactly (Matt. 3:3; Mark 1:3; Luke 3:4), while the Fourth Gospel conflates Isa. 40:3a with 3b (John 1:23).[20] The voice is of one calling in the wilderness, "Prepare the way of the LORD." By implication, the way begins there, in association with the one who calls in the wilderness, namely, John. Now it may be argued that since this is the reading of the LXX, primarily used by Diaspora Jews, the Gospel writers knew and copied it and applied it to John; John himself could not have accepted that reading of the text. Certainly, it is unlikely that John used a Greek translation of Scripture as his authoritative text; he most probably used a Hebrew version and knew Aramaic translation traditions from synagogue readings.

However, the LXX represents interpretive norms of the time it was translated (third century BCE) that may have been current as much in the Land of Israel as in the Diaspora. For example, it is intriguing that one-third of the deviations between the Samaritan Pentateuch and the MT are along the lines of the LXX and that one text of Jeremiah found near Qumran (4QJer^{b}) is close to being a Hebrew model of the version in the LXX.[21] Furthermore, four Greek biblical manuscripts were found near Qumran, which indicates that Greek versions were read in the heart of the Land of Israel.[22] We know from the DSS not only that the Hebrew text of the Scriptures could vary, but also that interpretive norms could vary, to an astonishing degree. We do not know for certain how the Aramaic translators of the passage in the synagogues of the first century rendered this verse, but it is most likely that they translated it similarly to the way it is found in the later *Targum Pseudo-Jonathan;* in other words, since the Hebrew was vague, they left it vague. This means that it was up to scribes and other teachers of the Law to make of the verse what they wished and to interpret it along the lines of either the Qumran manuscripts (and the later MT) or the LXX. In other words, given the words as found in the Hebrew text, the placement of the quotation marks could be debated, and the voice itself could have been that of someone in the wilderness or a disembodied voice from anywhere.

20. See M. J. J. Menken, "The Quotation from Isa. 40, 3 in John 1, 23," *Bib* 66/2 (1985) 190-205.

21. E. Tov, "Proto-Samaritan Texts and the Samaritan Pentateuch," in *The Samaritans,* ed. A. D. Crown (Tübingen: Mohr-Siebeck, 1989) 400.

22. See P. W. Skehan, E. Ulrich, and J. Sanderson, *Qumran Cave 4: Palaeo-Hebrew and Greek Biblical Manuscripts,* DJD 9 (Oxford: Oxford University Press, 1992).

The location of a sectarian community at Qumran on the edge of the Dead Sea, within the region of the wilderness of Judea, seems to correlate very well with what we have in 1QS. The community of 1QS exists in the wilderness, and Qumran is certainly located there. The employment of Isa. 40:3 may well have been a direct result of a reading of the verse in the light of the chosen location. It was necessary for this community itself to exist *in the wilderness* in order to make straight the paths of God and walk along them. This passage in the *Community Rule* is, in fact, the strongest indicator in favor of 1QS being related to the Essene group living at Qumran itself, for in an earlier version of the *Community Rule* (perhaps used by other celibate Essene groups not living in the wilderness), the passage requiring wilderness residence, and therefore the reference to Isa. 40:3, is absent ($4QS^d = 4QS^b$), though the latter reference (1QS 9:19-20) appears in an intermediate version ($4QS^e$). However, John does not appear to have asked people to remain with him in the wilderness. His teaching suggests that he thought they should go home to their own towns and jobs — even as toll collectors and soldiers (Luke 3:10-14) — and when we meet disciples of John in the Gospels (e.g., in Mark 2:18-19) they are never on their way back to a base camp in the wilderness. In fact, the easiest understanding of the *Sitz im Leben* of Mark 2:18-19 suggests that the disciples of John and the disciples of the Pharisees *in Galilee* were keeping a fast at the same time. There is no suggestion that John wished to form an exclusive community in the desert dedicated to the learning of the Law, frequent ablutions, a holy meal, and a host of rules and regulations governing life together. John seems to have wanted people to be obedient to the Law in anticipation of judgment and to accept his own teaching in this regard, but to remain where they usually were. He may have been one who was calling in the wilderness, but "the way of the LORD," having begun there with him, led repentant people to a life of righteousness in their own hometowns.

Therefore, if John did use the text of Isa. 40:3a as part of his prophetic call, the fact that both the community of 1QS and the disciples of John may have found it important does not amount to anything very significant. The Hebrew Scriptures were the property of all groups in Second Temple Judaism. If the same text was used, but with a completely different hermeneutical emphasis, this shows that the two groups were not related. The mere use of a text proves nothing in terms of relationship.[23]

23. Contra J. Jeremias, *New Testament Theology: The Proclamation of Jesus* (London: SCM, 1971) 43 n. 3.

Having said all this, it cannot of course be assumed that John himself made special use of Isa. 40:3 in relation to his purposes. The evidence for his employment of the verse is to be found in Christian material, and Christians may have had their own particular reasons for connecting the verse with John. Christian exegesis of Isa. 40:3 identified the "LORD" whose path was being prepared with Jesus, though the verse in fact refers to the Lord God, YHWH, not to the Messiah. Christians may have interpreted the verse as a reference to John's activity and applied it to him, having made the prior identification of the Lord as being Jesus. What is significant is that John apparently did not use the verse to justify the establishment of an actual wilderness community.

Baptism and the "Baptist Movement"

John made no statement known to us that he considered the Temple in Jerusalem defiled and therefore irrelevant to the way of righteousness, whereas this was a fundamental belief of the Essenes, including the Qumran group (cf. 1QS 1:11-13; 8:6-10; 9:4-5). The view that John participated, with Essenes, in a heterodox, anti-Temple "Baptist movement" out of line with "mainstream" Judaism[24] is based on two untenable assumptions: first, that there existed a kind of "mainstream"

24. For the proposition that a Jewish "Baptist movement" existed, see W. Brandt, *Die jüdischen Baptismen oder das Religiose Waschen und Baden im Judentum mit Einschluss des Judenchristentums* (Giessen: Topelmann)1910 and J. Thomas, *Le mouvement baptiste en Palestine et Syrie (150 av.J.C.–300 ap.J.C.)* (Gembloux: Duculot, 1935). C. H. H. Scobie adopts this hypothesis uncritically when he states that the Scrolls "support the view which sees John in the context of a number of roughly similar groups active in the Jordan valley area and making up a non-conformist, baptist, sectarian movement within the Judaism of the period. This movement forms the background of John's ministry and undoubtedly influences his thought at many points." See C. H. H. Scobie, *John the Baptist* (London: SCM, 1964) 69. Wink also accepts the thesis, characterizing the "baptist movement" as being "a movement of protest against contemporary piety" in which Temple sacrifices were rejected and replaced by baptisms. The groups were, apparently, "heterodox, schismatic, highly individualistic, quick to shift to the latest 'revelation,' and capable of borrowing from one another without establishing relationships of dependency" (Wink, *Gospel Tradition,* 108). Joseph Thomas' argument is completely speculative and based on a shallow reading of apocryphal and pseudepigraphal texts, but his work has never been subjected to a proper modern critique and is often cited in regard to John; see, e.g., D. E.

Judaism that was not particularly concerned with ritual purity or immersions, and second, that there were numerous groups exhibiting anti-Temple sentiment in pre-70 Judaism for whom immersions were a substitution for Temple sacrifices.

Contrary to the first assumption, all groups would have used immersions as prescribed in Torah. Later Jewish sects mentioned by patristic authors such as Epiphanius and Hegesippus — the Nasaraioi, the Masbotheans, the Daily Bathers[25] — need not necessarily have existed at the time of John, despite what Epiphanius states in regard to the Daily Bathers (*Panarion* 19.5.6-7). Epiphanius is not the most reliable historical source; he is notorious for his invention of heretical groups out of hearsay. Even if they did exist in John's time, the characteristic of all of these groups is extremism — frequently repeated rites of immersion — as we get with the Essenes. But no one has managed to prove that John was concerned that his disciples participate in repeated daily ablutions.

Rabbinic literature makes mention of a later group of "Morning Bathers" who were careful to purify their bodies each morning (*t. Yad.* 2:20; *b. Ber.* 22a), even if already pure, but they need not have been part of a movement as such. This is also the case with the hypothetical group that produced the *Sibylline Oracles* (Book IV)[26] or any so-called "Jewish-Christian" Ebionites, Elkasaites, or others who may have practiced frequent purificatory bathing.[27] Josephus' teacher Bannus washed often in cold water by day and by night "for the sake of purity" (*Life* 11), but he seems to have lived quite alone, not as part of a sectarian community. Moreover, despite his aloneness, Josephus finished his period of teaching under Bannus only to return to normal life and align himself with the Pharisees. We may possibly wonder if Bannus was positive about the

---

Aune, *Prophecy in Early Christianity and the Ancient Mediterranean World* (Grand Rapids: Eerdmans, 1983) 129, 382; Meier, *Marginal Jew*, vol. 2, 27. For a short critique of the views of J. Thomas, see M. Black, "Patristic Accounts of Jewish Sects," in *The Scrolls and Christian Origins: Studies in the Jewish Background of the New Testament* (London: Nelson, 1961) 54-58. As Black notes, "*prima facie* the garbled and disjointed reports of the later [Christian] Fathers do not inspire confidence" (p. 56).

25. Thomas, *Le mouvement baptiste*, 34-44; Scobie, *John the Baptist*, 33-40.

26. Thomas, *Le mouvement baptiste*, 46-60. See also Webb, *John the Baptizer and Prophet*, 120-21.

27. See Scobie, *John the Baptist*, 36. For an argument in favor of a praxis-based definition of Jewish-Christianity, see J. E. Taylor, "The Phenomenon of Early Jewish-Christianity: Reality or Scholarly Invention?" *VC* 44 (1990) 313-34.

Pharisaic position on the Law and lifestyle in general, which gave Josephus a predisposition in favor of going along with their rulings. Bannus' own particular lifestyle was probably not adopted in opposition to Pharisaic practice, but simply indicated an extreme adherence to the principles of bodily purity and an attitude of total faith in God.

Issues of ritual purity were extremely important to the Pharisees and later rabbis also, as the sixth division of the Mishnah well demonstrates, but — contrary to the second assumption noted above — nothing in our sources connects purification rituals with an anti-Temple stance. Immersion was never a substitute for Temple sacrifices.[28] In the *Community Rule,* substitution for the sacrifices of the Temple is made through individual members of the community doing good works to effect atonement (1QS 9:2-6). A similar notion is found in Philo's writings, where true sacrifice is made by the worshipper bringing the self to God (*On the Special Laws* 1.269-72). Philo himself could explain that when the heart was pure no sacrifices were strictly necessary (*On the Life of Moses* 6.2.107; *On Noah's Work as a Planter* 108), but the ritual of the Temple was still required to train one in piety and implant in one a zeal for holiness (*Who Is the Heir* 123).[29] Moreover, evidence in apocryphal and pseudepigraphal literature for people atoning for sin through various procedures shows that repentance and faith need not at all reflect rejection of the Temple cult; the evidence suggests only that these were seen as alternatives or complements to the Temple rites in some circles, especially, one may imagine, in the Diaspora.

28. O. Betz argues that John's statement that God could raise up children to Abraham from "these stones" (Matt. 3:9; Luke 3:8) means that there would be a living temple of people that would replace the Temple made of stones (O. Betz, "Was John the Baptist an Essene?" 211). By contrast, the usual (and better) reading is that John was pointing to the omnipotent power of God, who could create living human beings from the inanimate matter of the earth (so, e.g., Meier, *Marginal Jew,* vol. 2, 29). Similarly, John's putative priestly descent (Luke 1:5) means nothing (cf. Webb, *John the Baptizer and Prophet,* 193). That John is not described as serving in the Temple does not mean that he rejected it, since ordinary priests provided only occasional Temple service; see Chilton, *Judaic Approaches to the Gospels,* 20-26. As Chilton says, to maintain that John's baptism challenged the efficacy of sacrifical forgiveness invokes "a supposed dualism between moral and cultic atonement which simply has no place in critical discussion of early Judaism" (ibid., 21).

29. See D. Winston, "Philo and the Contemplative Life," in *Jewish Spirituality from the Bible through the Middle Ages,* ed. A. Green (New York: Crossroad, 1986) 198-231, esp. 216-17.

What all this suggests is that if John's baptism had to do with ridding the body of ritual impurity, as did other Jewish immersions, then this would tally with the concerns of the people of his time, for whom issues of purity were becoming increasingly important. Parallels may indicate a mentality, rather than a movement; they may indicate that different parties participated in the same thought-world, but they do not show us a pattern of influences from one group to another. General influences may have occurred naturally, without direct contact between groups. It would have been enough for some people just to hear about a group that aimed for optimum purity by means of frequent ablutions to start imitating this practice in order not to be outdone.

Asceticism

It is generally understood that John was ascetic in his lifestyle. John's asceticism is attested in a saying of Jesus, preserved in the Q tradition, where it is claimed that John came "neither eating bread nor drinking wine" (Luke 7:33-34; cf. Matt. 11:18-19; Luke 1:15). This is probably not meant to indicate that John ate and drank almost nothing, despite the exaggerated version of Matt. 11:18-19, where John is set up as an extreme antithesis of Jesus. Rather, taking the statement as written, we may assume his diet did not include bread and wine, the usual fare of townsfolk. Therefore, John's asceticism was of a particular type. It should not be understood in the light of later Christian asceticism, in which monks went out to the desert in order to defeat the powers of sin resident in the flesh by denying all comforts of the body. Nor should John's lifestyle be classed with the Essenes' supposed asceticism simply because their asceticism is thought to be "out of line with orthodox Judaism," as C. H. H Scobie puts it.[30] In an important essay on the subject of early Jewish asceticism, Steven D. Fraade has pointed out that the definition of "asceticism" can be inadequate and based on familiar

30. Scobie, *John the Baptist,* 39. The eagerness to find parallels continues in regard to John's disciples. Betz points out that the disciples of John were known to fast (Mark 2:18 and parr.) and recite a special prayer (Luke 11:1), and he notes that these acts of piety appear in Qumran texts also ("Was John the Baptist an Essene?" 211). These acts of piety, though, appear among *all* Jewish groups of the period in question.

models that define it too narrowly; Jewish groups may thus be considered deeply ascetic or not ascetic at all, depending on one's primary definition of the term.[31] Looking to the Greek term ἄσκησις, Fraade considers its origin as a "practice and exercise that leads to moral as well as physical excellence"[32] and notes that for the ancients, including Jews, ἄσκησις was not a negative denial of the world but a testing and training of one's faculties (often through abstention from what was normally permitted) in the pursuit of moral and spiritual perfection.[33] Fraade finds clear evidence of asceticism in the Old Testament Apocrypha and Pseudepigrapha and shows that ascetic ideals are by no means absent in later rabbinic literature, although there was often an ambivalent attitude on the part of the rabbis.[34] Philo describes one group of Jewish ascetics, the Therapeutae, as a celibate community living according to a very strict regimen of Torah study and meditation, and sustained by the barest diet imaginable (*On the Contemplative Life* 1–39, 64–90). Moreover, Judaism had clear provision for a form of ascetic life by means of the Nazirite vow.

John may have taken a vow as a נזיר (*nazir*), which meant he would not cut his hair, contract corpse uncleanness, or touch grapes or their by-products (Num. 6:1-21). The nativity story of Luke describes John as never drinking wine or strong drink (1:15). Both Samson and Samuel were considered to be *nazirim* (*m. Naz.* 9:5) and the nativity story of John as found in Luke's Gospel is heavily reliant on their birth stories. In the Mishnah, it is accepted that a vow may be made for life (*m. Naz.* 1:2). In the case of a lifelong *nazir,* haircutting was permitted as long as offerings of cattle were made at the Temple (*m. Naz.* 1:2; cf. Num. 6:14). As a *nazir,* one could not comb one's hair, though washing was allowed (*m. Naz.* 6:3). If John had taken such a vow, then he would have had long — probably matted — hair and a beard.

But this is pure speculation, for we cannot know whether he had taken such a vow, even with the models of Samson and Samuel behind

31. S. D. Fraade, "Ascetical Aspects of Ancient Judaism" in *Jewish Spirituality from the Bible through the Middle Ages,* ed. A. Green (New York: Crossroad, 1986) 253-88, esp. 253-56.

32. Ibid., 256.

33. Ibid., 257.

34. Ibid., 269-72. Much pro-ascetic sentiment is there; note, e.g., regarding the *nazir:* "And if one who denies himself only one thing (wine) is holy, how much more so one who denies himself everything."

him. Nowhere is it said that John was a *nazir.* He may have had long, matted hair and a beard simply because he was living in the wilderness and did not tend to his appearance. His diet may not have included wine or strong drink because these were not found naturally. He may have been concerned to preserve himself clean from all kinds of impurity. These factors may have led people to suppose he had taken the vow of a *nazir.* What we may be permitted to conjecture is that the nativity account found in Luke suggests that people saw him as either a *nazir* or someone resembling a *nazir.*

Probably the best parallel we have for John's lifestyle is the aforementioned Bannus, who lived nearly thirty years after John. Like John, he is not described as being affiliated with any one sect. According to Josephus, Bannus lived in the wilderness and was "wearing only clothing that trees provided and eating what grew on its own accord" (*Life* 11). John too seems to have trusted that he would find enough to live on in his natural environment. The wilderness is not necessarily a desert. In Hebrew, מדבר refers to uncultivated land, as does the equivalent Greek word ἔρημος. When Bannus decided to eat only what grew of its own accord, he was choosing not to eat anything that was grown in cultivated fields, so that his food was truly natural growth given by God. We are told that John also lived on "locusts and wild honey" (Mark 1:6; Matt. 3:4). Again, they were neither subject to human control nor the result of human labor. According to a later reckoning, there were 800 species of kosher locust available for consumption (*Lam. Rab.* Intro. 34; cf. *m. Ter.* 10:9; *m. Ḥul.* 3:7; *b. Ḥul.* 65a–66b; cf. Lev. 11:20-23). Wild honey is mentioned at Judg. 14:8-9. It should be remembered that the Essenes are described by Josephus as eating bread loaves (*War* 2.130). The *Community Rule* describes the communal meal as being bread and wine (1QS 6:4-6; cf. 1QSa 2:17-21), and according to Luke bread and wine were precisely what John did not eat (Luke 7:33-34; cf. Matt. 11:18-19; Luke 1:15).

In regard to clothing, we know from Josephus that the Essenes wore white (*War* 2.123, 137); Bannus wore what he found on trees, while John dressed in some kind of item of clothing made from camel's hair (Mark 1:6; Matt. 3:4) tied around his waist with a strip of skin. John did not even wear a proper man-made belt; the word used, ζώνη, is a simple tie or band (often worn by women); a proper man's belt was called a ζωστήρ. The tie was probably not a loincloth made of leather. A leather loincloth was worn underneath a garment, like modern underpants, and was therefore not visible. A leather loincloth would have been cut in a detailed manner in order to provide a comfortable fit (see photo on p. 36) and worn with a piece of cloth underneath. It was worn to secure this piece of cloth and was tied at the sides. It is doubtful that anyone would have thought to make a special comment on John's undergarments. The point of the skin tie around his waist, however, may be that it was not made by human labor. It was just a tie, made from the skin of some creature, possibly one found naturally, though presumably one that could be considered clean when dead.

As is well known, the description of this item of clothing echoes the description of Elijah wearing exactly the same thing (2 Kgs. 1:8); the wording found in the LXX (4 Kgdms. 1:8) is almost identical to the description in the Gospels. As (Greek) readers, we are meant to get the hint that John looked like Elijah, though this need not lead us to assume that since the Gospel writers wanted to connect John with Elijah, the description of what he wore must be invented. John may have worn this clothing himself without any intention that anyone should connect him with the prophet.

As for Bannus' garment (Josephus, *Life* 11), camel's hair can be collected from the trees around caravansaries where camels have been tethered. In winter, camels grow thick, shaggy coats which they shed in spring, so that during these months there is camel hair around and about on vegetation that camels rub against. When Josephus refers to Bannus wearing what trees provided, he may well have been referring to the camel's hair that stuck to the branches, and not necessarily to "leaves or, perhaps, bark," as Thackeray suggested.[35]

When Mark describes John's attire he says only that "John was wearing camel hair and a skin tie around his loins" (Mark 1:6a). Matthew alters this slightly, substituting τὸ ἔνδυμα for ἐνδεδυμένος, so that his description reads in English translation: "And this John had his clothing from camel hair and a skin tie around his loins" (Matt. 3:4a). This does not tell us a great deal, but most likely the reference is to some kind of camel hair cloth rather than to bits of camel hair found on trees, as these would, one imagines, too easily fall off with repeated immersions in water. Camel or goat hair was used for sackcloth, and sackcloth itself would have

35. See H. St. J. Thackeray, trans., *Josephus: The Life [and] Against Apion,* LCL 1 (Cambridge, MA: Heinemann, 1926) 7 *a.* Alternatively, Bannus may have made a "grass" skirt from bark, as is quite common in traditional cultures of the Pacific.

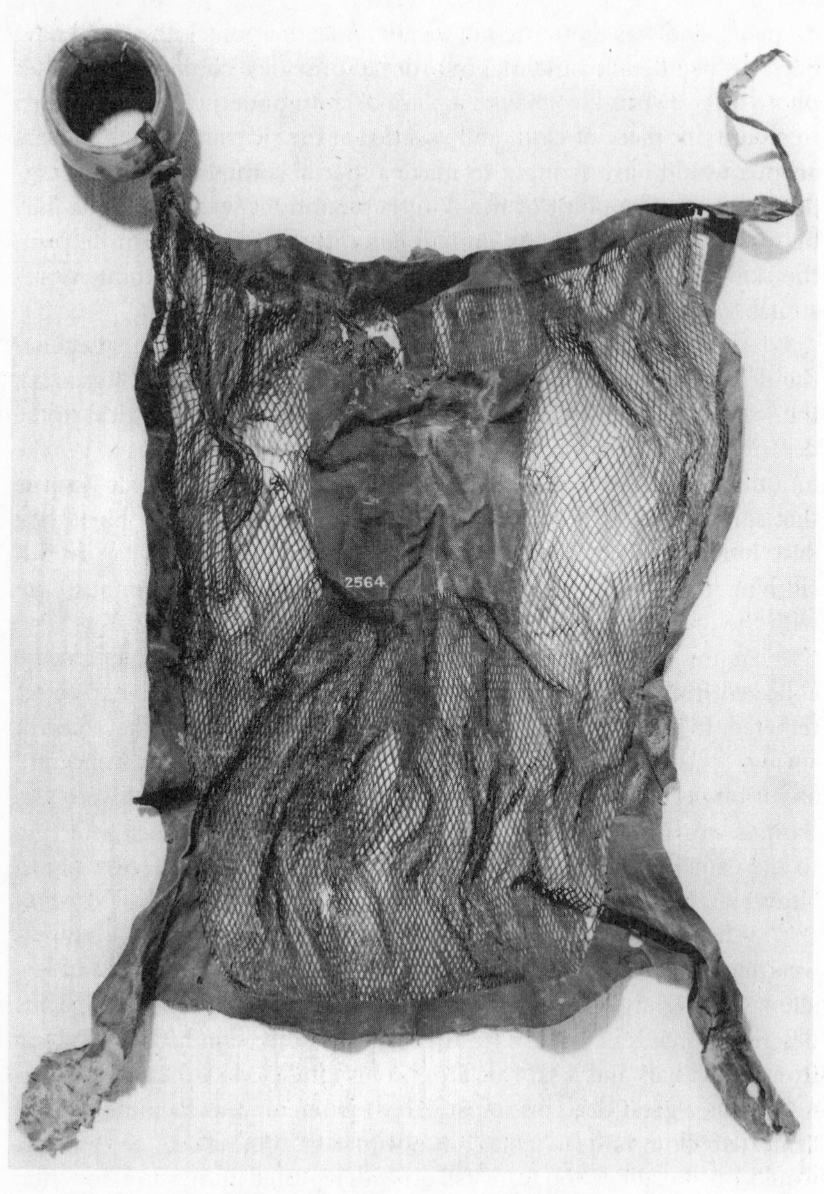

Leather loincloth from Egypt, Middle Kingdom: BM 2564
Courtesy of the Trustees of the British Museum

been a highly appropriate material for John to wear, not because he wanted to look like Elijah, or any other prophet, but because it was the appropriate attire for someone who was repentant.

In Hebrew and Aramaic, שק refers to the camel or goat hair material used for sackcloth, but the constituent hair is important in the meaning, analogous to how we may call a jumper made out of wool a "woolly." In Greek, σάκκος seems to have lost this specific primary meaning and could refer not only to a hair sack but to a woman's hair net.[36] If in Aramaic oral tradition John was spoken of as wearing שק, "camel hair cloth," a Greek translator might have been justified in rendering this as τρίχας καμήλου, "camel hair," as here, missing the implicit assumption that it was in fact hair *cloth.* That John wore material made of hair, however, is understood by Matthew, for τὸ ἔνδυμα suggests a garment made of cloth.

Sackcloth was primarily used for those in mourning,[37] but it also indicated repentance (Jonah 3:5-10; Matt. 11:2/Luke 10:13). It was not really a mark of asceticism, but it was worn in particular by those who sought God (Dan. 9:3). Wearing sackcloth showed special reverence and humility before God (1 Kgs. 21:27-29; Isa. 58:3-5; Neh. 9:1-2; Isa. 69:11). This practice may have evolved out of the custom for a vanquished foe to come before the victorious king after a battle in sackcloth, in order to plead for mercy (cf. 1 Kgs. 20:31-2). To plead for mercy from God, therefore, one donned sackcloth. In Jonah 3:10 the actions of fasting, putting on sackcloth, and calling upon God cause God to withdraw his anger. By these actions God sees that the people have turned from their wicked ways.

As a development of this, it appears that it was expected that prophets would wear sackcloth, for prophets were people of great faith who called on God. 2 Kgs. 1:8 may indicate in Hebrew that Elijah wore something made of hair, although the Greek version refers instead to Elijah being a "hairy man." Zech. 13:4 in Hebrew also refers to a prophet's "garment of hair," but the Greek version has a "hairy skin," which may refer to Genesis 27, where Jacob tricks his father by pretending to be his brother Esau. It may also reflect a Greek understanding that prophets, like philosophers, would generally have full beards. Whatever the case, the fact that the LXX does not associate hair cloth with prophets as readily as the

36. See I. Jenkins and D. Williams, "Sprung Hair Nets: Their Manufacture and Use in Ancient Greece," *AJA* 89 (1985) 411-18. I am grateful to Ms. Hero Granger-Taylor of the British Museum for this reference.

37. See G. Stählin, "σάκκος," *TDNT* 7 (1971) 58-60.

Hebrew text does means that Mark and Matthew, who wrote for Greek-speaking communities, may have missed any allusion in Aramaic source material that John's sackcloth associated him with prophets of old in general. The reference to a skin tie was certainly understood by them, conveniently, as a clear reference to Elijah. However, we do have a reference to Isaiah wearing sackcloth (Isa. 20:2), and in the Jewish-Christian book of Revelation (11:3) two Elijah-like prophets wear it.

At any rate, it seems likely that John may have worn sackcloth not to associate himself with prophets of the distant past but to demonstrate his humility before God and an attitude of continued repentance. This demonstration of faith may have struck people as particularly appropriate for a prophet, but sackcloth was no prophetic uniform. Sackcloth would certainly not have constituted "soft clothing," as Q's Jesus ironically indicates (Matt. 11:8; Luke 7:25). It should probably be noted that sackcloth was very cheap, rough material and may also have been recovered from caravansaries, since it was used to transport foodstuffs and goods in packsaddles and saddlebags.[38] Sackcloth was *not* the attire of an Essene. As mentioned above, Josephus tells us that Essenes always dressed in white (*War* 2.123, 137), probably to draw attention to their superior purity. White clothing would remind people of the attire of the Temple priests and Levites, who were supposed to be pure. Sackcloth was usually black. If made of camel hair, it would have been brown. It would always have looked rough.[39]

In following this lifestyle of total dependence on what God provided, John is the perfect example for someone whose trust is in God and a living paradigm of the advice Jesus himself gives to his disciples according to the Q tradition (Matt. 6:25-34 = Luke 12:22-31):

38. Among fragments of goat hair cloth from Masada are a number that derive from sacks. In some of these, as well as in fragments from other sites in Israel, camel hair has been spun together with the goat hair. I am indebted again to Ms. Granger-Taylor for this information. Both camel and goat hair cloth would have been rather scratchy to wear, and it seems unlikely that "Bedouins" made cloaks out of it, as Meier speculates (*Marginal Jew,* vol. 2, 48), unless they were very pressed for resources.

39. Ernst Lohmeyer pointed out that the camel is an unclean animal (Lev. 11:4), and if John dressed in camel hair he may have done so as a protest against purity regulations; see E. Lohmeyer, *Das Urchristentum 1: Johannes der Täufer* (Göttingen: Vandenhoeck & Ruprecht, 1932) 124-29. Lohmeyer confused different types of uncleanness. Camel hair and sheep's wool were permitted to be mixed together, as long as the greater part of the mix was camel hair (*M. Kil.* 9:1; cf. *M. Neg.* 11:2).

> Look at the birds of the sky: they do not sow or reap or gather (wheat) into barns, and your Father in heaven feeds them. Are you not of more value than they are? And can any of you by worrying add a single hour to your life span? And why do you worry about clothing? Consider how the lilies of the field are growing: they do not toil or spin, but I tell you that even Solomon in all his glory was not clothed like one of these. But if God so clothes the grass of the field, which exists today and tomorrow is thrown into the oven, will he not much more clothe you — little-faith people? Therefore do not worry, saying, "What will we eat?" or "What will we drink?" or "What will we wear?" for it is the Gentiles who strive for all these things, and your Father in heaven knows that you need all these. But seek first the Kingdom of God and his righteousness,[40] and all these things will be added to you also. (Matt. 6:26-33)

John may well have been used as an illustration of just how God would provide for those who simply trusted themselves to his care, just as Bannus might also have been later on. In eating no bread, only what could be found naturally, there was no need to sow, reap, or gather wheat into barns. Old sackcloth requires no toiling or spinning. Jesus may once have proven the point by his own action, for he seems to have chosen to live as John lived after his baptism by John in the Jordan.

Just to look at this point briefly, in the first account of Jesus' sojourn in the wilderness (Mark 1:12-13), Jesus is driven out there by the Holy Spirit, where he stays forty days to experience temptation by Satan. The form of temptation is not specifically described, and it is not suggested that he fasted. Mark states that Jesus was "with the wild beasts, and the angels looked after (διηκόνουν) him" (Mark 1:13). The word διακονέω seems to have had the sense of "provide with the necessities of life" (cf. Matt. 27:55; Mark 15:41), which includes food, shelter, clothing, and whatever else may be required by the one being looked after in any particular instance.[41] Therefore, in the account of Matthew

40. Several variants of this sentence exist in the Greek manuscripts, but this is the most probable original reading of the Matthean text. Luke 12:33 omits the reference to righteousness; it may have been Matthew's addition.

41. J. N. Collins argues that διακονέω should be translated as "minister," with the idea that those who minister must go on a mission and on errands, i.e., be messengers; see J. N. Collins, *Diakonia: Re-Interpreting the Ancient Sources* (New York: Oxford University Press, 1990). This rather evangelical interpretation is helpful as a cor-

(4:1-11; cf. Luke 4:1-13), where the Marcan temptation in the wilderness is combined with a separate Q tradition of specific temptations by Satan, Jesus ends a period of fasting by being "looked after" by the angels (Matt. 4:11); it is understood that they gave him food. In Mark, the reference to angels providing the means of life seems to indicate that, through the mercy of God, Jesus found enough food and drink to survive in the wilderness for a long period of time, as John had done.

Of course, given this tradition of the teaching of Jesus, John may have been recognized as living reasonably well in the wilderness. If God provided for those who trusted in him, then it would have been good if John looked fairly healthy and fit.[42] If John fasted, then this was quite in keeping with usual Jewish practice and does not mean that he fasted to excess. Fasting was, after all, traditionally associated with repentance and piety.

In summary, John's asceticism was of a certain type — one that aimed to prove a point by means of a wilderness diet and very rough clothing, which indicated total humility; it was very much the asceticism of Bannus.[43] Either they both derived the impetus for such a lifestyle from the same conceptual background, or else Bannus knew of John's example and copied him, as Jesus may have done for a period.[44] We need not assume, though, that an ascetic "movement" sprung from their

---

rective to the usual translation of διακονέω as "serve," but it seems wiser to keep to a broad and general English translation. To render the word as "minister" has an ecclesiastical connotation. In response to Collins' argument (p. 222), when Paul was in prison he surely stated that he wanted Onesimus so that he might "look after" him (Phlm. 13), since prisoners were to be fed and looked after by family and friends, who would be of service to them. Indeed, he may have asked Onesimus to run errands as well, but the point was that this just happened to be something that constituted "looking after" Paul.

42. S. L. Davies rightly notes that John may have eaten great quantities of locusts and honey, for all we know ("John the Baptist and Essene Kashruth," *NTS* 29 [1983] 569-71). The point of his diet was not that he ate little, but that he apparently ate from a very restricted range of absolutely pure and natural foodstuffs. It is probably worth noting that locusts and honey were delicacies in comparison with people's usual fare of bread and legumes; see M. Broshi, "The Diet of Palestine in the Roman Period: Introductory Notes," *IMJ* 5 (1986) 50-51.

43. So M. Goodman, *The Ruling Class of Judaea: The Origins of the Jewish Revolt Against Rome, A.D. 66-70* (Cambridge: Cambridge University Press, 1987) 79-80.

44. It is possible that all these found some inspiration in the example of the Rechabites of Jeremiah 35; cf. 2 Kgs. 10:15-17; 1 Chr. 2:55. I am grateful to Prof. Paul Morris for this observation.

example. As Martin Goodman notes, the fame of such men as John and Bannus "suggests that this sort of extreme asceticism was exceptional."[45] While exceptional, however, it may have been set up as exemplary action. Philo noted that people of great goodness would cultivate solitude and avoid cities (*Every Good Man Is Free* 63; *On Abraham* 22–23; *On the Special Laws* 2.44; cf. *On the Life of Moses* 2.34), and he viewed the renunciation of property positively (*On the Change of Names* 32). In later rabbinic literature, the concern about tomorrow's food is an example of little faith (*b. Soṭ.* 48b; *Mekilta Exod.* 16:40; cf. 16:9); it would follow that having no concern about food and completely trusting in God's providence are examples of faith. This same connection between faith in God and trusting in him to provide food is found in Jesus' teaching at Matt. 6:25-34 (= Luke 12:22-31) and in his specific prayer, where God is asked to provide each day our necessary (ἐπιούσιος) food (Matt. 6:11; Luke 11:3).[46] Those who pray are trusting in God to provide food, rather than worrying about producing it themselves.

While worrying about food is a sign of little faith, the extreme measures of John and the extreme advice given to his disciples by Jesus are not found in later rabbinic literature. John's example would, however, have been recognized as indicating the extent of his faith in God, as would Bannus' example. Such a degree of faith in God would naturally have attracted people who wished to hear words of wisdom from such men, as the young Josephus was attracted to Bannus.

There is also an issue of purity involved in the wilderness lifestyle that made a political statement. Eating a diet of what is found naturally recalled the actions of Judas Maccabeus who, after the vanquishing of Jerusalem by Antiochus Epiphanes, "got away to the wilderness, and kept himself and his companions alive in the mountains like wild animals.

45. Goodman, *The Ruling Class of Judaea,* 80.

46. Without digressing too far into the immense scholarly literature on the subject, it may be noted that ἐπιούσιος can be translated in several ways. A rare word, it may well have been created in order to render the sense of Aramaic די מחסרו, "enough for what he lacks," as suggested by S. T. Lachs, *A Rabbinic Commentary on the New Testament: The Gospels of Matthew, Mark, and Luke* (Hoboken, NJ: KTAV, 1987) 120. The Aramaic expression is found in the short prayer of the disciples of Rabbi Meir (ca. 150 CE); see *t. Ber.* 3:11. Lachs therefore proposes that the underlying Aramaic of the Lord's Prayer was די מחסרנו, "sufficient for what we lack." Most likely, the Greek word derives from the verb "to be," εἶναι, with the preposition ἐπί.

They continued to live on what grew wild so that they might not share in the defilement [of the Temple and the city]" (2 Macc. 5:27; cf. 10:6).

The group that produced the *Damascus Document* had no dietary restrictions beyond those defined in Torah and did not in general exhibit such a degree of exemplary faithfulness. They were concerned to keep the purity of prescribed food, so that in eating honey they did not consume the larvae of bees (CD 12:13), and they could eat locusts roasted or boiled (CD 12:14), but nothing indicates that these were preferred foodstuffs. The suggestion by Stevan L. Davies, that if John was an Essene he would have been "required to eat only certain herbs and locusts and wild honey" in order to maintain Essene vows concerning food purity in the desert,[47] helpfully points to the importance of the food's purity, but misses the point that *any* Jew would have been forced to eat such food if living off the wilderness. Moreover, Josephus' comment that those excluded from the Essene community could not eat normal Jewish food and were forced to eat grass until they died of hunger or were allowed back into the group (*War* 2.143-44) seems to reflect a notion that their people could not live on what God provided at all, but only in community with other pure Essenes. This is the very *opposite* of what John and Bannus (and, for a time, Jesus) seem to have wanted to demonstrate: God does provide for the faithful, from nature itself.

John's Location

The proximity of John and Qumran has proved intriguing to several scholars,[48] but, as stated above, nothing suggests that John established a desert community that practiced frequent purificatory bathing or even that he fitted into one. In immersing people possibly as close as ten kilometers or so away from Qumran, he likely knew about a community there and about Essenes in general, and he may have been familiar with

47. S. L. Davies, "John the Baptist and Essene Kashruth."

48. See, e.g., J. A. T. Robinson, "The Baptism of John and the Qumran Community," 11-27; cf. J. Jeremias, *New Testament Theology,* 43: "The very nearness of the place of baptism to Qumran makes the assumption of relationship between the two a likely one."

some of their beliefs. But geographical proximity does not in itself require influence or connection. He was closer to large towns like Jericho, Abila, or Livias (see map on p. 44). Thus all kinds of movements and ideas may have influenced John.

John is described by Luke as "living in the wildernesses" (Luke 1:80), which may refer to his propensity to live in uncultivated areas in general. As stated above, the wilderness was uncultivated land. In Greek there is also a sense of the ἔρημος being far from human habitation. The crowds go out "into the wilderness" to hear John (Matt. 11:7; Luke 7:24; cf. Mark 1:4; Matt. 3:1).

The reference to John living in these uncultivated areas comes at the end of the nativity story of John in Luke's Gospel and is ambiguous. In full, it reads: "And the child [John] grew and became strong in spirit, and was in the wildernesses till the day of his public appearance to Israel." This has suggested to scholars such as Otto Betz that John must have grown up with the Essenes in Qumran. As Betz states, "How could this little child, the only son of aged parents, grow up in the wilderness? Well, the Essenes lived there, leading a kind of monastic life."[49] Since Josephus notes that the Essenes took other people's children and instructed them (*War* 2.120), John might have been such a child.

However, Luke 1:80 is surely not to be read as indicating that a little child was sent off into the wildernesses, let alone the wilderness of Judea around Qumran.[50] The first part of the verse closes John's infancy narrative in the same way that similar words close that of Jesus at Luke 2:40. Luke 1:80a is a formulaic, stereotypical statement derived from passages relating to Isaac, Samson, and Samuel (Gen. 21:8; Judg. 13:24 LXX; 1 Sam. 2:21).[51] Since Luke has constructed the Baptist birth story to echo the history of these figures from Israel's past, we should expect the description of John's growth also to echo scriptural precedents.[52] The second part concerning the wildernesses prefigures what Luke returns to in chapter three; John is positioned there when the word of God comes to him. Luke 3:2 reads: "The word of God came to John the son of Zechariah in the wilderness." This, as Raymond Brown notes,

49. Betz, "Was John the Baptist an Essene?" 209.

50. As assumed by VanderKam, "The Dead Sea Scrolls and Christianity," 189.

51. R. E. Brown, *The Birth of the Messiah: A Commentary on the Infancy Narratives in Matthew and Luke* (London: Chapman, 1977) 376-77.

52. Ibid., 377.

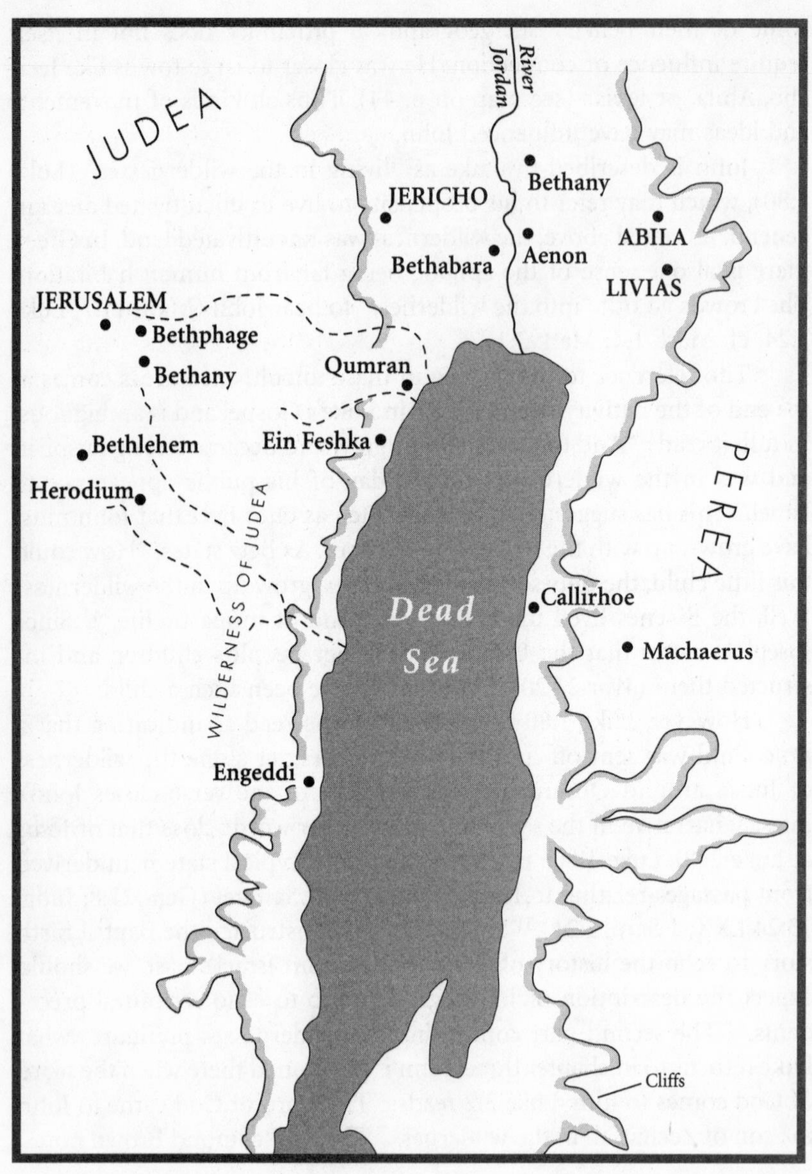

Map of the area of the Jordan River region associated with John, the Wilderness of Judea, and the Dead Sea

is "an appropriate continuation of 1:80" designed to make a "smooth transition" from the infancy narrative to the beginning of John's prophetic activity.[53] Therefore, it seems that in 1:80 Luke is setting the scene for what he is about to say in 3:2. It is unlikely, then, that John grew up in the wildernesses (note the plural) from babyhood.[54]

In the Fourth Gospel, John is described as being "in Bethany beyond the Jordan" (John 1:28) and "at Aenon near Salim, because there was much water [lit., many waters]" (John 3:23). These places are known only approximately.[55] Only Matthew describes the location as the wilderness of Judea (Matt. 3:1). In fact, Matthew describes it as such rather arbitrarily, because he is linking the placement of John with the province from which people came: Judea (Matt. 3:5). He later modifies a reference in Q, preserved in Luke 3:3 ("and he went into all the region about the Jordan, preaching a baptism of repentance for the remission of sins") in order to make it a reference to people: "Then went out to him Jerusalem and all Judea . . ." (from Mark 1:5) ". . . and all the region about the Jordan" (Matt. 3:3). In other words, according to Matthew, John did not go *into* the region about the Jordan; rather, people came *out* from there. Matthew therefore omits the reference to John's location along the Jordan river — which is where we would expect to find him immersing, since large amounts of water were important — and places John in the wilderness of Judea, where we find no water apart from in the wadis, and then only seasonally. It seems likely that Matthew had no idea about the geography of the region at all and felt that John had to be in the desert if he was to conform to Isa. 40:3. The region about a river is usually quite fertile and lush, and Matthew perhaps wished to stress the "desert" aspect over against the "wilderness" and to remove John from anywhere that might be fertile. "Desert," ערבה, is found in Isa. 40:3b as a parallel term to the "wilderness," מדבר, of 40:3a. The word מדבר is derived from the verb דבר, "to drive (sheep, goats)"; the word for "desert," ערבה, comes from the verb root ערב, "to be dry." Matthew puts John in a well-known dry place.

53. Ibid., 376. See also Meier, *Marginal Jew*, vol. 2, 26-27.

54. See also the critique of this notion by H. Lichtenberger, "Johannes der Täufer und die Texte von Qumran," 141-42.

55. The positions of places in the map on p. 44 are based on the locations determined by M. Avi-Yonah, *Gazetteer of Roman Palestine* (Jerusalem: Hebrew University of Jerusalem, 1976).

C. H. H. Scobie comments that the wilderness of Judea also included the last stretch of the river Jordan as it neared the Dead Sea, south of Jericho.[56] This is not quite true. This area is wilderness, and it becomes increasingly inhospitable the nearer one draws to the Dead Sea, but it is not the wilderness of Judea, strictly speaking (מדבר יהודה; cf. Judg. 1:16; Ps. 63:1). The wilderness of Judea is characterized by rugged, mountainous aridity, whereas the Jordan valley is in a different geographical zone and has a completely different character — river valley as opposed to hill district. Josephus describes the Jordan going through "a long wilderness" before it comes to the Dead Sea (*War* 3.515), but he does not say it meets the wilderness of Judea. As one looks down at the Jordan valley from the hills west of Jericho, it does not seem entirely natural to consider the valley and the wilderness of Judea to the south as part of the same geographical region (see map on p. 44).

Luke's reference to the "region about the Jordan" (Luke 3:3) may indicate that John roamed up and down, so we do not need to tie him to one locality with any great precision. If he gathered his food from the wild, he would have had to wander, and while the lower reaches of the Jordan may have held some attraction on account of their symbolic values, he may have moved much farther north as well. The region about the lower Jordan is bleak. The river lies in a trench well below the level of the valley, beneath sides of unstable marl that are impassable when wet. There are trees growing closely together and great masses of reeds, which makes access difficult.[57] Venomous vipers and wild boars still live there, and in John's time other wild beasts may have roamed around the banks of the river. The sixth-century Madaba mosaic map shows a lion chasing a deer not far to the east, and Mark's Gospel probably quite rightly notes in regard to Jesus' sojourn in the wilderness that he was "with the wild animals" (Mark 1:13).

There are two natural fords of the Jordan River near Jericho, the "fords of the Jordan" (Judg. 3:28) and "fords of the wilderness" (2 Sam. 15:28). It may have been around these that John first baptized, since they allow easy crossing of the river. However, the Jordan is not a raging torrent and can be crossed at other places by a small boat. John may

56. Scobie, *John the Baptist;* Meier, *Marginal Jew,* vol. 2, 43-44.

57. See the description by J. Murphy-O'Connor, "John the Baptist and Jesus: History and Hypothesis," *NTS* 36 (1990) 359 n. 2.

have gone elsewhere up the Jordan valley where there was a good supply of water for baptism, as Luke 3:3 indicates.

As mentioned above, in the Fourth Gospel it is understood that John "first" appeared along the Jordan (John 10:40) but was then in Aenon, near Salim, in Samaria (John 3:22-24).[58] The Madaba mosaic shows an Aenon east of the Jordan, across from Bethabara, and also an Aenon on the west bank identified as the Aenon near Salim. The name comes from the Hebrew word for "spring," עין. If John did move on to the west bank he would have been in the Roman-administered territory of Judea. He may have felt it safer to locate himself mainly in Perea on the east side of the Jordan, where Herod Antipas ruled, though if so he misjudged Herod's paranoia.

The fact that Herod Antipas, tetrarch of Galilee and Perea, arrested John and threw him into prison in the fortress Machaerus, east of the Dead Sea, seems to indicate that this was the nearest stronghold to where John was arrested that could be used for his incarceration; therefore, John was probably arrested in Perea.[59] This may explain why the Fourth Gospel tends to place John mainly in the region "beyond the Jordan," that is, Perea, rather than in Judea (John 1:28; 3:26; 10:40, cf. *War* 3.46 for Perea and its boundaries).

In conclusion, John's sphere of activity was mainly along the Jordan valley, Samaria, and Perea, not in the wilderness of Judea bordering the Dead Sea. Therefore, he did not share the same desert with the community at Qumran. Even if he did, and even though he may have once baptized people in the Jordan at a point fairly close to the Dead Sea, this does not mean he was associated with the Qumran group. Luke 1:80 is weak evidence on which to base a suggestion that John may have grown up at Qumran; the verse may be explained by looking at the literary purposes of the Gospel writer.

Moreover, we may remember also that only Pliny specifically mentions the Essenes in connection with the western shore of the Dead Sea, above Engeddi. Philo writes that the Essenes live in many cities and villages of Judea (*Hypothetica* 11.1), though he later qualifies this by

58. For an argument in favor of the historicity of this section, see Jeremias, *New Testament Theology*, 45-46.

59. So J. D. Crossan, *The Historical Jesus: The Life of a Mediterranean Jewish Peasant* (San Francisco: HarperSanFrancisco, 1991) 231. Oddly, Murphy-O'Connor suggests he was arrested in Galilee ("John the Baptist and Jesus," 369).

stating that they prefer villages (*Every Good Man Is Free* 75-76). Josephus also writes that they are in every town and village (*Ant.* 2.119-20). Both Philo and Josephus note that they number 4,000 men (*Hypothetica* 11.1; *Ant.* 18.18), which presumably is a rough approximation. Whatever the case, the wilderness community at Qumran would appear to be the exception to the usual localization of Essenes in urban centers or in villages. If one really wanted to speculate about Essene influence on John on the grounds of close proximity, one might do better to look to urban centers and villages close to the Jordan River.

The evidence reviewed above appears to indicate that John should not be associated with the Essenes. Isa. 40:3 was used in the rule book of the Qumran group to justify its existence as a community in the wilderness, but John does not appear to have used the verse in this way. While his baptism took place in the wilderness, people were expected to go home to their regular occupations. The notion that there was a "Baptist movement" — to which both the Essenes and John belonged — out of line with "mainstream Judaism" rests on outdated presuppositions regarding Second Temple Judaism. John and the Essenes used immersion, and both types of immersion may have been for purification, but this probably derives from the fact that issues of purity were very important to all groups of Jews at this time. John was an ascetic in a particular way, trusting that God would provide food enough for him to live in uncultivated regions; he rejected cultivated food like bread and wine, whereas the Essenes considered these staples of their diet, as did most others. His clothing of camel hair sackcloth indicated his humility before God; he did not wear the white garments of an Essene. He lived in the wild parts of the region around the lower Jordan, not on the western shores of the Dead Sea where the Qumran community was located. Physical proximity means nothing in terms of tracing influence or connection. In short, the overwhelming impression is that John should probably not be seen as having any direct relationship with the Essenes, least of all the isolated group at Qumran, whether prior to or during his own prophetic activity by the river Jordan. Having laid aside a connection between John and the Essenes at the outset, we can now proceed to investigate further the figure of John and his place within Second Temple Judaism. We will begin with a consideration of the nature of his baptism.

CHAPTER 2

Immersion and Purity

In the last chapter, we considered the evidence for John being linked with the Essenes in some way. In passing, the point was made that John's baptism may have had something to do with ritual purity and immersion, but, if so, this did not link John exclusively with the Essenes. Rather, it may be that in understanding immersion and the importance of ritual purity in Second Temple Judaism, John's baptism will be better understood. Indeed, Josephus expressly tells us that John's baptism was "a purification of the body" (*Ant.* 18.117). In this chapter, we will explore this in detail and then consider how certain ideas found in the Qumran *Community Rule* may well illuminate why John baptized people. In this, it will be argued, John need not have been influenced directly by Essene groups, but rather by a certain exegesis of the book of Isaiah. It must be noted that issues of purity in Second Temple Judaism were extremely complex, and this discussion considers only factors relevant to the identification of John's baptism.

John's Immersion: Procedure and Practice

Clearly, if there was one feature of John that struck his contemporaries as significant, it was that he immersed people. He was therefore called "the Immerser": in Greek ὁ βαπτιστής (e.g., Matt. 16:14 = Mark 8:28 = Luke 9:19; cf. Josephus, *Ant.* 18.117) or ὁ βαπτίζων (Mark 1:4; 6:14, 24). The word βάπτισμα means "immersion," from the verb βαπτίζω, which, in the LXX, is used of Naaman's seven self-immersions in the river Jordan (ἐβαπτίσατο, 2 Kgs. 5:14; cf. Jdt. 12:7; Greek Sirach 31:30). Josephus uses the verb βαπτίζω for "immerse" both literally (*War* 1.437; *Ant.* 15.55) and metaphorically (*War* 2.476; 4.137; *Ant.* 10.169) and also for "to sink (a ship) underwater" (*War* 2.556; 3.368; *Ant.* 9.212; *Life* 15) and "to sink (a person) underwater," that is, "to drown" (*War* 1.437; 3.423; 3.525, 527; *Ant.* 15.55). The Hebrew word equivalent to βάπτισμα (and βαπτισμός or βάπτισις, so *Ant.* 18.117) would be טבילה, which refers to full immersion and proselyte baptism. In the New Testament, the verb βαπτίζω refers to Jewish ritual immersion at Luke 11:38, where a Pharisee is surprised that Jesus has not immersed himself (ἐβαπτίσθη, the aorist passive, literally "was immersed") before eating. According to Mark 7:4, "Jews" (Pharisees?) βαπτίσωνται, immersed themselves, after coming in from the market before eating (cf. Heb. 6:2; 9:10). Elsewhere, both βάπτισμα and βαπτισμός (Col. 2:12) refer to Christian baptism.[1] The title, "The Immerser," may refer to someone who immerses himself often, but it is generally understood to mean that he immersed others. Mark quotes John as saying: "I immerse you with [or "in"] water . . ." (Mark 1:8a), which suggests that John was understood to be the agent of immersion. He is active, and those whom he immerses are to some extent passive. They come to him for immersion, and his agency is important. The only known parallel outside the New Testament for anyone immersing someone else is in Josephus' story of the drowning of the last Hasmonean high priest Aristobulus III, when agents of Herod pushed him underwater (thereby "immersing" him) and held him there (*War* 1.437; *Ant.* 15.55). It may be imagined that John similarly stood with people in the water and pushed them under.

However, there is no clear parallel in any current Jewish immersion rite for someone acting as an immerser alongside the person who is being immersed in the water. In Jewish immersion rites, the person goes down into the water and immerses himself or herself. No one pushes the person underwater. Therefore, it may be argued, John's immersion of people could not have been concerned with the removal of ritual

1. R. L. Webb, *John the Baptizer and Prophet: A Socio-Historical Study* (Sheffield: JSOT Press, 1991) 163 n. 2. See R. P. Booth, *Jesus and the Laws of Purity: Tradition History and Legal History in Mark 7* (Sheffield: JSOT Press, 1986) 24. See also A. Oepke, "βάπτω, etc.," *TDNT* 1 (1974) 529-46; βαπτίζω seems to be an intensive or iterative amplification of the verb βάπτω, which also means "dip, immerse."

uncleanness, like other Jewish immersions. It must have been for something else.

Aristobulus was, of course, an unwilling subject of immersion, whereas those who came to John for immersion were presumably eager for it. We do not know precisely how John actively immersed people. He may well have held on to them. If he did, this would not have invalidated the purificatory effectiveness of the immersion. As the Mishnah has it, "He who kept hold on a man or on utensils and immersed them — they are unclean" unless "he rinsed his hand in the water" beforehand (*m. Miqw.* 8:5). That the Mishnah here mentions someone keeping hold of another human being indicates that the practice of someone actively immersing someone else was known. Indeed, in the case of children, the sick, or the disabled, assistance must have been necessary at times. The Mishnaic rule required simply that the person who held on to those who were being immersed rinse his or her hand first, since water would still adhere to the hand. Alternatively, according to Rabbi Simeon, there had to be a moment (an unspecified length of time) during which someone's hold of items, including people, that were being immersed was relinquished. He is recorded as stating that the immerser should "loose his hold on them so that the water may come into them" (*m. Miqw.* 8:5). Although this literary evidence is late, these views may have been known before their codification at the end of the second century. The Mishnaic evidence suggests that even if John did hold on to people, his immersion might still be classified as being purificatory, as were other Jewish immersions.

Interestingly, in the account of the baptism of Jesus "by John" (ὑπὸ Ἰωάννου), the active participle of the verb ἀναβαίνων, "coming up," is used for Jesus' coming up out of the water, despite the fact that he was in some way immersed (ἐβαπτίσθη) by John. It is not written that John "brought him up" (Mark 1:9-10; cf. Matt. 3:16). If Jesus came up by himself, we may conjecture that he went down by himself also, or else that John let him go at some point.

The distinction between the passive and the active was not necessarily hard-and-fast. In Hellenistic Greek the passive of βαπτίζω could also mean "go under," whether literally or figuratively.[2] According to Joachim Jeremias, the Aramaic corresponding to the Greek passive βαπτισθῆναι (Mark 1:9 and parr.) is the active Qal form טבל, meaning

2. Oepke, "βάπτω," 530.

"undergo immersion, immerse oneself."[3] The Greek preposition ὑπό with the genitive case as here may mean "by" but can also mean "under" or "beneath," "by reason of," or "through."[4] It can express subjection to someone's authority. In other words, we need not assume that John had to be physically touching the person who was immersed throughout the entire operation. The action could have been self-administered, with John directing or participating. However, he must have been more than a witness, because a witness could never be understood as "immersing" someone else. In the rabbinic period, a new convert to Judaism had to immerse himself or herself in a ritual bath in the presence of three witnesses (*b. Yebam.* 46b), but these witnesses did not actually "baptize" the person.

It is possible that John went underwater at the same time as the person he was causing to be immersed. In Acts 8:36-39 the Christian διάκονος ("servant" or "assistant") Philip baptizes the Ethiopian eunuch by going down into the river with him, immersing himself at the same time. In one ancient version of Luke 3:7, those baptized by John in the Jordan do so ἐνώπιον αὐτοῦ, "in his presence."[5] Bodily contact is not suggested. As just noted, the title "the Immerser" does not necessarily imply that John was immersing someone else.

Since John's baptism was the basis for later Christian baptism,[6] we may look at the latter for helpful comparisons. Evidently, the candidate was not actually touched by the baptizer. In the *Didache,* the earliest known Christian manual, the candidate is "baptized into the name of the Father, the Son and the Holy Spirit in running water (of a river)" (*Did.* 7:1). It is specified that if there is no running water then other water is permitted, and if no cold water, then warm is all right, and if neither of these is available then water is to be poured over the head three times into the threefold name (*Did.* 7:1-4). There is no mention of physical dunking by someone else. Incidentally, the distinction between cold and warm water might allude to a suspicion of warm springs, as opposed to cold bodies of water. Josephus' teacher Bannus bathed in

3. J. Jeremias, *New Testament Theology: The Proclamation of Jesus* (London: SCM, 1971) 51.

4. LSJ, 1874-75.

5. Jeremias, *New Testament Theology,* 51.

6. See A. Yarbro Collins, "The Origin of Christian Baptism," *StudLit* 19 (1989) 28-46; cf. G. W. H. Lampe, *The Seal of the Spirit: A Study in the Doctrine of Baptism and Confirmation in the New Testament and the Fathers* (London: Longmans, 1951) 19-46.

cold water (*Life* 11), probably to resist luxuriating in the warm pools along the Dead Sea and elsewhere, as Herod Antipas did at Callirhoë. Whether some considered warm spring water less effective than cold water for purification is unknown; the rabbis considered "smitten" (salty or warm) natural water effective for cleansing (*m. Miqw.* 1:8). However, the sulfuric odor of warm springs or the high metal content of the water may have suggested to some that this water was not as pure as that from a natural cold spring, river, lake, or sea. The *Didache* reflects a pragmatic approach.

The notion that Christian baptism generally involved the pouring of water comes through in Titus 3:5-7 and other places where the Spirit being "poured out" over Christian believers is considered to be baptism in the Holy Spirit (e.g., Acts 10:44-48; 11:15). This is associated with a Christian reading of Joel 2:28-29 (MT 3:1-5), which predicts that God will pour out his Spirit on people prior to the end. In Christian baptism, the pouring out of the Spirit was linked with the pouring out of water on the heads of the people. On the numerous occasions in the Acts of the Apostles where baptism occurs, there is only one case — that of the Ethiopian eunuch — in which immersion takes place in a natural body of water. From this we should probably assume that it became the norm in the (Gentile) Church to "immerse" people by means of pouring out water over their heads. It was possibly a matter of expediency and picked up on a strand of Diaspora Jewish tradition that held that pouring water over someone was equivalent in effectiveness to full immersion in running water, at least in some cases not related to appearing at the Temple.[7]

In the Christian manual the *Apostolic Tradition* of Hippolytus (ca. 230), the water in the font was to be "flowing" or else water was to be poured over it (*Apost. Trad.* 21). Archaeology confirms that early baptisteries had fonts that were too shallow to be used for complete immersion. The house-church at Dura Europos in Mesopotamia, also dated ca. 230, contains a font that would have permitted the person to kneel within it, while water was poured over his or her head. In the

7. In *m. Ber.* 3:5 pouring water over someone is equivalent in effectiveness to full immersion in the case of a man who has had a seminal emission. According to Lev. 15:16 a man was to bathe his whole body for such an emission. See E. P. Sanders, *Judaism: Practice and Belief 63* BCE*–66* CE (London: SCM, 1992) 222-23. According to Philo, after sex it was necessary for a man to perform an ablution of splashing or sprinkling, instead of bathing (*On the Special Laws* 3.63). See also E. P. Sanders, *Jewish Law from Jesus to the Mishnah: Five Studies* (London: SCM, 1990) 263-71.

Lateran baptistery in Rome, a jet of water would have gushed into the font, so that the person could be immersed by standing in the flow.[8] In the case of such a pouring type of baptism, one is necessarily "immersed" by someone who actually does the pouring of the water over the body. Indeed, in early Christian art John the Baptist is depicted as baptizing Jesus in the Jordan by pouring water over his head.[9] Christian practice was read back into the interpretation of John's baptism. It was supposed that if John actually immersed people, then he must have poured water over their heads.

A peculiarity of Christian baptism should be noted here: the person who actually poured out water was not necessarily considered to be a true baptizer. For example, in the *Didascalia Apostolorum* deaconesses are to assist women and no doubt pour water over them (for modesty's sake),[10] but it is the bishop who does the "real" baptizing, with the pronouncing of the Trinitarian formula and the imparting of the Spirit — only men could officially baptize (*Didasc. Apost.* 16 [3:12]; cf. 14 [3:9]). The pneumatic immersion was considered the definitive part of the ritual.

Nothing is said in early Christian texts of any bodily contact between the baptizer and the person baptized. The *Apostolic Tradition* emphasizes the nakedness of the candidate for baptism, and the specification that women should not even have any jewelry on them connects the actual procedure of Christian baptism with a basic Jewish concept of bodily purification, in which continued contact with any other item — apart from certain things that did not interpose — renders the immersion invalid. That early Christian baptism generally required candidates to be naked (*Didasc. Apost.* 16 [3:12]; Cyril of Jerusalem, *Catecheses* 20:2) reflects the legacy of a concern for purity that we find in Jewish tradition.

As with representations in early Christian art depicting John pouring water over Jesus' head, so with nakedness: Jesus is frequently depicted naked in the river Jordan at his baptism by John. However,

8. See C. E. Pocknee, "The Archaeology of Christian Baptism," *Theo* 74 (1971) 309-11; J. P. Sodini, "Les baptisteres byzantins: un éclairage sur les rites," *MB* 65 (1990) 45-47.

9. For the iconographical repertoire of John the Baptist, see J. E. Taylor, "A Graffito Depicting John the Baptist at Nazareth?" *PEQ* 119 (1987) 143-45.

10. See E. J. Christiansen, "Women and Baptism," *StudTheo* 35/1 (1981) 1-8.

John probably would not have required those coming to his immersion to be naked. Traditionally, in Judaism, nakedness in front of others was shameful (cf. Gen. 2:25; 3:7). Public nakedness was the punishment of an adulterous woman (Isa. 3:17; 47:3; Hos. 2:3, 9-10; Jer. 13:26; Ezek. 23:26). The nudity of the gymnasium, brought in by Hellenizers ca. 174 BCE (1 Macc. 1:14-15; 2 Macc. 4:12-15; cf. *Ant.* 12.241), was not accepted by traditionalist Jews. The same abhorrence of nakedness is found in the *Community Rule* of the Essenes (1QS 8:12, 13-14). In going down into a מקוה (*miqveh*) naked, one was either alone or else in the company of those of the same sex, in front of whom nakedness was not quite so unseemly. In the case of public מקואות (*miqva'ot*) one may have kept something of one's clothes on.[11]

Josephus reports that the Essenes required men to wear a linen loincloth, περίζομα, and women some kind of garment, ἔνδυμα, during an immersion (*War* 2.161). The Essene garments may have been made from linen or, more commonly, wool. Interestingly, in the Mishnah, there

11. For nakedness and the self-administration aspect in Jewish immersions, see Lampe, *The Seal of the Spirit*, 24-25; H. H. Rowley, "Jewish Proselyte Baptism and the Baptism of John," *HUCA* 15 (1940) 323-24; Sanders, *Judaism: Practice and Belief*, 225. Juhl Christiansen notes in regard to John's baptism, "We can only conjecture about the absence of clothes . . . it may have taken place without people undressing" (Christiansen, "Women and Baptism," 2). This matter has only come to the fore with the consideration of women being involved. In later proselyte baptism, witnesses had to be of the same sex as the baptizand (*b. Yebam.* 46). Sanders notes in regard to public immersions in *miqva'ot* that if people went down naked — the usual practice — they had to put on unclean clothes afterwards, which was a problem. He states: "The existence of public immersion pools indicates that many people did not observe rules of garment-purity. Several impurities render the clothes impure. How can one walk to a public pool in impure clothes, immerse, and not touch one's impure clothes again?" (*Judaism: Practice and Belief*, 521 n. 28). Sanders notes that the Pharisees considered the garments of ordinary people impure (*m. Ḥag.* 2:7; *Judaism: Practice and Belief*, 440). The common people may not have been fastidious, but it seems doubtful that people would have put on unclean clothing after immersion. One way around the problem would have been to immerse with one's clothes on, immerse other unclean material (bedding, for example) and garments at the same time, and then just dry off naturally outside in the air. This would have been uncomfortable, but Sanders rightly points out that the whole procedure was uncomfortable (*Judaism: Practice and Belief*, 225). Alternatively, one could go with someone who was clean, who could carry some clean, dry clothing; various methods were possible. Whatever the case, one need not imagine that people necessarily went down naked, since keeping one's clothing on, if permitted, rendered it clean at the same time.

is the view that threads of wool or flax and the ribbons on the heads of girls all interpose and render the immersion invalid. Rabbi Judah apparently stated that those items made of wool and those of hair do not interpose, because the water enters into them (*m. Miqw.* 9:1). This statement, along with what we learn of Essene practice, seems to indicate that there was debate about what might be worn during an immersion. What is almost certain is that people would not have gone naked in front of other people of the opposite sex in order to be immersed. If John himself wore a haircloth garment while immersing, his clothing may have been acceptable by some standards for purification, provided that water entered into the garment and onto his body unobstructed.

Pouring water over someone's head was not considered the most effective form of ritual purification by later rabbinic standards. By far the most effective form of baptism was immersion in a natural body of water, in the sea, or in a *miqveh* cut into rock and filled with rain. The widespread use of *miqva'ot,* shown by discoveries throughout the Land of Israel, indicates that these installations were common by the first century, though details of *miqveh* construction and procedure might have varied depending on sectarian affiliation.[12] By taking the form of immersion in the river Jordan — and in other places where there was an abundance of water (cf. John 3:23) — John's baptism would have been acceptable as a means of Jewish purificatory ritual for bodily uncleanness, even by later rabbinic standards.

The best parallel we have for the baptism of John may be the immersion of the Ethiopian eunuch by Philip, which was clearly not a case of pouring but of going underwater in a natural flow or reservoir encountered by the travelers on the road between Jerusalem and Gaza. Byzantine Christians identified the site as a natural spring.[13] The inter-

12. Sanders, *Judaism: Practice and Belief,* 223.

13. Jerome (*Ep. ad Eustochium* 11.1) identifies the site on the "old Gaza road." Theodosius (*De Situ Urbis Jerusalem* 5) places it two miles from Mamre. The Piacenza Pilgrim (*Itinerarium* 32) has it close to Eleutheropolis in a valley; cf. also Hugeburc, *Vita Willibaldi* 24. See for these texts J. Wilkinson, *Jerusalem Pilgrims Before the Crusades* (Warminster: Aris & Phillips, 1977) and his Map 5 (p. 23), which gives the first identification of the spring north of Mamre very near Bethsur. The Spring of Philip appears to have moved closer to Eleutheropolis to accommodate the logistics of a pilgrim itinerary. For the importance of logistical considerations in the identification of Byzantine holy sites, see J. E. Taylor, *Christians and the Holy Places: The Myth of Jewish-Christian Origins* (Oxford: Clarendon, 1993) 219-20, 340.

esting thing about Philip's baptisms is that they differed from what was becoming the norm in the Church. While they were performed "in the name of the master/lord Jesus" (Acts 8:16), but his immersions did not involve the baptism of the Holy Spirit. Peter and John came to Samaria in his wake to impart the Spirit by means of the imposition of hands (Acts 8:17). As such, the type of water-only baptism he administered was much closer to the baptism of John than to later Christian water-and-Spirit baptism. In the story of the immersion of the Ethiopian eunuch (Acts 8:26-39), a proselyte who has just come from worshipping at the Temple in Jerusalem, Philip and the Ethiopian go down into the water together, where "he immersed (ἐβάπτισεν) him" (Acts 8:38). So Philip was more than a witness; he acted alongside the Ethiopian and could be described as immersing him. It is not stated that Philip pushed the Ethiopian's head underwater or touched him, only that he went down into the water with him and came up out of it with him.

All this argues against the view that John's baptism must have been quite different from other Jewish immersions because he actively baptized by putting people underwater.[14] It is impossible to argue that this was definitely not the case, on account of the paucity of the evidence, but if it was not necessarily the case, we may be justified in trying to consider John's baptism in line with other Jewish immersions rather than as something wholly unique and distinct. Moreover, even if he did somehow put people underwater — if he let go of them so that the water could reach all parts of the body — and even if they then came up out of the water without holding on to him, his immersion of people would still have been considered effective. It cannot be proven on the evidence of the New Testament that John definitely held on to the person he was baptizing throughout the entire procedure. The evidence of the baptism of Jesus suggests that he did not, and Philip's baptism of the Ethiopian eunuch gives us the same impression. John may have gone down into the water with people and emerged with them, and he may have somehow supervised a group of people at the same time. Therefore, either way, John's baptism may well have been concerned with bodily purification, as Josephus expressly states. We can remember also that the baptism of John is associated with

14. So Lampe, *The Seal of the Spirit,* 19, 25; cf. J. P. Meier, *A Marginal Jew: Rethinking the Historical Jesus. Volume Two: Mentor, Message, and Miracles* (New York: Doubleday, 1994) 51.

purification in the Fourth Gospel, where "purification" and "baptism" appear to be equated (John 3:25-26).

What then is "bodily" or "ritual" purification? For non-Jews, these concepts are generally unfamiliar and can be baffling. We will therefore explore these issues further before proceeding, in order to clarify understanding of what is involved.

Bodily Purity: Ṭohŏrâ

To outsiders, any religious system involving praxis that is interwoven with the processes of daily life will seem complex. For those who have grown up in the system, the praxis is ingrained, normative, and simply done. Jacob Milgrom has noted that the purity laws of Judaism are part of a system, and one needs to understand the underlying nature of the system in order to comprehend the significance of the laws of purity, טהרה *(ṭohŏrâ)*. The purity laws are given their justification in the Torah and may be found in particular in Leviticus 11–15. The basic notion is that God is entirely pure and holy and resides in Israel. Therefore, those who wish to do the will of God and serve him must endeavor to be pure and holy; the closer one gets to the Temple, where God resides, the purer and holier one should be.[15] As Jacob Neusner stresses, ritual purity has absolutely nothing to do with hygiene.[16] To put it another way, purity is not about using soap, or having regular baths, or washing off *dirt*. Nevertheless, the language used is similar, and ritual impurity is an actual state — a kind of unseen contamination — that is not liked by God, even though it is not a condition symbolically representing sin. There is nothing morally sinful about being impure. One cannot avoid it. Becoming impure happens quite naturally all the time. One simply aims to get rid of this impurity in order to return to a state of purity, if possible. One distinguishes between the pure and the impure, as it is said in the Torah: Israelites are "to distinguish between the holy and the common, and between the unclean and the clean" (Lev. 10:10).

15. J. Milgrom, *Leviticus 1–16: A New Translation with Introduction and Commentary* (New York: Doubleday, 1991) 118-36.

16. J. Neusner, *The Idea of Purity in Ancient Judaism. With a Critique and a Commentary by Mary Douglas* (Leiden: Brill, 1973) 1.

All kinds of things can render a body unclean, in particular: contact with a corpse (Num. 19:10-13; cf. bodies of creatures, Leviticus 11); skin diseases (Leviticus 13); and bodily discharges (Leviticus 15; also Deut. 21:1-9; 23:10; cf. Josephus, *Ag. Ap.* 2.198, 203; *Ant.* 3.263).[17] Immersion was not necessary to remove every form of ritual impurity, but it was called for in the following types of situations: someone who has had a contagious skin disease (Lev. 14:8-9); someone with a genital discharge, a זב (Lev. 15:13); someone who has touched a corpse (Lev. 22:4-6; Num. 31:23-24); a man with a seminal emission (Deut. 23:11; Lev. 15:16); someone who eats an animal that has died a natural death or been savaged (Lev. 17:15); someone who touches the bed of a זב or sits on his chair (Lev. 15:6); someone who touches a זב (Lev. 15:7-8, 11-12) or is spat on by a זב (Lev. 15:8), or has carried anything under a זב (Lev. 15:10); someone who touches the bed or seat of a menstruant, a זבה (Lev. 15:21-22, 25-27).[18] Jacob Milgrom has also argued that the presumption that a person will be unclean until evening, found in some of passages in Leviticus 11, implies the minimal necessity to immerse and is simply shorthand for immersion (cf. Lev. 11:32, where the shorthand is spelled out for objects; also Lev. 17:15; 22:5-6). Taking these additional instances into account increases the number of cases calling for immersion. If this is right, then one would have to immerse after touching, picking up, or eating the carcass of an unclean animal (Lev. 11:24-28, 31, 39; cf. 40).[19]

In Lev. 15:13 a person is cleansed from the impurity caused by discharges by immersion in "running water," מים חיים (lit., "living water"), that is, in a river, spring, lake, or in the sea (cf. Lev. 14:5-6, 50-52; Num. 19:17; Deut. 21:4). This type of naturally collected water was considered to have been provided directly by God and was therefore deemed far more effective than water collected by human means. Scripture explicitly demands that immersion take place in running water only in the case of a זב (Lev. 15:13), but Milgrom has argued quite persuasively that the demand is implied in the case of a normal menstruant,

17. See Neusner, *The Idea of Purity,* 15-24.

18. On the levitical purity laws, see Milgrom, *Leviticus 1–16,* esp. his table of purification procedures and effects (pp. 986-91).

19. Milgrom, *Leviticus 1–16,* 667; cf. H. K. Harrington, *The Impurity Systems of Qumran and the Rabbis: Biblical Foundations* (Atlanta: Scholars Press, 1993) 117-19; also 11QT 51:2-3.

a menstuant with an irregular flow, or a woman who has recently given birth (cf. Lev. 12:2).[20]

In Israel during the Second Temple period, purification from uncleanness could also be accomplished by full immersion in a מקוה *(miqveh)*, a specially constructed immersion pool. The Pharisees may have immersed in a *miqveh* more frequently than others, for example when coming in from the market (cf. Mark 7:4) or before eating (cf. Luke 11:38).[21]A *miqveh* was considered to be almost as good as natural water, but not quite. In the six grades of water defined by the rabbis, *miqveh* water falls in the middle at grade three, but "running water" in its natural state is the best, at grade six (*m. Miqw.* 1:1-8). Those with genital discharges and women with an irregular menstrual flow were to immerse in this kind of water only (*m. Miqw.* 1:8). The typical *miqveh* was constructed out of rock and was filled largely with rainwater — not drawn water — to make it as "natural" as possible. Only three logs (= ca. 0.9 liters) of drawn water could be added to the principal of forty seahs (= ca. 500 liters; *m. 'Ed.* 1:3; cf. *m. Miqw.* 4:4), or else it would be invalid. In this case, "natural" means "heavenly"; a *miqveh* had to be as close to that ideal as possible. As Hannah Harrington has noted, a passage in *Sifre Shemini* (9:1) states this explicitly: "Just as a spring is made by the hands of Heaven, so an immersion pool is to be made."[22]

Immersion in running water was only one method of cleansing from impurity. The passage of time, and especially waiting until the sun's rays had ceased, effected the final removal of impurity in certain cases. A woman was unclean for seven days after bearing a male child and fourteen after a female child, though to cleanse the blood of un-

20. Milgrom, *Leviticus 1–16*, 923-24.

21. In the market, people bustled around and one could not avoid being pushed against someone who was unclean. See the discussion in Booth, *Jesus and the Laws of Purity*, 151-216, based on many of Neusner's conclusions. Logistically, this must mean that *miqva'ot* would have been fairly close to where the Pharisees lived, or else a Pharisee risked becoming unclean on the way home. Purity was especially connected with eating food, since Pharisees wished to eat meals in a state of purity; see J. Neusner, "Mr. Sanders' Pharisees and Mine: A Response to E. P. Sanders, *Jewish Law from Jesus to the Mishnah*, *SJT* 44 (1991) 73-95; idem, "Mr. Sanders' Pharisees and Mine," *BBR* 2 (1992) 143-69; idem, "Mr Maccoby's Red Cow, Mr Sanders' Pharisees, and Mine," *JSJ* 23 (1992) 81-98; B. D. Chilton, *Judaic Approaches to the Gospels* (Atlanta: Scholars Press, 1994) 165-68; Harrington, *The Impurity Systems of Qumran and the Rabbis*, 267-81; cf. D. R. de Lacey, "In Search of a Pharisee," *TynBul* 43 (1992) 353-72.

22. Harrington, *The Impurity Systems of Qumran and the Rabbis*, 135.

cleanness resulting from childbirth a blood sacrifice had to be made. This took place thirty-three days after the birth of a male child and sixty-six days after the birth of a female (Lev. 12:2-8). Some kinds of impurity could be removed by sprinkling water on the body (Num. 19:18; cf. 31:19, 23) or by other washing. If one failed to wash when washing was prescribed in the Law, as in the case of sexual intercourse (Lev. 15:18), then the uncleanness remained (cf. Num. 19:13). Corpse impurity required sprinkling with spring water in which the ashes of a red heifer had been mixed (Numbers 19). Most importantly, in terms of Scripture, blood purifies, as when blood from the red heifer is sprinkled towards the entrance of the Tent of Meeting (Num. 19:4). Alternatively, there is fire (Num. 31:23-24).

The Torah specifies that in some cases of uncleanness a sin offering be made in the Temple. This largely has to do with cases in which the uncleanness is the result of abnormal conditions, particularly sickness. So, for example, no sin offering is required for uncleanness resulting from menstruation (Lev. 15:19-25) or sexual intercourse (Lev. 15:18), but sin offerings are required for skin disease (Lev. 14:10-32), irregular emissions (Lev. 15:2-25), or bleeding other than from menstruation (Lev. 15:26). As Robert Webb has rightly pointed out, sin (חטאה) in the Hebrew Bible can refer to things being out of order, rather than morally wrong.[23] The "sin" involved, however, concerns the outer rather than the inner; it is bodily sin rather than wrongdoing springing from the heart.

While the laws of uncleanness had relevance beyond the Temple, impurity of the body was especially important for those intending to go to the Temple. People who were not clean were not allowed to enter the Temple (Josephus, *War* 5.227). Levitical law stipulates: "Thus you shall keep the children of Israel separate from their uncleanness, so that they do not die in their uncleanness by defiling my tabernacle that is in their midst" (Lev. 15:31). Non-Jews had to remain in the court of the Gentiles, beyond the *soreg,* or partition,[24] but could participate in some

23. Webb, *John the Baptizer and Prophet,* 99.

24. The court referred to in *b. Yoma* 30a and *t. Yoma* 1:14 is probably the inner court — part of the complex that comprised the sanctuary proper — rather than the Court of the Gentiles. Josephus states that Jews had to purify themselves before entering this area (*Ant.* 12.145), but what was required beyond the area is not absolutely clear. Purity was required in different degrees the nearer one got to the Holy of Holies, but it seems likely that people made some effort to be pure even in the outer court.

ways in the sacred cult by proxy. The court of the (impure) Gentiles was huge and able to accommodate a great many people, but the court of the Israelites, with the court of the women included, took up less than one-seventh of the total area of the Herodian Temple complex. Certainly, those who wished to eat of the meat of sacrificed animals had to be in a clean state (Lev. 8:19-21).

The ceremony of the Day of Atonement (see Leviticus 16) was partly conducted in order to rid the sanctuary itself of any uncleanness that it may have contracted on account of people not keeping the purity rules. The sanctuary was sprinkled with blood "because of the uncleannesses of the people of Israel and because of their transgressions and all their sins" (Lev. 15:31; 20:3; Num. 19:13, 20). The various things that might have defiled the purity of the sanctuary were thereby removed. The sins and transgressions of the people of Israel, though not uncleannesses, were borne away by a goat, sent into the wilderness (Lev. 16:20-22).

What all this serves to show is that a desire to live in obedience to the Law made bodily purity a significant concern. In first-century Judaism the Temple continued to be an important focus of religious life until its destruction in 70 CE. For those sufficiently proximate to Jerusalem, there were festivals that entailed going to the Temple and that therefore required a state of bodily purity. To what extent can we assume that ordinary people kept the purity laws in general?

One passage in rabbinic literature suggests that the rabbis at least considered that most people were unclean. The Mishnah notes that the unclean walked in the middle "current" of the road or bridge in Jerusalem and that the clean walked on the perimeter (*m. Šeqal.* 8:1); clearly the area in the middle of the road would accommodate the bulk of the traffic. This tradition applies to the period before 135 CE, since after this date Jews were banned from the city.[25] One imagines Pharisees and those endeavoring to remain clean shuffling along the sides. Even so, it appears that Pharisees would always immerse themselves after coming in from public places such as the market.[26] Only during festival times in Jerusalem when people were intending to go to the Temple could it be assumed that the majority were clean.[27]

25. Eusebius, *Hist. Eccl.* 4.3.1-6.

26. See Booth, *Jesus and the Laws of Purity,* 200-201.

27. The widespread use of *miqva'ot* indicates that religious people did wish to maintain purity, or considered it of some concern, but Pharisaic standards required a

There were probably many *miqva'ot* (purificatory baths) on the Temple Mount (*b. Yoma* 30b; *m. Tamid* 1:1). It was decided by the rabbis that prior to going to the Temple people should immerse themselves in a *miqveh* even if they thought they were ritually clean, just to be on the safe side (*m. Yoma* 3:3; *y. Yoma* 40b).[28] This may have been Pharisaic practice, possibly followed by many.

Now, if all this reflects the rationale for immersion, how did John's immersion fit with this system? One may imagine that to Jews in general John's call for immersion would have been understandable as a call to become ritually clean. Those who had fallen away from the praxis of Judaism and consequently neglected the rules of ritual cleanness would have understood that John's immersion in the running water of the Jordan would cleanse them, upon their return to the fold. Those who had obeyed the Law and kept to the praxis of purity may have considered John's immersion to be a kind of extra measure, as in the case of going to a Temple *miqveh*. It was a generally good thing to do. But this does not give us a sufficient explanation for why John's immersion was so special.

It certainly would have come as a shock to people coming forward to be immersed if John called them, rather fiercely, "offspring of vipers" (Matt. 3:7; Luke 3:7). These are not kind words. Moreover, John had to "preach" or "proclaim" (Mark 1:4) an immersion that was not precisely the same as

---

higher degree of purity than what was common. Sanders thinks that Palestinian Jews kept most of the biblical purity laws (*Judaism: Practice and Belief*, 229), whereas Neusner thinks they did not (*Reading and Believing: Ancient Judaism and Contemporary Gullibility* [Atlanta: Scholars Press, 1986] 54), but both these scholars may be right, for the point is that purity is not an objective state to be tested empirically, but a subjective state defined by the observer. Therefore, one person's purity could be another's impurity. Essenes apparently considered only those within their sect pure. By Pharisaic and later rabbinic standards, most people were regarded as impure or could not be relied upon to be pure. However, most people may have considered themselves to be pure, by different standards, unless they had abandoned the praxis of Judaism.

28. The Temple was equipped with a massive storage system for water, as yet only partially defined; see D. Bahat with Ch. T. Rubinstein, *The Illustrated Atlas of Jerusalem* (New York: Simon & Schuster, 1990) 47-50. No *miqva'ot* as such have been found on the Temple Mount, but if excavations were permitted these would no doubt come to light. If they were constructed in accordance with the rulings we find in later rabbinic literature, then they would have been cut into rock at a lower level than the pavement. People would have had to go underground in order to immerse, probably close to the main gates leading into the Temple proper, or *soreg*.

the others and yet that shared the same general concern with them — removing ritual purity. If John's immersion was for the removal of impurity, why does it seem unique? It would have been impossible to remain clean permanently after John's immersion. A woman became unclean with every menstrual period or childbirth. A man's seminal emission, whether in sexual intercourse or not, made him unclean. One could not neglect burying the dead. As we saw above, so many things could make one unclean; there was no avoiding them. Absolutely nothing in our sources gives us any reason to presume that John's immersion invalidated any other subsequent form of immersion or ablution, sprinkling, or anything else that removed ritual impurity as prescribed in the Law. We are still left pondering the distinctive purpose of John's immersion.

Traditionally, John's baptism has been seen as an initiation rite of some kind. It is tempting to jump to this conclusion. There is a fundamental problem in seeing John's baptism as just another Jewish ritual immersion, for we do not have any apparent reason for it. The most appealing parallel given by scholars thus far has been proselyte immersion, in which a convert to Judaism is immersed and becomes clean upon joining the people of Israel. We will therefore now consider whether John's immersion might have been some kind of initiation rite, or conversionary immersion.

Proselyte Baptism

The immersion of Jewish proselytes may be considered initiatory in that it was part of the conversion procedure for those who wished to become Jews.[29] One of the key problems with citing proselyte baptism as a

29. Some have seen proselyte baptism as widespread at the time of John and as such probably used by John as a model; see I. Abrahams, *Studies in Pharisaism and the Gospel* (Cambridge: Cambridge University Press, 1917); H. H. Rowley, "Jewish Proselyte Baptism"; T. F. Torrance, "Proselyte Baptism," *NTS* 1 (1954) 150-54; J. Jeremias, *Infant Baptism in the First Four Centuries* (London: SCM, 1960); K. Pusey, "Jewish Proselyte Baptism," *ExpTim* 95 (1984) 141-45. C. H. H. Scobie (*John the Baptist* [London: SCM, 1964] 95-102) and Webb (*John the Baptizer and Prophet,* 122-30) follow S. Zeitlin ("The Halaka in the Gospels and its Relation to the Jewish Law in the Time of Jesus," *HUCA* 1 [1924] 357-63) and A. Büchler ("The Levitical Impurity of the Gentile before the Year 70," *JQR* 17 [1926-1927] 1-81) in finding the beginning of the practice in the late first century and

precedent or analogy for John's practice is chronological. This ritual cannot be traced with certainty to the first century. The first real description of it comes in the Babylonian Talmud (e.g., *b. Yebam.* 46a–48b; cf. *Midrash Sifre* Num. 15:14). Before this time the evidence suggests that circumcision of males was considered to be the way to gain the actual entrance into the House of Israel (Jdt. 14:10; Josephus, *Ant.* 13.257-58; 318-19); there is no information about how converting women could be accepted other than by marriage. Presumably, a sacrifice of atonement in the Temple was all that was necessary before 70 CE.

Comments in *T. Levi* 14:6, which refer to an unlawful purification of Gentile women,[30] most likely refer to lawful purificatory ablutions of the usual kind, not to an initial immersion.[31] Philo writes often of proselytes but never mentions the necessity of immersion.[32] The earliest possible reference to proselyte baptism comes in Epictetus, *Dissertationes* 2.9.19ff., but this was written ca. 108 CE.

Other references to immersion refer to ordinary ritual immersions not intrinsically connected with the entrance procedure. A debate is recorded between the schools of Hillel and Shammai concerning whether a man circumcised on the day before Passover could immerse himself and eat his Passover offering (*m. Pesaḥ.* 8:8; cf. *m. ʿEd.* 5:2), but it is clear that the entry into Israel was effected already by circumcision (Exod. 12:48).[33] The Jerusalem Talmud contains a reference to con-

---

therefore not an influence on John. S. J. D. Cohen argues for a second-century date for the conversion ceremony; see Cohen, "The Rabbinic Conversion Ceremony," *JJS* 41 (1990) 177-203. However, G. Alon has argued that immersion of proselytes was taking place early in the Second Temple period, because Gentiles contracted impurity by their dealings with idols; see Alon, *Jews, Judaism and the Classical World: Studies in Jewish History in the Times of the Second Temple and Talmud* (Jerusalem: Magnes, 1977) 146-89.

30. This is cited by Jeremias, *Infant Baptism*, 25-28, as evidence for an initiatory baptism for proselytes.

31. So Yarbro Collins, "The Origin of Christian Baptism," 33.

32. See Scobie, *John the Baptist*, 29; Yarbro Collins, "The Origin of Christian Baptism," 33-34.

33. There may be an implicit concern here with whether the sacrifice of atonement had been completed; so Webb, *John the Baptizer and Prophet*, 125-27, though this is not the key issue. The interesting thing is that according to the Shammaites the impurity of the Gentile male was equal to semen-impurity, which required immersion and sunset, whereas according to the Hillelites he had to be cleansed of an impurity equivalent to corpse-uncleanness, which involved a period of a week to become pure; so Sanders, *Judaism: Practice and Belief*, 73-74.

verted Roman soldiers who were immersed on the day before Passover and ate their sacrificed lambs in the evening, while the later Babylonian Talmud contains at the same point a reference to the importance of immersing proselytes as part of the entrance procedure (*b. Yebam.* 46a). This seems to have resulted from a consensus which held that Gentiles were unclean and needed to be purified at the point of their entrance into Israel (Josephus, *War* 2.150; *Ant.* 14.285; 18.93-94; *m. Tohar.* 7:6; *t. Yoma* 4:20; *t. Pesaḥ.* 7:13; cf. Acts 10:28; John 18:28). They were not allowed into the Temple proper on account of their uncleanness (*m. Kel.* 1:8; 1 Macc. 9:34; Philo, *On the Embassy to Gaius* 212; Josephus, *Ant.* 12.145-46; *t. Yoma* 4:20).[34]

The consensus about the intrinsic impurity of Gentiles may not have been wholly unanimous, because there is some evidence that may point to another view (*b. Pesaḥ.* 91b–92a; cf. *m. Neg.* 7:1; *t. Ohol.* 1:4), that is, that Gentiles may not have been able to contract corpse uncleanness (*b. Naz.* 61b) or leprous impurity (*m. Neg.* 3:1).[35] But one should

34. See Büchler, "The Levitical Impurity." Sanders considers the different grades of impurity and notes that while Gentiles were treated as impure, their general impurity was less than that of a Jewish menstruant, who could not enter the outer court of the Temple (*Judaism: Practice and Belief,* 75; cf. Josephus, *Ag. Ap.* 2.102-05; *m. Kel.* 1:6-9). I am not sure that this inference can be drawn. As mentioned in the previous note, the Hillelites considered Gentiles corpse-impure. Also, the exclusion of menstruating women from the Temple courtyard did not mean that those who could enter were less impure than they. This would make menstruating women the most impure of all Jews at any time, too impure for even the outer court. But menstrual impurity is not to be classed as the most serious impurity; it is on the same level as that of a man's seminal emission, that of a discharge by anyone, or that of a man who has sex with an unclean woman (cf. Leviticus 15, esp. vv. 32-33). The reason that menstruating women were excluded probably had more to do with the fact that they might leave drops of blood behind (cf. Lev. 15:19-23); no other impurity had this risk factor. Therefore, the law makes a specific prohibition. Leviticus 12 deals with the subject of the purity laws following childbirth and decrees that, for different periods following the birth of a male or a female, the new mother "shall be unclean . . . as in the days of the impurity of her menstruation" and declares that "she shall remain in the blood of purification . . . [and] shall not touch anything holy, or come to the sanctuary, until the days of her purification are completed" (12:4). What is interesting is that the outer court must have been deemed holy, at some stage, and that this verse was interpreted to apply to this area as well as to the Temple proper.

35. See Sanders, *Judaism: Practice and Belief,* 72-76. The main proponents of the view that Gentiles may not have been able to contract impurity were Büchler, "The Levitical Impurity," and Zeitlin, "The Halaka in the Gospels," but their views have been challenged by Alon, *Jews, Judaism and the Classical World.*

probably not stress the exception to prove the rule. Gentiles may not have been able to contract these impurities if they were considered to be already in a state of such impurity that new impurities did not have any effect. Already in the Tanakh there is the view that Gentile lands are impure (Josh. 22:19; Amos 7:17; cf. *b. Šabb.* 14b), as are the objects of idolatry (Gen. 35:2). If Gentiles handled idolatrous objects and lived in impure lands, it may follow that they were impure. The evidence that Gentiles were considered impure by Jews is so great that the evidence against it seems unconvincing. Even if some Jews considered Gentiles not necessarily unclean, we do not have a single text indicating that Gentiles were considered positively pure. They were either unclean, or neither clean nor unclean, being outside the system.

Therefore, even without positive evidence, proselyte immersion may have taken place before the second century CE, because if Gentiles were unclean or "neutral" then it would naturally follow that upon becoming Jews they would keep the laws of ritual cleanness. At what point would a Gentile become clean? Safely, only with an immersion after becoming Jewish. In the case of men, immersion would have taken place shortly before or after circumcision. In the case of women, immersion would have marked off their state of uncleanness or neutrality as Gentile women from their state of cleanness as Jews. In itself, then, ritual immersion was not an initiation into Israel. It simply removed the uncleanness of the body that had existed before and marked the person as a clean Jew as opposed to an impure one.

However, a debate is recorded between Eliezer ben Hyrcanus and Joshua ben Hananiah, both of whom lived in the second generation of the Tannaim (ca. 90-130 CE). Rabbi Eliezer is quoted as stating that a proselyte male who had been circumcised but not immersed was still a proper proselyte, while Rabbi Joshua held that one who had been immersed but not yet circumcised was a proper proselyte (*b. Yebam.* 46a). This indicates that immersion was coming to be seen as an ingredient of the process of conversion to Judaism early in the second century. Rabbi Eliezer seems to have preserved the traditional view, while Rabbi Joshua emphasized that cleanness is what distinguishes a Jew from a Gentile and is therefore the definitive mark of a Jew.

It seems a little strained to argue, as some have done, that the practice of proselyte immersion was suddenly instituted all at once after the destruction of the Temple; we should probably consider the evidence of the debate to indicate its growing adoption as an integral part of the conversion ritual by the early second century, while its origins would have to be found earlier. Without evidence of proselyte immersion, we would have to assume that Gentiles converting to Judaism were somehow rendered clean automatically with inclusion in Israel, or else with the passage of time. This may well have been the case, but in view of the importance of immersions and ablutions in the Land of Israel in Second Temple Judaism, it seems likely that by this period something more was required. If the Hillelite view was that a Gentile was separated from corpse impurity upon inclusion in Israel, then possibly a week was required after immersion before one could be considered clean (*m. Pesaḥ.* 8:8). This statement would indicate that there was a Hillelite recommendation for a ritual involving the removal of corpse impurity in the case of new converts.

In rabbinic writings, the Hebrew word טבילה is used of ordinary immersions in *miqva'ot* as well as of proselyte baptism, thus linking the two practices. Essentially both were for purification. Proselyte baptism came to be required to rid a person of the impurities of having been a Gentile. Jewish proselyte baptism was therefore not an initiation rite strictly speaking; it actually removed bodily impurity. It was once and for all in that one only needed to have such past impurity removed on a single occasion, but it did not exempt one from performing other ablutions and immersions. The debate between Rabbis Eliezer and Joshua hinged on the issue of whether being clean or being circumcised was what really counted as the critical entrance requirement for a male proselyte. Immersion did not mean that the proselyte was mystically changed or reborn in the water. It was noted that, "One who has become a proselyte is like a child newly born" (*b. Yebam.* 48b), but this was not because of the immersion but because of his/her new participation in the community of Israel, with resulting new legal status (*m. Šeb.* 10:9; *m. Yebam.* 11:2; *m. Ḥul.* 10:4).[36]

In summary, it has been usual to look to later Jewish proselyte baptism as defined in rabbinic literature and find here an example of an initial immersion that all converts to Judaism had to undergo as well as a parallel to John's baptism. There may have been an assumption that a Gentile, being unclean, had to be immersed upon conversion to Judaism, for all Jews had to be ritually clean. Proselyte baptism has accordingly been

36. Pusey, "Jewish Proselyte Baptism," 144.

cited as a possible inspiration to John, even though the evidence for its practice before and at the time of John is inconclusive. Discussions of proselyte baptism do well to highlight the critical significance of issues of purity, but they do not explain why John immersed Jews, many of whom had presumably been keeping to most of the usual practices of ablutions and immersions prescribed in the Scriptures, unless they had abandoned Jewish praxis altogether. Moreover, to consider John's immersion initiatory would imply that there existed a community that people joined by a rite of initiation. It is by no means certain that John founded such a community.[37] Proselyte baptism is therefore not a useful parallel, because John did not convert people, strictly speaking; calling to repentance is not calling to conversion. Repentance is rather the return to a state in which the person should have been all along.

Immersion as Symbolic Initiation?

Another frequently expressed view sees John's baptism as an outer rite symbolizing an inner washing of sins in preparation for the end.[38] On this view John's baptism was a rite of initiation. This idea seems rash

37. Ellen Juhl Christiansen rightly notes that there appear to have been "no community boundaries to cross" in regard to John's immersion; see *The Covenant in Judaism and Paul: A Study of Ritual Boundaries as Identity Markers* (Leiden: Brill, 1995) 200; cf. 192-99.

38. For example, J. D. Crossan thinks that John's baptism was "the physical symbol of spiritual reality already established before" (*The Historical Jesus: The Life of a Mediterranean Jewish Peasant* [San Francisco: HarperSanFrancisco, 1991] 231); A. M. Hunter considered it a rite that "symbolised moral cleansing and initiation into a new community" (*The Work and Words of Jesus* [Philadelphia: Westminster, 1950] 35). H. Lichtenberger expresses a common view when he calls it a "symbolisch-sacramentaler Handlung und schliesslich der seinen Tod herbeiführenden Konfrontation mit dem Herrscher"; see his study "Johannes der Täufer und die Texte von Qumran," in *Mogilany 1989: Papers on the Dead Sea Scrolls Offered in Memory of Jean Carmignac,* ed. Z. J. Kapera, vol. 1 (Krakow: Enigma, 1993) 149. See Webb, *John the Baptizer and Prophet,* 202 n. 119 for those scholars who consider John's baptism to be an initiation rite. In the Jesus Seminar on John, scholars responding to the statement "JB's baptism was understood as an initiation into a Jewish sectarian movement" affirmed its probability: 19% thought the statement certain; 29% thought it probable; 42% thought it possible; and only 10% considered it improbable; see W. B. Tatum, *John the Baptist and Jesus: A Report of the Jesus Seminar* (Sonoma, CA: Polebridge, 1994) 125-26.

given the fact that a symbolic ritual in preparation for the end is not found in any Jewish rite of immersion.[39] Fundamentally, this line of thinking derives from an anachronism that sees John's immersion in terms of later Christian baptism.

Later *Christian* baptism became a complex ritual that accrued features of the initiatory processes of the Hellenistic mystery cults, and it came to seem very different indeed from any Jewish practice, despite occasional parallels. Paul's notion that a person dies with Christ in going down into the water and rises with Christ as a new spiritual being upon coming up, by means of the outpouring of the Holy Spirit (Rom. 6:3-11), may largely have been responsible for this development. But already the idea that the Holy Spirit is received at or soon after baptism led to the development of the idea of Christian baptism as an initiatory rite in which a person changed inwardly, gaining "gifts," χαρίσματα, from the Holy Spirit.[40]

John's baptism has been considered alongside Christian baptism, and the assumption has been that it must have constituted an initiation rite that changed a person once and for all. So, for example, Gunther Bornkamm called John's baptism an "eschatological sacrament" that was "the last preparation and sealing of the baptised for the coming 'baptism' of the Messiah" that would preserve believers from the day of wrath to come.[41] Since John's baptism appears to have been administered only once, while Jewish immersions were often repeated, it is assumed that John's immersion must have marked a person in some way and signified some altered state.[42] His baptism was then "conversionary" and unrepeatable.[43]

However, we just do not know that John's immersion was unrepeatable. Presumably, John did not live long enough to have to cope

39. So J. Neusner, *A History of the Mishnaic Law of Purities,* vol. 14: *Miqvaot, Literary and Historical Problems* (Leiden: Brill, 1976) 2-5.

40. For important discussions of Christian baptism, see Lampe, *The Seal of the Spirit;* R. Schnackenburg, *Baptism in the Thought of St. Paul: A Study in Pauline Theology* (Oxford: Blackwell, 1964); and W. F. Flemington, *The New Testament Doctrine of Baptism* (London: SPCK, 1948).

41. G. Bornkamm, *Jesus of Nazareth* (London: Hodder and Stoughton, 1960) 47. J. P. Meier resists the sacramental designation, but then slips into a similar conceptualization as a result of his identification of John's baptism as symbolic (*Marginal Jew,* vol. 2, 50-54).

42. See Tatum, *John the Baptist and Jesus,* 125-26.

43. Webb, *John the Baptizer and Prophet,* 197, 202.

with the problem of people who had lapsed after their immersion by him. Moreover, this issue did not become a problem in Christian circles until somewhat later in the first century, when we find a remarkably austere position presented in the letter to the Hebrews (6:1-8). According to Heb. 6:4-8 it is impossible to restore again to repentance those Christians who have once been enlightened, shared in the Holy Spirit, and then fallen away, since they are "crucifying again the Son of God and are holding him in contempt." But it would be wrong to assume that only one of John's immersions was required per lifetime, even in the case of lapsing, for this was still not resolved in the Church in third-century North Africa, during the debates between Cyprian and Stephen of Rome. As Bruce Chilton notes, "Even Hebrews must argue against the proposition that one might be baptized afresh" and "only the attribution to John of a later, catholic theology of baptism can justify the characterization of his baptism as a symbol of a definitive 'conversion.'"[44] It would be unwise, then, to see John's baptism as a sacrament conferring some kind of seal on those who went through it. This view seems anachronistic and centered on understanding John from the perspective of later Christian theology.

To confuse matters, it may be that in the early Gentile Church John's baptism was counted with Christian baptism as being in some way initiatory. A Gentile understanding of the gospel stories could easily have led to this assumption. In Acts, John's baptism seems to have been considered adequate for participation in the community of Jesus' first disciples, though after Pentecost and the reception of the Holy Spirit, distinctive Christian baptism had a different, two-pronged character: it involved water and the Holy Spirit, as opposed to water alone (though Philip was permitted to continue a water-only baptism by full immersion, as long as apostles such as Peter and John made sure to follow in his tracks). The idea that being immersed with the "immersion of John" gave one a certain status in the community of Jesus' disciples is reflected in the story that the man chosen to replace Judas had to be someone who had been with Jesus and the others "beginning with [or: from] the immersion of John" (Acts 1:22; cf. John 1:35-51). Yet there is the idea that those who were baptized by John — or were immersed in accordance with the kind of baptism John performed — had only an inferior sort of immersion and had to be baptized again with the Holy Spirit.

44. Chilton, *Judaic Approaches to the Gospels,* 27.

The Pentecost experience apparently completed the process, so that those immersed were immersed not only in water but also by the Holy Spirit (Acts 2:1-4).

So water-only immersion for ridding the body of ritual uncleanness became inadequate as a qualification for participation in the community of Jesus' disciples as this community became rather more sectarian in nature, founded on the belief that the participants were all in receipt of an immersion by the Spirit. At this point we should consider the evidence of Acts 18:24–19:7.

Apollos and the Immersion of John

In Acts 19:1-7, Paul discovers in Ephesus about twelve people who had been immersed "into John's baptism," and the usual translation would be that they had not heard of a "Holy Spirit." Even if this story is historically accurate, which is very hard to assess, we should probably read it cautiously. For example, it is fairly clear from the narrative that these people were Jews, but, if so, it is extremely unlikely that they could have been ignorant of the concept of the Holy Spirit (cf. Isa. 63:10; Ezek. 2:2). Indeed, there may be a case for the alternative reading in Acts 19:2; λαμβάνουσίν τινες is attested in some important early manuscripts ($\mathfrak{p}^{38,41}$, D*, it^{d*}, syr^{hmg}, cop^{sa}), replacing ἔστιν, so that the text reads, "But we had not heard that *anyone received* a Holy Spirit" rather than, "But we had not heard that *there is* a Holy Spirit." The usual text given provides us with something more than a difficult reading that might give us cause to consider it authentic; the premise is not only difficult but absurd. What they were unaware of, clearly, is the notion that the Holy Spirit would be imparted at baptism, a belief so essential to Pauline theology. Although it is frequently assumed that these people were disciples of John, the text states only that they were "some disciples" who were "believers" (19:1-2). As "believers," in Lucan terminology, they must have recognized Jesus as Messiah, and this indicates that they were part of the Christian community at Ephesus,[45] not a separate group of

45. See E. Haenchen, *The Acts of the Apostles: A Commentary* (Philadelphia: Westminster, 1971) 554-57. Haenchen notes (p. 553) that the author of Acts always means to refer to a Christian by the use of μαθητής without any other specification. Further-

hypothetical "Baptists."[46] Presumably, they had missed out on charismatic gifts, since they had come over to being disciples of Jesus via a water-only baptism and had been accepted as part of the Christian community in Ephesus without another baptism of the Spirit. It is unlikely that they were baptized by John himself, for "the immersion of John" may well have been a term used for the type of baptism done by John rather than a specific reference to a baptism performed by John himself.[47] Indeed, the disciples appear to be connected with Apollos, who was "trusting only in the immersion of John" (Acts 18:25); they may then have been baptized by Apollos in Ephesus.

The entire story needs to be read in the light of the whole of chapter 18 of Acts. Priscilla and Aquila, with Paul, arrive in Ephesus from Corinth (18:2-3, 18-19). Paul goes on to Caesarea and elsewhere (18:20-21) while Priscilla and Aquila stay behind in Ephesus. There is no suggestion that a Christian community existed at Ephesus prior to their arrival. When they first come there, Paul enters the synagogue and receives a positive reception; the Jews there even ask him to stay longer (18:19-20). It is implied that Priscilla and Aquila are accepted by the synagogue, and when Apollos comes to Ephesus he too goes there in order to talk to the Jewish community about Jesus. It is here that Priscilla and Aquila hear him. Acts 18:24–19:8 reads:

---

more, Paul asks if they received the Holy Spirit "when you believed," which must imply that they were Christians; see also F. F. Bruce, *The Acts of the Apostles: Greek Text with Introduction and Commentary,* 3rd rev. ed. (Grand Rapids: Eerdmans, 1990) 405-06.

46. Webb notes that whether "these are disciples of John or of Jesus is not entirely clear. The fact that they had received John's baptism suggests that they had been at one time followers of John." Webb concludes, though, "The pericope suggests that John's ministry and baptism continued to have an influence in the early church, even as far away as Ephesus, and that the assimilation of John's disciples was a matter of concern in the early church" (*John the Baptizer and Prophet,* 69). See also E. Käsemann, "The Disciples of John the Baptist in Ephesus," in his *Essays on New Testament Themes* (London: SCM, 1982) 136-48; C. K. Barrett, "Apollos and the Twelve Disciples of Ephesus," in *The New Testament Age: Essays in Honor of Bo Reicke,* ed. W. C. Weinrich (Macon: Mercer, 1984) 29-39; Scobie, *John the Baptist,* 187-88. What seems to have been a concern is how to deal with John's message and his immersion in the light of developing Christian theology; we do not need to assume that disciples of John existed in far-away Ephesus. Rather, it is interesting that immersion was a key issue here as well as in the Land of Israel.

47. J. Murphy-O'Connor wonders, if the reference is really to baptism by Jesus, who may have continued to baptize in the name of John after John's incarceration; see his study, "John the Baptist and Jesus: History and Hypothesis," *NTS* 36 (1990) 367.

> And a certain Jew named Apollos had come to Ephesus. He was an Alexandrian by birth [and] a learned man, powerful in the Scriptures. This man had been instructed in the way of the Lord, and he spoke and taught accurately things about Jesus, being fired up with the Spirit, [though] trusting only in the immersion of John. So this man came to speak boldly in the synagogue. When Priscilla and Aquila heard him, they took him to one side and explained the way [of God] more accurately. Then when he wanted to go over into Achaia, the sister and brother (οἱ ἀδελφοί) encouraged him and wrote to the disciples to welcome him. When he arrived he helped many of those who had believed through grace, for he powerfully refuted the Jews in public by demonstrating by the scriptures that Jesus was the Anointed.
>
> And it happened that while Apollos was in Corinth, Paul — having passed through the upper country — came to Ephesus and found some disciples. So he said to them, "Did you receive the Holy Spirit when you believed?" But they said to him, "But we have not heard that anyone received a Holy Spirit!" He said, "With (εἰς) what [kind of immersion] were you then immersed?" And they replied, "With John's immersion." So Paul said, "John immersed [with] an immersion of repentance, telling the people that they should believe in the one coming after him. That is [that they should believe] in Jesus." Upon hearing this they were baptized in the name of the Lord Jesus. And when Paul laid his hands upon them the Holy Spirit came upon them, and they spoke in languages and prophesied. There were in all about twelve men. And he went into the synagogue and continued to engage in dialogue and persuade [the Jews] about the kingdom of God for three months.

Paul clearly considers John's immersion highly suspect here. The "immersion of John" is inadequate by itself, for, according to Paul, John always meant to indicate that the "one coming" after him was Jesus (Acts 19:4). His immersion of repentance was then just an interim measure that would prepare people for a greater baptism in the Spirit under the auspices of Jesus. As a result of Paul's clarification, they are baptized again "in the name of the lord Jesus," that is, they accept the "proper" Christian baptism, which included the reception of the Spirit through the laying on of Paul's hands (Acts 19:6). We therefore have evidence of people who had been baptized in water and thought they had become disciples of Jesus, believing him to be the Messiah, and who had come up against the apostle Paul, who re-interpreted John's message for them, claimed a water-only baptism of repentance to be inadequate, and demanded that they accept a Christian baptism, as he defined it. Given this situation, it is possible that there was some embarrassment or confusion in the Church about what "John's immersion" did, even though it was still used alone by some disciples of Jesus. The confusion was not resolved until Paul's understanding of baptism became the normative one in the Church as a whole.

As we have seen, the story of the disciples comes immediately after the story of Priscilla and Aquila's meeting with the Alexandrian Jew, Apollos, in Ephesus (Acts 18:24-28). Apollos is described as a believer in Jesus as Messiah who trusted only (ἐπιστάμενος μόνον) the immersion of John. He is welcomed by Priscilla and Aquila, who are impressed by his eloquence and learning and by his ability to teach "accurately things concerning Jesus" (18:25). Unlike Paul, they completely accept him, though after they have explained things "more accurately," whatever this means. There is no suggestion here that Priscilla and Aquila felt that Apollos should have been re-baptized into the name of the Lord Jesus. It appears from the text that they believed he was fired up by the Holy Spirit, since only by this means could he speak so powerfully from the Scriptures. When he wishes to travel to Achaia, Priscilla and Aquila encourage him and write to the disciples in Corinth, where they had just come from, to welcome him there. There is no reference whatsoever to a Christian community in Ephesus prior to the arrival of Apollos; no other Christians have been mentioned apart from Priscilla and Aquila, who attend the synagogue.

Apollos appears elsewhere in the New Testament as someone who baptized people but who clearly differed from Paul in his theology (1 Cor. 1:10-12; 3:4-10, 22; 4:6; 16:12; cf. Titus 3:13). After Apollos had been in Ephesus, trusting only in John's immersion, we then find twelve men who are disciples. Paul's arrival at Ephesus after Apollos' departure and his insistence on the re-baptism of those who had been baptized there with "John's immersion" is a story signifying a change in how the Church was to behave in relation to water-only baptism derived from John's practice. John's message itself was defined in its relation to Jesus, something the believers at Ephesus had not realized. At Corinth, Apollos appears to have advised people about immersion quite differently than Paul (1 Cor. 1:10-17; 3:4-10). Like Peter and John following in the wake of Philip, Paul clearly felt that someone should follow in the wake of Apollos, and arguments erupted about their respective baptisms.

But what Pauline Christians thought about the baptism of John, even during this very early period and within a Jewish-Christian context, need not be our standard for interpreting it. If, for example, John's immersion of people was in line with other Jewish practices in being for the ritual purification of the body, as Josephus specifically states it was, then churches within the Gentile world would have had a very minimal appreciation of its significance. For Paul, working within the context of the Gentile world in an attempt to convert Gentiles to Christianity, despite his concern also with the synagogue, a water immersion to rid the body of Jewish ritual impurity would have been hard to explain.[48]

Paul did not think it was necessary for Gentiles to become Jews or behave like Jews in order to be saved from destruction at the time of judgment, so if immersion had anything to do with the effective removal of Jewish ritual impurity, it needed to be radically reinterpreted for a Gentile audience. For Paul, immersion was a way of becoming part of the one body of Jesus Christ (Rom. 6:3-11; 1 Cor. 12:13; 2 Cor. 1:21-22; 5:17; Gal. 3:26-47; 6:15; Eph. 1:14; 4:4-5; cf. 1 Pet. 3:21; Col. 2:10-14; Titus 3:5-7).[49] His interpretation therefore picked up the conceptual framework of Hellenistic mysteries, in which a person might be initiated into a cult by means of immersion in water (or, in the case of Mithraism, blood), thereby becoming one with the god.[50]

Initial Immersion at Qumran

John immersion is best grounded, not in the conceptual ambiance of the Diaspora, or in a later religious development, but in the Land of Israel. In Chapter 1 we reviewed the evidence for a link between John

48. Sanders rightly notes that pagans understood the concept of purification in regard to the holy (*Judaism: Practice and Belief*, 229-30). Pagans may not, however, have understood the significance of immersion to be clean as a kind of general mode of piety and would have considered many of the Jewish rules defining the causes of impurity odd.

49. For Paul's theology of baptism, see Schnackenburg, *Baptism in the Thought of St. Paul.*

50. For pagan initiation, see J. Ferguson, *Greek and Roman Religion: A Source Book* (Park Ridge, NJ: Noyes, 1980) 167-68; A. Oepke, "βάπτω," 530-34.

and the Essenes and concluded that it seems unlikely that there was any close connection. However, there is one curious similarity that deserves attention. The most interesting parallel between John and the community of 1QS may be in the underlying presuppositions in the practices of immersion, if John's baptism is indeed to be understood as having to do with Jewish ritual purification, like the immersions of the Essenes.[51] As we have seen, there were numerous kinds of ablutions and immersions in Second Temple Judaism as a whole and among the Essenes in particular,[52] but at Qumran there seems also to have been a notion that an initial immersion was significant in ridding the body of ritual uncleanness that had accrued while one was outside the community. The group at Qumran appears to have believed that since only those who were inside the community were walking on the true way of righteousness, and that any purifications of the body were effective only if undertaken by those who were truly obedient to God, then all Jewish purificatory procedures undertaken outside the community were invalid. Immersions and ablutions by Jews who were not members of the group (or related groups?) were ineffective. A Jew who was not part of the community was unclean. This is clearly spelled out in 1QS 3:3-6.

ולוא יצדק במתיר שרירות לבו וחושך יביט לדרכי אור בעין תמימים
לוא יתחשב לוא יזכה בכפורים ולוא יטהר במי נדה ולוא יתקדש בימים
ונהרות ולוא יטהר בכול מי רחץ טמא טמא יהיה כול יומי מואסו במשפטי
אל לבלתי התיסר ביחד עצתו

51. That John's baptism was concerned with ritual purification has recently been suggested by Chilton, *Judaic Approaches to the Gospels,* 1-37 and was supported by 38% of the participants in the Jesus Seminar on John; another 38% thought the association probable; see Tatum, *John the Baptist and Jesus,* 119-20. Webb also places John's baptism in the context of Jewish immersion, but he links it with repentance as a "repentance-baptism" (*John the Baptizer and Prophet*). Perhaps as an indication of confusion among some Christian scholars concerning ritual purity, the same Jesus Seminar group responded to the statement "JB's baptism was understood to purify from uncleanness" with some hesitation: 19% thought it certain; 43% thought it probable; and 38% thought it only possible; see Tatum, *John the Baptist and Jesus,* 124-25. Since a Jewish immersion rite by definition purifies from uncleanness, the difference in response, and even the two statements themselves, testifies to some muddled thinking.

52. For an exploration of the eschatological importance of purity and of God's atoning action in the purification from sin in the Dead Sea Scrolls, see B. Janowski and H. Lichtenberger, "Enderwartung und Reinheitsidee: Zur eschatologischen Deutung von Reinheit und Sühne in der Qumrangemeinde," *JJS* 34/1 (1983) 31-62.

> He shall not be made righteous in the stubbornness of his heart, for though looking to the ways of light he is dark. He shall not count himself among the perfect ones. He shall not be made blameless by acts of atonement and not be purified by waters for impurity or be made holy by seas and rivers or be purified by any water for [ritual] washing. Unclean, unclean will he be all the days he despises the precepts of God, up until he receives instruction in the community of his counsel.

Indeed, once he "ordered his steps to walk perfectly in all the ways commanded by God," then things would be different. Purification would then be effective. The text of 1QS 3:6-9 continues:

כיא ברוח עצת אמת אל דרכי איש יכופרו כול
עוונותו להביט באור החיים וברוח קדושה ליחד באמתו יטהר מכול
עוונותו וברוח יושר וענוה תכופר חטתו ובענות נפשו לכול חוקי אל יטהר
בשרו להזות במי נדה ולהתקדש במי דוכי

> For by a spirit of the counsel of truth concerning human ways all his iniquities will be atoned so that he may look upon the light of life. And by a holy spirit of the community in his truth he will be purified from all his iniquities; by a spirit of uprightness and humility his sin will be atoned. And by means of the humble submission of his soul to all the precepts of God his body will [then] be purified when sprinkled with waters for impurity and made holy with waters for cleansing.

The final statement appears to sum up what has been covered. The "humble submission of his soul towards all the precepts of God" is what makes immersion effective, just as atonement, that is, the inward purification of iniquities, is effected by the spirits of the counsel of truth concerning human ways, the holy spirit of the community in his truth, and the spirit of uprightness and humility. These spirits are all somehow inseparable — aspects of the spirit of light as opposed to darkness — and are manifested in a person's humble submission to all the precepts of God. The "precepts of God," however, are not simply those outlined in the Torah, but also those defined by the Qumran community.

The passages quoted above are concerned with two things: atonement and bodily purification. The first is an inner state; the second, an outer one. God's forgiveness results in atonement or inner cleansing, just as purifying waters effect outer cleansing for a person who has wholly undertaken to walk in the way of God. Elsewhere in the Qumran literature it is clear that atonement — the inner cleansing — was itself effected by the practice of justice (1QS 9:2-6), that is, by the works of the Law (4Q174, the Florilegium; cf. Pesher on 2 Sam. 7:10) as defined by the community. The practice of the Law, or justice, prompts God to forgive sins, thereby effecting atonement. This was not self-evident or immediate. Moreover, if one failed to abide by the laws of the community, one risked being considered impure; one's misdemeanor indicated a lack of inner purity, which would seem to mean that outer cleansing had ceased to be effective. For this reason, possibly, sinners in the community were excluded from the Purity — the pure meal and related matters — for various lengths of time, as if sin resulted in a corresponding bodily impurity commensurate with the degree of moral violation. Repentance here apparently did not mean instant atonement (cf. 1QS 7:9-10; 8:22-26; 9:2). Pure members of the community could not touch those who had committed sins or their property (1QS 8:23-26); they were unclean.

Texts like 1QS 2:25–3:9 cannot be used to argue that in the Qumran community *bodily* immersion was thought to cleanse a person from *inner* defilement, as Robert Webb has suggested.[53] Rather, 1QS 3:8-9 makes clear that the practice of righteousness as defined by the community was what made cleansing of the flesh (בשׂר) effective. The distinction between the metaphorical cleansing of the heart and the actual purification of the body is always maintained, as it is within Judaism as a whole.[54]

53. Webb suggests that the passage uses parallelism to equate purification by atonement with cleansing of the flesh (*John the Baptizer and Prophet,* 146-51). Although there is poetic parallelism and repetition here, it seems forced to argue that the document is simply stating the same thing twice. Webb believes that the person had to exhibit the right attitude while undertaking the immersion, and he argues that this attitude of piety would be recognized as atoning for a person's sins (ibid., 152). But the sectarians demanded much more than the exhibition of the right attitude at the moment of immersion; prospective members had to prove themselves by righteous behavior that was carefully monitored over some time (Josephus, *War* 2.137-38).

54. In Jewish immersions it is the body that is cleansed of ritual impurity (טומאה). The inner being (the heart, לבב) is sometimes described in the Scriptures as being metaphorically polluted by sin (e.g., Isa. 1:16-17; 4:2-4; 66:20; Ps. 26:6; 51:1-10; 73:13; Prov. 30:12; Jer. 2:22; 4:14), but actual water could not touch the inner being; so Neusner, *The Idea of Purity.* Wholehearted obedience to the Law, which effected atonement, would

So, for example, in the *Community Rule* a righteous man is purified inwardly, by means of a spirit of holiness, from all the deeds of evil: "and he [God] will sprinkle upon him the spirit of truth like waters (כמי) for impurity (נדה) from all the abominations of falsehood" (1QS 4:21-22). This is clearly a simile, with the use of כ, "like"; the action of the spirit of holiness from God is compared to the sprinkling of water on a body for purification. It is not stated that actual sprinkling of water on the body removes the inner impurity of all the abominations of falsehood.

The belief that only repentance and the practice of righteousness, as defined by the community, made purification effective is also found in 1QS 5:13-15, where it is stated that one outside the covenant of the community "shall not go into the water in order to [then] participate in the purity of the holy ones, for they will not be purified unless they repent of their wicked deeds; for all who transgress the word are unclean." The uncleanness is total. Everything that they do is therefore directed towards impurity (לנדה), as is everything that they actually touch: "All their deeds are towards impurity before him and all their possessions are unclean" (1QS 5:19-20).[55]

According to 1QS 6:17-21 a person had to undergo a year of probation and close examination by a trustworthy member of the community before being allowed to participate in the "Purity"(טהרה); then, after two years, he was allowed to drink the common drink (1QS 6:17-21). Josephus says of the Essene group of his source material that the new candidate was excluded for only one more year (*War* 2.138), but the principle is the same. To ensure that bodily purity was actually effected, proof of inner purity was necessary. According to Josephus, once properly purified for the first time, a man who wished to enter the Essene community would still not be able to attend group meetings and meals (*War* 2.138-39) but would be considered on probation, undoubtedly participating in the group's other ablutions (*War* 2.129-32).[56]

---

act like water, purifying the defilement of the heart; cf. Maimonides, *Mishneh Torah, Miqva'ot* 11:12.

55. Their possessions are regarded as unclean because if the body was impure, then things that were touched would become unclean also.

56. For a useful, concise discussion of ablutions at Qumran, see Webb, *John the Baptizer and Prophet,* 133-62. For specific details and a discussion of the relationship between biblical law, the sectarian rules of the Dead Sea Scrolls, and rabbinic literature, see Harrington, *The Impurity Systems of Qumran and the Rabbis.*

It is difficult, then, to see the initial immersion as initiatory, since it was not the decisive step towards inclusion in the community, but only something resulting from a practice of righteousness accounted acceptable by God.

There has been a tendency to see initial immersion at Qumran not only as initiatory, but also as a possible inspiration to John precisely because of its alleged initiatory character.[57] However, the point of correlation between John's baptism and the initial immersion of 1QS and of Josephus' Essenes is probably not that these constituted initiation rites, but the idea that immersion is pointless without prior cleansing of the heart (the inner self) through repentance and the practice of righteousness. This is not immediately clear in the Gospel material, largely because the Gospels were written for a Gentile Christian audience, to whom issues of Jewish ritual purity were not relevant. However, that John's baptism was for purification of the body after repentance is made explicit in what Josephus writes about John in *Ant.* 18.116-17. We need to look at this passage now in closer detail. According to Josephus, John was

> a good man who was exhorting the Jews to practice virtue and righteousness towards each other and to act with piety towards God, and [thereafter] to come together for immersion. Because then indeed the immersion would be acceptable to Him [God], if it was not about pleading forgiveness for certain sins they had done, but for a purification of the body, now that the soul had been cleansed already by righteousness.[58]

57. See, e.g., J. A. T. Robinson, "The Baptism of John and the Qumran Community: Testing a Hypothesis," in his *Twelve New Testament Studies* (London: SCM, 1962) 11-27; W. H. Brownlee, "John the Baptist in the New Light of Ancient Scrolls," in *The Scrolls and the New Testament,* ed. K. Stendahl (New York: Harper, 1957) 33-53.

58. H. Lichtenberger has noted the similarities between Josephus' description of John's immersion and the Essenes', but he puts these down to Josephus' own wish to characterize John as being like an Essene. It seems that Lichtenberger takes for granted the Gospels' view that new life follows baptism and that he assumes from this that Josephus' description is idiosyncratic. See Lichtenberger, "The Dead Sea Scrolls and John the Baptist: Reflections on Josephus' Account of John the Baptist," in *The Dead Sea Scrolls: Forty Years of Research,* ed. D. Dimant and U. Rappaport (Leiden: Brill, 1992) 340-46; idem, "Die Texte von Qumran und das Urchristentum," *Jud* 50 (1994) 68-82.

In fact, the Gospels do implicitly support this interpretation of John's baptism in noting that John believed that immersion was not to be undertaken without a person *first* "bearing good fruit" (Luke 3:7-8; cf. Matt. 3:7-8):

> He said therefore to the crowds that came out in order to be immersed by him: "You viper's offspring! Who warned you to flee from the coming wrath [of God]? [If you wish to be immersed] then you must bear fruits worthy of repentance.

So "bearing good fruit" was not supposed to come *after* someone's baptism. People came to John specifically to be immersed, and they were roundly condemned. They were apparently seen as sinners who could not be immersed without the practice of righteousness. Repentance and its proof (bearing good fruit) — after which God's loving forgiveness was guaranteed — was supposed to take place *before* immersion. The same notion is reflected in 1QS; both John and the Qumran community held righteousness to be the priority, which rendered immersion for the purification of the body "acceptable to" God (*Ant.* 18.117). However, their definitions of what constituted the way of righteousness appear to have been quite different. John did not call those he immersed to live in an exclusive community of people, armed with a plethora of rules about conduct in order to maintain their exclusivity.[59]

If all this is so, then we may take a significant step towards understanding why John immersed Jews at all. Even though Jews of his time might claim to be "children of Abraham" (Matt. 3:9; Luke 3:8), in his eyes they were not truly Abraham's spiritual offspring unless they were accounted righteous by God, that is, were inwardly clean. If they were not truly obedient to God and did not "bear good fruit," then they were unclean outwardly. Purity was inside-out; the inner influenced the outer.

Possible supportive evidence for this belief is found in a saying of Jesus in Matt. 23:25-26 (probably garbled in Luke 11:39-41), derived

59. Chilton notes, "John's baptism was . . . an implicit claim that there was no advantage in the pools of Qumran, the double-vatted *miqvaoth* of the Pharisees or the private baths of aristocratic groups such as the Sadducees. He enacted what amounted to generic purification" (*Judaic Approaches to the Gospels,* 29-30).

from Q. Here Jesus criticizes the Pharisees for practicing bodily ablutions while ignoring the inside of the person:

> Woe to you, scribes and Pharisees, hypocrites, because you clean the outside of the cup and the plate, but inside they are full of extortion and intemperance. Blind Pharisee, first clean the inside of the cup in order that its outside may also come to be clean. (Matt. 23:25-26)

In Luke's version, the statement goes: "Give for alms those things that are inside, and see, everything is clean for you" (Luke 11:41), a wording that fits with a Gentile Christian wish to disregard all the prescriptions of ritual purity found in Jewish law.[60] However, Matthew's version seems to state that the careful cleansing of the outside of a vessel (and so, by analogy, of the body) is useless if the inside (by analogy, the heart or inner being) is dirty. As with cups, so with persons; the careful cleansing of a person's body from ritual impurity is useless if the heart is defiled by things that are contrary to the Torah.[61] Once the inside is clean, then it is possible to cleanse the body. Clearly, the process is similar to that which we find in the *Community Rule:* repent, practice righteousness and obedience; then the heart will be inwardly cleansed by atonement and, subsequently, the body may be outwardly purified by immersion in water.

60. As Wellhausen conjectured long ago, it is possible that Luke was familiar with a mistranslation of the saying from Aramaic. "Cleanse" in Aramaic is דכו, while "give alms" is זכו; see M. Black, *An Aramaic Approach to the Gospels and Acts*, 3rd ed. (Oxford: Clarendon, 1967) 2. Booth believes that Luke is inserting his special (mistranslated?) source, related here to Mark 7:1-23, into Q material (*Jesus and the Laws of Purity*, 24).

61. Jesus does not say that the outside of a vessel (symbolizing the human body) never requires (ritual) cleansing; he simply gives the opinion that it cannot be made clean if the inside is dirty. Once the inside is clean, then the outside may "come to be" (γένηται) clean. Jesus may have been adopting an anti-Shammaite position on the (ritual) cleaning of dishes here, since the Shammaites considered that the outside of a vessel could be clean even if the inside was unclean, whereas in Hillelite tradition the state of the inner part of the dish was decisive; so Neusner, "First Cleanse the Inside: The Halakhic Background of a Controversy Saying," *NTS* 22 (1976) 486-95. Jesus may also have been ridiculing the Shammaite position as an analogy for what should take place with human ritual cleansing; it was the very opposite of what needed to happen for people. The point is that Jesus appears to have argued that inner cleansing of the heart through repentance and righteous conduct had to take place before bodily ritual cleansing could be effective.

A detour on the subject of Jesus' attitude toward purity is not necessary here,[62] but certainly the above passage shows a striking similarity with what may have been John's view. What we do not appear to have, though, is actual Essene *influence;* ultimately the root of this idea is not to be found within the wings of Essene sectarianism, but in the book of Isaiah — a text that was a resource for all Jews. In Isa. 1:12-20, God tells the people that nothing they do in terms of ritual is of any value without righteousness, justice, and obedience to the Law. The passage plays on images of purity: sinful actions are bloody and scarlet and are metaphorically washed to be as white as wool or snow. Bringing offerings is futile, burning incense is useless, festivals are loathsome, and prayer is ineffective: "When you stretch out your hands, I will hide my eyes from you; even though you make many prayers, I will not listen. Your hands are full of blood" (1:15). This is spelled out more specifically in Isaiah 58, where fasting too is considered pointless when people remain unjust and oppressive. When people do the "true fast" of loosing

62. In Mark 7:1-23 (cf. Matt. 15:1-20) Jesus is portrayed as maintaining that all foods are clean and that purification is unnecessary. In Mark 7:14, Jesus claims that it is not what goes into the body that defiles the person (as a *person*) but what comes out (of the heart). In the saying, there seems to be a clear distinction drawn between moral (inner) defilement and outer (bodily) defilement (Mark 7:18-19a, 20-23), for bodily impurity caused (perhaps) by eating (incorrectly prepared) food with unwashed hands is temporary; the food passes out of the body and into the ditch without a permanent tainting effect. But Mark wishes to emphasize the inner and negate the outer. The story is designed to illustrate Mark's conclusion: "Thus he declared all foods clean" (7:19b). Such a prescription is unlikely to have come from the mouth of Jesus. In Peter's vision of Acts 10, when he sees a sheet full of unclean creatures and hears a voice saying "kill and eat," Peter says, "By no means, Lord, for I have never eaten anything profane or unclean" (Acts 10:13-14). Later Jewish-Christians found table fellowship with Gentiles intolerable, even if they were also Christians (Gal. 2:11-14). See for this point G. Vermes, *Jesus and the World of Judaism,* 46. For a careful and convincing discussion, see Booth, *Jesus and the Laws of Purity.* According to Booth, "Jesus . . . did not deny the fact of cultic impurity in the logion, but only treated it as of less gravity than moral impurity" (p. 219). The washing of hands before eating was possibly only a custom of the *ḥaberim* (Pharisees), which they are here seeking to impose upon Jesus' disciples in an effort to force them to conform to their prescriptions of purity. The Pharisees do so because they recognize that Jesus is "true" and that he teaches "the way of God truthfully"; therefore, his disciples should undertake a higher standard of purity (p. 202). Often overlooked is the fact that the *Gospel of Thomas* preserves a saying of Jesus that appears to equate going into a *miqveh* for the removal of ritual impurity with acceptance of his message: "Lord, there are many around the cistern, but nobody in the cistern" (Log. 74).

the bonds of injustice, releasing the oppressed, sharing bread with the hungry, covering the naked, visiting relatives, and honoring the Sabbath (58:13-14), then "You shall call and YHWH will answer; you shall cry for help and he will say, 'Here I am'" (Isa. 58:9).

From established biblical sentiments such as these, it would not have been difficult for John to extrapolate the uselessness of immersion without prior righteousness. No rites and acts of piety are effective without prior acceptance by God. This entails obedience to the Law in all its moral and ethical aspects, for the Law has its source in the love of a just and righteous God. The deeds of those who wish to be obedient to the Law must reflect the divine nature. Without justice, cultic and pious acts will not be accepted. In other words, we can trace the idea that immersion was ineffective without prior righteousness directly to the book of Isaiah, so we do not need to assume that John experienced direct influence from the Essenes.

The book of Isaiah is also clear in stating that those who are truly walking along the way of righteousness have to be (ritually) clean:

> A highway shall be there [in the wilderness]
> and it shall be called the holy way.
> The unclean shall not pass over it,
> but it shall be for those who walk the way
> and the citizens[63] will not go astray. (Isa. 35:8)

Here the language is not metaphorical. The unclean, like the uncircumcised, are repugnant to God (cf. Lev. 11:43; Ezek. 36:24-29a). In Isa. 52:1 the "uncircumcised and unclean" shall no longer enter Jerusalem when God acts in judgment. People are advised to "leave, leave, go out from there. Do not touch any unclean thing. Go out from the midst of it [Jerusalem]; purify yourselves, you who carry the vessels of YHWH" (Isa. 52:11). Those who carry the vessels are not only priests but all those who carry vessels to the Temple (cf. Isa. 66:20).

For John, then, purification would necessarily follow and constitute, just precisely, an "immersion of repentance for (εἰς) the remission

63. The Hebrew word אוילים can mean "foolish people" as well as "citizens." The Aramaic *Targum Pseudo-Jonathan* translates it as "the unlearned"; see B. D. Chilton, *The Isaiah Targum: Introduction, Translation, Apparatus, and Notes* (Wilmington, DE: Glazier, 1987) 70.

of sins" (Mark 1:4 = Luke 3:3) as distinct from any other immersion specified in Jewish law. We will examine this phrase in more detail below. For now, we can simply note that John seems to have earned his title "the Immerser"[64] because he was doing something innovative within the context of Judaism as a whole — immersing repentant Jews with the notion that, prior to repentance, they had been unclean. It seems likely that, for this reason, he is described by Mark as "proclaiming" (κηρύσσων) such a baptism (Mark 1:4); any other kind of Jewish immersion would not have needed to be proclaimed. This suggestion is not intended to downplay the eschatological significance and apocalyptic urgency of what John was doing, but it is important not to assume that an eschatological consciousness meant that the baptism had to be something other than an immersion rite understandable in the context of other Jewish immersions. The end was coming soon, and God would act in judgment; those who were not righteous would perish, while those who were righteous would be saved. To be clean was part of being righteous. The unrighteous could not become clean; they were in a permanent state of ritual impurity.

But if there is a parallel here between the initial immersion at Qumran — which followed on from a person's repentance and commitment to the teaching of the sect — and the baptism of John, is this parallel unique among Jewish groups? Possibly not. Philo too considered it absurd that someone who had cleansed the body (the outer) could pray and sacrifice in the Temple with his mind (the inner) sullied by sin, for only those who had resolved to forsake evil could approach the Temple. In Philo's view, one who lacks repentance and resolution should keep away since he is δυσκάθαρτος, "uncleansible" (*On the Unchangeableness of God* 7–9). God would see into the inner recesses of the mind. Philo repeatedly stresses that the sacrifices of bad people do nothing. The inner person has to be purified first in both thought and deed, and only then will the sacrifice be acceptable to God, not because of the sacrifice itself, but because of the right inward state of the worshipper (*On Noah's Work as a Planter* 164; *On the Special Laws* 1.191, 203-04, 275, 283-84; 2.35). Given this, we may speculate that there was a current mentality in which diverse subjects (Philo, the 1QS group, and John)

64. The "immerser," βαπτιστής (Matt. 3:1; 11:11, 12; 14:2, 8; 16:14; 17:13; Mark 6:25; 8:28; Luke 7:20, 23; 9:19) or the "immersing one," βαπτίζων (Mark 1:4; 6:14, 24); cf. Josephus, *Ant.* 18.116.

all participated. John was making explicit in regard to immersion what may have been self-evident in principle, given the text of Isaiah.

This was not the only mentality, however. There is also evidence of a completely different use of immersion, evidence that clarifies the similarities and differences between John and the 1QS group. Josephus points out that John's baptism was "not about pleading forgiveness for certain sins they had done" (*Ant.* 18.117). The implication here is that some people did use immersions as part of a process of pleading forgiveness. There are three texts in roughly contemporaneous Jewish literature that reflect this other use of immersion: the Greek *Testament of Levi* (cf. 4QTLevi ar[a]); book four of the *Sibylline Oracles*; and the Greek *Apocalypse of Moses.*[65] In these three texts, people aiming to "straighten" their ways and prove themselves worthy to God immerse themselves. In one manuscript of the *Testament of the Twelve Patriarchs* (MS *e*), an addition beginning at *T. Levi* 2:3 has Levi wash his garments in "pure water" and his whole body in "living water." Levi then utters a lengthy prayer and is taken on a tour of the heavens. In the *Sibylline Oracles* 4.162-70 (ca. 80 CE) people are advised to abandon sin, immerse themselves, pray for forgiveness, and make propitiation by praising God in order to avoid God's wrath. In the *Apoc. Moses* 29:6-13 Adam repents for forty days and stands in the river Jordan to beg God for forgiveness. These texts are important, and will be discussed in more detail below from a different angle.

John's immersion stands in contrast to the sort of immersion reflected in these texts. As we have seen, according to Josephus and the Gospels, John did not accept that people should come to baptism before repentance as a way of exhorting God to forgiveness. On seeing people coming for baptism, Q's John calls them a "brood of vipers" who are afraid of the "wrath to come," and he tells them to bear fruit that befits

65. For a useful compilation of these three texts, see Webb, *John the Baptizer and Prophet,* 116-22. H. Lichtenberger has suggested that *Sib. Or.* 4.161-69 may refer to John's baptism because it refers to (1) immersion in running water; (2) the unique, saving significance of baptism in view of the coming judgment; (3) repentance as a prerequisite of baptism; and (4) an imminent judgment of fire. Regarding (1), immersion in running water was not unique to John's immersion. As for (2), it is piety that is stressed, not immersion in itself; immersion is considered an act of piety. As for (3), repentance is not a prerequisite for baptism here; rather, God grants repentance after seeing a variety of acts of piety indicating a turning away from evil. Only (4) is assured, but belief in a judgment of fire was widespread. See Lichtenberger, "Reflections on the History of John the Baptist's Communities," *FolOr* 25 (1988) 46-47.

repentance *before* immersion (Matt. 3:7-10; Luke 3:7-9). Josephus also characterizes John's immersion as being quite different from the "exhortation" immersions.

The *Community Rule* from Qumran, then, does help us understand John's baptism better, by drawing attention to a current of biblical interpretation, even though it probably does not establish a clear connection between John and Qumran. The similarity between the initial immersion of the Qumran community and John's immersion probably stems from a common use of the book of Isaiah. Thus, the idea that one could be made clean in body only if one was pure in heart is probably to be derived from an interpretation of the book of Isaiah that was current among several groups in Second Temple Judaism. There is no reason, therefore, to suggest that the Essenes influenced John on this matter, although, of course, we cannot conclusively say they could not have done so.

Repentance-Baptism?

In his extensive study of John's baptism, Robert Webb has sought to combine the Gospel's descriptions of John's baptism with that of Josephus so that repentance, righteousness, and baptism are all linked together in a complete system of "repentance-baptism." Webb believes that the distinction made by Josephus between the soul (ψυχή) and the body is made for a Roman audience and that Jews did not really distinguish between a person's soul and body.[66] This would mean that John's baptism was for a kind of *moral* purification, so that through John's mediation a bodily washing effected a cleansing of the whole being. Webb states, "We could speculate that in his role as baptizer, John, the mediator of forgiveness, might have pronounced the person forgiven, just as a priest pronounced a person after offering a sacrifice in the temple."[67] Webb's "repentance-baptism" is, then, a quasi-initiation; it is both an immersion for the removal of ritual uncleanness and a sacrament for absolution from sin through John acting as God's priest.

Unfortunately, Webb's conclusions rest on a fundamentally false premise concerning what Jews of the period believed. To say that Jews

66. Webb, *John the Baptizer and Prophet*, 167.
67. Ibid., 193.

did not distinguish between body and soul is not correct.[68] "Soul" may be a Greek concept, and it is true to say that the existence of disembodied souls was not accepted by Jews. For Jews a human being was not an immortal soul clothed in a corruptible body, but a total entity. The Pharisaic notion of a resurrection at the end of time presupposes that a person had to have some kind of body in the new age. But, as we have noted already, Jews of the first century did distinguish between the inner and outer being of a person. The inner was the heart (לבב) while the outer was the body or flesh (בשׂר). It is somewhat inaccurate to say that Jewish ablutions in Second Temple literature "cleansed the person,"[69] meaning inner and outer together. The heart was understood as the seat of the innermost feelings and impulses;[70] God has a heart (cf. Gen. 6:8), as do human beings. It can be understood as one's mind, character, disposition, and understanding — one's deepest being. The heart was not thought to be cleansed along with the body in Jewish ablutions. It was the impurity of the body that was removed by immersion; whatever existed in the heart was a separate matter and was not touched by water.

Therefore, a person's heart could not be rendered free of inner contagion caused by sin by means of cleansing the body.[71] The laws of ritual uncleanness presuppose that the body has its own distinctive type of outer ritual impurity. The term "ritual impurity" is perhaps not the best way of referring to this state, since, as Neusner has noted, ritual impurity may be seen to stand against substantive or actual impurity. Bodily purity (טהרה) and impurity (טמאה) were considered to be actual states of physical contamination, even though these states had nothing to do with being hygienically dirty or clean. Bodily impurity was understood to be a kind of contamination that might not be apparent but that nevertheless actually exists. Immersion, ablutions, sprinklings, or (in some cases) the passage of time rendered one clean again, depending on the character of the impurity. Bodily purity is necessary for the person to interact normally and, especially, to participate in a sacred function. Outward bodily impurity does not mean that one has become inwardly or morally contaminated; the distinction between the inner and outer being remains clear.

68. See above, notes 53 and 54.

69. Webb, *John the Baptizer and Prophet*, 167.

70. BDB, 523-25; W. L. Holladay, *A Concise Hebrew and Aramaic Lexicon of the Old Testament* (Grand Rapids: Eerdmans, 1971) 171-72.

71. Contra Webb, *John the Baptizer and Prophet*, 195.

Conversely, inward, moral "contamination" does not render one bodily impure. The language of inner contamination and defilement, requiring cleansing by obedience to the Law and good works, is metaphorical; the notion of bodily impurity was actual. The practice of washing the body clean of ritual impurity led to imagery in which a person's ethical behavior caused inner impurity that could be washed clean through a change in behavior. But the two — metaphor and actuality — seem never to have been confused in any Jewish rite of ablution. However, both purity of the heart and purity of the body were necessary for complete holiness, so that in some sectors of Jewish society, such as among the Essenes, outward bodily purity seems itself to have constituted a moral requirement.[72] This does not blur the distinction between heart and body, but it puts matters of the body's purity into the moral domain.

The use of cleansing language as a "metaphor of morality,"[73] as Neusner puts it, is found mainly in prophetic literature. As we have seen, in Isa. 1:12-15 God is described as saying that Temple worship is futile — as are sacrifices, prayers, and festivals — for God is not pleased with his people because their "hands are full of blood." Therefore the people are exhorted:

> Wash yourselves, make yourselves clean.
> Remove the evil of your actions from before my eyes,
> Cease to do evil, learn to do good;
> seek justice, rescue the oppressed;
> defend the orphan, plead for the widow. (Isa. 1:16-17)

Similar imagery occurs elsewhere, for example in Ps. 26:6; 51:1-10; 73:13; Prov. 30:12; Jer. 2:22; 4:14; and Isa. 4:2-4; 66:20. The "washing" is defined as living a righteous life. The heart is therefore cleansed. It is this inner being — the "heart" — that Josephus refers to as a "soul" for the sake of his Roman readers in *Ant.* 18.117, but the conceptual framework of his comment is entirely Jewish.

The three passages from Jewish literature noted above as indicating a different, hortatory use of immersion are cited by Webb to argue that outer bodily washing could effect cleansing from inner moral defile-

72. J. Neusner and B. D. Chilton, "Uncleanness: A Moral or an Ontological Category in the Early Centuries A.D.?" *BBR* 1 (1991) 63-88.

73. J. Neusner, *The Idea of Purity,* 11; see also 11-13, 36-38.

ment. If we look more closely at these texts, though, they appear rather to preserve the distinction between metaphorical and actual.

The passage from the *Testament of Levi* discussed by Webb[74] forms part of an addition at *T. Levi* 2:3 in an eleventh-century Greek manuscript of the *Testaments of the Twelve Patriarchs* (MS *e*). The late date of this manuscript would at first seem to render it worthless for our purposes, but the manuscript preserves in Greek material found in a (pre-Christian) Aramaic Levi document from Qumran (4Q TestLevi[a] or 4Q213). The relevant Greek text (*T. Levi* 2.3B1-2 in the versification adopted by Webb) partially survives in the Aramaic and reads, in Webb's translation,

> Then I washed my clothes and cleansed them in pure water
> and in living water I wholly bathed myself,
> and all my ways I made straight.

The straightening of this particular way pertains to bodily impurity. Levi's prayer, which follows (*T. Levi* 2.3B7-8, 11, 14; cf. 4QTestLevi[a] 1:12-15), refers to cleansing of the heart but does not link this cleansing of the heart with the washing of the clothes and body. Having straightened all his ways and purified his body, Levi is then accepted by God and allowed into heaven, where he is told that he is the Lord's priest (2:5-10).

The second text, the *Sibylline Oracles* 4.162-70, which was probably composed by a Jewish writer ca. 80 CE,[75] reads,

> Ah, wretched mortals, change these things, and do not
> lead the Great God to all sorts of anger, but abandon
> daggers and groanings, murders and outrages,
> and wash your whole bodies in perennial rivers.
> Stretch out your hands to heaven and ask forgiveness
> for your previous deeds and make propitiation
> for bitter impiety with words of praise; God will grant repentance
> and will not destroy. He will stop his wrath again if you all
> practice honorable piety in your hearts.[76]

This is an exhortation to people to change from wickedness and impiety

74. Webb, *John the Baptizer and Prophet*, 116-20.

75. Ibid., 120-21.

76. Trans. J. J. Collins in *OTP*, vol. 1, 388.

to God. The process of change is outlined by reference to certain actions on the part of the repentant person: (1) abandoning wicked ways; (2) washing the body in perennial waters; (3) praying for forgiveness; and (4) praising God. All these together constitute the process of practicing piety. Washing of the body here does not purify the heart. All the actions combined are meant to nudge God into forgiveness and to stop his wrath.

In the Greek *Apocalypse of Moses,* a misnamed work that is closely related to the Latin *Life of Adam and Eve,* Adam counsels Eve after their expulsion from Paradise (29:11-13):

> Let us repent for forty days in order that God might have compassion on us and give us food better than that of animals. I will do forty days but you [will do] thirty-four days, because you were not formed [until] the sixth day in which God completed his creation. But arise and go to the Tigris river, and take a stone and place [it] under your feet, and stand clothed in the water up to [your] neck, and do not let a word escape out of your mouth, for we are unworthy and our lips are not clean. But Adam went to the Jordan river . . . and was praying in the water.[77]

As in the case of the passage from the *Sibylline Oracles,* the immersing action here is a kind of penitence that is supposed to elicit God's forgiveness.

In these texts, there is no suggestion that immersion is not worthwhile until a person has repented and borne good fruit. This point is worth stressing because it seems to constitute the fundamental distinction between John's baptism and other Jewish immersion rites. In John's practice, repentance does not take place at the same time as the immersion, as Webb supposes, making it a "repentance-baptism"; rather, the inner cleansing precedes the outer cleansing. Without inner cleansing, the outer cleansing is completely useless.[78]

The texts given by Webb therefore appear to confirm that immersion was being used to plead forgiveness from certain sins, but they do not help illuminate John's baptism, nor do they indicate that bodily

77. Webb, *John the Baptizer and Prophet,* 121-22.

78. The same differentiation between actual, bodily impurity and metaphorical, inner impurity is found much later in Maimonides, *Mishneh Torah,* Miqva'ot 11:12. See Neusner, *The Idea of Purity,* 18-31.

washing removed inner contamination caused by sin. God's forgiveness, prompted by a person's sincere repentance, and good works, effected this inner cleansing, and henceforth a person's outer cleansing would be "acceptable to" God, as Josephus indicates.

Moreover, if John were the mediator for the forgiveness of sins, which supposedly took place at baptism, then it is surprising that we find absolutely no evidence of this important role in the literature. In fact, the words of the angel Gabriel in Luke's nativity story stress that John's role was to turn people back from unrighteousness to righteousness:

> He will be filled with the Holy Spirit [i.e., he will be a prophet], even from his mother's womb, and many of the children of Israel will turn back to the Lord their God. And he will go before him [God] in the spirit and power of Elijah, 'to turn back the hearts of fathers to their children' [Mal. 4:5-6; Sir. 48:10] and the disobedient to the purpose of the righteous, to make ready a people prepared for the Lord. (Luke 1:15b-17)

This passage is consistent with a perception of John as one determined to turn the unrighteous to righteousness. Zechariah's prophecy at the circumcision of John reflects the same understanding (Luke 1:76-79). Here John's baptism does not at all play a part in what was supposed to be important about him. If John's baptism itself were an integral part of the actual process of repentance and forgiveness, it is curious that these passages make no mention of it. In defining John's activity as having to do with "turning people back" to righteousness, the passages reflect a Hebrew and Aramaic understanding of repentance, as we shall see below, and may therefore reflect very ancient traditions about John. In this section, John's immersion itself seems to be subsumed under his primary objective of preparing newly righteous people for the Lord. The people who walked the way of the Lord had to be clean, as Isa. 35:8 expressly states: "A highway shall be there, and it shall be called the holy way. The unclean shall not pass over it, but it shall be for them who walk the way."

An Immersion of Repentance for the Remission of Sins

Thus far we have explored the issue of what John's immersion actually did and why it was necessary. It has been suggested that his immersion was designed to rid the body of impurity, as all other Jewish immersions were designed to do. However, John's immersion was different in that for him no ritual for the purification of the body would have been acceptable to God, and thereby effective, unless one were repentant or righteous and kept God's Law. In view of the nearness of the coming end, this was a serious issue. We will examine now in more detail what repentance meant, and why John's immersion could be called "an immersion of repentance for the remission of sins" (Mark 1:4; Luke 3:3; cf. Acts 13:24; 19:4). This definition of John's baptism distinguishes it from other immersions. As we have noted, in the Marcan text, John *proclaims* his immersion.[79] By immersing in the way he did, he earned the title "Immerser," for it was something novel and extraordinary and yet comprehensible in the context of biblical precedents. Jews clearly saw John's immersion as both understandable, given what they knew of immersions, and distinct. It was not important at the time to define what his baptism did (rid the body of impurity), for everyone knew that was what an immersion was about. But it was important to define *why* his baptism was necessary — it was concerned with repentance for the remission of sins.

Let us go over the ground once more, concentrating now on understanding the meaning of the phrase βάπτισμα μετανοίας εἰς ἄφεσιν ἁμαρτιῶν (Mark 1:4 = Luke 3:3), "an immersion of repentance for/towards the remission of sins." According to Josephus, John was particularly concerned that people should embrace a life of righteous behavior. Immersion was secondary. He states that John, called "Immerser," was

> a good man who was exhorting the Jews to practice virtue and righteousness towards each other and to act with piety towards God, and [thereafter] to come together for immersion.

That Josephus avoids mentioning anything of John's eschatological predictions is consistent with the fact that Josephus avoids mentioning

79. Apparently not understanding why such an immersion might need to be "proclaimed," Matthew modified the Marcan text so that John proclaims something more comprehensible, viz., a prophetic message: "Repent, for the kingdom of heaven is at hand" (Matt. 3:1-2), which is followed by Isa. 40:3. Luke keeps to Mark's wording of "proclaiming" an immersion (Luke 3:3) and quotes all of Isa. 40:3-5, but not as if it were spoken by John.

eschatology in general in his writings.[80] But we need not assume that Josephus is radically altering the main thrust of John's message here. Josephus emphasizes that John was concerned that people should behave with virtue and righteousness towards each other and act with piety towards God. The language is Josephus' characteristic vocabulary for the fundamentals of Jewish religion. He says in the *Antiquities* (16.42) that all Jewish customs are concerned with "piety and righteousness."[81] To Josephus, piety, εὐσεβεία, was centered in the Temple cult (cf. *Ant.* 8.122-24; 10.45; 14.65). It involved obedience to God and Torah (*Ant.* 6.148; *Ag. Ap.* 2.184), the observance of food and purity laws (*Life* 14; 75; cf. *War* 7.264), Sabbath observance (*Ag. Ap.* 1.212), circumcision (*Ant.* 20.44-48), and sacrifice (*Ant.* 14.65). Righteousness and piety are the particular characteristics of good Jewish kings (*Ant.* 7.338, 342, 356, 374, 384; 9.236). Steve Mason notes that in both 4 Maccabees and Josephus εὐσεβεία means "pleasing God by adhering faithfully to his law."[82] In asking people to be pious, therefore, John also asked people to be good Jews, with all the ramifications that this involved — Temple cult, purity laws, and obedience to the moral and cultic Law.

The problem that has faced scholars is how to reconcile the portrait of John provided by Josephus and that provided by the Gospels. How can they both be true? We have seen how Josephus' description of John's immersion appears to match fairly well with what may be discerned in the Gospel tradition, once an anachronistic reading of the information is stripped away. But how can a βάπτισμα μετανοίας εἰς ἄφεσιν ἁμαρτιῶν be an immersion for ridding the body of impurity? There seems at face value to be a contradiction here. The passage in Josephus describes John as asking people who were already living virtuous, righteous, and pious lives to come together and be baptized: τοῖς Ἰουδαίοις κελεύοντα ἀρετὴν ἐπασκοῦσιν καὶ τὰ πρὸς ἀλλήλους δικαιοσύνῃ καὶ πρὸς τὸν θεὸν εὐσεβείᾳ χρωμένοις βαπτισμῷ συνιέναι. There is no reference to repentance, which is all important in the Gospel descriptions of John's immersion. Josephus seems to report that people

80. See S. N. Mason, "Fire, Water and Spirit: John the Baptist and the Tyranny of Canon," *SR* 21/2 (1992) 179.

81. S. N. Mason, *Flavius Josephus on the Pharisees: A Composition-Critical Study* (Leiden: Brill, 1991) 85-89; idem, "Fire, Water and Spirit," 178.

82. Mason, *Flavius Josephus on the Pharisees*, 88.

who were already righteous went to John to be immersed, while the unrighteous stayed away. But really it is unlikely that John was calling people who had always been righteous to come for immersion. Implicit in Josephus' text is the assumption that there was a process of transformation involved. Josephus does indicate that the people who were coming to John had already changed from living lives of disobedience to righteousness by stating that "the soul had been cleansed already [or previously] by righteousness": ἅτε δὴ καὶ τῆς ψυχῆς δικαιοσύνῃ προεκκεκαθαρμένης.[83] He tells us that the righteous people coming to John had had their "souls" cleansed already by righteousness. In other words, a transformation had taken place prior to their immersion. Yes, they were righteous upon immersion; but shortly before they had required soul-cleansing. Prior to soul-cleansing, then, they cannot have been righteous. Moreover, people who had always understood themselves to be living righteously would not have had any need to come to John, for they required no soul-cleansing. Their souls having been cleansed by righteous conduct, their bodies needed to be purified also.[84] Josephus therefore tells us that it was a turning to righteousness that effected remission of sins or soul-cleansing. Baptism was for the body's purification and followed from this.

In the New Testament, it is stated that crowds gathered at the Jordan River, where they were baptized, "confessing their sins" (Mark 1:5b = Matt. 3:6). Essentially, there is only one account here, that of Mark, which has been used by Matthew and Luke. In the Marcan version, there is a definite sense that repentance, baptism, and remission of sins are all packaged together. The same packaging is found in relation to Christian baptism in Acts 2:38: "Repent, let each one of you be baptized in the name of Jesus the Messiah for the remission of your sins, and you shall receive the gift of the Holy Spirit." Elsewhere in Luke-Acts remission of sins is linked only with repentance (Luke 24:27; Acts 2:38; 5:31).[85] We have to unpack the package if we are to understand John's immersion.

83. The expression "cleanse the soul" is a metaphorical way of referring to forgiveness of sins; see Webb, *John the Baptizer and Prophet,* 190.

84. So Meier, *A Marginal Jew,* vol. 2, 229-31. Josephus' language indicates that John aimed his message at those he considered to be disobedient to the Law.

85. See Webb, *John the Baptizer and Prophet,* 171-72 for the authenticity of the phraseology.

The Greek phraseology of "a baptism of repentance for the remission of sins," βάπτισμα μετανοίας εἰς ἄφεσιν ἁμαρτιῶν (Mark 1:4; Luke 3:3; cf. Acts 13:24), may be explained by examining the possible underlying Aramaic prepositions. The genitive case, μετανοίας, "of repentance," would have been rendered in Aramaic by the prefix די or ד. This prefix is capable of many meanings, not simply "of." It can indicate purpose, "in order that," or result, "resulting from," or cause, "because of" (cf. Dan. 3:22).[86] The phrase could also be rendered in the construct state, translated by "of." In the *Community Rule* from Qumran, the construct form מי נדה, literally "waters of impurity" (1QS 3:4, et al.) may be translated "water *for the removal of* impurity," a phrase deriving from Scripture (e.g., Num. 31:23). The εἰς of the Greek phraseology may itself be translated as "with a view to"; that is, repentance will result in the remission of sins. In Aramaic, the prefix ל can express the same. It can mean "to" or "towards" but also "because of," "for," "in regard to," "concerning."[87] While the precise Aramaic must remain a matter for speculation, these prefixes are what we find in the Syriac translations of the Greek Gospel texts, and they render the phraseology extremely vague. In Syriac, a dialect of Aramaic, the phraseology could easily accommodate a translation consistent with Josephus: for example, "an immersion resulting from repentance for the remission of sins." Repentance and the remission of sins are linked; the remission of sins is what follows from repentance.

86. Holladay, *A Concise Hebrew and Aramiac Lexicon*, 402.

87. Ibid., 167-70. The prefix ל would relate to the final purpose of the repentance, not the immersion. The ד following the reference to immersion would indicate the specific character of this immersion as opposed to any others, i.e., it is related to repentance, while others are not. It does not mean that immersion and repentance were inextricably intertwined in some kind of atoning water-rite. It simply means that this immersion does not take place without repentance, which in turn takes place with a view to the forgiveness of sins. Turned around, however, the phraseology has the prior condition for the effectiveness of the immersion last — forgiveness of sins following repentance renders the immersion acceptable to God (so Josephus). The steps of the process may be masked beneath the ambiguities of Aramaic prefixes; an immersion that is acceptable to God on account of the forgiveness of sins that comes from true repentance and righteous acts has been condensed into Aramaic shorthand. It has then been rendered in Greek in a way that makes it difficult to see what is taking place. Since the precise meaning of John's immersion was irrelevant in the early Church, such phraseology did not need to be explained. All that was necessary was to make sure that Christians knew it was different (and inferior) to Christian baptism; so Acts 19:4, "John immersed [with] an immersion of repentance"; cf. Acts 1:5; 11:16; 13:24; 18:25-26.

To be precise, then, the New Testament describes John's practice not as an immersion for the remission of sins (with a view to repentance), but as an immersion of repentance (for the remission of sins). In Acts, the phraseology is shortened to precisely this formulation (Acts 13:24; 19:4). The phrase "immersion of repentance" is also found in the *Gospel of the Ebionites* (Epiphanius, *Panarion* 20.13.6). In Matt. 3:11 John states, "I immerse you in water for repentance." If one wanted to distinguish John's immersion from any other type of immersion, one would need to link it with the reason it was necessary: repentance. If one wanted to be even more specific, one would stress that the repentance was for or towards inward cleansing, that is, the remission of sins by God. The process is this: (1) one repents and practices righteousness; (2) one's sins are remitted (= one is cleansed inwardly); (3) one immerses; (4) one's immersion is considered acceptable by God, and one becomes outwardly clean. Remission of sins comes from repentance and its proof in righteous behavior, as defined by John — not from immersion.[88] The immersion follows on from the repentance that has led to a remission of sins. This may seem like playing with semantics, but the relationship of the parts in this description is extremely important for our understanding of the meaning of John's immersion. It was not a package: each part had a sequential relationship to the other parts. It is repentance (for/towards the remission of sins) that is initial and fundamental; immersion follows, and is linked to it, because without repentance there is no point in being immersed at all. Only when a sinner repents will the immersion be effective. The process cannot go back to front. John's immersion was not primary (or initiatory), as though one were accounted righteous afterwards. This notion was precisely what he rejected outright.

Where Josephus writes of righteousness and piety and implies that repentance had taken place, the Gospels describe repentance but also assume that righteousness was necessary. In the Q tradition, John calls out to those wishing to be immersed and tells them that they should

88. Acts 2:38a has Peter saying: "Repent and be immersed each one of you in (ἐπί) the name of Jesus the Messiah for (εἰς) forgiveness of your sins." Here the second part of the equation, concerning repentance, has become detached from the first part, so that it is possible to read this unclear exhortation as indicating that forgiveness of sins is related to the immersion rather than the repentance. Elsewhere in Acts, however, it is clear that repentance (and faith) releases people from the debt of their sins; see, e.g., 3:19; 5:31.

not be coming forward until they have borne fruit befitting repentance (Luke 3:7).[89] Good fruit is used metaphorically of righteous deeds in later rabbinic literature: "The fruit of a righteous man is his good conduct" (*Gen. Rab.* 16:3). As we noted above, this fits exactly with what Josephus reports, that John immersed after righteousness had been attained. In its wider context, the message is eschatological:

> You vipers' offspring! Who warned you to flee from the coming wrath [of God]? [If you wish to be immersed] then you must bear fruits worthy of repentance. And do not begin to say among yourselves, "We have a father in Abraham," for I say to you that God is able to raise up children for Abraham from these stones! For even now the ax is laid to the root of the trees, and every tree not producing good fruit will be cut down and thrown into a fire. (Luke 3:7-9)

We will return to this important passage again for further discussion in the next chapter. For now, we can interpret it fairly straightforwardly to mean that the end is so near that the ax of the orchardist (God) is already primed to cut down the trees (people) in the orchard (Israel), so that there will be no trees left that do not bear good fruit (righteous deeds). The image of the tree to be cut down would have been easily recognized as coming from Isa. 10:33-34 (cf. Dan. 4:11, 14-20). The claiming of Abraham as one's father was nothing if not accompanied by good works. John's immersion itself is not identified in this statement as conferring any particular exemption from the coming judgment; righteousness born of a repentant heart was the important factor. Whatever immersion did, it was secondary to this and apparently useless without it. This reading of the Q text in Luke matches precisely what Josephus states about John's emphases. Repentance itself entailed the practice of righteousness. The link between repentance and the practice of righteous behavior was itself fundamental in Second Temple Judaism. We will look at this in more detail in the next chapter.

In conclusion, John's immersion was wholly in keeping with other Jewish immersions of the time in having to do with ridding the body of uncleanness, but it also entailed the different idea that previous immersions and ablutions were ineffective for Jews without the practice

89. While in Luke 3:7 the reference is to the crowds who come to John, in Matt. 3:7 the reference is to Pharisees and Sadducees.

of true righteousness. Immersion itself could not be used as a method of exhorting God for forgiveness. John's practice was not an initiatory rite or a "repentance-baptism." It had its own integrity and followed on from people turning back to the way of God, just as becoming clean followed on from people's acceptance into Israel as God's obedient servants. John addressed those who could not count themselves as righteous, and asked them to turn back to God's way. While they were straying from obedience, they could not be pure in body, for the body could not be clean if the heart was defiled. With repentance and its proof in the practice of righteousness, the heart was rendered pure; God cleansed the heart and granted remission of sins. Now pure inside, one could become pure outside, and therefore immersion naturally followed. Bodily purity was important for those who wished to be acceptable to God and obedient to his Law, especially given the fact that the end was so near. John's immersion, then, was distinctive, and yet also entirely understandable in the context of Second Temple Judaism.

CHAPTER 3

Teaching and Predictions

Before a review of what John may have taught, it should be noted that all of John's teaching is found within Christian literature, and therefore its integrity is difficult to assess. We have no independent body of material, or list of John's sayings, collected by any Jewish group. John does not appear in rabbinic literature. As we have seen, what Josephus states concerning John has been useful for understanding the nature of his immersion, but he tells us very little about John's message, other than that he wanted Jews to live lives obedient to God. This, however, may be worth reiterating. All the discussion so far points to John's turning back those who had not been obedient to the Law, to a life of obedience.

John's radical assertion that lustrations were ineffective without inner purity, was, of course, a teaching in itself. However, it is likely that John not only proclaimed his immersion, but also made it the core of a small body of teaching that encompassed more than immersion. For example, if he deemed purifications ineffective, he may also have considered other pious or ritual acts, most especially praying and fasting, as ineffective in themselves. "Ineffective" here means that God would not accept these acts, as Josephus spells out in regard to John's immersion. The most strongly attested and well-known evidence indicates that John's message had an eschatological perspective. This perspective, though, does not preclude a concern with ethical conduct in the here and now. Although the usual eschatological understanding of John's message is very important in a total appraisal of what he taught, this feature of his message will in this chapter be somewhat underplayed, as a counterbalance to the predominant image of John as preacher of apocalyptic doom.

John the Teacher

In the New Testament John is called a "teacher" (διδάσκαλος, Luke 3:12) or, in Aramaic and Hebrew, a "rabbi" (John 3:26). Fittingly, then, he had disciples (Mark 2:18; 6:29; Matt. 9:14; 11:2; 14:12; Luke 5:33; 7:18; 11:1; John 1:22, 32, 35, 37; 3:25, 27; Acts 19:1-7) or, more correctly, "students"; the word μαθητῆς (masc.) or μαθήτρια (fem.) means "learner, student," deriving from the verb μανθάνω, "learn, study."[1] But the New Testament writings consistently avoid John's teaching. Luke alone attributes to John material comprising ethical sayings (Luke 3:10-14; cf. 11:1). Some disciples stayed close to John (Matt. 11:2 = Luke 7:18; cf. Mark 6:29; Matt. 14:12), but many went back to their own homes (cf. Matt. 9:14 = Mark 2:18 = Luke 5:33).

How did one become a disciple of John? Not by immersion. Immersion completed a process of becoming clean inwardly and outwardly; it was not an initiation into a select group of disciples. One became a disciple, a "student," of another person by receiving instruction from that person. It seems quite clear from our sources that people became disciples of John prior to their immersion. This is only logical, for people needed to know how to attain inner purity before immersion took place (cf. Luke 3:9-14). John was seen to have the answers. Josephus describes people who were highly excited by John and ready to do anything he advised them. Some of those he immersed may have wished to stay close to him, receiving further instruction and remaining loyal devotees. Nevertheless, the implication of John's teaching in Luke 3:10-14 is that he expected that most would return to their usual jobs in towns and villages.

As in other religions, so in Judaism discipleship was not a loose relationship with a person whom one respected as a reputable scholar or sage, but a well-defined relationship entailing close involvement between disciple and teacher. While our material on this subject in Judaism generally comes from the rabbinic period, and is too late to be con-

1. LSJ, 1078-09.

sidered definitively useful for Second Temple Judaism as a whole, it can be set alongside more contemporary material in order to understand the nature of what was taking place, especially since, as K. H. Rengstorf notes, the New Testament portrayal of disciples is very similar to the rabbinic picture of תלמידים.[2] In regard to Greek terminology, Rengstorf notes that there is "no μαθητής without a διδάσκαλος. The process involves a corresponding personal relation."[3] The same was true of the relationship between the תלמיד and the rabbi. A תלמיד had the obligation of looking after his master/teacher in quite a close way. In return, the teacher formally taught his disciples a body of teaching.[4] However, it appears in Second Temple Judaism that, if someone was considered to be a prophet, then those who wished to learn the prophet's particular prophetic teaching were also probably known as תלמידין (Aramaic). The evidence for this is found in Josephus and is supported by the Targums. To look at the latter first, the "sons of the prophets" of 2 Kings (2:3, 7, 15; 4:1, 38; 5:22) are in Aramaic "disciples of the prophets," תלמידי נביאיא, and the מִשפחות, "guilds," of 1 Chron. 2:53, 55 are תלמידיא, "the disciples." Josephus confirms that these ideas were known in the first century, since he too translates "sons of the prophets" as "disciples of the prophets" (*Ant.* 20.28, 68). The saying concerning the "sons of the Pharisees" (Matt. 12:27; Luke 11:19) may also represent an Aramaic idiom that could refer to disciples of certain sages as "sons" (or "children").

Those considered prophet-teachers would probably not have taught their disciples in the same formal way found in later rabbinic academies. Nevertheless, the process of the disciples' learning was based on the teacher giving instruction in an accepted pedagogical framework. As we read frequently in regard to Jesus, he "taught" his disciples and had a body of teaching (e.g., Mark 1:22; 4:2; Matt. 7:29; Luke 19:47; Acts 1:1), which the disciples undoubtedly would have sought to learn and commit to memory, as was customary.

The content of John's teaching was most likely "the way of God" or "the way of righteousness." In the Jesus tradition, John the Baptist is said to have come "in the way of righteousness" (Matt. 21:32). The

2. K. H. Rengstorf, "μαθητής," *TDNT* 4 (1967) 415-61.

3. Ibid., 416.

4. The masculine language here is used deliberately; in rabbinic Judaism there was no such thing as a תלמידה, "female disciple."

Pharisees and Herodians of Mark 12:14 (cf. Luke 20:21) tell Jesus, "Teacher, we know that you are true, and do not take notice of any person, for you take no regard for people's position, but truly teach the way of God." "The way of God" could itself be abbreviated as "the way," as is shown in Acts (9:2; 18:25-6; 19:9, 23; 22:4; 24:14, 22). Christians used general terminology to refer specifically to their ideology, as did the members of the Qumran community (1QS 4:12; 9:16-21; CD 1:9, 13; cf. 1:16, 20-21). To walk in the way of God or of righteousness meant complete obedience to all aspects of the Law, both in one's heart and in one's actions. The integral connection between all aspects of the Law is found in Deut. 10:12-13:

> And now Israel — what does YHWH ask of you? To fear YHWH your God, to walk in all his ways, and to love him, and to serve YHWH your God with all your heart and all your soul, and to keep the commandments of YHWH and his statutes which I [Moses] command you this day for your good.

In the Christian manual the *Didache,* the "way of life" is called "the way of the teaching," that is, the teaching of Jesus (*Did.* 2:2; 6:1; cf. 1:1–4:12; cf. *Ep. Barnabas* 18–20). In Acts 24:14-15 Paul speaks of the way in these terms: "I worship the God of our ancestors, believing everything that is according to the Law, and which is in the writings of the prophets." Paul's interpretation of what this meant may have been idiosyncratic, but the basic affirmation could be readily accepted.

To make the metaphor complete, it is necessary to walk along the way, as Prov. 8:20 has it. The way of the Lord is the Law of the Lord: "Those of the house of Jacob will say, 'Come and let us walk in the teaching of the law of YHWH.'"[5] With these biblical metaphors in view, it is significant that in rabbinic literature the word הלכה, a religious ruling, comes from the verb הלך, "to walk." The religious ruling is a "walking" along the way of righteousness — בדרך צדקה/צדק, which is God's Law (תורה).

Here we are not dealing with technical terminology that would link John with a specific movement — the Essenes or the Pharisees, for example — but with general terminology common to all kinds of Jewish

5. B. D. Chilton, *The Isaiah Targum: Introduction, Translation, Apparatus, and Notes* (Wilmington, DE: Glazier, 1987) 6.

groups. For example, in the Dead Sea Scrolls the phrase "ways of true righteousness" (e.g., 1QS 4:2) reflects the same consciousness and conceptual framework found in Pharisaic and later rabbinic Judaism. The Teacher of Righteousness (מורה הצדק, 1QpHab 1:13; 2:2; 5:10, etc.; or מורה צדק, CD 1:11) was precisely a teacher who enabled his disciples to walk along God's ways and avoid ways of iniquity and falsehood. The phrase "teacher of righteousness" ("righteousness-teacher") is found also in Midrashic literature.[6]

"Righteousness" here is, of course, not a fixed concept. Much would have been understood by all Jews as comprising righteous behavior and piety, founded on Scripture, but the definition of "righteousness," like "purity," depended on one's own particular perspective. One person's righteousness may not be that of another. Individual teachers prescribed individual interpretations of Scripture that defined righteousness for their own disciples in particular ways. We know this from the various *halakhot* of rabbinic literature, which are rulings by individual teachers given to their disciples. Rabbinic literature gives ample evidence of debates between teachers on correct interpretations and proper rulings. To define a set of particular teachings on righteousness for one's disciples did not mean that one was forming an exclusive sect, though a sect could grow out of the interpretations and ideas of a particular teacher, as we know from the early Nazarene "sect," αἵρεσις, the disciples of Jesus. A "sect" was, in a sense, a philosophical school within Judaism, based on specific interpretations and beliefs, but still founded on the same bedrock of Scripture (which could be supplemented by other texts, some of which were considered authoritative by different groups). John might have been understood by some to have founded a "sect" or a "school" comprised of disciples, but essentially what we have in our sources is vestigial.

We never find a fully fledged "Baptist sect" in evidence in the first century (the Mandaeans of a later time being irrelevant to the present discussion). As we saw, the story of Apollos in Acts 18 does not indicate that a "Baptist sect" existed in Ephesus. The impression gained is that the disciples of John were no more cohesive as a group than were the disciples of other teachers of the time. They probably endured for a

6. M. Bregman, "Another Reference to the Teacher of Righteousness in Midrashic Literature," *RevQ* 37 (1979) 97-100.

while, but were simply one small part of the immense diversity within Second Temple Judaism.

Certainly, those who had been to John for immersion considered themselves to be his disciples. Put simply, one could be John's disciple and still not yet be immersed, but one probably could not be immersed by John without being his disciple. If people believed that he was proclaiming his immersion under prophetic inspiration, they may well have wished to stay with him for a period of time to learn from him. Once home, they may have distinguished themselves as "disciples of John" by following the basic teachings he prescribed and by advocating the necessity of "an immersion of repentance" for those who had strayed from the Law or who would otherwise not count themselves as righteous. Fundamental in this would have been the explication of repentance.

Repentance

As we saw in the last chapter, in the description given in Luke's infancy narrative John's call to repentance is considered to be his most distinctive characteristic. In Hebrew, the word **תשובה**, "repentance," has as its root the verb **שוב**, "turn"; the same was true of Aramaic, with **אתיב**, "turn" (in its Aphel form) meaning "repent." The words of the angel Gabriel in Luke's nativity story stress that John's role was to turn people back from unrighteousness to righteousness: "He will be filled with the Holy Spirit [i.e., he will be a prophet], even from his mother's womb, and many of the children of Israel will turn back to the Lord their God. And he [John] will go before him [God] in the spirit and power of Elijah, "to turn back the hearts of fathers to their children" (Mal. 4:5-6; Sir. 48:10) "and the disobedient to the purpose of the righteous, to make ready a people prepared for the Lord" (Luke 1:15b-17). Zechariah's prophecy at the circumcision of John reflects the same understanding of John's role (Luke 1:76-79):

> And you, child, will be called prophet of the Most High;
> for you will go before the Lord to prepare his ways:
> to give knowledge of salvation to his people
> in (ἐν) the forgiveness of their sins,

on account of (διά) the innermost feelings of mercy of our God,
by which the sunrise from on high has broken upon us[7]
to shine on those who sit in darkness and the shadow of death,
to make our feet straight along (εἰς) the way of peace.

In the prophecy of Zechariah, John prepares the ways of the Lord, which in Luke 1:15b-17 is an activity interpreted as "turning people back" to God from disobedience of the Law to obedience or righteousness. This is done "to give knowledge of salvation to his people in the forgiveness of their sins." In other words, knowledge of salvation comes in the forgiveness of sins; people can be assured of being spared condemnation at the final judgment because their sins have been forgiven. Repentance requires people to turn back to the right path. Zechariah's prophecy coheres with the imagery and language of texts like the Wisdom of Solomon 5:6-7, where those under judgment say:

So we have strayed from the way of truth;
the light of righteousness has not shone upon us,
and the sun has not risen upon us.
We have explored every path of lawlessness or ruin,
and we have wandered through trackless deserts,
and the way of the Lord is one we have not known.

7. Reading the aorist form of the verb, ἐπεσκέψατο. Some ancient manuscripts use the future tense of the verb, ἐπισκέψεται, so that the "sunrise from on high" that "will break upon us" refers to Jesus rather than to John. The authentic wording, however, was most likely the aorist. The change may have come about because of the lack of any specific mention of Jesus as Messiah in this section of the prophecy; see C. H. H. Scobie, *John the Baptist* (London: SCM, 1964) 53. Brown notes that the word ἀνατολή, "sunrise," was used by Greek-speaking Jews to refer to the expected king of the house of David (R. E. Brown, *The Birth of the Messiah: A Commentary on the Infancy Narratives in Matthew and Luke* [London: Chapman, 1977] 390-91), but this does not mean that we should interpret every passage in which there is a metaphorical sunrise as messianic. Brown himself notes that in the passage of Malachi concerning Elijah's return (Mal. 3:1-24) there is a reference to the "sun of righteousness" that "will rise with healing in its wings." It seems quite clear here in Luke 1:78 that the reference is to John; cf. John 5:35, where John is a "burning and shining lamp." It is therefore also John who shines on those who sit in darkness "to make our feet straight along the the way of peace" (Luke 1:79; cf. Mal. 3:1). For a fuller discussion, see W. Wink, *John the Baptist in the Gospel Tradition* (Cambridge: Cambridge University Press, 1968) 65-68, who favors the future ἐπισκέψεται.

For John, repentance was clearly not something that simply blossomed in the heart full of emotion and good intentions. It had nothing to do with believing any fundamental dogmas; it had to be proven. The תשובה, or turning around (cf. Isa. 3:15), was a turning back to God in obedience and trust. It was central in the message of the prophets (e.g., Isa. 10:20-21; Jer. 3:22-23; 18:8; 26:3-5; 34:15; Zech. 1:3-4; Mal. 3:7). To obey God meant to follow the Law and to do his will — to do good. Through this, God would grant remission of sins, so that final judgment and condemnation would be averted from the righteous (Isa. 55:7; Jonah 3:9-10; Ezek. 33:13-16).[8] Essentially, this part of John's teaching would have been widely understood, since it derived entirely from the prophetic tradition.

The use of the verb שׁוב, "turn," connects the concept of repentance with the metaphorical phrase "to walk in the way of righteousness" (cf. Prov. 8:20).[9] The imagery conjures up a person on a journey who has been walking along the wrong path but who, upon realizing and regretting the error, turns around and finds the right path along which to continue the journey. People who so turn around can count themselves among the righteous who will be spared destruction at the end. As Jesus is recorded as saying, "Enter by the narrow gate, because the gate is wide and the way is easy that leads to destruction, and those who enter it are many. But the gate is narrow and the way is hard that leads to life, and those that find it are few" (Matt. 5:13-14; cf. Luke 13:23-4).

For John, repentance was not a case of exhibiting a good attitude, or of pleading with God for forgiveness, or of expressing belief. It involved obedience to God, which demonstrated one's true, heartfelt intention. God's right path was manifested in Scripture. Torah was a fundamental expression of God's will. In Neh. 9:29 repentance is specifically described as turning towards the Law. Isa. 55:7 spells out the association between God's forgiveness and repentance:

> Let the wicked forsake his way and the evil person his thoughts, and let him return to YHWH, and he will have mercy upon him. And [let him return] to our God, for he will abundantly pardon.

8. See R. L. Webb, *John the Baptizer and Prophet: A Socio-Historical Study* (Sheffield: JSOT Press, 1991) 184-85.

9. See Prov. 16:31; 21:16; Ps. 1:6; 23; *1 Enoch* 82:4-7; cf. Dan. 12:3; *'Abot* 5:18.

In the Aramaic *Targum Pseudo-Jonathan* of Isaiah, it is written, "let him return to the service of the Lord, that he may have mercy upon him, and to the fear of our God, for he will abundantly pardon."[10] Here the Targum makes explicit what is implicit in the Hebrew text: returning to the Lord means doing his service. This means living righteously, in obedience to the Law, and doing good.

Prophetic literature itself provides the idea that remission of sins was not necessarily linked with making sacrifices in the Temple, for atonement was made by repentance and righteous conduct rather than the sacrifice of an animal (cf. Lev. 5:5-10; 14:19-20; 15:15, 30). We find this notion fairly well attested as part of the prophetic tradition (cf. Ps. 51:16-17; 1 Sam. 15:22; Prov. 15:8). The prophet Hosea, for instance, did not believe that the Temple was redundant, only that sacrifices should be seen as secondary to ethical and moral concerns. As Hosea (6:6) states:

> For I desire loving-kindness, and not sacrifice;
> the knowledge of God, rather than burnt offerings.

In the *Community Rule* from Qumran (1QS 9:4-5), a similar idea is expressed:

> They shall atone for guilty rebellion and for the sins of unfaithfulness that they may obtain loving-kindness for the Land without the flesh of holocaust and the fat of sacrifice. And prayer rightly offered shall be as an acceptable fragrance of righteousness, and perfection of way as a delectable free-will offering.[11]

And according to 1QS 8:3-4,

> They shall preserve the faith in the land with steadfastness and meekness and shall atone for sin by the practice of justice and by suffering the sorrows of affliction.[12]

10. Chilton, *The Isaiah Targum,* 108.

11. Trans. G. Vermes, *The Dead Sea Scrolls in English,* 4th ed. (Harmondsworth: Penguin, 1995) 82.

12. Ibid., 80. See also 4Q174 Florilegium.

The rejection of the primacy of Temple sacrifice for atonement was probably not simply a quirk of the Essenes, who considered the present Temple defiled (cf. Josephus, *Ant.* 18.19; Philo, *Every Good Man Is Free* 1.75). This rejection would have been known by all Jews from the prophetic tradition. Considering that the high priest was chosen by the Roman procurators and that those who administered the Temple were those who appeared to collaborate with the occupying power, the validity of the Temple sacrifices may have been questioned more widely than simply among the sectarian Essenes.[13] For example, the group responsible for the *Psalms of Solomon* believed that the righteous person makes atonement for sins of ignorance by "fasting and affliction of his soul" (3:8), and that God purifies the soul when "confession and acknowledgment [of sin] is made" (9:6). These are the essential components of the initial stages of תשובה. This relegation of the Temple cult to secondary importance, with the Temple nevertheless still maintaining its relevance, must also have been felt by many Jews in the Diaspora, for whom pilgrimage to the Temple was a once-in-a-lifetime event, if that.

If John stressed that "turning around" to righteousness effected atonement, then he would have been participating in a current that did not consider atonement (the remission of sins) effected only through Temple sacrifices by priests. On the other hand, sacrifice in the Temple may still have been relevant and important, for all we know, so that everything would be done in accordance with the Law. If the Gospel tradition has omitted to tell us that John asked his converts to go to the Temple and sacrifice, this is not to say that he could not have done so. Our information concerning John is extremely abbreviated. As noted in Chapter 1, there is nothing about John's practice of immersing that should lead us to assume that it was considered to be a replacement for Temple sacrifices and procedures, even though his immersion had to do with repentance and atonement.

In other words, we do not need to see John as anti-Temple simply because he endorsed the primacy of repentance and righteousness over sacrificing in regard to atonement and forgiveness.[14] Jesus himself in

13. See C. A. Evans, "Opposition to the Temple: Jesus and the Dead Sea Scrolls," in *Jesus and the Dead Sea Scrolls,* ed. J. H. Charlesworth (New York: Doubleday, 1992) 235-53.

14. Contra Webb, *John the Baptizer and Prophet,* 203-05.

the Marcan tradition advises a healed (cleansed) leper to go to the Temple and do everything in accordance with the Law (Mark 1:40-45 = Matt. 8:1-4 = Luke 5:12-16). John too may have asked his disciples to act according to the Law in regard to the Temple. Since the Gospels were written mainly for a Gentile audience after the destruction of the Temple, it would not be surprising if references to the Temple were deleted, but we know that for the early Jewish-Christians in Jerusalem the Temple remained the prime focus of piety and teaching (Acts 3:1; 5:12, 21-25, 42, etc.). So there is no reason to assume, on the basis of the link between remission of sins and repentance, that John's attitude to the Temple cult was negative. A focus on the importance of תשׁובה does not amount to an anti-Temple stance. The prophetic tradition had both an emphasis on personal righteousness and turning towards God and a recognition of the importance of the Temple cultus. It was a case of emphasizing matters of the heart in relation to the cult, not of rejecting the cult outright.

The Confession of Sins

According to Mark (1:5b; cf. Matt. 3:5), people baptized by John had to confess their sins. This appears to have been a teaching of John's — that people should confess their sins to indicate publicly their repentance. Strictly speaking, recognition and confession of sins to God is part of the personal process of repentance. So, Rabbi Berekha, in the name of Rabbi Ba ben Bina, gave as an example of confession, "My Lord, I have sinned and have walked in a far-off path. I will no longer do what I have done. May it be Thy will, O Lord my God, that you grant me atonement and forgive all my sins and pardon all my sins" (*y. Yoma* 45c).[15] In linking baptism with confession, therefore, Mark appears to link baptism with the very moment of repentance. But while confession of sins to God is part of personal repentance, Mark does not indicate to whom the people coming to be baptized are confessing. They are simply ἐξομολογούμενοι, "making full acknowledgment of" their sins in public.

Josephus states that John asked people to "come together" or "as-

15. Trans. S. T. Lachs, *A Rabbinic Commentary on the New Testament: The Gospels of Matthew, Mark, and Luke* (Hoboken, NJ: KTAV, 1987) 38.

semble" (συνιέναι) for baptism, which seems to indicate that he waited for a mass of people to gather. Luke describes Jesus' prayer as taking place "when all the people had been baptized" (Luke 3:21). Josephus indicates that Herod Antipas grew anxious when Jews had gathered together, excited by John's teaching (*Ant.* 18.118); they were apparently willing to do anything he advised. John did not then immerse people in ones and twos, or even suggest they go to a *miqveh* by themselves. The New Testament agrees with Josephus that crowds came out to John at the Jordan, apparently for a particular event — a mass immersion. Therefore, it seems likely that the immersions that took place were public, and that part of the process involved a person indicating to God, John, and also to some of the assembled crowd that he or she was truly repentant by confessing past sins. However, neither Josephus, Luke, nor Mark was interested in giving us a precise description of what took place. We can but speculate.

As we saw in the last chapter, it is unlikely that John actually decided on the spot whether or not a person was worthy of immersion. His disconcerting attack on the people coming to him ("You offspring of vipers!") seems to have been designed to make them hesitate, but there is nothing to suggest that John himself sorted people out. If someone was not truly righteous, or had not borne good fruit, then the immersion would not have been truly acceptable to God, anyway; ultimately, everything rested with God, and not with John. He cannot have been a mediator. God would soon come to judge; it was not for John to do God's job. In teaching people that they had to repent and bear good fruit, and come to immersion with the requirement that they publicly acknowledge their sins to everyone there, John was probably going as far as was necessary. The public announcement of sins would have been a major obstacle for anyone who was not truly repentant. Few people would have done this lightly. There seems to have been no public announcement of anyone's good works; they were for God's viewing alone. The final decision was with God.

After undergoing instruction from John, most people who came for immersion would have had a fairly clear idea of what was required before immersion could be effective. The process of instruction would itself have sorted out those who were sincere from those who were not. People may have been expected to go away, to prove repentance, and then return indicating what they had done, before immersion.

John's Ethical Teaching: Luke 3:10-14

We have very little material indeed that might help us fit John into the theological and pedagogical framework of Second Temple Judaism, but John's specific teaching as given in Luke 3:10-14 may enable us to make a start. There has been considerable debate about the genuineness of this material, but, on balance, there are probably more reasons than not to accept the basis of the material as authentic. The reasons for rejecting the passage as authentic rest on various assumptions. Bultmann thought it ridiculous that soldiers would have gone on a "pilgrimage" to John.[16] However, as Webb points out, there is no reason to assume that Jewish men serving as soldiers (in the forces of Herod Antipas) could not have found John religiously persuasive. The term στρατευόμενοι in Luke 3:14 refers to those serving (temporarily) as soldiers rather than to professional soldiers.[17] As Webb notes, the words used for toll collectors (τελῶναι) and men serving as soldiers (στρατευόμενοι) are not Lucan, even though other words in the passage (πράσσω, 3:13; συκοφαντέω, 3:14; cf. 19:8) do have a Lucan ring. These words, moreover, are hardly specific to Luke alone, but are found in the LXX, which was a resource for all Greek-speaking Jews and Christians.[18] The examination by E. H.

16. R. Bultmann, *The History of the Synoptic Tradition* (Oxford: Blackwell, 1963) 145. Doubts concerning the authenticity of this passage were first raised by J. Wellhausen, *Das Evangelium Lucae* (Berlin: Reimer, 1904) 13. According to Wellhausen, the passage has features, such as the "eigentümlich griechischen Ausdrücke" (p. 5), that make it likely that it was Luke's invention. E. Bammel suggests that something similar was found in Q and that Luke used this as a "coat-hanger" for his own ideas since the original contents were more radical than the evangelist's own position; see E. Bammel, "The Baptist in Early Christian Tradition," *NTS* 18 (1971-72) 105-06. It is hard to imagine anything more radical than John's teaching that everyone should give away everything except one's essential clothing and food; his words imply that at least half one's possessions should be given to the poor. Scholarly opinion remains divided about the authenticity of this passage; see W. B. Tatum, *John the Baptist and Jesus: A Report of the Jesus Seminar* (Sonoma, CA: Polebridge, 1994) 134-35.

17. Webb, *John the Baptizer and Prophet,* 358 n. 16.

18. Ibid. H. Schürmann has also pointed out the presence of non-Lucan vocabulary in this passage and conjectures that Luke used a source that he reformulated in his own style; see H. Schürmann, *Das Lukasevangelium,* vol. 1 (Freiburg: Herder, 1969) 169 n. 53. Webb concludes that the pericope "probably reflects genuine Baptist material with respect to the ethical positions espoused for various groups, but . . . its form and terminology are due to translation and subsequent shaping of the tradition" (*John the Baptizer and Prophet,* 359 n. 16). I. H. Marshall notes that Luke's special material con-

Scheffler, which relates the passage to the overall socio-economic concerns of Luke's narrative, especially in regard to the condemnation of the wealthy and the exaltation of the poor,[19] may well be right, but Luke need not have edited some hypothetical "severe" teaching to amplify his own themes. These themes are not exclusive to Luke in all of early Jewish and Christian literature. Moreover, John Meier points out that this section agrees with the presentation of John in Josephus as a moral teacher.[20] Given Josephus' description, some kind of teaching as found here is precisely what we might expect from John.

Luke's special material (L) — which may not have been homogeneous — may well have contained a body of historically authentic traditions about John the Baptist. After all, one of the most important passages for the dating of the events connected with Jesus (cf. Luke 2:1-2) is found in Luke alone in relation to John, *not* Jesus. As far as can be ascertained, the Lucan chronology contains accurate information concerning the regional rulers in the period.[21] Therefore, it seems strained to argue that, after such good historical information, come statements concerning John's teaching that are a wild invention. Even though the teaching fits well with Luke's interest, and with L as a whole, this cannot be a reason to reject its authenticity outright. We might be

---

tains no other traditions concerning John and that this passage therefore most likely comes from Q; see Marshall, *The Gospel of Luke* (Grand Rapids: Eerdmans, 1978) 142. J. S. Kloppenborg omits Luke 3:10-15 from Q, presumably because there is no Matthean parallel; see Kloppenborg, *The Formation of Q: Trajectories in Ancient Wisdom Collections* (Philadelphia: Fortress, 1987) 74.

19. E. H. Scheffler, "The Social Ethics of the Lucan Baptist (Lk. 3:10-14)," *Neot* 24 (1990) 21-36.

20. J. P. Meier, *A Marginal Jew: Rethinking the Historical Jesus. Volume Two: Mentor, Message, and Miracles* (New York: Doubleday, 1994) 61-62.

21. Joseph Caiaphas appears to have been high priest from 18/19 CE until 37 CE. Pontius Pilate was *praefectus* of Judea from either 19 (doubtfully) or 26 CE until 37 CE, when he was recalled to Rome. Herod Antipas was tetrarch of Galilee and Perea from 4 BCE until 39 CE, when Gaius Caligula sent him into exile. Philip was tetrarch of Ituraea and Trachonitis from 4 BCE until his death in 34 CE, after which his territory was absorbed into the Roman province of Syria. The dates of Lysanias are unknown. For the date of Pilate's prefecture beginning in 26 CE, see D. R. Schwartz, *Studies in the Jewish Background of Christianity* (Tübingen: Mohr-Siebeck, 1992) 182-217. Luke does say that Annas and Caiaphas were both high priests, but this may have derived from a popular understanding on account of the immense power of Annas. Even the Fourth Gospel mentions that Caiaphas was high priest "that year," as if Annas and Caiaphas were alternating; Jesus is taken to Annas first on the night of his arrest (John 18:13-14).

assured of its authenticity if it did not fit with these features, on the basis of the criterion of dissimilarity, but lack of absolute assurance of authenticity does not mean that we should jump to a conclusion of utter skepticism. The passage reads:

> And the crowds asked him, saying, "What then should we do?" So he answered and said, "The one who has two tunics should share with the one who has none, and the one who has food should do likewise." And toll collectors came to be immersed and they said to him, "Teacher, what should we do?" So he said to them, "Do [or take] no more than that which has been allotted to you." Men serving as soldiers also questioned him, saying, "And we — what should we do?" And he said to them, "Do not rob or extort, and be content with your wages." (Luke 3:10-14)

To set this teaching in context, it should be noted that it reflects a particular perspective on true righteousness. It reinforces the letter of the Law in order to prescribe a way of behaving that is consistent with the spirit of the Law and with the nature of God. That people should obey the Law is implicit. The reasons people should do so are quite simple: the ax has been "laid to the root of the trees" (Matt. 3:10 = Luke 3:9), and judgment is nigh. In view of this eschatological urgency, people are to repent of their sinful ways and embrace a life of righteousness in obedience to God. This was more than a prophetic announcement from John. The threat of future judgment was known to many groups. A common view appears to have been that, in order to offset the threat of future judgment, people could store up "treasure in heaven" in the form of righteous deeds. Q's Jesus notes this (Matt. 6:19-21 = Luke 12:33-34). In the *Testament of Levi* (13:5) it is advised: "Do righteousness upon earth that you may have treasure in heaven." In *Tg. Ps.-J.* Isa. 26:10, it is stated, "good deeds . . . will protect you in the time of distress." In rabbinic literature we have statements such as, "Repentance and good works are a shield against punishment" (*m. 'Abot* 4:13; cf. *Gen. Rab.* 39:3; *y. Ta'an.* 65b). John's eschatological prediction of coming judgment and his teaching on righteousness are therefore integrally related, and they would have been considered two sides of the same coin by the people who came to him.

But more than this, these exhortations to righteousness need to be seen in the context of the Lucan passage as a whole, for Luke makes it clear that these words were addressed specifically to those who were coming for immersion and who — having repented — wished to know what fruits (deeds) would be considered worthy of repentance (Luke 3:8-9). "Good fruit" means "righteous deeds" in later rabbinic literature (cf. *Gen. Rab.* 16:3). In other words, these actions were necessary before John's immersion could be effective. Without these examples of "good fruit," no one could expect to be immersed and be cleansed, for God would not have forgiven the person's sins. If inner cleansing had not taken place, then neither would outer, bodily cleansing. The passage flows on directly from the statement concerning this good fruit: "you must bear fruits worthy of repentance . . . and every tree not producing good fruit will be cut down and thrown into a fire . . . and the crowds asked him, saying, 'What then should we do [in order to be immersed/bear good fruit]?'"

There are two parts to John's specific teaching as recorded by Luke. The first part (3:10-11) is a general prescription for οἱ ὄχλοι, the crowds who came to him for immersion, accepted him as a prophet-teacher, and sought both his immersion and advice on how to make it effective. The second part concerns the problems encountered by people who wished to repent and follow the Law in professions that society tended to consider reprehensible. There are, accordingly, specific questions from toll collectors (3:12-13), who address John as διδάσκαλε, teacher, and then from men serving as soldiers (3:14). We shall look at the latter section first.

Luke 3:12-14

> And toll collectors came to be immersed and they said to him, "Teacher, what should we do [in order to bear good fruit]?" So he said to them, "Do [or take] no more than that which has been allotted to you."
>
> Men serving as soldiers also questioned him, saying, "And we — what should we do [in order to bear good fruit]?" And he said to them, "Do not rob or extort, and be content with your wages."

John's reply does not presume that toll collectors had to cease being toll collectors in order to be righteous. They could be "righteoused," to use Sanders's term, in their jobs by being fair and collecting no more than was allotted to them. The toll collector (Aramaic, מוכסא) and tax collector (גבאי) are despised in later rabbinic literature (*m. B. Qam.* 10:2; *b. B. Qam.* 113a; *b. Sanh.* 25b; *b. Šeb.* 39a). The tax collectors, though not the toll collectors, rendered things unclean (*m. Ḥag.* 3:6; *m. Tohar.* 7:6; *t. Tohar.* 8:5-6). Both tax and toll collectors were often understood to be money-grubbing and uninterested in following the Law. Tax collectors could not become members of the חברים (*t. Dem.* 3:4). "Repentance is hard for tax collectors and toll collectors" (*t. B. Meṣ.* 8:26; cf. *b. B. Qam.* 94b); repentance involved restitution of all that they had wrongfully taken from people, plus a fifth (*t. B. Qam.* 10:14) or else a donation of the sum to the common good, by, for example, building a cistern (*b. B. Qam.* 94b).[22] This stereotype is also found on the lips of Matthew's Jesus, who equates toll collectors with Gentiles as people who cared nothing for the Law (Matt. 5:46-47). But both John and Jesus appear to have accepted that toll collectors could somehow live righteously while continuing to follow their own particular (though rather unfortunate) careers. When in a Matthean saying of Jesus addressed to the chief priests and scribes it is written that, in respect to John, "toll collectors and prostitutes enter the Kingdom of Heaven before you" (Matt. 21:31), the shock value could not be greater. Jesus here does not say "ex-toll collectors and ex-prostitutes." This would mean that toll collectors and prostitutes have been accepted by God, while the chief priests have not. Those who should have been the standards of righteousness in society were being left behind, while those who were generally considered the least righteous succeeded in being vindicated, despite their vocations. The lost sheep were found.

John's advice to toll collectors indicates that he believed it possible to repent, obey the Law, and remain a toll collector. However, there was a requirement that applied specifically to the temptations of their profession: they should be scrupulously fair and take only what had been officially allotted to them. Toll collectors were sub-tenants of much richer

22. J. Jeremias, *New Testament Theology: The Proclamation of Jesus* (London: SCM, 1971) 111. The distinction between the tax collector and the toll collector is important; see J. A. Fitzmyer, *The Gospel According to Luke I–IX: Introduction, Translation, and Notes* (Garden City, NY: Doubleday, 1981) 469-70. See also P. W. Hollenbach, "John the Baptist," in *ABD*, vol. 3, H– J, 896-97, though he does not make the distinction. F. Herrenbrück, *Jesus und die Zöllner: Historische und Neutestamentlich-exegetische Untersuchungen* (Tübingen: Mohr-Siebeck, 1990), notes that the τελῶναι should be understood as Hellenistic tax farmers, not Roman *publicani.*

toll farmers (like Zacchaeus of Luke 19:2, an ἀρχιτελώνης). They made a bid for the toll income of a district, and whatever the circumstances they had to get the agreed sum plus their own additional profit.[23] Implicitly, John proscribed bribery and extortion, but his words are most simply read as a prohibition against doing anything beyond what was required in one's toll collecting in an effort to make more money. If this kind of money-grubbing, which so often was seen to go with the job, was halted, then toll collectors could be righteous. There is also a passivity here, for toll collectors are to remain as toll collectors, rather than join John in the wilderness. This passivity may derive from the notion that the end was so near that changing one's job to embrace a wilderness lifestyle was hardly worthwhile; the ax was already laid to the root of the trees. One should accept one's vocation and live justly in the meantime.

As for the second specific recommendation, given to men serving as soldiers, a striking parallel to Luke 3:12-13 is found in the advice that Josephus gave to his troops (*Life* 244): "I thanked them and advised them not to attack anyone nor to sully their hands with robbery, but to set up camp in the plain and be content with their rations." It was a standard of good and just behavior for those who would find favor with God. Josephus clearly hoped and believed that God would be on his side, and he wanted his soldiers to impress God by their exemplary standards. The men who came to John were almost certainly Jewish, not Roman, soldiers. The Jewish officers appointed by Agrippa II were mostly descended from Babylonian Jews settled in Bathyra in Batanaea by Herod the Great.[24] The story of John assumes that all the people coming to John were Jews (Matt. 3:9 = Luke 3:8; Josephus, *Ant.* 18.116).

Special righteousness in respect to the temptations of one's specific vocation was therefore required before immersion could be effective. In both cases, however, there was an implied prescription that one should be content with what money might come one's way without hoping for

23. Jeremias, *New Testament Theology,* 110.

24. M. Goodman, *The Ruling Class of Judaea: The Origins of the Jewish Revolt Against Rome,* A.D. *66-70* (Cambridge: Cambridge University Press, 1987) 42 n. 21; 47-48; 162 n. 9. Hollenbach suggests that the soldiers may have been "direct supporters of the tax-collectors" or the Jerusalem establishment ("John the Baptist," 897), but it seems more likely, given their placement by the Jordan, that they were employed by Antipas. They may well have been sent there by the tetrarch to keep watch on John and the crowds, only to find themselves responding to John's powerful speeches. Antipas may well have wondered about his power over the people if John could win the tetrarch's own soldiers!

more. There was a detachment from "mammon." Not only fair dealing was required, but also a passive acceptance of one's financial lot.

Matthew 21:31-32

Before moving on, it is worthwhile to consider Matt. 21:31-32, a saying of the Jesus tradition indicating that prostitutes came to John:

> Amen, I tell you that the toll collectors and the prostitutes go into the kingdom of God ahead of you [i.e., the chief priests and elders]. For John came to you in the way of righteousness, and you did not believe him, but the toll collectors and prostitutes believed him, and when you saw you still did not afterward change your minds and believe him.

There seems no good reason to doubt that the saying reflects accurate information about what was believed in regard to the kind of people who came to John. If toll collectors *and prostitutes* did not go to John in repentance, then the opponents of Jesus in the story could not have been affronted (Matt. 21:45). They would have replied that he had gotten it completely wrong. Even doubting the authenticity of Jesus' words here, the story could not have been credible if it were not fairly common knowledge that these people were attracted by John's message. Moreover, toll collectors appear in relation to John not only in Luke 3:12-13 but also in Luke 7:29. The appearance of toll collectors is fairly well attested and sure. The prostitutes appear only in Matt. 21:31, but their appearance at all in connection with such a revered figure as John is so astonishing that there seems no reason to doubt that they were understood at the time of Matthew to have been associated with John. Luke may have deliberately dropped them from his reference at Luke 7:29, for the words "*all the people* and the toll collectors . . . having been immersed with John's immersion" read so awkwardly as to suggest that Luke was aware of some saying that included prostitutes among those baptized by John.[25] If Luke 3:12-14 does

25. See Schürmann, *Das Lukasevangelium,* vol. 1, 422. Meier notes the "contorted order" of the clause and suggests that the words "and the tax collectors" are an afterthought (*Marginal Jew,* vol. 2, 167-70). If "all the people" had read "the prostitutes" there would be less contortion, though I agree that the pericope as it stands is almost entirely Lucan commentary.

preserve traditions of John concerning despised groups in society, it may be that in the evangelist's source material there was also some advice given to repentant prostitutes who came to him for immersion.

Prostitutes would have had to indicate in some way that they had borne good fruit worthy of repentance. Were they also to continue to be prostitutes? This is an interesting question. The rabbis clearly considered prostitution sinful, but in ancient Israel prostitution was not unlawful under all circumstances.[26] A father was not to prostitute his daughter (Lev. 19:29), though he was allowed to sell her as a concubine (Exod. 21:7). A priest was forbidden to marry a prostitute or a divorced woman, and a priest's daughter who became a prostitute was to be burned (Lev. 21:7-9), but the rule for priests was not the rule for everyone. Prostitution was certainly frowned upon (Tob. 4:12; Prov. 7:9-23), but there was no specific law forbidding it. Certain notable prostitutes appear in Scripture — Rahab, for example (Josh. 2:1; 6:25). Samson visited one (Judg. 16:1). Prostitutes could appeal to the king for judgment (1 Kgs. 3:16-28), and they walked openly in the streets (Isa. 23:16). There were probably large numbers of prostitutes in Israel near to Roman military garrisons (Josephus, *Ant.* 20.356; cf. *b. Šabb.* 33b; *b. Pesaḥ.* 113b).[27] The idea that prostitutes could be righteous would nevertheless have been shocking. The saying of Jesus in Matt. 21:31 is designed to play on the shock value of the statement. Yet would John, whose ethical standards were extremely high, have allowed that such women could be accepted by God upon immersion, if they, somehow, "bore good fruit"? Did he advise ethical conduct *within* their profession? What kind of advice would he have given to these women, if indeed we are to imagine that he objected only to abuses within their profession?

It is highly unlikely that John thought professional prostitutes capable of living righteously while still keeping to prostitution. The key point to recognize here is that Matt. 21:31 does not necessarily refer to professional prostitutes; it is very unlikely, I think, that the verse refers to women who earned their money from having paid sex. In rabbinic literature, a woman may be referred to as a "harlot," זונה

26. See V. L. Bullough, *The History of Prostitution* (New Hyde Park, NY: University Books, 1964) 25-31.

27. On the association of prostitutes and Roman soldiers, see J. Gibson, "Hoi Telōnai kai hai Pornai," *JTS* 32 (1981) 429-33.

(from root זנה, "to go astray") for all types of reasons — if she had had premarital sex, for example, or committed adultery. The rabbis wished to define what was meant by the term זונה, because a זונה was not permitted to marry a priest (Lev. 21:7). They arrived at a very loose definition. A passage from the Babylonian Talmud (*b. Yebam.* 61b) proves this point:

> Surely it was taught: Zonah implies, as her name [indicates, a faithless wife]; so R. Eliezer. R. Akiba said: Zonah implies one who is a prostitute. . . . R. Judah said: Zonah implies one who is incapable of procreation. And the Sages said: Zonah is none other than a female proselyte, a freed bondwoman, and one who has been subjected to any meretricious intercourse. R. Eleazer said: An unmarried man who has had intercourse with an unmarried woman, with no matrimonial intent, renders her thereby a zonah![28]

The Greek word πόρνη, as used in Matt. 21:31, is equally pejorative and general and is used to translate זונה in the LXX. Even if professional prostitutes are referred to in relation to John, it should be remembered that in a country of extreme poverty, in which women were a vulnerable group, prostitution proper might have been the only way of surviving for women who were divorced, widowed, or somehow on their own and in need of money. The word could also refer to a woman who, though living with a man, was not married to him, that is, to a woman who was maintained by a man without a formal marriage contract. A woman could very easily earn the reputation of being a "prostitute," even if she were not actually earning money from sex. In the story of Jesus' meeting with the Samaritan women, he refers to the man she is living with as her "husband," to which she replies that she has none. He then notes that indeed she has had seven "husbands," though in fact the one she is living with now is not her real husband (John 4:16-18). In common appraisal, this unmarried and sexually active woman would have been considered a prostitute. Interestingly, in this story, Jesus does not advise her to go and "sin no more"(cf. the adulterous women of John 8:1-11). This subject is clearly one that requires more study, but it will suffice

28. Trans. I. W. Slotki in *The Babylonian Talmud,* ed. I. Epstein (London: Soncino, 1936).

for now to note that "prostitutes" — broadly classed as sexually active, unmarried women or those who had *at any time in the past* been sexually active in such a way as to earn the reputation of being זונות — may have been addressed by John and been given advice concerning righteousness. Moreover, an ex-prostitute would still have retained the stigma of being a זונה even if she was henceforth entirely celibate. The word did not refer to a profession, but was applied to women who were thought in some way, some time in their lives, to have engaged in sexual misconduct and to "infertile" women.

John likely equated true prostitution with the sin of fornication. Far from condoning prostitution as a means of earning one's living, it is much more likely, given comparative examples in early Christian and rabbinic literature, that John advocated marriage or celibacy, even though in the latter case this may have meant that a woman would be deprived of any financial support. A conviction that God would provide for the obedient, in their case as in all others, may have been all that John could offer. If John instructed "prostitutes" to adopt celibacy, his instruction would have been compatible with Christianity's later practice of extolling celibacy for destitute, unmarried women (whether virgins, widowed, or divorced) and looking after them, since they would otherwise have had no way to earn an adequate living, and prostitution would have been a constant temptation (see, e.g., Acts 9:41; 1 Tim. 5:3-16). In the case of *b. Yebam.* 61b, where a זונה is one who has at any time in the past had intercourse with a man outside marriage, a freed bondwoman is considered a זונה because it is assumed that her former master has used her sexually. Josephus expands on the priestly prohibition concerning prostitutes by stating that priests should not marry slaves or captive women (*Ant.* 3.276), presumably for the same reason. A proselyte might have been lax about the supposed mores of Gentile society and pagan religion.

A further point to note in regard to the so-called "prostitutes" is that Matt. 21:31-32 is the only specific mention of women among the disciples of John. This is important, because discipleship in later Judaism and in Graeco-Roman philosophy was typically a male preserve. Two key exceptions to this norm were found elsewhere in Judaic culture, in the community of Therapeutae living by the Mareotic Lake near Alexandria (Philo, *On the Contemplative Life*) and in the community of the disciples of Jesus (see, e.g., Acts 8:3; 9:2, 36). Again, this subject requires greater study, but it should be noted here that women were probably among the disciples of John, and were, like the men, immersed after undergoing a period of instruction.

Luke 3:11

The guide to specific conduct in John's teaching recorded in Luke is all secondary to the general prescription given in Luke 3:11, addressed to everyone, including toll collectors, men serving as soldiers, and "prostitutes," who asked him what to do over and above obedience to the Law in order to show repentance. How could one prove oneself by acts of righteousness? How could one bear good fruit in a way that would demonstrate to God that one was worthy of his acceptance? John's way of righteousness was radical and demanding:

> And the crowds asked him, saying, "What then should we do [in order to bear good fruit]?" So he answered and said, "The one who has two tunics should share with the one who has none, and the one who has food should do likewise." (Luke 3:11)

John's prescription does not read as just another plea for charity in line with traditional Jewish almsgiving, as Scobie dismissively suggested.[29] What he asked people to do to prove repentance would have been considered extraordinary. He asked for people who may have had only one spare tunic themselves (people who might themselves be considered poor) to give away this spare tunic to the begging poor, who dressed in rags. Given this directive, those who had *more* than one tunic would surely have felt the force of the prescription acutely; at a bare minimum, John's statement could be interpreted as asking people to give away at least half of what they had to the begging poor, whether they were toll collectors, soldiers, women labeled as "prostitutes," or anyone else. John hardly demanded less than what Jesus was to ask of the "rich young man" (Matt. 19:16-30; Mark 10:17-31; Luke 18:18-30), which was to give away all his possessions to the poor. Turned around, the prescription indicates that anything above one tunic would be unnecessary, and anything beyond sufficient food was also superfluous for one's needs.

29. Scobie, *John the Baptist,* 86; cf. Isa. 58:6-7; Prov. 14:31.

Zekhut

The real key for understanding John's exhortation to share food and clothing with those who have none (Luke 3:11) may be found in later rabbinic statements concerning acts of זכות (*zekhut*). Strictly speaking, *zekhut* means "a favorable judgment, acquittal; right; merit" (*m. Sanh.* 4:1; 5:4, 5; 6:1),[30] but it came to be applied to the protecting influence of freely chosen good conduct over and above what was required by the Law. Presumably, the word came to be applied in this way because people began to think that certain types of behavior would lead to acquittal in the heavenly court. Jacob Neusner defines *zekhut* as "the heritage of virtue and its consequent entitlements."[31] This gives the bearer an entitlement to heavenly favor when needed, not simply in regard to final judgment. Neusner traces the concept back to the period of the formation of the Mishnah (cf. *m. Qidd.* 4:14; *m. Soṭa* 3:4-5), but thinks that it became more important in successor writings such as the Jerusalem Talmud (ca. 350 CE). An act of *zekhut* could be one done for the good of another person, to whom one responded with genuine, heartfelt love. It was central to the rabbinic understanding of God and the Law and was not necessarily dependent on people's general day-to-day obedience to the Law.[32]

It was believed that good deeds act to the credit of those who perform them. In certain stories of the Jerusalem Talmud, these good deeds include spending a long time in the synagogue praying or studying Torah and speaking words of Torah, but they also include simpler things indicating goodness, like never delighting in an associate's embarrassment, never going to get money from someone in the marketplace, or never losing one's temper (e.g., *y. Ta'an.* 3:11).[33] Most importantly, a significant act of *zekhut* can give one merit even if one has been a sinner. The giving away of material possessions to the needy is a prime instance of an act of *zekhut.* Examples pointed out by Neusner from the Jerusalem Talmud illustrate this point:

30. See the definitions in M. Jastrow, *A Dictionary of the Targumim, the Talmud Bavli and Yerushalmi, and the Midrashic Literature* (New York: Pardes, 1950) 398.

31. J. Neusner, *The Transformation of Judaism: From Philosophy to Religion* (Urbana: University of Illinois Press, 1992) 253.

32. Ibid., 255-56.

33. See *y. Ta'an.* 3:11, trans. in Neusner, *The Transformation of Judaism,* 247.

> A certain ass driver appeared before the rabbis [the context requires: in a dream] and prayed, and rain came. The rabbis sent and brought him and said to him, "What is your trade?"
>
> He said to them, "I am an ass driver."
>
> They said to him, "And how do you conduct your business?"
>
> He said to them, "One time I rented my ass to a certain woman, and she was weeping on the way, and I said to her, 'What is with you?' and she said to me, 'The husband of that woman [me] is in prison [for debt], and I wanted to see what I can do to free him.' So I sold my ass and I gave her the proceeds, and I said to her, 'Here is your money, free your husband, but do not sin [by becoming a prostitute to raise the necessary funds].' "
>
> They said to him, "You are worthy of praying and having your prayers answered." (*y. Ta'an.* 2.4.1)[34]

The reputation of an ass driver was hardly much better than that of a toll collector, but his act of *zekhut* enabled him to pray so effectively that it rained. This is the classic example in rabbinic literature of someone's acceptance by God. Here is another example cited by Neusner:

> In a dream of Rabbi Abbahu, Mr. Pentakaka ["Five sins"] appeared, who prayed that rain would come, and it rained. Rabbi Abbahu sent and summoned him. He said to him, "What is your trade?"
>
> He said to him, "Five sins does that man [I] do every day, [for I am a pimp:] hiring whores, cleaning up the theater, bringing home their garments for washing, dancing, and performing before them."
>
> He said to him, "What sort of decent thing have you ever done?"
>
> He said to him, "One day that man [I] was cleaning the theater, and a woman came and stood behind a pillar and cried. I said to her, 'What is with you?' And she said to me, 'That woman's [my] husband is in prison, and I wanted to see what I could do to free him,' so I sold my bed and cover, and I gave the proceeds to her. I said to her, 'Here is your money, free your husband, but do not sin.' "

34. Trans. Neusner, *The Transformation of Judaism,* 255; cf. Neusner, "The Feminization of Judaism: Systemic Reversals and Their Meaning in the Formation of the Rabbinic System," *ConJud* 45 (1994) 44.

> He said to him, "You are worthy of praying and having your prayers answered."[35]

This story is extraordinary; the man is extremely sinful by rabbinic standards, but his act of *zekhut* makes him acceptable to God. As Neusner notes, "The singularity of the act of *zekhut,* which suffices if done only one time, encompasses its power to outweigh a life of sin," for the act of *zekhut* is "the mirror image and opposite of sin."[36] Moreover, in the center of the Judaism of the dual Torah, Neusner argues, "Torah is contingent and instrumental, whereas *zekhut* is uncontingent and the system's sole . . . independent variable."[37]

In his teaching, John admonished those who came to him for immersion and who wished to prove repentance to do what, in later rabbinic parlance, were classified as acts of *zekhut.* If you have two tunics, give the second one to someone who does not have a tunic. If you have any food beyond what is necessary to existence, give it to someone who has no food. This applies to toll collectors, soldiers, and disreputable women. Disciples of John could find continued favor with God by conducting their businesses fairly, while performing the basic rule to begin with. John imposed this rule on those who wished to prove repentance: to give anything beyond the bear necessities required for one's own life to the poor. This reflects a similar detachment from "mammon" found in the teachings of Jesus (Matt. 6:24-34 = Luke 12:22-31; 16:13; cf. *Gospel of Thomas* 64, 95). Later rabbis would have acknowledged this detachment from material possessions as admirable and indicative of great faith, as they acknowledged in the case of Hanina ben Dosa.[38]

Caring for the poor and needy is central to the justice system of the Torah (Lev. 19:9-10; cf. 23:22) and is spelled out explicitly as a key theme in the prophetic literature (e.g., Isa. 3:15; Amos 5:11). Nothing could be more indicative of one who was acceptable to God than to give away anything not required for one's own basic existence to the poor. Literature roughly contemporaneous with John also emphasizes God's

35. Trans. Neusner, *The Transformation of Judaism,* 256; cf. Neusner, "The Feminization of Judaism," 45.

36. Neusner, *The Transformation of Judaism,* 256.

37. Ibid., 251.

38. Cf. G. Vermes, *The Gospel of Jesus the Jew* (London: SCM, 1981) 77.

concern for the poor and the needy (e.g., *Ps. Sol.* 18:2). The *Testament of Isaac* (which may, however, be a Christian text) has God saying that if anyone would give a poor person food on the day of the festival of Isaac, then "I will give him to you in my Kingdom" (*T. Isaac* 6:11). And, of course, a concern for the poor is powerfully indicated in the teachings of Jesus (e.g., Mark 10:21; Matt. 11:5; Luke 6:20-25; 19:8); his apostles were to go out only with things necessary for their existence, with no provisions and no change of sandals or clothing (Matt. 6:25-33).[39] Their lifestyle proved continuing repentance and humility in regard to their own virtue. By later reckoning, this behavior would have counted as acts of *zekhut.* Whether this type of action was expressly called an "act of *zekhut*" during the first century may be debated, but the awareness of the intrinsic benefit of such actions seems to be apparent here.

Matthew 3:9 = Luke 3:8

The concept of *zekhut* may also enable us to understand the scornful words of John in regard to those Jews who came to him: "And do not begin to say among yourselves, 'We have a father in Abraham.'" It is common for New Testament scholars to think that with these words John was spurning an ethnic criterion for salvation. The effect is to make John into some kind of "non-Jewish Jew" who reacted against a supposedly widespread view in Judaism that a biological link with Abraham was all that really mattered.[40] This view reflects a racial consciousness

39. See J. D. Crossan, *The Historical Jesus: The Life of a Mediterranean Jewish Peasant* (San Francisco: HarperSanFrancisco, 1991) 273.

40. Scheffler sees John as rejecting "nationalistic particularism" ("The Social Ethics of the Lucan Baptist," 23). Schürmann identifies it as an attack on national privilege (*Das Lukasevangelium,* vol. 1, 182). E. Linnemann thinks that the reference relates to people who reject immersion, claiming national privilege; see her study "Jesus und der Täufer," in *Festschrift für Ernst Fuchs,* ed. G. Ebeling et al. (Tübingen: Mohr-Siebeck, 1973) 228-29; so also P. Hoffman, *Studien zur Theologie der Logienquelle,* 2d ed. (Münster: Aschendorff, 1975) 27. C. R. Kazmierski traces the inheritance back to God's *promise* to Abraham, which could be invoked as "ethnic privilege"; see his study "The Stones of Abraham: John the Baptist and the End of Torah (Matt. 3,7-10 par. Luke 3,7-9)," *Bib* 68/1 (1987) 30; idem, *John the Baptist: Prophet and Evangelist* (Collegeville, MN: The Liturgical Press/Michael Glazer, 1996) 112-13; see also Fitzmyer, *Luke I–IX,* 468. With this kind of understanding, John is seen to be against Israel as a nation; so Kazmierski, "The Stones of Abraham," 34. Meier thinks that the affirmation, "We have

that is absent in our texts, and it perpetuates a false stereotype of Jews being concerned with physical rather than spiritual matters. The actual texts tell a different story: Abraham was not the biological father of Jews alone, but the "father of many nations" (Gen. 17:4); Arabs (Nabateans) were believed to be descended from Abraham (Josephus, *Ant.* 1.186-93, 213), and Idumeans, understood to be descendants of Esau (1 Macc. 5:65; cf. Josephus, *Ant.* 12.328), were converted under John Hyrcanus (*Ant.* 13.257-58).[41] Itureans, converted to Judaism in 104 or 103 BCE (*Ant.* 13.318-19), were not physical descendants of Abraham. Physical descent from Abraham *cannot* have been the issue here, or else Nabatean pagans would be equally addressed by John, and Jewish Itureans and other converts would be excluded.

Moreover, the entire deuteronomistic history (Joshua–2 Kings) was directed to show that ethnicity and nationality counted for nothing in terms of God's acceptance; communal ongoing obedience to the Law was what counted.[42] It would be surprising if none of the people in the crowds coming to John had understood this. Rather, the clue to John's meaning may come in the later literature concerning the *zekhut* Abraham gained from the עקידה (*aqedah*), his near sacrifice of Isaac. This act reflected Abraham's total obedience to the will of God, and it was passed on to Israel, including those who had married or converted into Israel). *Genesis Rabbah* 56.2.5 reads:

Abraham for our father," "bespeaks a collective consciousness as the chosen people that was meant to instill trust in God's covenant-promises but which instead could breed smug complacency. It is to shatter that complacency that the Baptist shatters the significance of a *biological* link with Abraham" (*Marginal Jew,* vol. 2, 29; italics mine). See also the discussion by Ellen Juhl Christiansen, *The Covenant in Judaism and Paul: A Study of Ritual Boundaries as Identity Markers* (Leiden: Brill, 1995) 185-92. The phrase "sons/children of Abraham," along with similar expressions, was widespread (see, e.g., *Ps. Sol.* 9:8; 18:3; 3 Macc. 6:3; *T. Levi* 15:4) and seems to refer to a religious ideal, not to Jews as a racial group connected biologically with Abraham.

41. See F. Millar, "Hagar, Ishmael, Josephus and the Origins of Islam," *JJS* 45 (1993) 23-45. The apostle Paul accepts this also (Rom 4:16-18; cf. 4:1). For Paul the issues turned on a binary opposition of "Law" and "faith."

42. See O. H. Steck (1967), *Israel und das gewaltsame Geschick der Propheten: Untersuchungen zur Überlieferung des deuteronomistischen Geschichtsbildes im Alten Testament, Spätjudentum und Urchristentum* (Neukirchen-Vluyn: Neukirchener Verlag, 1967) 196-215. Paul attacks a Law-related view of Abraham's inheritance: "If the inheritance [of Abraham] comes by the Law, it no longer comes through a promise. . . ."

> Said Rabbi Isaac, "And all was on account of the *zekhut* attained by the act of prostration.
>
> "Abraham returned in peace from Mount Moriah only on account of the *zekhut* owing to the act of prostration '. . . and we will worship [through an act of prostration] and come [then, on that account] again to you' (Genesis 22:5)."[43]

Furthermore, as *Genesis Rabbah* continues, on account of the act of prostration — the near sacrifice of Isaac — the Israelites were redeemed, the Torah was given, Hannah was remembered, the exiles were brought back from Babylon, the Temple was rebuilt, and the *dead will live.*[44] Here Israel's hope in a resurrection at the end is explicitly stated to rest in part on the inherited *zekhut* passed down by the act of the *aqedah.* To claim Abraham as one's father pointed to Abraham's act of prostration and its powerful *zekhut.* Calling Abraham one's father was a spiritual affirmation of inclusion in Israel as God's servant-nation that was obedient to the Law. The notion that *zekhut* could be inherited comes through also in passages such as *m. 'Abot* 2:2, where for those who work with the community "*zekhut* of their fathers strengthens them, and their [fathers'] righteousness stands forever." The communal dimension is made explicit: "Moses attained *zekhut* and bestowed *zekhut* on the community" (*m. 'Abot* 5:18). John appears to have rejected this communal notion outright, stating:

> And do not begin to say among yourselves, "We have a father in Abraham," for I say to you that God is able to raise up children for Abraham from these stones. (Luke 3:8)

For Jews and converts to Judaism, the claim to inherited merit on the basis of the *aqedah* is baseless. God can, if he so wishes, make new

43. Quoted in Neusner, *The Transformation of Judaism*, 272; cf. idem, "The Feminization of Judaism," 48. *Genesis Rabbah* contains many examples of the *zekhut* of the patriarchs providing a treasury of merit that now belongs to Israel and works to the good in times of crisis. Again, it must be stressed that this is not a biological or physical matter, for inclusion in Israel was not necessarily a matter of physical descent. The heritage of virtue passed down from the patriarchs belongs to those who are part of the family of Israel, who obey the Law; to be converted to Judaism essentially entails an adoption into this spiritual family and a sharing of its heritage. One could also lose one's heritage, regardless of one's ethnicity, if one forsook the family, Israel, by not obeying the Law.

44. Neusner, *The Transformation of Judaism*, 272.

children for Abraham — body and spirit — out of stones lying around on the ground, just as he created the first human being out of the dust of the earth. One cannot look to a community that followed God's Law and expect inherited *zekhut;* it has to be earned individually in the present time by each person in his or her own life; only then can s/he truly continue the spirit of Abraham.[45]

John apparently rejected any notion of acquired communal or religious merit. In looking to eschatological judgment, he pointed instead to personal responsibility. Furthermore, by rejecting a communal religious consciousness, John set the basis for Christianity's radical individualism, for Jesus — heavily influenced by John — would take this notion as axiomatic in his own schema of salvation.

Also pronounced in John's teaching is the link between good works indicating that one is truly a child of Abraham and God's judgment in the here and now. John's teaching is intended to lead to "the remission of sins," which is a favorable judgment by God. The Greek phrase ἄφεσιν ἁμαρτιῶν, "remission of sins," employs the terminology of a legal judgment — acquittal. Only this acquittal can make bodily cleansing possible. In this language there is also an anticipation of imminent judgment, where one's acquittal in the present will, it is hoped, be sealed in the eschatological court. While obedience to the Law is implicit in what John recommends, righteous acts, perhaps even acts of *zekhut,* are directly referred to in Luke 3:10-11. Such acts are essential to prove repentance to God and can be performed immediately. The less dramatic lifestyle of obedience to Torah is supposed to follow, but a supererogatory act of loving-kindness is clearly a good fruit that everyone can see. Such acts of giving away one's nonessential clothing and food exemplify a life in which one becomes, metaphorically, a tree bearing good fruit of all kinds, though some are less spectacular than others. One can bear good fruit even by ethical conduct in jobs that are ordi-

45. The notion of racial salvation for all ethnic Jews, regardless of religiosity, seems to be unknown in this period. Scobie notes rightly that all John's hearers were Jews, but he goes on to say that John meant that *physical descent* from Abraham was not enough (*John the Baptist,* 83). To be fair, Scobie also notes that there was a "common belief that God had been, and might still be, especially merciful towards Israel for the sake of his servant Abraham," who, along with the other patriarchs, had a "treasury of merit" that could be passed down to the generations following him (p. 84). However, Scobie appears not to have understood the implications of his own observation.

narily regarded as sinful, impure, or of doubtful moral worth. Each individual has to work this out alone. Nevertheless, supererogatory acts of loving-kindness are necessary and ongoing. Such was John's radical social prescription.[46]

A striking parallel to Luke 3:10-14 is found in the story of Zacchaeus, in the Jesus tradition, from Luke's special material (Luke 19:1-10). As Dennis Hamm has convincingly argued, this is the story of a toll collector who repents and undertakes to live a life of righteousness, exemplifying the kind of "conversion" called for by John.[47] The story reads:

> And he [Jesus] entered and was passing through Jericho. And look there was a man named Zacchaeus, and this person was a chief toll collector and he was rich. He was trying to see who Jesus was, and he was unable because of the crowd, for he was short. So running on ahead he climbed up into a sycamore tree in order to see him, for that man [Jesus] was about to pass through. And when he came to the place, Jesus looked up and said to him, "Zacchaeus, hurry, come down, for today I must stay in your house." So he hurried and came down, and received him gladly. But all who saw it murmured, saying, "He has gone in to stay with a man who is a sinner." So Zacchaeus stood up and said to the Master, "Look, Master, I will give half of my possessions to the poor, and if I have extorted [anything from] any-

46. The radical nature of John's call in favor of the poor was noted by E. Lohmeyer, *Das Urchristentum 1: Johannes der Täufer* (Göttingen: Vandenhoeck & Ruprecht, 1932) 53-56, though he perceived an extremely politicized and revolutionary agenda on John's part. Following Lohmeyer, P. W. Hollenbach has argued that John challenged the societal order of his day, advocated social justice, and propounded an ethic that struck at structural injustice. See P. W. Hollenbach, "Social Aspects of John the Baptist's Preaching Mission in the Context of Palestinian Judaism," *ANRW,* II.19.1, 850-75; idem, "John the Baptist," *ABD,* vol. 3, H–J, 887-99. This is an attractive thesis, but I think that it makes explicit what in John may have been only implicit. Hollenbach's view that John's derisive words to the "offspring of vipers" were addressed only to the priestly aristocracy is too speculative. Moreover, his thesis places too much stress on human action in bringing about societal change. For John, it was God who would bring about social revolution, by acting in history at the end. It was he who would vindicate the good and champion the oppressed. What could be done by human beings was limited.

47. D. Hamm, "Zacchaeus Revisited Once More: A Story of Vindication or Conversion?" *Bib* 72 (1991) 249-52. "Repentance" seems more correct than "conversion," however.

> one, I will give four times [as much money] back. Then Jesus said to him, "Today, salvation has taken place in this house, because indeed this man is a son of Abraham. For the Son of man (ὁ υἱὸς τοῦ ἀνθρώπου) came to seek and save that which was lost." (Luke 19:1-10)

Jesus may just as well have said that Zacchaeus deserved to pray and have his prayers answered. Zacchaeus — a toll collector with a reputation of being a sinner — was lost, but Jesus here accepts that his acts of giving away half of his great wealth to the poor, and of restoring four times the amount he has ever taken unfairly from people, are supererogatory acts of loving-kindness — what the rabbis would have called "acts of *zekhut*." Zacchaeus does not volunteer all of his possessions, but his action would still have been regarded as going far beyond what would ordinarily have been required. The Law required only that one should make full restitution plus one-fifth of whatever one had taken unfairly (Num. 5:6-7; cf. Lev. 5:24 = LXX Lev. 6:4). For this reason, Zacchaeus' repentance — shown by "bearing fruit" befitting that repentance — makes him in Jesus' eyes a true "son of Abraham."[48]

John's Predictions

We will consider John's reputation as a prophet in Chapter 5. For now, we will consider the substance of his predictions as forming part of his

48. "Son of Abraham" (cf. Luke 19:9) is paralleled by "daughter of Abraham" at Luke 13:16. When the poor Lazarus dies, he goes to the "bosom of Abraham" (Luke 16:22-23), which reflects his vindication and acceptance as a righteous man in the sight of God. The view that Zacchaeus is a son of Abraham by virtue of his hospitality has been argued by A. C. Mitchell, who looks to the Jewish Diaspora and traditions of the LXX for his exegesis; see A. C. Mitchell, "Zacchaeus Revisited: Luke 19,8 as a Defense," *Bib* 71/2 (1990) 153-76. However, that Zacchaeus is hospitable is not the reason for his being called a son of Abraham in this story, even if his action may recall Abraham's hospitality in Genesis 18 (both MT and LXX). Moreover, the Greek language of the story is a thin veneer over the underlying Aramaic language and syntax. Aramaic characteristics include: the repeated use of the *waw* conjunction; the rhythm; the expression "look" or "behold"; the expression "the Son of Man," though it may now be used in accordance with Luke's understanding of the phrase as a title; and the expression "that one." Therefore, looking to the Greek Diaspora rather than the Aramaic milieu of Palestine for understanding the story may be misguided.

body of teaching. This material, which concerns a coming figure and impending judgment, is universally accepted by scholars as being authentic. John preached the nearness of the end and the importance of deciding now to walk along the right path. Someone coming soon would separate the righteous from the wicked like wheat from chaff. There were no ambiguities; you were either one thing or the other, so Matt. 3:12 (cf. Luke 3:16-17; and *Sifre Deut.* 53), which states:

> I immerse you with water for repentance, but he who is coming after me is mightier than I am — he whose sandals I am not worthy to carry — this one will immerse you in holy spirit and fire. His winnowing fork is in his hand, and he will clear his threshing floor and gather his wheat into the granary, but the chaff he will burn with an unquenchable fire.[49]

or, as Mark 1:7 has it:

> The one mightier than I comes after me — I am not worthy to stoop down and untie the strap of his sandals. I immerse you with [or: in] water, but he will immerse you in holy spirit.

Related to this prediction is a metaphor that describes the people of Israel as trees in an orchard. Trees that do not bear good fruit are about to be cut down and thrown on to the fire; only the trees that do bear good fruit will remain standing.

> You vipers' offspring! Who warned you to flee from the coming wrath [of God]? [If you wish to be immersed] then you must bear fruits[50]

49. Scheffler thinks that the use of aorist infinitives for the future tense in Q (Luke 3:17) slightly detaches the activities of clearing the threshing floor and gathering the wheat from the judgment of the wicked ("The Social Ethics of the Lucan Baptist," 24). The effect of this wording is to connect the gathering of the righteous with the activity of Jesus.

50. Luke 3:8 has the plural, "fruits (καρποὺς) worthy of repentance," which may be intended to link up with the examples given in vv. 10-14. However, the use of the plural noun here is consistent with the fact that John is addressing his hearers with plural imperatives. Arguably, it is the Matthean version (3:8) that alters the Q plural to the singular καρπόν. In this version, John addresses only Pharisees and Sadducees (Matt. 3:7) whom John exhorts, "Bear fruit worthy of repentance," the implication being that

> worthy of repentance. . . . For even now (ἤδη) the ax is laid to the root of the trees; then every tree not producing good fruit will be cut down and thrown into a fire. (Luke 3:7b-8a, 9 = Matt. 3:7b-8, 10)

John's reputation as a preacher of apocalyptic doom rests on these passages.[51] John Kloppenborg dubs the sermon "bitter and reproachful."[52] At the same time, these words are considered by scholars to be the most likely authentic sayings of John the Baptist.[53] Indeed, that the coming one would put unrighteous people into a great bath of fire, like trees thrown onto a raging pyre, seems to have been a central image of his predictions. But John did not, it seems, see himself as a grim figure. Far from it. The one coming after him would comport himself in stark contrast to John, who gently immersed people in water for their repentance. By John's own statement, then, he was the mild one; it was the one coming after him who would be ruthless and accept no further repentance.

---

this fruit is John's immersion itself (cf. Matt. 3:11); see Merklein, "Die Umkehrpredigt bei Johannes dem Täufer," 36-37 for this interpretation of Matthew's "fruit," though he argues that Matthew preserves the orignal wording. See also Kazmierski, "The Stones of Abraham," 31.

51. Wellhausen stressed John's doom pronouncement in the Q tradition (*Das Evangelium Lucae,* 5), and his view has been influential; cf. Scobie, *John the Baptist,* 62. Scheffler considers the toning down of this doom aspect an example of Lucan redaction ("The Social Ethics of the Lucan Baptist"). However, even in Q the expectation of judgment is supposed to lead people to repentance, the bearing of good fruit, and immersion with a view to a righteous life. Concern with present obedience to God is implicit. The gathering of the wheat in Q (Matt. 3:12 = Luke 3:17) also indicates that John's message was concerned with "good news" for the righteous (cf. Luke 3:18). Hollenbach expresses a common view when he writes, "John's opening salvo was a stark message of doom familiar from portions of the Old Testament prophets, except that he added the possibility of escape through the baptism of repentance" ("John the Baptist," 893). However, Hollenbach considers the scholarly emphasis on judgment alone as misleading.

52. Kloppenborg, *The Formation of Q,* 106.

53. See Becker, *Johannes der Täufer und Jesus von Nazareth* (Neukirchen-Vluyn: Neukirchener Verlag, 1972) 109 n. 21; Bammel, "The Baptist in Early Christian Tradition"; Merklein, "Die Umkehrpredigt bei Johannes dem Täufer." The passage is apparently authentic because it lacks a Christological perspective. For voting by the Jesus Seminar, see Tatum, *John the Baptist and Jesus,* 128-35. The probability that the apocalyptic parts of John's recorded teaching are authentic is affirmed by the Seminar, while the didactic elements preserved in Luke 3:11, 13-14 are thought to be only possibly authentic — so 53% of the voters, with 35% voting against authenticity because of the supposedly peculiar Lucan interests of the traditions.

By calling people who came to him for immersion "vipers' offspring," John indicated that they were scared, wanting to slither away from their own punishment, as a snake slithers away into a corner or under a rock to avoid being bashed by a stick. John's language in modern colloquial usage might be rendered "You bunch of chickens!" Yet there may be another nuance; the offspring of a venomous snake might recall Gen. 3:15, where God says to the snake of Eden: "I will put enmity between you and the woman, and between your offspring and hers. Her offspring will bash your head, and you [i.e., through your offspring] will strike at his heel." Those who come to immersion without proof of repentance are therefore not only scared, but potentially the offspring of the first tempter. Only if repentance was proven by "good fruit" could their repentance, and subsequent immersion, be acceptable to God. But scaring people into repentance was not what John seems to have aimed for. He was full of disdain for unrighteous people who seemed to cower before the possibility of judgment.

In formulating this eschatological scenario, John appears again to have been influenced by the book of Isaiah. As we have seen, in the New Testament the central scriptural verses associated with John are Isa. 40:3-5 (Luke 3:4; cf. Mark 1:3; Matt. 3:3; John 1:23). We need not assume that John himself quoted these verses precisely to define his mission; but he may have used the book of Isaiah to explicate his immersion, as we saw in Chapter 2, and more generally to shape his eschatological views. If he did so, he would have been using one of the more popular books of Scripture. In Judaism during the Second Temple period, the book of Isaiah as a whole was very likely considered to be one of the three most important books of Scripture. Among the 200 biblical manuscripts of the DSS, there are 39(+2?) scrolls of Psalms, 31(+3?) of Deuteronomy, and 22 of Isaiah.[54] These three books are also the most frequently quoted in the New Testament. While only the first few lines of a much larger passage of Isaiah are given in the New Testament in relation to John, it may be helpful to consider Isaiah 40 a little more extensively, in particular as it is found in the Aramaic *Targum Pseudo-Jonathan.* While it cannot be proven that any of the Aramaic traditions of translation were known at the time of John, it seems quite likely that some of them were known. Many of the sayings

54. See Lawrence H. Schiffman, *Reclaiming the Dead Sea Scrolls: The History of Judaism, the Background of Christianity, the Lost Library of Qumran* (Philadelphia/Jerusalem: The Jewish Publication Society, 1994) 163.

of Jesus have been shown to be closely related to the Targum (e.g., Mark 4:12, cf. *Tg. Ps.-J.* Isa. 6:9, 10; Matt. 26:52, cf. *Tg. Ps.-J.* Isa. 50:11; Mark 9:48, cf. *Tg. Ps.-J.* Isa. 66:24; Matt. 7:2 = Mark 4:24, cf. *Tg. Ps.-J.* Isa. 27:8).[55] It is interesting, then, that a passage of the *Tg. Ps.-J.* Isa. 40:3-8 uses an image that John employed in his teaching, namely, that of the chaff (Matt. 3:12; Luke 3:17). The Hebrew MT does not contain this image, but here we find it in the Targum:

> A voice of one who cries:
> "In the wilderness clear the way before the people of the Lord,
> level in the desert highways before the congregation of our God.
> All the valleys shall be lifted up,
> and every mountain and hill be made low;
> the uneven ground shall become a plain and a banked place a vale.
> And the glory of the Lord shall be revealed,
> and all the sons of flesh shall see it together,
> for by the Memra[56] of the Lord it is so decreed."
> A voice of one who says, "Prophesy!"
> And he answered and said, "What shall I prophesy?"
> All the wicked are as the grass,
> and all their strength *like the chaff of the field.*
> The grass withers, its flower fades, for the spirit from the Lord blows upon it.
> Surely the wicked among the people are reckoned as grass.
> The wicked dies, his conceptions perish; but the word of our God stands forever.[57]

The same image of chaff occurs in *Tg. Ps.-J.* Isa. 41:15-16, where the Gentile oppressors of Israel are compared to chaff that is winnowed by God on a strong threshing sledge. The wicked are compared to chaff elsewhere in the Hebrew Scriptures (Isa. 17:13; 29:5; Ps. 1:4; 35:5; Job 21:18; Hos. 13:3; cf. Wis. 5:14),[58] but only in the Targum is this image

55. See Chilton, *The Isaiah Targum,* xxv-xxviii and idem, *A Galilean Rabbi and His Bible: Jesus' Use of the Interpreted Scripture of His Time* (Wilmington, DE: Glazier, 1984), also published in England, with the subtitle *Jesus' Own Interpretation of Isaiah* (London: SPCK, 1984).

56. For the meaning of *Memra* in the Targum, see Chilton, *The Isaiah Targum,* lvi.

57. Chilton, *The Isaiah Targum,* 77.

58. See Scobie, *John the Baptist,* 61.

placed close to the passage that has been most associated with John. In this passage, the chaff is blown away by a whirlwind. However, elsewhere in the Targum the wicked are burned up in the fires of Gehenna (1:26, 31; 5:16-25; 26:11; 30:27, 33; 31:9).

Tg. Ps.-J. Isa. 40:9-11 continues to ask prophets "who herald good tidings to Zion" or "herald good tidings to Jerusalem" to say, "the kingdom of your God is revealed!"[59] The coming time referred to is after judgment, when the glory of the Lord will be revealed to the righteous (40:5). The voice who cries in the wilderness commands that a way be prepared for "the people of the Lord" or "the congregation of our God." Accordingly, when the prophets "herald good tidings" to Zion/Jerusalem they say, "the kingdom of your God is revealed" (cf. *Tg. Ps.-J.* Isa. 24:23).[60] Now, after describing John's apocalyptic scenario — that the coming figure would gather the wheat into the barn and burn up the chaff — Luke adds, "And then also with many other exhortations he told the people the good news" (Luke 3:18). The "good news" is defined as it is defined in the Targum; the good news is for the righteous, who look forward to judgment and the kingdom of God. None of the key expressions is found in the Hebrew version of this passage or in the LXX. In particular, the "kingdom of God" is found in neither the Hebrew nor the Greek. The MT tends to refer to God as king, whereas the Targum refers to the kingdom; so, for example, the MT of Isa. 52:7 has:

> How beautiful on the mountains,
> are the feet of the messenger
> announcing peace,
> of the messenger of good news,
> who proclaims salvation
> and says to Zion, "Your God is king."

while the *Tg. Ps.-J.* Isa. 52:7 reads:

> How beautiful on the mountains of the land of Israel
> are the feet of him who announces,
> who publishes peace,

59. Chilton, *The Isaiah Targum,* 77-78.
60. Cf. Luke 16:16 = Matt. 11:12-13.

who announces good tidings,
who publishes salvation, who says to the congregation of Zion,
"The kingdom of your God is revealed."[61]

The expression "kingdom of God" is also found in the *Mekilta Exod.* 17:14, the *Assumption of Moses* 10:1,[62] and the *Alenu* prayer. The congregation again appears, along with the kingdom of God, whereas these expressions are absent in the Hebrew text. It may be worth noting that the Aramaic term here, כנשׁתא, ordinarily translates the Hebrew word קהל; and קהל in the LXX is frequently translated as ἐκκλησία, the term the early Christians used for themselves, the "Church." In the Targum, the congregation of God is made up of those who perform the Law and who will return to Zion in glory at the Day of the Lord (*Tg. Ps.-J.* Isa. 1:26-31; 19:25; 26:2-3; 30:15; 37:32; 38:17; 46:3-4; 49:23; 64:3). They are those who do not sin and "those who have repented from sin" (7:3; 10:21-22; 33:13; 57:19). Repentance itself is linked with the Day of the Lord (12:1-5; cf. 13:15). One should repent while there is time (21:12), for the wicked person who repents will be called "my servant" (42:19) and be forgiven (6:10), while those who persist in wickedness will be burned up (1:26, 31; 5:16-25; 26:11; 30:27, 33; 31:9).

All this suggests strongly that if the Aramaic traditions of the Targum were known at the time of John, he may very well himself have announced, "The kingdom of God is revealed [or: upon you]" as part of his eschatological message to the people who came to him. While Luke has John telling the good news (εὐηγγελίζετο, Luke 3:18), Matthew has John specifically state, "the kingdom of heaven is at hand" (Matt. 3:2; cf. 4:17). One may wonder if these versions are both preserving in different form some line in Q that described John as telling the good news that the kingdom was revealed.[63]

The motif of fire burning up the wicked is found not only in the Targum but also extensively in the Hebrew Scriptures and particularly in apocalyptic literature. The fire is often pictured as a river (Dan. 7:9-11; cf. 1QH 3:27-32) or lake (Rev. 19:20; 20:10, 14; 21:8; cf. Ezra 13:10) into which the wicked are immersed (baptized). *1 Enoch* 90:26 has:

61. Chilton, *The Isaiah Targum,* 102.

62. Lachs, *Rabbinic Commentary on the New Testament,* 72.

63. See below, 309-14.

> In the meantime I saw how another abyss like it, full of fire, was opened wide in the middle of the ground; and they brought those blinded sheep, all of which were judged, found guilty, and cast into this fiery abyss, and they were burned.[64]

The bad trees are uprooted in *Jub.* 7:27-39; 20:6; 21:22 and also burned in 22:22-23; 36:9-11. The trees are cut down in Isa. 10:33-34; Sir. 6:4; 23:25; and Wis. 4:3-5. The expression "Day of the Lord" comes from Amos 5:18-20; Zeph. 1:15, 18; Isa. 13:9; Ezek. 7:19. All this is well-known. It serves to show, however, that John was using contemporary expectations to visualize the final scenario. He was not inventing anything new.

According to both Matthew and Luke, John predicted that the righteous would be immersed in holy spirit and the wicked in fire (Matt. 3:11; Luke 3:16). It is possible that the reference to the holy spirit was found by Matthew and Luke in Mark 1:8 and joined with a saying in Q that referred only to the wicked being immersed in fire.[65] Elsewhere in Q, addressing only the unrighteous, John warns that they will be burned unless they repent and do good works (Matt. 3:10 = Luke 3:9). Caution is in order here, though, because John's supposed prediction of an immersion in holy spirit may have been inserted into material about John, to make him predict later Christian baptism in the holy spirit.

Consideration of the imagery may lead one to question whether mention of "holy spirit" goes back to John himself. John's baptism appears to have involved a full-body immersion, and the imagery of the "immersion of fire" ties in with his practice. One imagines someone entirely immersed in a lake of fire. However, the so-called "baptism in the holy spirit" was not an immersion in the same way. People were not imagined as going into a large body of aqueous spirit. In the Scriptures, the (or: a) holy spirit is *sprinkled* over people's heads, just as water may be sprinkled or poured out for some kinds of purification (see, e.g., Joel 3:1-5; Ezek. 36:25-27; 39:29; Zech. 12:10; cf. 1QS 4:21). In Ezek. 36:27 the spirit is poured into people's hearts so that they will

64. Trans. E. Isaac in *OTP,* vol. 1, 71. See also Scobie, *John the Baptist,* 66-70; for further examples, see S. N. Mason, "Fire, Water and Spirit: John the Baptist and the Tyranny of Canon," *SR* 21/2 (1992) 170-71.

65. So Mason, "Fire, Water and Spirit"; for a critique of this position, see Scobie, *John the Baptist,* 70-73. See also Kloppenborg, *The Formation of Q,* 106-07.

be able to follow God's Law instinctively in the glorious period following the vindication of the righteous after judgment (and the destruction of sinners; cf. 1QS 3:6-8). In 1QS 4:20-21 God is expected to purge all the remaining falsehood and wickedness from those who are to live at the end. The inner cleansing process is effected by sprinkling of a holy spirit of truth:

> And he [God] will cleanse him of all evil actions by a spirit of
> holiness
> and he will sprinkle upon him a spirit of truth like waters for
> impurity from all the abominations of falsehood.
> And he will be saturated in the spirit for impurity
> in order to instruct the upright in the knowledge of the Most
> High. . . .

But here we may pause, for in the *Community Rule* we do get a sense that the "sprinkling" involves a very thorough drenching in spirit. It is not a mild splash. In Isa. 32:15 (cf. 44:3), the spirit is poured out and "the desert becomes a fertile field." It is like torrential rain that drenches a person through and through. Given this imagery, perhaps a saturation or immersion of this type was envisaged by John. It is certainly possible that John predicted not an immersion in an aqueous body of holy spirit, but a thorough drenching and saturation in it. In the Mishnah tractate *Miqwa'ot,* water of rain drippings that have not stopped is clean (1:6), though nothing is said about anyone immersing in downpours. To what extent complete saturation in rainwater might be called an "immersion" can remain a moot point, but this seems to be what the imagery used by John indicates. Like rainwater also, a downpour of holy spirit comes from the heavens. So there is no compelling reason against accepting that John did indeed predict an immersion either in fire (as a river or lake) or in holy spirit (as a torrential downpour from heaven).

That there was some promise of reward for the righteous in John's teaching seems quite likely; far from a baptism of fire being the consistent feature of John's predictions, reference to fire is lacking at Mark 1:8 and Acts 1:5 and 11:16. In fact, in Acts 11:16 we have a preserved saying of the Jesus tradition: "John immersed with water, but you will be immersed in holy spirit." Saturation in holy spirit seems to have been part of a larger complex of widely varying apocalyptic expectations. The righteous could expect a wonderful long life in a Gentile-free land, focusing on a cleansed and renewed Temple (cf. *Ps. Sol.* 17:25, 33). The resurrected righteous dead would join the living to dwell there. God would rule his kingdom on earth. All war and ill-health would cease. Righteousness, love, and faithfulness would prevail. Women would bear children without pain.[66] Perhaps John predicted such things. Whatever the case, there is a positive side to John's message in Q: the righteous would be safely gathered like wheat into a barn (Matt. 3:12; Luke 3:17). People could make of that what they liked, but it implies that John promised a definite reward to those who repented.[67]

Furthermore, to argue that Christians invented John's reference to an immersion in holy spirit entails a serious problem. If John accepted the teaching of Ezekiel — that the righteous would find God's spirit coming into them *after* judgment — Christians could not have made his teaching refer to Christian baptism in the Spirit. If Christians had done so, John's prophecy would have been blatantly anachronistic, for immersion in fire and spirit *follows* judgment, whereas Christian baptism in the Holy Spirit *precedes* it. It seems unlikely, then, that Christians put the prediction of immersion in spirit onto John's lips, for had they invented it outright one would expect some qualification to indicate that the immersion in spirit would precede the punishment of the wicked in fire.[68] In short, Q must have contained both elements: immersion in holy spirit and in fire.

As far as our two versions (Q and Mark) of John's teaching go, there is no reason to choose between them for an authentic single saying. There are good reasons to suppose that the Marcan version of John's saying is perfectly authentic as it stands. The most important factor to note is the internal logic of the statement. Those addressed as "you" in Mark 1:8 are those whom he has immersed. He addresses them collectively, saying, "I immersed you (ἐγὼ ἐβάπτισα ὑμᾶς) with water, but he [who comes after me] will immerse you with holy spirit." The aorist,

66. See E. Schürer, *The History of the Jewish People in the Age of Jesus Christ (175 B.C.–A.D. 135)*, vol. 2, rev. and ed. G. Vermes et al. (Edinburgh: Clark, 1979) 529-44.

67. For an argument in favor of the originality of the Marcan wording "I baptize you with water, but he will baptize you with [the] holy spirit" (Mark 1:8), see Meier, *Marginal Jew*, vol. 2, 38-39; the Q version of the saying (Matt. 3:11; Luke 3:16) has "with [the] holy spirit *and fire*."

68. See Schürmann, *Das Lukasevangelium*, vol. 1, 174 and R. Laufen, *Die Doppelüberlieferungen der Logienquelle und des Markusevangeliums* (Bonn: Hanstein, 1980) 106, who argue that this is the reading of Q.

ἐβάπτισα, indicates an action *having taken place.* John therefore gives an assurance to the repentant righteous, who have become inwardly and outwardly clean, that they will be counted among those who will be immersed in holy spirit, when a greater figure than John comes.

However, in the Q block, John addresses people he has identified as "offspring of vipers" (Luke 3:7-9). They have come to him for immersion but have been challenged to show proof of repentance. Indeed, some of them might have been truly repentant and already doing acts of loving-kindness and general righteousness, but they are subsumed into a crowd of potential disciples who seek immersion but have yet to show proof that it would be effective in their case. The Q section breaks off after John provides the metaphor of good people and bad people being like good trees and bad trees (Matt. 3:10 = Luke 3:9). Then, Matthew and Luke both insert the Marcan saying, which was addressed to those who were already immersed (not the crowds), but they add the prediction of fire, which seems to come from something in Q. After this, Matthew and Luke return to Q, in which the addressees remain all those listening to John prior to immersion — they are like wheat or chaff (Matt. 3:12 = Luke 3:17-18). The wheat will be gathered into the barn, and the chaff will be burned by fire. We can surmise that originally Q had three predictions in regard to those who came to be immersed but who had not yet been immersed, all involving a promise of reward or a punishment by fire; but it is necessary to remove the Marcan intrusion in order to ascertain the original wording of Q pertaining to the promise of holy spirit/fire and the figure who was to come.

Matthew (3:11-12) and Luke (3:16-18) follow Mark (1:7-8) quite closely, and whatever stood in Q must have been similar. However, in terms of immersion, they both have the present tense, βαπτίζω, rather than the past, ἐβάπτισα. As regards the addressees of Q, it would make sense if "you," ὑμᾶς, from Mark were left aside and John said only "I baptize with/in water," ἐγὼ βαπτίζω ὕδατι, referring to his own action (cf. John 1:26, where this is exactly what John indicates). We then would remove the illogicality of the existing texts of both Matthew and Luke, in which John promises that those he immerses are going to have an immersion in both holy spirit and (punitively) fire. As Meier notes, in this case what is the point of being immersed?[69] Matthew includes the

69. Meier, *Marginal Jew,* vol. 2, 38.

words "for repentance," which may also derive from Q, being absent in Mark. The Q version was not addressed at all to those John had immersed, but to those who hoped for immersion but had yet to prove themselves worthy of it.

In regard to the coming figure, Mark has: "The one mightier than I is coming after me, and I am not worthy to stoop down and untie the strap of his sandals" (Mark 1:7). Luke follows this closely, but omits "after me" (ὀπίσω μου) and "stoop down" (κύψας). Matthew also omits the latter, introduces the term ὁ ἐρχόμενος, "the coming one," which may come from Q (cf. John 1:27), and refers to sandals being carried rather than loosed or untied. The saying has parallels in another Q block about John at Matt. 11:2-6 = Luke 7:18-23 (cf. Matt. 21:9 and parallels). Both Matthew and Luke add the prediction of "and fire" to the one concerning an immersion in holy spirit. In summary, if we weed out Mark, Q may have appeared as follows:

> I immerse with water for repentance,
> but the coming one — the sandals of whom I am not worthy to carry —
> will immerse with holy spirit and fire.

Redesigning the Gospel text can be a tendentious operation; one may be accused of fitting the text to match one's interpretation. This reconstruction is not done to support any particular exegesis here, but only in order to make sense of the Q source and to account for the garbled state of the Gospel text. In my view, only if there are key grammatical indicators for a conflation of texts, and semantic holes and inconsistencies that can only be accounted for by some rearrangement, should a reconstruction be attempted. What is provided here must remain contingent and speculative. If this is Q, it may be an authentic saying. It relates closely to what is found in Mark, addressed to those who have been immersed, as well as to a number of other passages relating to a coming figure and John's immersion. With this as Q, the modifications of Matthew and Luke in conflating it with Mark may be understood.

It is clear that John predicted that a figure would come after him who was by far his superior. As we have seen, this prediction is found in both the Marcan and Q traditions (Mark 1:7-8; Matt. 3:11-12; Luke 3:16-17) and also in Acts (1:5; 11:16; 13:23-25; 19:4) and John 1:26-27,

33. In Q, the coming figure is one who executes judgment.[70] It has been suggested that John predicted the coming of God himself. God would clean the threshing floor (Matt. 3:12 = Luke 3:17) after the winnowing that separates the wheat from the chaff has taken place.[71] However, as Webb notes, the reference is not quite so simple, for other passages referring to the "coming one" strongly imply that this figure is a person, who may be understood as an agent of God.[72] After all, if John asked Jesus whether he was "the coming one," ὁ ἐρχόμενος (Matt. 11:2-6 = Luke 7:18-23), then John must have expected a human being.[73] For the Church, of course, the agent of God was to be identified with Jesus (cf. Acts 19:4). The figure of Paul defines the equation in Acts 13:25 by stating that John said throughout his mission:

> I am not who you suppose me to be,
> but look he is coming (ἰδοὺ ἔρχεται) after me
> [and] I am not worthy to untie the sandal of his feet.

John Meier has pointed out the similarities between this version of what John said and what is found in the Fourth Gospel, especially the singular of "sandal" and the use of ἄξιος rather than ἱκανός for "worthy," indicating possibly a variant oral tradition.[74] Interestingly, too, the Semitism "the

70. So J. H. Hughes, "John the Baptist: The Forerunner of God Himself," *NovT* 14 (1972) 196, who considers the reference metaphorical; cf. Ps. 60:8; 108:9. C. H. Kraeling argued long ago quite rightly that comparing oneself with YHWH, even with humility, would have sounded ridiculously presumptuous (*John the Baptist* [New York: Scribner, 1951] 54). P. G. Bretscher suggests that the sandals do not in fact belong to the coming one, though his view has not gained wide support; see his article, "Whose Sandals? (Matt. 3:11)," *JBL* 86 (1967) 81-87.

71. The image given by John indicates that the winnowing has already taken place and that the figure who has cleaned the threshing floor is about to burn the chaff; so Webb, *John the Baptizer and Prophet*, 103-11. Webb suggests it was John's activity that was the winnowing, but in early Jewish literature the separation of the good from the bad is an eschatological action of God or his agent; see Schürer, *History of the Jewish People*, vol. 2, 497-513. It seems improbable that John would have presumed that he could take on this divine role. If anything, John might have thought that people were "winnowing" themselves by choosing whether to follow God's Law or not. By one's own actions a choice is made to be wheat or chaff, sheep or goat, fruitful tree or fruitless tree.

72. Webb, *John the Baptizer and Prophet*, 261-306.

73. Ibid.

74. Meier, *Marginal Jew*, vol. 2, 33. Meier also notes the omission of the reference to one stronger, but we have already suggested that this was not in Q, either.

sandals of his feet" points to an Aramaic logion underlying the awkward Greek. A slave might untie (or: carry; cf. Matt. 3:11) his master's sandals. John's self-deprecation was such that he could not consider himself worthy of this menial task, in respect to the coming figure.[75]

The Fourth Gospel indeed reflects the same prediction made by John (John 1:26-27), with the disclaimer that he was not the Anointed One, Elijah, or "the prophet" (John 1:20-21; cf. 1:29-31; Luke 3:15). John's elusive reference to "the coming one," ὁ ἐρχόμενος (as in Q), may indicate that he wished to make a general reference to any of these three possible figures, and that he would not tie himself down to a belief in the coming of any one figure anticipated in the scenarios of eschatological expectation. Any of these three figures could be understood by some people as an agent of God. There were figures other than YHWH himself who were expected to act in eschatological events: for example, the Davidic Messiah; the Aaronic or priestly Messiah; the angel Michael or Melchizedek, the Danielic, human-like, angelic figure or "Son of Man"; and an anointed prophet or Elijah *redivivus.*[76] In particular, in John's prediction, there are clear echoes of language relating to the prophet Elijah, who was expected to come just before the end (Sir. 48:10; cf. Mal. 3:1; 4:6). For example, Mal. 3:1 reads: "Look he is coming, says the Lord of Hosts." The Hebrew phrase **הנה בא**, "Look, he is coming," is found precisely in its Greek form, ἰδοὺ ἔρχεται, in Acts 13:25, quoted above. Many listening to this may have thought he was referring to Elijah.[77] In the DSS, two fragments seem to

75. Ibid., 284 n. 65. However, a Jewish slave or disciple was not necessarily *required* to untie a master's sandals, e.g., *b. Qidd.* 22b; *b. Ketub.* 96a. It was one of the most menial tasks. Hoffman argues that the comparison was devised as a response to the problem of John's relationship to Jesus; see P. Hoffman, *Studien zur Theologie der Logienquelle,* 32-33; cf. Merklein, "Die Umkehrpredigt bei Johannes dem Täufer," 32. Given the Christian understanding that John's "coming one" was Jesus, there is certainly some reason for the inclusion of this saying in the NT, but this does not explain the saying's invention in the first place. German scholarship in particular has stressed that this saying may be secondary, ever since M. Dibelius, *Die urchristliche Überlieferung von Johannes dem Täufer* (Göttingen: Vandenhoeck & Ruprecht, 1911) 54 and R. Bultmann, *History of the Synoptic Tradition,* 107, 117. But the saying is too well attested in multiple sources for it to be secondary. In the Jesus Seminar on John, 13% voted for definite authenticity, and 44% voted for probable authenticity; see Tatum, *John the Baptist and Jesus,* 128-30.

76. Webb, *John the Baptizer and Prophet,* 219-60.

77. For the titular aspect of ὁ ἐρχόμενος, see Laufen, *Die Doppelüberlieferungen der Logienquelle,* 407-08; also Hoffman, *Studien zur Theologie der Logienquelle,* 28-31;

relate to this belief in a returning Elijah: 4Q558 has a line ending with "behold," followed by reference to Elijah being sent (by God),[78] while 4Q521 (frag. 2 iii) reads: "fathers/parents will return to sons/children," recalling Mal. 3:24 and Sir. 48:10, associated with Elijah.[79]

As we have seen, John wished people to repent and live righteously. Eschatological predictions had ramifications for present behavior. The "chaff" (of Matt. 3:11-12 = Luke 3:16-17) are those who do not keep the Law and live unrighteously, rather like the "goats" of the Jesus tradition's analogy in Matt. 25:31-46. The comments recorded by Matthew and attributed to Jesus concern how the righteous are expected to behave: they are to clothe the naked and feed the hungry. These expectations reflect perfectly the directives that John gave his disciples. As we have seen, John probably told people who asked him how to bear good fruit that they should give a second tunic to the one who had none and share food (Luke 3:10-11). The further characteristics of the "sheep," the righteous, that are given by Jesus are perfectly in keeping with these instructions: to give drink to the thirsty, to welcome the stranger, to visit the sick and those in prison. As we saw, this definition of supererogatory righteousness, constituting acts of *zekhut*, ultimately derives from the prophetic tradition (Isa. 58:7, 10; Ezek. 18:7; Job 31:32), which itself built upon the Mosaic Law. Never were these moral principles expressing loving-kindness to one's fellow human beings thought to supersede all the rest of the Law, which might then be dispensed with, as Ezek. 18:5-9 makes clear:

> If someone is righteous, and does justice and righteousness . . . if one does not oppress anyone, but restores to the debtor his pledge, does not commit robbery, gives his bread to the hungry, and covers the naked with clothing . . . if he walks in my statutes and observes my ordinances, acting faithfully, then he is righteous and will surely live, says the Lord YHWH.

Schürmann, *Das Lukasevangelium,* vol. 1, 183. There may also be echoes of Isa. 5:26 here; cf. 1 Thess. 4:14-17; so G. D. Kirchhevel, "He that Cometh in Mark 1:7 and Matt. 24:30," *BBR* 4 (1994) 105-12.

78. For 4Q558, see J. Starcky, "Les quatres étapes du messianisme à Qumrân," *RB* 70 (1963) 498; J. J. Collins, *The Scepter and the Star: The Messiahs of the Dead Sea Scrolls and Other Ancient Literature* (New York: Doubleday, 1995) 116.

79. For 4Q521, see E. Puech, "Une apocalypse messianique (4Q521)," *RevQ* 15 (1992) 475-519; Collins, *The Scepter and the Star,* 117-22.

A person who is truly obedient to God and his Law will do these things as part of his or her righteous life. Morality and the Law are intertwined, for God is a moral God who wants his people to live justly. Eschatology too is intertwined with the maintenance of God's Law, for eschatological expectation of the coming of God to separate out the good and bad and administer reward or punishment was an incentive to present behavior. This is expressed by the prophet Malachi, who announced that a "messenger of the covenant," Elijah (Mal. 3:1; 4:5), would "prepare the way" before God. God would then come to his Temple and bear witness against the wicked — the sorcerers, the adulterers, those who swear falsely, people who oppress workers, widows, and orphans and who thrust aside the alien (3:5). In other words, God says that he will condemn those who "have turned away from my statutes and have not kept them." The solution is simple: "Turn to me [repent], and I will turn to you" (3:7). The wicked will be burned up like dead wood, and the righteous will leap like calves over their ashes (4:1-3). In the meantime, they should "remember the teaching of my servant Moses, the statutes and the ordinances for all Israel that I commanded him at Horeb" (4:4). John's message was very similar in theme and language.

In John's scenario, awareness of the nearness of judgment should influence present behavior. The congregation of God, which lives righteously, may itself bring near the kingdom. In rabbinic literature, accepting God's sovereignty and living virtuously in accordance with God's will is considered to be acceptance of "the yoke of the kingdom of heaven" (עול מלכות שׁמים). The yoke of the kingdom of heaven is "the yoke of Torah" (*m. 'Abot* 3:5). As the Mishnah has it, "A man should take upon himself first the yoke of the kingdom of heaven and therefore the yoke of the commandments" (*m. Ber.* 2:2). God's kingship implies that all will walk on the way of God, which, as we have seen, is the way of Torah — the way of righteousness. John's message seems to have been generally in keeping with this kind of concept. Living righteously — walking along the way of God — brings near the universal eschatological reality of the kingdom of heaven, for the kingdom of heaven means essentially that the rule of God exists among a congregation of people on earth. It was then partly realized, and growing, and yet also in the near future in fullness. The Matthean tradition of Jesus' teaching also connects the coming of the kingdom with righteousness: "but seek first his kingdom and *his righteousness,* and all these shall be yours as well"

(Matt. 6:33). In Luke's version of this saying (12:31) the reference to righteousness is not included.

All this is worth stressing, because although it is usually recognized that John predicted the coming end and God's judgment, this prediction is often detached from its proper connection with an exhortation to keep God's Law in the present. For example, Scobie notes, in considering whether John might have had anything in common with the Pharisees as opposed to the Sadducees, "John may have felt more sympathy with the Pharisees, with whose general outlook and whose eschatology he had much in common. Yet their legalistic temper and concern with the tradition which was built up around the Law is foreign to John's radical prophetic outlook."[80] Recent studies have, of course, shattered the stereotype of the "legalistic" Pharisee.[81] Yet Scobie curiously sees a "radical prophetic outlook" to be totally opposed to the tradition built up around the Law. In fact, the two do not exist in opposition within Judaism; the wholehearted keeping of the Law was central to the message of the prophets. Biblical prophecy was never concerned with instituting a faith-centered religion that would marginalize the Law; rather, it was concerned with calling people to complete moral, ethical, cultic, and spiritual obedience to God, as enshrined in the Scriptures — especially the Law.

It is very unlikely indeed that John considered that only those he immersed would be saved from punishment. Absolutely nothing about John's message requires us to assume that he intended to immerse people to form an exclusive group that might deem themselves to be God's faithful remnant in the last days. The Targum of Isaiah's definition of the righteous as those who do not sin as well as those who have repented from sin (7:3; 10:21-22; 33:13; 57:19) illustrates the commonly accepted notion that those who repented, even if rather late, would be included with the righteous on the same terms when it came to final judgment. The wicked person who repents would also be called "my servant," as the Targum has it (42:19). If John shared this view, which seems very likely, then the repentant sinner he immersed would have been included with the already righteous as God's servants. The figure of Jesus in the Gospels specifically comments that he has not come to call the righteous, but the wicked to repentance (e.g., Mark 2:16-17; Matt. 18:12-14; Luke 15:1-32), and we may presume that John felt much the same way. There is simply no point

80. Scobie, *John the Baptist,* 33.

81. See the following chapter.

in calling the righteous to *repentance;* it is illogical. John is described as calling the disobedient to repent and follow the Law, but at no stage did he consider that only those who came to him would be counted as God's servants; nor is there a suggestion that the righteous should also come to him for immersion to ensure their own salvation, as if immersion was some kind of quasi-magical sealing rite.

There is nothing sectarian or exclusive here. Some of those who came to him as repentant sinners and who were immersed by him, along with those who were accounted righteous already, looked to him as their particular teacher. There were many teachers in Judaism, and their disciples did not immediately form themselves into a sect as such. They were just disciples of a certain teacher. John's disciples seem not to have constituted an exclusive sect claiming that it alone could expect salvation while all others would be consumed by fire. They probably embraced the careful following of the Law — the way of righteousness — in expectation of an imminent judgment, and they looked forward to the purging of Israel of all things wicked. If they distinguished themselves at all it would have been by the supererogatory acts of loving-kindness that John demanded: to live only with the barest minimum of possessions and to give away the rest to those in great need — in short, to live as ethically as possible. In this way, what was initially required as good fruit to prove that repentance had taken place would have been maintained in order to live a life of ongoing acceptance by God that would, in due course, ensure salvation at the end. However, it would have been uncharacteristically arrogant of John to suggest that no one in the whole of Israel apart from those who came to him was already righteous.

The Teaching of John in the Teaching of Jesus?

We have already assessed the historical reliability of the passages relating John's specific teaching in Luke 3:10-14. However, it could be argued that teaching about righteousness attributed to John was in fact derived from Jesus and put back on to the lips of John so as to make him fall into line with the Christian message.[82] On the other hand, the opposite

82. So M. S. Enslin, "John and Jesus," *ZNW* 66 (1975) 5-6; Scobie, *John the Baptist,* 16.

may have been the case: Jesus' teaching may have been in part derived from John's, and Christians may have quarried recollections of John's teaching and placed profound logia on the lips of Jesus. Chronologically, of course, Jesus came after John, and he probably became his disciple and was immersed by him. He must have learned something from him by the Jordan.

There are certainly striking similarities between the teaching of John and Jesus. Matthew repeats John's words "the ax is laid to the root of the trees" (Matt. 3:10 = Luke 3:9) so that Jesus says it in Matt. 7:19 (cf. 15:13). The dismissal of the idea that Jews could have claims to salvation on account of calling Abraham their father (Matt. 3:9; Luke 3:8) is found on the lips of Jesus in John 8:33-39. The slogan "offspring of vipers" (Matt. 3:7; Luke 3:7) is used by Jesus at Matt. 12:34 and 23:33. As John Meier notes, since these Matthean additions have no synoptic parallels, it is probable that Matthew borrowed expressions from the Q material on John the Baptist and gave them to Jesus.[83] The sharing of tunics (Luke 3:11) is vaguely echoed by Jesus in Matt. 5:40 (cf. Luke 6:29).

The Gospel of Matthew shows the greatest tendency to integrate the teaching of John with that of Jesus.[84] In Matthew, Jesus' parables of the wheat and tares (13:24-30, 36-43), the dragnet (13:47-50), the sheep and goats (25:31-46), the ten virgins (25:1-13), and the marriage feast (22:11-14) are all, as T. W. Manson has noted, "just variations, more or less elaborate, on the theme of John the Baptist — wheat and chaff" (cf. Matt. 3:12 = Luke 3:17).[85] If Jesus was once a disciple of John, he may have followed themes in John's teaching so closely in his own teaching that disciples of Jesus may have had difficulty in determining which saying belonged to John and which to Jesus. And there may have been a policy of assigning doubtful traditions to Jesus rather than to John, just to be on the safe side.

It would be hard to argue that Jesus' message concerning righteousness in view of the closeness of judgment was radically different from that of John. Jesus' teaching on matters of behavior, as found in the "Sermon on the Mount" (Matt. 5:1–7:27 and Lucan parallels), largely

83. J. P. Meier, "John the Baptist in Matthew's Gospel," *JBL* 99/3 (1980) 389-90.

84. Wink, *Gospel Tradition*, 33-41.

85. T. W. Manson, *The Teaching of Jesus: Studies of Its Form and Content*, 2d ed. (Cambridge: Cambridge University Press, 1943) 37.

derives from the Q source, and Q was very much concerned with John the Baptist.[86] It is anyone's guess how much of John's teaching may have been buried in this body of tradition. The Gospel writers do not seem to have felt any concern about similarities between Jesus' and John's teaching, but they ensured that John's teaching was completely eclipsed by Jesus' and incorporated into the *kerygma* of the early Church. Jesus' teaching itself may therefore be looked at for further clarification of John's concerns. It is impossible, given the evidence we have, to make a definitive distinction between what must have been John's teaching concerning basic righteousness and what must have been exclusively Jesus' own. All that may be concluded from the evidence is that Jesus undertook to teach much more widely than John did and that he taught in connection with a healing mission. He spoke in parables and engaged in debate. However, thematically, John and Jesus appear to have shared a significant amount of teaching material.

Interestingly, Luke preserves the idea that Jesus' disciples actually wanted him to do things as John did in relation to his disciples. One of Jesus' disciples says to him, "Master, teach us to pray as John taught his disciples" (Luke 11:1), and Jesus responds by teaching them "the Lord's Prayer." The offering of prayers is considered characteristic of John's disciples in Luke 5:33, but in Luke 11:1 the specific question to Jesus is phrased somewhat ambiguously: δίδαξον ἡμᾶς προσεύχεσθαι, καθὼς καὶ Ἰωάννης ἐδίδαξεν τοὺς μαθητὰς αὐτοῦ. The wording does not necessarily suggest that Jesus should teach his disciples a prayer different from that taught by John to his disciples; καθώς can mean "just as" or "exactly as."[87]

The common interpretation is that Jesus was asked to teach his disciples a short prayer in the same general sort of way that John taught his disciples a (different) short prayer. Equally, however, it could be that the disciples wanted exactly the same prayer as that taught by John to his disciples. Therefore, we may consider this prayer one that just might have been taught by John. Luke (11:2-4; cf. Matt. 6:9-15) gives the prayer as:

86. Wink, *Gospel Tradition,* 18-26; Bammel, "The Baptist in Early Christian Tradition," 99-101; Kloppenborg, *The Formation of Q,* 322-25.

87. LSJ, 857. Matt. 21:6, "the disciples went and did *exactly as* (καθώς) Jesus had told them." Matt. 26:24, "But the son of humankind/the man goes *exactly as* (καθώς) it has been written of him."

Father,
May your name be held holy.
May your kingdom come.
Give us each day our necessary food[88]
and remit/forgive us our debts/sins,
for also we have remitted/forgiven all those indebted to us.
And lead us not into a trial.[89]

As Lachs has noted, this kind of prayer was not meant to replace the prayers of the synagogue, but was one from a particular prayer genre known in Hebrew as תפלה קצרה, "short prayer," which was particularly to be recited in places of danger.[90] Certainly, if the context of the prayer was usually a stressful one, perhaps encountered during the early travels of the disciples who accompanied Jesus on the road around Galilee, this would explain why it ends by asking God to spare those praying from a trial. Such a prayer would naturally fit as well with the message of John as of Jesus. Perhaps not surprisingly, the parallel passage in Matthew's Gospel has no introductory reference to John's teaching of a short prayer to his disciples. It is hard to imagine why Luke might have invented such a peculiar introduction, so that Jesus is apparently copying John, prompted by his disciples. Whatever prayer John taught his disciples is likely to have been very similar. If Jesus was a former disciple of John, he would have known it. If others from his own close circle of disciples, such as Peter and Andrew, were also once disciples of John (so John 1:35-42; cf. Acts 1:22), they also would have known the short prayer John taught and would undoubtedly have used it.

This prayer fits well with John's teaching as a whole. Its tight

88. As noted above, ἐπιούσιος is a rare word and seems to have been created in order to render the sense of the Aramaic די מחסרנו, "sufficient for what we lack"; see S. L. Lachs, *Rabbinic Commentary on the New Testament*, 120.

89. For useful discussions of the Lord's Prayer, see J. Jeremias, *The Prayers of Jesus* (London: SCM, 1967) 82-104; C. G. Montefiore, *Rabbinic Literature and Gospel Teachings* (London: Macmillan, 1930) 125-37; Lachs, *Rabbinic Commentary on the New Testament*, 117-24; J. H. Charlesworth, ed., with M. Harding and M. Kiley, *The Lord's Prayer and Other Prayer Texts from the Greco-Roman Era* (Valley Forge, PA: Trinity Press International, 1994), esp. the bibliography compiled by Harding on pp. 101-257.

90. Lachs, *Rabbinic Commentary on the New Testament*, 118-19. Lachs gives this short prayer of Rabbi Eleazar as an example: "Perform your will in Heaven, and bestow satisfaction on earth upon those who revere you and do what is good in your sight. Blessed are you who hears prayer" (*t. Ber.* 3:2; cf. *m. Ber.* 4:4).

connection between eschatological and practical considerations places it in the same theological tradition, even if it was wholly invented by Jesus. In saying the "Lord's Prayer," the disciples of Jesus prayed together for the coming of God's kingdom and his rule on earth, when the righteous will live and the unrighteous perish. In saying this prayer, they asked God to provide for their own (collective) basic sustenance, but no more than that. They asked for forgiveness of sins (which ensured purity of heart), with a repentant spirit, remitting from debt (or forgiving) also all those indebted to them. They prayed to be saved from a trial, perhaps the trial of judgment, but also from any trial in their daily lives that God himself might allow to test their repentance and righteousness. The disciples of John may have prayed something similar.

Even without beginning to consider the enormous importance of caring for the poor and detachment from possessions that was characteristic of the earliest Christian Church, John's teaching was tremendously influential in the formation of Christianity. Precisely how much of John's teaching passed to Jesus, to his disciples, or directly into the Christian tradition is impossible to determine, but the impact of John's teaching should not be underestimated. Only the most cynical view would assert that, despite chronology and the attested dependence of Jesus and his earliest disciples on John's work, his teaching and prophecy were recast from scratch along Christian lines, so that nothing of John's real message remains for us to distinguish, except perhaps something entirely doom-laden and severe. It seems likely that much more of John's message has remained than has hitherto been recognized and that it is embedded in the heart of the Christian ethos.

In conclusion, we can say that in general John's teaching had its basis in the prophetic tradition, particularly in the book of Isaiah. He not only stressed obedience to the written Law but also extrapolated from the Law ways of living a moral lifestyle for repentant people, even those who were not usually considered just or acceptable to God. Above all, he asked one thing of those who wished to prove repentance and come to immersion: to give away everything unessential of their food and clothing to the begging poor, even if the penitent themselves possessed only one spare tunic, or very little surplus food. Such radical acts of *zekhut*, supererogatory acts of loving-kindness, were "good fruits," "fruits worthy of repentance" that would ensure forgiveness by God. The righteous were good, fruit-bearing trees in God's orchard, Israel. John also predicted an imminent judgment by a coming figure, possibly Elijah, and his prediction functioned to spur people on to present action. John did not recommend that people such as toll collectors or men serving as soldiers leave their jobs, probably because he thought that the end was going to be so soon. John may also have given special counsel to women who were reputed to be "prostitutes," but we do not know precisely what that may have been. Some of John's teaching may have been absorbed into the Jesus tradition. Jesus himself, as a former disciple of John, may have taught as John taught and handed on John's short prayer to his own disciples.

CHAPTER 4

John and the Pharisees

In Chapter 1 it was argued that John "the Immerser" was probably not an Essene. Since it is a prime purpose of this study to understand John within the context of Second Temple Judaism, we will now explore whether John may have had links with another group: the Pharisees. To begin with, we shall consider who the Pharisees were and examine the extent of their judicial power. We will consider their social influence and their reputation for righteousness. Only when this has been reviewed can we begin to assess the historical reliability of statements regarding the Pharisees and John in the Fourth Gospel and, following this, the Synoptics. The subject of the Pharisees within Second Temple Judaism is itself extremely complicated, and here only the main issues for our study will be discussed. Specific characteristics of Pharisaic belief and practice will be broached only when relevant. Since in the Fourth Gospel those called "Pharisees" are effectively those in charge in Jerusalem, the issue of the historicity of this portrayal will be our chief concern. I plan to argue that, once correctly understood, the Fourth Gospel gives us our best evidence that the relationship between the Pharisees and John was positive. It is in the synoptic Gospels that we find attempts to put Jesus and John together in opposition to the Pharisees.

The Pharisees and Power

The fundamental matter to consider here is the extent of the Pharisees' judicial power. Much has been written about the Pharisees and where they might fit within the context of Second Temple Judaism; the reader may wish to consult some of these broader studies for the main tenets of Pharisaic teaching and praxis.[1] In regard to judicial and religious power, however, two main points of view may be distinguished, one that minimizes the influence of the Pharisees judicially and administratively during the early part of the first century, and another that tends to stress that the Pharisees were influential on both counts during this time.

On the one hand, there is the hypothesis proposed by Jacob Neusner,[2] which follows the observations of Morton Smith.[3] Neusner contends that Pharisaism went through three distinct phases. In the first phase, during Hasmonean rule from the second to first centuries BCE, Pharisees sought to excel in observance of religion and exact expounding of the Law (cf. Josephus, *War* 1.110-12), but they also aimed to achieve their aims through political means. In the second phase, during

1. Especially noteworthy among many are the studies by L. Finkelstein, *The Pharisees: The Sociological Background of Their Faith,* 2d rev. ed. (Philadelphia: Jewish Publication Society of America, 1940); A. Finkel, *The Pharisees and the Teacher of Nazareth: A Study of their Background, their Halachic and Midrashic Teachings, their Similarities and Differences* (Leiden: Brill, 1964); J. Neusner, *The Rabbinic Traditions about the Pharisees before 70,* 3 vols. (Leiden: Brill, 1971); J. Bowker, *Jesus and the Pharisees* (Cambridge: Cambridge University Press, 1973); E. Rivkin, *A Hidden Revolution: The Pharisees' Search for the Kingdom Within* (Nashville: Abingdon, 1978); A. J. Saldarini, *Pharisees, Scribes, and Sadducees in Palestinian Society: A Sociological Approach* (Wilmington, DE: Glazier, 1988); S. N. Mason, *Flavius Josephus on the Pharisees: A Composition-Critical Study* (Leiden: Brill, 1991); E. P. Sanders, *Judaism: Practice and Belief 63 BCE–66 CE* (London: SCM, 1992) 380-490. See also D. Goodblatt, "The Place of the Pharisees in First Century Judaism: The State of the Debate," *JSJ* 20 (1989) 12-30; K. G. C. Newport, "The Pharisees in Judaism Prior to A.D. 70," *AUSS* 29 (1991) 127-37; and D. R. de Lacey, "In Search of a Pharisee," *TynBul* 43 (1992) 353-72.

2. Neusner, *Rabbinic Traditions about the Pharisees;* cf. idem, "Josephus' Pharisees — A Complete Repertoire," in *Josephus, Judaism, and Christianity,* ed. L. H. Feldman and G. Hata (Detroit: Wayne State University Press, 1987) 274-92. Neusner's views are essentially followed by L. Grabbe, *Judaism from Cyrus to Hadrian,* vol. 2 (Minneapolis: Fortress, 1992) 467-84.

3. Morton Smith, "Palestinian Judaism in the First Century," in *Israel: Its Role and Civilization,* ed. M. Davis (New York: Jewish Theological Seminary of America, 1956) 67-81.

the reign of Herod the Great (37-4 BCE) and up to the fall of Jerusalem in 70 CE, they were forced to withdraw from the political arena to become a strictly sectarian, inward-looking movement. In the third phase, after the Temple's destruction, the Pharisees regained political authority by means of an agreement with Rome in which they undertook to keep the country peaceful in return for political and religious leadership; hence the rise of "normative" Judaism based on Pharisaic lines.

It is Neusner's conclusions about the Pharisees of the middle period that have caused much rethinking in regard to the Pharisees' relationship with Jesus. In his extensive form-critical study of rabbinic writings concerning issues up to the year 70, Neusner has identified 317 separate traditions attributable to Pharisaic masters of the Houses of Hillel and Shammai. The overall majority (67%) of these focus on table fellowship, purity laws, and tithing. There are also some rules about the keeping of the Sabbath and festivals, and some family rules, but there is virtually nothing on political matters or concerns of the wider community. Neusner has therefore proposed that the main concerns of the Pharisees of Jesus' time involved the maintenance of levitical purity laws — which had formerly been applicable only in regard to priests and Levites in the Temple — in the home environment. The Pharisees, according to Neusner's analysis, were fundamentally introverted during the period of John and Jesus.

On the other hand, there is the opinion of Ellis Rivkin,[4] who in many ways affirms the traditional picture of the Pharisees as the religious authorities of the time. For Rivkin, the סופרים (scribes) and possibly the חכמים (sages), but rarely the פרושים (Pharisees) of rabbinic literature, are to be equated with the true Pharisees of the New Testament and Josephus. The real Pharisees were a powerful scholarly class, influential throughout the judicial and educational structures of the land. Support for this portrayal of the Pharisees is found also in the work of Gedalyahu Alon[5] and Daniel Schwartz,[6] who argue for an active political role for the Pharisees throughout the Second Temple period.

4. Rivkin, *A Hidden Revolution;* cf. idem, "Defining the Pharisees: The Tannaitic Sources," *HUCA* 40-41 (1969-70) 205-49.

5. G. Alon, *Jews, Judaism and the Classical World: Studies in Jewish History in the Times of the Second Temple and Talmud* (Jerusalem: Magnes, 1977).

6. D. R. Schwartz, "Josephus and Nicolaus on the Pharisees," *JSJ* 14 (1983) 157-71.

On this side of the debate also we may place Martin Hengel who, in a recent article with Roland Deines, has presented the view that the Pharisees were active politically, religiously, and socially, while the chief priests of the time of Jesus needed to cooperate with the "Pharisaic scribes" in order to stay in power.[7] Caiaphas, who held the office of high priest from 18 to 36/37 CE, was, then, "a great diplomat" who "got on well with the Pharisees."[8] Hengel and Deines find complete accord in the descriptions of the Pharisees in the New Testament, Josephus, and early rabbinic literature.[9] The Pharisees, according to this view, were actively extroverted and authoritative during the time of John and Jesus.

In some ways, the picture drawn by Rivkin appears to approximate more closely that of Josephus, who states outright that the Pharisees "have the support of the populace" (*Ant.* 13.298) and that the ritual and social life of Jews operated according to their principles (*Ant.* 18.15, 17). Josephus applies this characterization consistently to the post-70 context, as well as to Hasmonean and Herodian times (e.g., *War* 1.110, 571; 2.162; *Ant.* 13.288-98, 400-431; 17.41-45; 18.17). However, Morton Smith has argued that Josephus, by stressing the influence of the Pharisees over the people, was indicating to the Roman government that Judea could not be ruled without Pharisaic support.[10] His language reflects the post-70 situation, when the Pharisees were powerful socially and politically, which was then read back into history. So, for example, in the story of Queen Salome Alexandra's succession in 76 BCE as described in the *Jewish War* (ca. 75 CE), Pharisees do not appear to be particularly powerful (1.106-12), but in the revised story found in the *Antiquities* (ca. 93-94 CE), the Hasmonean king Alexander Jannaeus advises his wife and successor Salome Alexandra to yield some power to the Pharisees because of their influence over the masses (13.401-02). Against Smith, however, Neusner does accept that during the reign of Alexander Jannaeus the Pharisees were politically powerful.

It seems unlikely that a group that had significant political influence a century before the destruction of the Temple could have been forgotten by the people and allowed to closet itself away in ritual clean-

7. M. Hengel and R. Deines, "E. P. Sanders' 'Common Judaism,' Jesus and the Pharisees," *JTS* 46 (1995) 1-70.

8. Ibid., 65.

9. Ibid., 66.

10. Smith, "Palestinian Judaism in the First Century," 76.

liness, only to emerge suddenly as the major political and religious force a few decades later. Both polarities in the debate may be somewhat too extreme here. The texts, in fact, provide us with divergent views. The "Pharisees" in the Fourth Gospel hardly seem to be the same group as those described by Josephus or Luke. References to "Pharisees" in rabbinic literature can be critical, even though the "sages" are esteemed. The material does not seem to present us with a consistent picture. Moreover, it is necessary to distinguish between various types of power. "Political power" as a term itself may be inappropriate for our period, for it is difficult to define precisely what this meant in terms of the workings of the institutions of the land. Politically, the Land of Israel was under the control of Rome, as an occupied area governed by a prefect or procurator. Those in power were those who collaborated with Roman interests, and the Jewish nation was represented by the Roman-approved high priest. The land was run by the Roman administration, centered in Caesarea, and by town and city administrations, some of which were fairly independent and could be non-Jewish in character. Judicially and religiously, however, the Jewish population was under the authority of the high priest, and the council of elders, or γερουσία (συνέδριον), a point we will return to soon. The Jewish religious center was Jerusalem and the Temple.

Neusner is probably correct that the Pharisees held no real political or religious authority in Herodian Judea. They had no function administratively. They were not responsible for the making of laws or for deciding legal judgments; this authority rested with the priests, who were ultimately responsible to the Romans. They did not control the workings of the Temple; these also were in the hands of the priests. It would be extremely hard on the basis of Josephus or the synoptic Gospels to conclude that they were anything more than a pressure group in the wealthy aristocratic echelons of Jerusalem, even without recourse to verifiable rabbinic traditions. But social influence is another thing. They may have held social influence over large sectors of the community. If a group has no actual political, administrative, religious, or judicial power, this does not mean that the group has no social power. Rabbinic traditions indicate that the high priest followed Pharisaic rulings when he entered the holy of holies on the Day of Atonement (*t. Yoma* 5:8; cf. *t. Para* 3:8; *m. Soṭa* 9:9). This may be recorded as a claim to authority in the rabbinic tradition, but Josephus does say that even the Sadducees abided by Pharisaic directives because the populace would not tolerate them if they did not (*Ant.* 18.17; cf. 13.298). According to the Tosephta, the wives of Sadducees sought rulings from Pharisaic sages on menstrual purity (*t. Nid.* 5:2, 3).

Furthermore, in the passages in Josephus that have been read as endeavors to convince the Romans that they should deal with the Pharisees (*Ant.* 13.288-98, 400-432; 17.41-45; *Life* 189-98), there is anti-Pharisaic sentiment, which undermines any simple agenda on the part of Josephus (e.g., *Ant.* 13.288). As Steve Mason has recently pointed out, Josephus' Pharisees are influential with the masses, but often in a negative way (*Ant.* 13.400).[11] The result of Salome Alexandra's confidence in the Pharisees is an unmitigated disaster.[12] As Mason puts it, the "consistent thread in all these stories is that the Pharisees are jealous of those in power and cause trouble for them."[13] Josephus' antipathy towards the Pharisees, despite the fact that he followed their rulings in his public life, was probably caused by the fact that several Pharisees, including Simon son of Gamaliel, were involved in an attempt to remove him from his position in Galilee (*Life* 191-98). In his view, the Pharisees were partly responsible for the collapse of the Hasmonean dynasty (*War* 1.110-14; *Ant.* 13.288-98) to which he traced his own priestly ancestry. If this is so, then Josephus was trying to make his readers reconsider whether Pharisaic control over Judea was really such a good thing. Mason would opt for a middle position, somewhere between the extremes of the Smith–Neusner and Rivkin scenarios. As Mason points out, the Pharisees could not have had a mandate over the Law during the early first century, because the evidence suggests strongly that it was the *priests* who held this mandate.[14] Mason's convincing argument is

11. See also Schwartz, "Josephus and Nicolaus on the Pharisees," 158-62. According to Josephus, the masses themselves were unruly and disruptive and had to be controlled.

12. S. N. Mason, "Pharisaic Dominance before 70 CE and the Gospels' Hypocrisy Charge (Matt. 23:2-3)," *HTR* 83/4 (1990) 369.

13. Mason, "Pharisaic Dominance," 370. To be noted also is Mason's dismissal of the notion that Josephus was himself a Pharisee; see Mason, *Flavius Josephus on the Pharisees*, 325-26, 347-53. In following Pharisaic rulings and advice in his public life, Josephus seems to have been doing what was considered acceptable by most people.

14. *Ag. Ap.* 2.185-86; cf. Mal. 2:7; 4 Macc. 5:4, 29, 35. See S. N. Mason, "Priesthood in Josephus and the 'Pharisaic Revolution,'" *JBL* 107 (1988) 657-61; idem, *Flavius Josephus on the Pharisees*, 236; also Sanders, *Judaism: Practice and Belief*, 398 n. 37 and Chapter 10.

that the Pharisees had a degree of religious and social influence, but no authority.[15]

The position of E. P. Sanders is similar, though more extreme as regards Pharisaic social influence: they had only a moderate amount. The Pharisees could not have held official or public control in the Roman period. As Sanders notes of the narrative in Josephus: "When they [the Pharisees] tried to intervene in public affairs by plotting, protesting or joining an uprising, their efforts were ineffective because of the power of the secular government. Josephus' long silences about them complement the accounts of sporadic attempts that failed: they were powerless. The actors who made it into history were Herod, his descendants, the Jerusalem aristocracy, and of course the Romans themselves."[16] Sanders sees the Pharisees as having some indirect power, by having an influence among the ordinary people (*Ant.* 13.288, 298; 18.17), but even that was not very significant since those who spoke out too loudly or acted rashly were killed.[17]

According to Sanders, not even the synagogues were run by Pharisees; they may have been influential, but they are not depicted as leading the synagogues in the Gospel material. Jairus is not called a Pharisee (Mark 5:21-24, 35-43); neither is the "ruler of the synagogue" of Luke 13:14. They are present in narratives set in synagogues (Mark 3:1-6), but they are not in charge.[18] Following Mason, Sanders notes that the priests were in charge of synagogue life.[19] Indeed, Philo states that a priest or an elder led the synagogue service (*Hypothetica* 7.13).[20]

15. On the Pharisees in Luke, see S. N. Mason, "Chief Priests, Sadducees, Pharisees and Sanhedrin in Acts," in *The Book of Acts in its Palestinian Setting,* ed. R. Bauckham (Grand Rapids: Eerdmans, 1995) 134-42.

16. Sanders, *Judaism: Practice and Belief,* 389.

17. Ibid., 395.

18. Ibid., 398.

19. E. P. Sanders, *Jewish Law from Jesus to the Mishnah: Five Studies* (London: SCM, 1990) 77-81.

20. Hengel and Deines have questioned this notion of Pharisaic displacement from synagogue authority, arguing instead that the priestly aristocracy in Jerusalem would have had no interest in creating competition for the Temple service by means of synagogue service, and, by implication, that only Pharisaic initiatives could account for the rise of the synagogue ("E. P. Sanders' 'Common Judaism,'" 33-34). However, this seems a rather narrow view. The high priest may have considered synagogues a useful network to use in order to collect Temple dues, and he may have utilized synagogues to stretch his religious jurisdiction to far-flung Jewish communities. There was nothing

Neusner notes also that the absence of rules about synagogue life in these traditions makes it hard to argue that "the sect claimed to exercise influence in the life of synagogues not controlled by its own members, or that they preached widely in synagogues."[21]

While Sanders and Neusner disagree about legal matters, purity regulations, and other aspects of the Pharisees,[22] there has been growing scholarly agreement in recent years that the Pharisees were without real political and religious power during the first half of the first century. Though active in synagogue life, particularly in Judea and Galilee, the Pharisees were not in control. This situation seems to be reflected in criticisms of the Pharisees in the Jesus tradition. In Mark 12:38-39 (Matt. 23:6; cf. Luke 11:43) it is stated that the Pharisees "love to have . . . the best seats in the synagogues." It is not actually said that they control the synagogues or legislate concerning them. The language reflects a situation in which Pharisees were influential and respected in synagogues, but not necessarily in charge. They sit on "the seat of Moses" (Matt. 23:1), which implies that they enjoy a special place of honor (a place of teaching and interpretation), but this still locates them in the realm of influence rather than actual control.[23]

Anthony Saldarini has argued that the Pharisees were an elite retainer class,[24] which means that we should not imagine them as ordinary people who just happened to subscribe to a particular religious ideology; they were more like a political party currently in opposition. This is useful, especially since it checks any assumption that the Pharisees constituted a kind of religious denomination within Judaism. Josephus describes the three main "sects" of Second Temple Judaism — the Pharisees, Essenes, and Sadducees — as philosophies rather than as

---

inherently competitive in the synagogue vis-à-vis the Temple. Hengel and Deines's suggestion (p. 33) that in the description of a synagogue service in Josephus (*Ant.* 16.43-46) ἔθη καὶ νόμος relates to the oral and written Torah and is "reminiscent of Pharisaic tendencies" has no basis in the language used by Josephus. Priests were necessary for the synagogue blessing (cf. *m. Ber.* 5:4; *m. Meg.* 4:3, 5-7); Pharisees were not.

21. Neusner, "Pharisaic Law in New Testament Times," *USQR* 26 (1971) 333.

22. See Sanders, *Jewish Law from Jesus to the Mishnah*, 166-73; idem, *Judaism: Practice and Belief*, 413-14; Neusner, "Mr Sanders' Pharisees and Mine," *BBR* 2 (1992) 143-69; idem, "Mr Maccoby's Red Cow, Mr Sanders Pharisees, and Mine," *JSJ* 23 (1992) 81-98.

23. For the "seat of Moses," see S. T. Lachs, *A Rabbinic Commentary on the New Testament: The Gospels of Matthew, Mark, and Luke* (Hoboken, NJ: KTAV, 1987) 365-66.

24. Saldarini, *Pharisees, Scribes, and Sadducees.*

denominations (*War* 2.119-66; *Ant.* 17.11-25). They are sects in the sense of philosophical schools. In his descriptions of all three sects, Josephus makes it clear that he is referring to a small minority of men (male reference intended) in the total population of the Land of Israel:[25] the Pharisees number "over six thousand" (*Ant.* 17.42), the Essenes "more than four thousand" (*Ant.* 17.20), and the Sadducees "but a few men" (*Ant.* 8.17). This means that the total number of men involved in the schools is a little over 10,000, which may be a liberal estimate, given Josephus' tendency to exaggerate numbers. (For example, he can write that the smallest village in Galilee contains more than 15,000 inhabitants [*War* 3.41].) It should be remembered that Josephus writes that there were 18,000-20,000 priests and Levites (*Ag. Ap.* 2.108) and that 1,500 of these received a tithe of the revenue to administer public affairs (*Ag. Ap.* 1.188).

In regard to the extent of Pharisaic influence, almost everyone agrees that it was largely in the region around Jerusalem and Judea proper,[26] rather than throughout the whole of the Land of Israel. In other words, their influence was not as great in Galilee as it was closer to Jerusalem, the religious center of the country, though Pharisees probably did exist in Galilee.[27] It may be significant, or at least not to be wholly discounted, that only two references in the entire Gospel of Mark refer to Pharisees *outside* Galilee. Otherwise, Galilee is presented as the

25. T. Ilan presents some interesting observations about the attraction of certain aristocratic women to the Pharisees and their dicta; see T. Ilan, "The Attraction of Aristocratic Women to Pharisaism during the Second Temple Period," *HTR* 88 (1995) 1-33. Josephus, though, never tells us that such women became Pharisees themselves. Rather, "by these men called Pharisees the women were ruled" (*Ant.* 17.41).

26. Terminology is not always clear. "Judea" proper was a region around Jerusalem between Idumea and Samaria. Its name derived from the territory of the tribe of Judah. But the whole area known by the rabbis as *'Ereṣ Yiśrā'ēl* was known as "Judea" by classical authors. This nomenclature probably resulted from the Hasmonean conquests of the second century BCE that expanded Jewish (= Judean) territory. To further confuse matters, the Roman prefects and procurators ruled a region known as Judea that comprised Samaria and Idumea, but excluded part of *'Ereṣ Yiśrā'ēl:* Golanitis, Galilee, and Perea. "Palestine" was not introduced as a term to cover the whole region until the second century CE and would therefore be anachronistic in this discussion. See L. H. Feldman, "Some Observations on the Name of Palestine," *HUCA* 61 (1990) 1-23.

27. J. D. G. Dunn, "Pharisees, Sinners, and Jesus," in *The Social World of Formative Christianity and Judaism: Essays in Tribute to Howard Clark Kee,* ed. J. Neusner et al. (Philadelphia: Fortress, 1988) 280-81.

central locus of Jesus' interactions with Pharisees.[28] Mark's reference to "disciples of the Pharisees" (2:18-19) in Galilee would indicate that there were people who followed specific Pharisaic directives and were engaged in tuition with Pharisaic teachers, without necessarily counting themselves as Pharisees proper.

The distinction between those who were חברים, "fellows" (always men) and those who were not is indicated in rabbinic literature (cf. *m. Ḥag.* 2:7; *m. Dem.* 2:3). The חברים endeavored to go along with the strict tithing and purity rules and could participate in the group dinners (חבורות).[29] The חברים and the Pharisees proper are therefore rightly equated by Neusner.[30]

In his attempt to find verifiable rabbinic traditions about the Pharisees, Neusner notes that the absence of rabbinic traditions about a particular matter does not mean that it could not have existed. In comparing the accounts in Josephus with rabbinic literature, we learn that "what interested one was of no concern to the other," but it does not follow that events not recorded in one or the other never took place in history. Neusner adds, furthermore, that it is not even a necessary inference that "stories present in both must have in fact taken place."[31] The early traditions of the Pharisees identified by Neusner show us what later rabbis chose to remember about them.[32] Neusner has therefore identified a basic minimum, rather than maximum, in terms of tradition, with the proviso that even within this minimum we may not be able to find historical accuracy. It is to Josephus and the New Testament that we need to look for further information.

That Pharisees made specific interpretations of law may be implied in the very name of the sect. A. I. Baumgarten has made an interesting case for the Greek word Φαρισαῖος coming from a Hebrew Qal active participle, פְּרוֹשִׁים, meaning "those who specify."[33] In support of this

28. R. L. Mowery, "Pharisees and Scribes, Galilee and Jerusalem," *ZNW* 80 (1989) 266-68.

29. For a basic description of the חברים, see E. Schürer, *The History of the Jewish People in the Age of Jesus Christ (175 B.C.–A.D. 135),* vol. 2, rev. and ed. G. Vermes et al. (Edinburgh: Clark, 1989) 398-99.

30. Neusner, *Rabbinic Traditions about the Pharisees;* and Schürer, *History of the Jewish People,* vol. 2, 388-403.

31. Neusner, *Rabbinic Traditions about the Pharisees,* vol. 3, 244.

32. So also Dunn, "Pharisees, Sinners, and Jesus," 266.

33. A. I. Baumgarten, "The Name of the Pharisees," *JBL* 102 (1983) 411-23.

he notes that the Greek word ἀκρίβεια, "exactness, strictness," is used in descriptions of the Pharisees by Luke (Acts 26:5; cf. 22:3), Josephus, and Josephus' source, Nicolaus of Damascus (in *Ant.* 17.41). In other words, these writers seem to imply that the group focused on the specific and accurate interpretation of biblical law (cf. *War* 2.162).[34] Again, however, it should be noted that interpretation is one thing, but the making of authoritative religious rulings on the basis of such interpretations is another. Strictly speaking, in rabbinic literature, the Hebrew word פְּרוּשִׁים is a Qal passive participle meaning "separated ones."[35] The Pharisees or חברים appear to have been seen as separating themselves mentally from other Jews, probably by means of an exceptional pursuit of purity (by their definition).[36]

The identification of Pharisees with the חכמים and סופרים, the sages and scribes, made by Rivkin,[37] has been very popular.[38] It has often been assumed that the scribes mentioned in the New Testament were, in general, Pharisees. The Gospel of Matthew has aided this identification since Matthew sometimes substitutes "Pharisees" for "scribes" in his source material: Mark or Q (Matt. 9:34, 12:24, cf. Mark 3:22; Matt. 21:45, cf. Luke 20:19 [Q]; Matt. 22:34, cf. Mark 12:28; Matt. 22:41, cf. Mark 12:35). It seems likely that Matthew inserted Pharisees here specifically in order to make them conspicuous as an opposition group to Jesus and that the equation of Pharisees with scribes owes more to the situation of Matthew's time of writing (after the destruction of the Temple) than to the situation of the time of Jesus.[39] Considering the tendency in later Christian literature to lump Jewish groups into one throng opposed to Jesus,[40] we may suspect that the beginning of the

34. See also Schürer, *History of the Jewish People,* vol. 2, 398 n. 57.

35. See, e.g., *m. Yad.* 4:6-8; *m. Ḥag.* 2:7; *m. Soṭa* 3:4; see Schürer, *History of the Jewish People,* vol. 2, 396-400; also M. Jastrow, *A Dictionary of the Targumim, the Talmud Bavli and Yerushalmi, and the Midrashic Literature,* vol. 2 (New York: Pardes, 1950) 1222, 1228, 1241-43. The Greek word Φαρισαῖος may possibly derive from an Aramaic passive participle, equivalent to Hebrew פרוש: פריש, pl. פרישיא.

36. Schürer, *History of the Jewish People,* vol. 2, 396-97; M. Goodman, *The Ruling Class of Judaea: The Origins of the Jewish Revolt Against Rome,* A.D. *66-70* (Cambridge: Cambridge University Press, 1987) 83.

37. Rivkin, *A Hidden Revolution.*

38. See D. R. Schwartz, *Studies in the Jewish Background of Christianity* (Tübingen: Mohr-Siebeck, 1992) 88-89.

39. Ibid., 90-91.

40. H. F. Weiss, "Φαρισαῖος," *TDNT* 9 (1974) 47.

tendency is to be found in the Gospel of Matthew. The passages preserving the distinction between scribes and Pharisees, being at variance with this tendency, would then contain some historical weight. After all, the phrase "scribes of the Pharisees" found in Mark 2:16 and Acts 23:9 (cf. Luke 5:30) seems to indicate that there might have been scribes belonging to other parties as well.

Daniel Schwartz has argued very convincingly that scribes were Levites.[41] Strictly speaking, a scribe is simply a person who *writes* in a society in which universal literacy is far from realized. But in reality the job was more than that; it involved to some degree an official legal function and probably teaching as well. The סופרים were those who wrote in a ספר, a scroll or document, and who were educated in interpretational norms and law. It appears to have been one of the vocations open to Levites (cf. *T. Levi* 8:17), along with that of Temple singers and policemen. However, Schwartz concludes that the scribes and the Pharisees were in opposition,[42] which seems unnecessary, for essentially the distinction is between a particular religious sect and a *job*. In Qumran literature, the משכיל, "man of understanding" or "instructor" in charge of teaching the doctrine of the sect, was a Levite.[43] In the *Rule of the Congregation* or *Messianic Rule* from Qumran (1QSa), Levites are to be attached to the groups of Israelites "to cause all the congregation to go and come."[44] As Geza Vermes notes, "this causing the people 'to go and come' obviously alludes to the spiritual guidance of the members of the Community."[45] The Pharisees may well have had their own Levites among them who took on the job of being scribes and teachers. Not all Pharisees were necessarily teachers. Some may have wished simply to lead quiet lives in accordance with the principles of holiness that had been set, earning a place of respect in the community by example. In Luke 11:37–12:1 there are separate woes to Pharisees and scribes/lawyers, possibly indicating differentiation.[46] Neusner notes that while both scribes and Pharisees could be considered חכמים in rabbinic literature,

41. Schwartz, *Jewish Background of Christianity,* 89-101.

42. Ibid., 100.

43. G. Vermes, *The Dead Sea Scrolls in English,* 2nd ed. (Harmondsworth: Penguin, 1975) 22-25.

44. Ibid., 25.

45. Ibid.

46. Luke 11:43 makes the distinction explicit: "And one of the lawyers said to him in reply, 'Teacher, when you say this, you insult us too.' "

at no point does Josephus equate the two (cf. *Life* 197-98, where none of the groups is equated with the scribes).[47] In Josephus, it seems clear that scribes are legal authorities or teachers of the Law; the Pharisees are a "sect" (a philosophical school); and the scribes are members of a profession.[48]

Therefore, where scribes and Pharisees are linked in Mark (7:5) and Luke (5:21; 6:7; 7:30; 11:23; 15:2), this may indicate scribes who were also Pharisees or who were associated with the Pharisees, but while scribes could be Pharisees, or disciples of the Pharisees, they could belong to any other religious party as well or be at the service of the high priest. Schwartz has gathered interesting information together to illuminate the function of the scribes of the high priest, who are especially linked with the juridical functions of the court he convened, or with courts in general. Schwartz identifies the scribes with the levitical ὑπηρέται, "servants," of local courts mentioned by Josephus (*Ant.* 4.241). The Mishnah refers to levitical חזנים, who served high priests (*m. Soṭa* 7:7; *m. Yoma* 7:1; *m. Tamid* 5:3; *m. Mak.* 3:12).[49] The same term is used for those who execute a court's decision, who are also identified as Levites (*Sifre Deut.* 15).[50] Josephus' ὑπηρέται and rabbinic חזנים may then be one and the same. Interestingly, Mark 14:53-55 seems to equate scribes with ὑπηρέται of the court.[51]

All this is intended to provide something of an impression of scholarly debate on the matter of Pharisees' degree of power (of various types) and on some of the issues at stake. On balance, it seems unlikely that the Pharisees held any judicial authority in our period, or that they controlled synagogues. The social influence of the Pharisees, however, may be more readily accepted. Pharisees were interested in teaching and interpreting the Law, and in giving directions to people about how to follow the Law. They should not be equated with scribes, however, even though there were scribes belonging to the Pharisee "philosophy." We will look at certain issues in more detail now, beginning with an examination of the popular reputation of the Pharisees as particularly righteous.

47. J. Neusner, "'Pharisaic-Rabbinic' Judaism: A Clarification," *HR* 12/3 (1972) 267.

48. Ibid., 267-69.

49. Schwartz, *Jewish Background of Christianity,* 96 n. 38.

50. Ibid., 96 n. 39.

51. Ibid., 92-98.

The Pharisees as Righteous

According to Josephus, the Pharisees had a reputation for being the most righteous of all Jews (*War* 1.110). This reputation for righteousness is reflected in certain passages in the synoptic Gospels. For example, where Mark has "some Pharisees and Herodians" (Mark 12:13-17; cf. Matt. 22:15-16), Luke (20:20) has people "who pretended to be righteous," as if this righteousness were indeed a commonly acknowledged characteristic of the groups.[52] Of course, they "pretended" in Luke's narrative because they are pitted against Jesus here in asking him a tricky question about paying taxes, but the implication is that they were known as being righteous or at least endeavored to be so. Throughout his narrative Luke presents the Pharisees as being held in high esteem as respected teachers with a reputation for righteousness, but he undermines them, seeking instead to show that this reputation is unjustified since they misunderstood the meaning of Jesus' teaching.[53]

In Luke 10:29, the lawyer (νομικός) who has asked Jesus what he should do to inherit eternal life queries, "Who is my neighbor?" — "wishing to make himself righteous" (θέλων δικαιῶσαι ἑαυτόν). The motive behind his question is often translated along the lines of his having a wish to "justify himself" (so, e.g., NRSV), but, as Ed Sanders has pointed out in regard to Paul's use of the verb δικαιοῦν, there is no simple English translation. To use "justify" carries a sense of defensiveness or legal excuse that is wholly absent in the Greek.[54] The verb δικαιοῦν means in fact "to regard someone who is right as being in the right."[55] Sanders himself suggests restoring the old English verb "to righteous," though this may sound odd. In Luke 10:29 the lawyer simply wishes to know whom he should think of as his neighbor so that he can live righteously. Jesus responds by telling him the parable of the good Samaritan, and the lawyer readily understands it, noting that the one who was the neighbor to the man who had been attacked was neither a priest, nor a Levite, but a Samaritan "who showed him mercy." Jesus

52. According to Chilton, the "Herodians" were probably not members of the Herodian dynasty but teachers favored by Herod and his family; see B. D. Chilton, "Jesus *ben David:* Reflections on the *Davidssohnfrage*," *JSNT* 14 (1982) 88-112.

53. See the discussion in Mason, "Chief Priests, Sadducees, Pharisees," 134-42.

54. E. P. Sanders, *Paul* (Oxford: Oxford University Press, 1991) 45.

55. Ibid., 47.

tells the lawyer to go and do likewise (Luke 10:37). He therefore prescribes a way of being righteous for the lawyer.

Luke's parable of the prodigal son (Luke 15:11-32) places the Pharisees in the position of the older son who served his father for many years, never transgressing any commands and always having free access to everything belonging to his father.[56] In Luke 16:15, Jesus criticizes the Pharisees, saying, "You are the ones 'righteousing' (οἱ δικαιοῦντες) yourselves before the people, but God knows your hearts. For what is prized among people is an abomination before God." In other words, according to the Lucan Jesus, the Pharisees' apparent righteousness is not true righteousness of the heart, because they have focused on gaining credit for righteousness from people. The statement presupposes that people considered the Pharisees righteous and that the Pharisees gained respect because of this. Jesus criticizes them for being too preoccupied with gaining this acclaim from people, rather than considering God. Luke describes the Pharisees here as being fond of money; such is the abomination, the βδέλυγμα, a word with associations of idolatry. It is significant that the saying follows directly from Jesus' pronouncement against "serving material possessions" or "mammon": "No servant is able to serve two masters. For one he will hate and the other he will love. For one he will be devoted to and the other he will despise. You are not able to serve God and mammon" (Luke 16:13; cf. Matt. 6:24). Material possessions were complete anathema to Jesus, who advised some of those who wished to follow him to sell all their possessions and give to the poor (Mark 10:21; Matt. 19:21; Luke 18:22). Jesus' standards were extreme, but this does not make the Pharisees' righteousness a sham, despite the traditions of criticism leveled against them. Jesus himself was one among several others, for example Hanina ben Dosa (*b. Ta'an.* 24b–25a), who reacted against materialism by spurning money and possessions.[57]

Criticism of the acquisition of material possessions aside, the Lucan Jesus acknowledges the righteousness of Pharisees at times. When the Pharisees inquire in Luke 17:20 when the kingdom of God will come,

56. Mason, "Chief Priests, Sadducees, Pharisees," 141: "All of this confirms that the Pharisees are the safe, righteous and healthy, who do not need Jesus' teaching, though in other [Lucan] contexts he finds them culpable for having squandered their privileged position."

57. See G. Vermes, *Jesus the Jew: A Historian's Reading of the Gospels,* 2d ed. (London: SCM, 1983) 77.

Jesus responds that the kingdom is "within you" (17:22). Mason notes that here "Jesus is declaring that the Pharisees have the Kingdom in themselves, as the 'older brother' with heaven's resources at their disposal, as the righteous and healthy of society; but . . . they squander their potential."[58]

In his prologue to the story of the Pharisee and the toll collector, Luke comments that Jesus told the parable to "those who trusted in themselves that they were righteous and counted the rest as nothing" (Luke 18:9). Since a Pharisee is a principal actor in the story, the implication is that it is the Pharisees who trusted that they were righteous and counted the rest as nothing. The parable (19:10-14) emphasizes that true righteousness springs from the right attitude of the heart: true repentance and humility before God. Thanking God for one's presumed righteous conduct is unjustified, for God's standards are so high that constant forgiveness should be asked for. Such a view is consistent with Jesus' hard line on individual morality (e.g., Matt. 5:21-24, 27-28). Trusting in one's own righteousness is wrong. As Jesus apparently snapped in response to someone addressing him as "good teacher," "Why do you call me good? No one is good but God alone" (Mark 10:17-18 = Luke 18:18-19; cf. Matt. 19:16-17).

But common failure to attain true goodness and righteousness by such high standards did not mean that striving for these goals was useless, and it was the Pharisees whose standard of excellence Jesus' disciples were supposed to exceed. In the Matthean tradition Jesus tells his disciples that "unless your righteousness exceeds that of the scribes and the Pharisees, you will never enter the kingdom of heaven" (Matt. 5:20). The statement implies that the disciples of Jesus should aim for an extraordinarily high standard and be "perfect as your Father in heaven is perfect" (Matt. 5:48, cf. Luke 6:36).[59] Again, this saying presupposes that the Pharisees were known to be particularly righteous. Jesus himself may have accused the Pharisees of getting the emphasis wrong, but this did not mean that anything found in the Law could be

58. Mason, "Chief Priests, Sadducees, Pharisees," 142.

59. The Aramaic word behind "perfect" of Matt. 5:48 and "merciful" of Luke 6:36 is the same: תמימא (cf. Hebrew תמים, from the root תמם). The word means "whole, perfect, complete; sincere, just, upright, honest, and righteous (in moral and ethical terms)." No English word captures all these senses. It is characteristic of one who completely follows God's Law. See BDB, 1070-71.

dispensed with (Matt. 5:18; Luke 16:17). The Pharisees were good examples to follow. The evidence of Paul and Acts tells a similar story. Paul notes that as a Pharisee he aimed to live "according to the righteousness in the Law" (Phil. 3:6; cf. Rom. 10:3).[60] There was no question for most Jews that it certainly was possible to be righteous and obedient to God. A Pharisee who had the reputation for righteousness might in fact have been a self-congratulating hypocrite, but it was still possible to be a righteous Pharisee without hypocrisy; it was possible to be "righteoused" by obedience to the Law.

According to Josephus, the Pharisees believed that people had a choice — to walk along the path of righteousness or of iniquity — and that the choice was within human power (*War* 2.163). In other words, "the will of human beings can act with virtue or evil" (*Ant.* 18.13). The decision to do what was right marked out the Pharisees. Josephus would have preferred nevertheless that people value the righteousness of the Essenes more highly. Josephus refers to Essenes swearing an oath of loyalty to practice piety towards God and to maintain righteousness (δίκαια φυλάξειν) towards other people (*War* 2.139). Yet Josephus does not indicate that a large part of the population esteemed the Essenes as being pious and righteous. The Essenes, he states, endeavored "to lead the approach of righteousness" (*Ant.* 18.18).[61] The Essenes were worthy of admiration (*Ant.* 18.20; cf. *War* 2.122) and seemed to exercise a kind of holy "solemnity" (*War* 2.119), but Josephus does not actually say that people admired them, whereas he states that the Pharisees were highly influential with the people (*Ant.* 18.15). They *appeared* to be more righteous than the others (*War* 1.110). They were considered the most accurate interpreters of the Law (*War* 2.110; 2.162). They had good relations with the community (*War* 2.166). The people were easily swayed because of the Pharisees' influence (*Ant.* 13.288).

Given all this, we may sense that the Pharisees did indeed have considerable social influence, enjoying the reputation of being the most righteous of all groups. On account of this reputation, people might naturally have looked to them for advice and leadership in certain situations, and for the specification of an accurate interpretation of the Law. However, if we are to determine whether they were religiously or

60. Dunn, "Pharisees, Sinners, and Jesus," 271-72.

61. See L. H. Feldman, trans., *Josephus in Nine Volumes. IX: Jewish Antiquities, Books XVIII–XX*, LCL (Cambridge, MA: Harvard University Press, 1965) 15-16 n. *e*.

politically authoritative, and able to make legally binding decisions, we will need to consider whether they participated in the judicial council of Jerusalem, headed by the high priest.

The Jerusalem Council

It has traditionally been assumed that the Pharisees were members of the Jerusalem judicial council in the early part of the first century and that they were involved in passing judgment on Jesus of Nazareth.[62] This is mainly derived from the presentation of the Fourth Gospel, where the Pharisees simply *are* the religious authorities in Jerusalem, or at least major players in the Jewish religious hierarchy. Matthew's polemical insertion of Pharisees where his source material has only "scribes" has also served to place them in the context of the court (Matt. 21:45; 22:34, 41; cf. 27:62). It therefore seems worthwhile to examine this traditional picture, since the identity of the Pharisees in the Fourth Gospel is important in terms of their relationship with John the Baptist.

In the synoptic Gospels, the meaning of the Greek word συνέδριον is very general, meaning any court, council, or assembly — not simply a Jewish court in Jerusalem. There are three instances of the word συνέδριον in the synoptic Gospels (Matt. 5:22; 10:17; Mark 13:9) where the meaning is clearly "court" in a general sense. In Matt. 5:22 the reference to a "Gehenna of fire" indicates that the συνέδριον is a heavenly court instituted at the time of final judgment. Matt. 10:17 and Mark 13:9 have συνέδρια, the plural form, and the reference seems to be to local courts.[63]

The court in Jerusalem was a different thing. The synoptic Gospels

62. For a classic exposition of the "Sanhedrin," see Schürer, *History of the Jewish People,* vol. 2, 199-226; see also Grabbe, *Judaism from Cyrus to Hadrian,* vol. 2, 386-95; J. S. McLaren, *Power and Politics in Palestine: The Jews and the Governing of Their Land 100 BC–AD 70* (Sheffield: JSOT Press, 1991) 210-18. For the meanings of various words translated as "Sanhedrin," see Sanders, *Judaism: Practice and Belief,* 473. In fact, the Greek word συνέδριον is, as Sanders notes, "a common Greek noun referring to a meeting of some sort." The Aramaic and Hebrew loanword סנהדרין refers more specifically to a deliberative body adjudicating a legal case. The Gospels reflect this understanding.

63. On village administration, see Schürer, *History of the Jewish People,* vol. 2, 184-90.

have this court involved in the handing over of Jesus to the Roman governor, Pontius Pilate. Mark 14:55 (cf. Matt. 26:59) has the chief priests καὶ ὅλον τὸ συνέδριον, "and the whole court," trying to get testimony against Jesus. They are unanimously opposed to him. The identification of the members of the συνέδριον refers back to "all the chief priests and the elders and scribes gathered together" (Mark 14:53; cf. 26:3). We are therefore given a clear indication of the composition of the court. The καί of Mark 14:55 (Matt. 26:59) is most likely emphatic, meaning "namely." The court is comprised of chief priests, elders, and scribes. Mark 15:1 has the same:

> And immediately, early [in the morning], the chief priests held a consultation with the scribes and the elders, namely (καί) the whole court, who bound Jesus and led [him] away and handed him over to Pilate.

In Luke 22:66 the result of the elders, chief priests, and scribes being gathered together is a συνέδριον. Interestingly, here Luke gives another term for the court: τὸ πρεσβυτέριον τοῦ λαοῦ, "the council of elders of the people." The passage reads:

> When day came, the council of elders of the people, both the chief priests and scribes, gathered together and led him into their court.

Elsewhere, those who are responsible for killing Jesus are identified as "the elders, the chief priests, and scribes" (Luke 9:22; cf. 20:19). In the synoptic Gospels, this group is also identified as not believing John. The chief priests, scribes, and elders are accused of killing John in the parable of the wicked tenants (Mark 12:1-12 = Matt. 21:33-46 = Luke 20:9-19), since the Gospels state that they understood that this parable was told against them (Mark 12:12 and parr.). However, we are not told specifically that the court took legal action against John. The implication may nevertheless be there.

In Acts 4:15 the words "but when they had ordered them to go aside out of the συνέδριον they began to confer with one another" would refer to going out of an assembly or court. The term συνέδριον here refers back to 4:5, "their rulers and elders and scribes" gathered together in Jerusalem, a group that included Caiaphas, John, Alexander, and "many of high-priestly descent." Peter addresses the body, "Rulers and elders of the people" (4:1).[64] The Sadducees are identified as agents of arrest and probably as representatives of this court.

Acts 5:21 has the high priest and his associates — who are all considered to be Sadducees — calling together τὸ συνέδριον καὶ πᾶσαν τὴν γερουσίαν τῶν υἱῶν 'Ισραήλ. It is not clear whether this description of the γερουσία refers to another body or to the court that has already been encountered. The word γερουσία may, like πρεσβυτέριον, be translated as "council of elders." At any rate, it is in this context, for the first time, that we encounter a prominent Pharisee — Gamaliel — who seems to have special influence. He is identified not simply as a Pharisee but also as a "teacher of the Law, respected by all the people" (Acts 5:34). This respect given him by the people immediately sets him apart from the chief priests, elders, and scribes, who are described in the Lucan narrative as fearing the people (Luke 19:48; 20:6, 19; cf. Mark 11:32; 12:12; Matt. 21:26, 46). Gamaliel defends the disciples of Jesus and his opinion prevails, presumably because of his popular power base, which the chief priests could not ignore.[65]

In Acts 6:12 Stephen is dragged before the συνέδριον by "the people, elders, and scribes." This court, like all the others in the synoptic Gospels and Acts, is presided over by the high priest. Later, Paul claims that the high priest and all the πρεσβυτέριον can testify to his action of persecuting the Church (Acts 22:5). The close relationship between the court and the high priest is clear. In Acts 9:1 Paul receives letters from the high priest to take to the synagogues of Damascus. This shows that the high priest was in charge of the legal issues affecting synagogues there. The reference to the πρεσβυτέριον in Acts 22:5 may indicate that it was decided in a convened court that Paul should be responsible for carrying these letters. The reference also points to the close relationship between the council and the high priest. The overwhelming impression we gain from the narrative of Luke-Acts is that the chief priests, scribes, and elders in Jerusalem were consistently hostile to Jesus and the early Church.[66]

Apart from the one reference to the Pharisee Gamaliel, there is

64. Schwartz argues that the scribes may have had to go outside for some of the business of the court proper, as is implied in Mark 14:53-55; see Schwartz, *Jewish Background of Christianity*, 92.

65. Mason, "Chief Priests, Sadducees, Pharisees," 150.

66. Ibid.

nothing in the Lucan narrative thus far that would lead us to associate Pharisees with this court presided over by the high priest. But suddenly, in Acts 23:6, we are told that the court, συνέδριον, has Pharisees in it: "the one part is of Sadducees and the other part of Pharisees." Only at this point are we informed about the philosophical persuasion of the members of the court, though perhaps we are to imagine that the chief priests, elders, and scribes have all along aligned themselves with either the Sadducees and Pharisees. Yet Luke has chosen not to mention Pharisees until this point, as if their presence in the court was insignificant or unnecessary to comment upon. It would seem unwise to assume from Luke's narrative either that there were no Pharisees in the court up until this point in time, ca. 57 CE, or that the court was equally divided between Pharisees and Sadducees around this time. Both may be literary exaggerations, and the historical truth may lie somewhere in between. In Acts 23 Paul plays off the Sadducean component against the Pharisaic component for his own ends; the result is an amusing story in which Paul comes off as the clever hero. It is certainly the same court, presided over by the high priest, in this case Ananias (Acts 23:2). That the court is convened by the Roman commander and not by the high priest may, however, signal that something has changed. In fact, in Josephus' account we find that the high priest (Ananus) could not convene a council without the Roman governor's permission (*Ant.* 20.199), but we are not told at what point this became necessary.

The situation at this later time is not, of course, the concern here. It will suffice to note that even if the author of Acts reports that in the late 50's the Jerusalem court was made up of one part Sadducees and one part Pharisees, and even if this is indeed historical, it in no way predisposes us to think that this was its composition in the 20's and 30's. However, if Pharisees did begin to find significant representation in the court in the years prior to the revolt, then this may explain why someone like the writer of Matthew, or of the Fourth Gospel, could assume that this must also have been the case during the time of Jesus.

The question of the nature and history of the judicial court or council in Jerusalem has been the subject of intense scholarly debate. Traditionally, there has been the notion that this court was called the "Sanhedrin" and that it was a consistent, fixed body, comparable to a body of the same name in rabbinic literature. In terms of what Josephus tells us about judicial councils, however, it may be a fundamental error to suppose that we are dealing with something consistent and cohesive, or even that the council was a "Sanhedrin," סנהדרין, which is a Hebrew loanword from Greek συνέδριον. The presentation of the council in the synoptic Gospels and, in particular, in Acts is vague.

Josephus calls the judicial council a γερουσία, "council of elders" (*Ant.* 5.15; 13.55). This Greek word and its equivalent, πρεσβυτέριον, reflect the Hebrew זקני העם (Exod. 19:7) or הזקנים (1 Sam. 16:4). While γερουσία derives from Greek antecedents (such as at Sparta), πρεσβυτέριον (τοῦ λαοῦ) was used in the LXX (e.g., Exod. 19:7 and 1 Kgs. 16:4 = 1 Sam. 16:4) for the judicial body. These terms appear at Luke 22:66 and Acts 5:21 (cf. Acts 22:5).

The judicial council was never a democratically elected body. Its administrative power was unclear. Throughout the Persian (539-331 BCE) and Hellenistic (331-63 BCE) periods, the high priest was the leader of the nation and supreme judge. Whatever court existed in Jerusalem would have been under his direct supervision. To what extent the high priest was guided by the γερουσία, or the γερουσία by the high priest, is impossible to ascertain. In Josephus' *Ant.* (12.138) the Seleucid king Antiochus III seizes Jerusalem (198 BCE) and reference is made to this council of elders.[67] When Jerusalem was made into a πόλις, a Greek city (ca. 175 BCE), the γερουσία remained an institution.[68] The βουλή and δῆμος — council and people — were the two main components of the political organization of every Greek city, and the Jerusalem βουλή was probably the same as the γερουσία. The institution was simply adapted and renamed. As Victor Tcherikover notes, the βουλή or γερουσία was always an aristocratic institution in both oriental and Greek cities.[69] It was certainly that in Jerusalem.[70] The use of the term πόλις continued on into the first century, so that the court or council could also be referred to as the βουλή (cf. *War* 2.331, 336; Mark 15:43). The official

67. So Goodman, *The Ruling Class of Judaea,* 113.

68. V. Tcherikover, *Hellenistic Civilization and the Jews* (New York: Atheneum, 1982) 162; Schürer, *History of the Jewish People,* vol. 2, 203.

69. Tcherikover, *Hellenistic Civilization and the Jews,* 162, 221, 302; idem, "Was Jerusalem a Polis?" *IEJ* 14 (1964) 61-78. Sanders notes that the members of the Hellenistic βουλή — comprising about 500 members — were to be elected by eligible voters; see Sanders, *Judaism: Practice and Belief,* 473. This probably still maintained the status quo of the aristocratic participation. Whether 500 members really served on the Jerusalem βουλή can remain an open question.

70. Mason, "Chief Priests, Sadducees, Pharisees," 159-60.

meeting place of the court was known as the βουλευτέριον and was located in or near the western cloister of the Temple (*War* 2.344; 4.243; 5.144; 6.354).

There may have been some reform of the γερουσία under Judas Maccabeus, but there is no reason to doubt that it remained a body made up of "the principal priests, the rich lay nobility, the great landowners and heads of clans," as Martin Hengel has suggested.[71] With the rule of the Hasmonean dynasty, in which the high priesthood and monarchy were combined (except in the case of queens, who could not become high priests), the γερουσία appears to have been under the supervision of the high priest/monarch.

In the reign of Salome Alexandra (76-67 BCE), Pharisees may have been highly influential in the γερουσία (*Ant.* 13.408-10; *War* 1.110-14). Josephus states that they were veritable "lords" during her reign. But such religious and political glory was short-lived. A civil war between her sons Aristobulus and Hyrcanus resulted in political instability, which the Roman commander Pompey, arriving in the East in 66 BCE, decided to sort out. He ostensibly restored Hyrcanus to the proper position as his mother's successor, but only as high priest, not as king.[72]

When the Romans occupied the whole region in 63 BCE political structures soon changed. Gabinius, governor of Syria from 57 to 55 BCE, divided the land so that it was administered by five συνέδρια (*Ant.* 14.91) or συνόδοι (*War* 1.170), based in Jerusalem, Gadara, Amathus, Jericho, and Sepphoris. These courts or councils were probably constituted by the nobles, the powerful wealthy class close to the Hasmonean dynasty.[73] Whatever they did, in 49 BCE it was the Jerusalem court — now called a συνέδριον — that summoned Herod to trial for ordering unlawful executions in *Galilee* (*Ant.* 14.165-79). The Jerusalem court remained a body supervised by the high priest (*War* 1.208-11)[74] and must have been authoritative in a way that the regional councils were not. According to Josephus, when Herod, backed by Rome, subsequently

71. M. Hengel, *Judaism and Hellenism: Studies in Their Encounter in Palestine during the Early Hellenistic Period,* vol. 1 (London: SCM, 1973) 26.

72. Hengel and Deines suggest that the Pharisees may have exerted influence on Hyrcanus II for a time, though their identification of Jews "of best repute" (*Ant.* 14.21) with Pharisees can be no more than a hypothesis; see Hengel and Deines, "E. P. Sanders' 'Common Judaism,' Jesus and the Pharisees," 57 n. 140.

73. Goodman, *The Ruling Class of Judaea,* 37 n. 11.

74. Ibid., 114.

took Jerusalem in 37 BCE, he executed all the members of this court (*Ant.* 14.175), namely, "forty-five chief men of the party of Antigonus" (*Ant.* 15.6), the deposed Hasmonean high priest. As for the Pharisees, it is at this point that Neusner sees them undergoing a radical change of emphasis as a result of Hillel's influence, so that they withdrew from political life.[75]

According to Josephus, Herod forced the population to swear an oath of loyalty to himself and the emperor, but the Pharisees refused (*Ant.* 17.41-46). Herod exempted them out of respect for a prominent Pharisee (Pollion or Samaias) who, when Herod was besieging Jerusalem, had advised the citizens to surrender. That he gave such advice was in no way meant to suggest that he was pro-Herod; the same Pharisee attacked the court for being intimidated by Herod's arrogance when he had appeared before them, and he said that they deserved whatever Herod would do to them because they had let justice be outraged on account of their cowardice. He advised the citizens to surrender, feeling that it was time for the court to receive its fate (*Ant.* 15.3), since it had failed to punish Herod for his illicit executions in Galilee. Josephus later reports that Pharisees were intent upon fighting and injuring Herod and that the dispensation given to them was not gratis, but depended on their paying a fine. This fine was in fact paid by the wife of Pheroras, and, upon discovering this, Herod executed both the Pharisees and those among his own household who were disposed towards them (*Ant.* 17.41-46). Two teachers, probably Pharisees, incited their disciples to tear down the image of the golden eagle that Herod had erected over the Temple gate (*War* 1.648-55; *Ant.* 17.149-67). If this is historical in its basic presentation, then Neusner's hypothesis that political withdrawal was essential for survival under Herod is highly probable. The Pharisees as a group seem to have been linked with opposition to Herodian power. It is hard to imagine that they were represented during that time on any judicial body in Jerusalem.

We may also question at this point whether the usual γερουσία,

75. Neusner, *Rabbinic Traditions about the Pharisees*, vol. 3, 306. The view of Sanders (*Judaism: Practice and Belief*, 478) that these forty-five supporters of Antigonus did not constitute all of the high priest's συνέδριον assumes that it had to have seventy or seventy-two members. There may have been only forty-five members in Antigonus' συνέδριον, for all we know. His point that this was not the same συνέδριον as the one convened by Hyrcanus, however, is important. Membership in the συνέδριον was not lifelong but rather depended on being chosen by whoever was in charge.

or "council of elders of the people," was in place. With Roman changes, we find Josephus using συνέδριον of the court in Jerusalem. But elsewhere, as Mason has noted, Josephus uses συνέδριον to refer to ad hoc meetings usually convened by the high priest (*War* 1.559, 571, 620, 640; 2.25, 81, 93; 6.342; *Ant.* 16.357-67; 17.46; 20.216, 217). The notion of its being an advisory council for the high priest (who was entirely aligned with Herod) may have eroded the basic concept of the court as somehow an independent judicial body composed of the elders of the people, over which the high priest presided. Moreover, after the cessation of direct Herodian rule of Judea, with the removal of Herod's incompetent son Archelaus in 6 CE, the Jerusalem court had to answer ultimately to the Roman prefect. Josephus explains that "the government of the state was aristocratic" (*Ant.* 20.251), a situation he traces back to Moses (*Ant.* 4.233; cf. 6.36), but what constituted the aristocracy was quite different under the Herodians than under the Hasmoneans or before. The high priesthood acted in accordance with Roman wishes (*War* 6.288-303; Acts 22:30). Herod had replaced the old succession of high priests with a new order that could be relied upon for loyalty to both himself and to Rome. He had drowned the last Hasmonean high priest, Aristobulus III, in his swimming pool in Jericho (*War* 1.437), and the high priests he appointed appear to have been from Babylonian or Alexandrian families. These men were despised by the populace. When Herod died, the people demanded that the Romans remove Herod's high-priestly order from power (*War* 2.7; 17.207).[76]

The high priest was still entrusted with the leadership, προστασία, of the nation (*Ant.* 20.251). Philo considered the high priest superior to any king as the divine was always superior to the human (*On the Embassy to Gaius* 278). But the legitimacy of the high priests after Herod murdered Aristobulus III was probably doubted by some. A high priest should have been chosen by a vote cast at an assembly (cf. *War* 2.7) or elected by lot (cf. *War* 4.155). He should have stayed in post until his death. But the high priests during the Herodian and Roman periods were appointed and deposed at the whim of the political leaders. During Herod's reign there were seven high priests, with an average length of office lasting less than five years each. Joseph ben Ellem held the post for just one day (*Ant.* 17.166). The Romans favored the family of Ananus ben Sethi, whose five sons held the high priesthood (*Ant.* 18.26; 20.198).

76. See Goodman, *The Ruling Class of Judaea*, 40-42.

Since the family owed its position to the Romans, their loyalty was assured. The high priest's garments were often kept in the Antonia fortress, headquarters of the Roman garrison in Jerusalem (*Ant.* 20.6-9). The dependency of the high priesthood on Rome could not have been more blatantly advertised.

The high priest headed the Jerusalem court and could convene a court as he saw fit (cf. Mark 14:53; Matt. 26:57). The court itself in this period was perhaps, as Martin Goodman has argued, "an extension of the High Priest."[77] It is significant that Josephus uses the word συνέδριον elsewhere to refer to a Roman senator's advisory council of friends (*War* 2.25), a *consilium*.[78] The Jerusalem συνέδριον may therefore have been an advisory council to aid the decision of the supreme judge, the high priest (*Ag. Ap.* 2.194), and could include anyone he deemed fit (*Ag. Ap.* 2.187, 194). Most of these appear to have been what the Gospels describe as "chief priests," ἀρχιερεῖς; they belonged to families from which the high priest might be drawn under the Herodian/Roman system.[79]

However, the high priest was seldom completely impervious to popular criticism, and at times he would have needed a few popular voices on a council. Pharisees may have begun to make inroads and started to serve more conspicuously in the court convened by the high priest a decade or so before the outbreak of the revolt against the Romans. According to Josephus, during the reign of Agrippa II and Berenice in 66 CE, under the procuratorship of Florus (64-66 CE), "the nobles (δυνατοί)

77. Ibid., 115; and see 111-12.

78. Ibid., 115. See also Sanders, *Judaism: Practice and Belief*, 472-80. Sanders (ibid., 485-86) distinguishes between the συνέδριον called by the high priest and the βουλή proper, which he identifies as a city council, though he admits that it did very little (cf. Josephus, *War* 2.293-405). However, the references in Josephus to a βουλή can be read as just another way of indicating the council convened by the high priest, as we find in Mark 15:43. That Florus could summon it, as could the Roman commander in Acts 23:6 (referring to a συνέδριον), indicates that the members of the high-priestly συνέδριον were known and could be called upon to assemble by the Roman administrators. We need not imagine that another assembly existed. If the membership varied, it may be that whoever called the body together could randomly remove those he did not particularly care for or call in others. See McLaren, *Power and Politics in Palestine*, 216, who suggests that there was a section of the community from whom members of the court could be gathered. Membership in any συνέδριον would therefore have been not a right, but a privilege bestowed on certain men in favor with the current powers.

79. Cf. *m. Ketub.* 13:1-2; *m. Ohol.* 17:5; Schürer, *History of the Jewish People*, vol. 2, 232-35; Goodman, *The Ruling Class of Judaea*, 119-20.

got together with the chief priests, as did the notables of the Pharisees and . . . took counsel on what was to be done" (*War* 2.411). Pharisees appear here, whereas they do not appear in Josephus' earlier accounts of council meetings. Simon, the son of Gamaliel, was able to sway the high priests, Ananus and Jesus son of Gamala, at the time of Josephus' troubles in Galilee in ca. 63 CE (*Life* 191-98). We may also consider the evidence of Acts 23:6, where Pharisees and Sadducees are both well represented in the court. If Pharisees were included in this court by the late 50's, their inclusion may indicate that the high priest was forced to consider their opinions because of their popularity with the people. Their inclusion was then a matter of pragmatism on the part of the high priests who, in the face of growing unrest, felt they could not act in disregard of Pharisaic advice. The comment by Josephus that Sadducees, upon attainment of some office, had to act according to the formulas of the Pharisees, may also relate to this time prior to the revolt (*Ant.* 17.17; cf. *b. Yoma* 19b), when the chief priests' increasingly vulnerable position made them more prone to consider popular sentiment.

At any rate, a συνέδριον summoned by the high priest was not necessarily a whole court with fixed legal procedures, since it was probably his decision alone that constituted the judgment. In Josephus' account of the execution of James, Jesus' brother, the high priest summons a "συνέδριον of judges" (*Ant.* 20.200), which apparently was a selection of citizens of his own choosing that acted as the judicial council. In other words, the council as an institution was conceptually consistent, but the membership of the council might alter depending on the circumstances and the decision of the high priest. Some references to the συνέδριον may be to a small group of leading citizens of the city whom the high priest used as advisers in a particular situation and who might meet anywhere, even in the house of the high priest. Other references might be to a large group sitting in judgment in the βουλευτέριον. One could be a member of the βουλή without necessarily participating in every single meeting to decide a case.

If there were Pharisees in the court at the time of John, they would have been personally chosen by the high priest because of their status, wealth, and influence. They needed to belong to the ruling class or be associated with it.[80] One person who is traditionally understood to have

80. See Goodman, *The Ruling Class of Judaea,* 29-50 and T. Rajak, *Josephus: The Historian and His Society* (London: Duckworth, 1983) 65-143 on the nature of this class.

been a Pharisee in the court was Joseph of Arimathea. In Mark's Gospel he is described as a "respected member of the council (εὐσχήμων βουλευτής) who was himself waiting eagerly for the kingdom of God" (Mark 15:43). Luke (23:50-51) has:

> And there was a man named Joseph, a member of the council (βουλευτὴς ὑπάρχων) who was good and righteous. He was not in agreement with their will and action. He came from Arimathea, a Jewish city, and he was waiting eagerly for the kingdom of God.

Matthew severs Joseph from the court by stating that Joseph was simply a "rich man from Arimathea" and rewrites the reference to his waiting for the kingdom of God to read bluntly, "he was also a disciple of Jesus" (Matt. 27:57). It is interesting that although Matthew does not want Joseph to be associated with the court that condemned Jesus, he says that he was a rich man, as though his wealth could be deduced from his membership of the court.[81]

In the Fourth Gospel, Joseph of Arimathea is also described as a disciple of Jesus, though a secret one. When he takes the body of Jesus down from the cross, he has with him Nicodemus, who is described in John 3:1 as a "Pharisee." If Joseph and Nicodemus were Pharisees, their presence on the court would have been due to their wealth and nobility and to the high priest's approval of them. Even in the case of Gamaliel, his presence in the court may have had much more to do with these factors than with his status as a learned teacher within the Pharisaic "philosophy." Josephus says of Gamaliel's son Simon that he was of "a very noble family" (*Life* 191). In other words, in the period of Jesus, the number of Pharisees in the court would probably have depended on the number of nobles in favor with the high priest who happened to be Pharisees. There is no reason to doubt, however, the hierocratic nature of the court. It should also be noted, given the above, that just because Joseph of Arimathea was a member of the βουλή does not mean that he was part of the high priest's συνέδριον on the night of Jesus' arrest. He may have been, but this is not stated in our material, and it is not a necessary inference.

To lay to rest the traditional picture once and for all, we will now

81. Wealth was probably an essential prerequisite for entry into the court; see Goodman, *The Ruling Class of Judaea,* 34-35, 46, 53.

consider the rabbinic evidence. What are we to make of detailed information given in rabbinic literature about a body known as the Beth Din (or Beth Din ha-Gadol, *m. Sanh.* 11:2)? The word "Sanhedrin" occurs only twice in the Mishnah tractate of that name, and only once do we find "Great Sanhedrin" (*m. Sanh.* 1:6; cf. *m. Mid.* 5:4). Although it has been customary in scholarship to equate the two bodies — the Beth Din or Sanhedrin of the Mishnah and the συνέδριον, γερουσία, πρεσβυτέριον, or βουλή of the synoptic Gospels and Josephus[82] — the descriptions of the two are so divergent as to make their equation almost inconceivable. In the Mishnah we have an assembly made up of seventy or seventy-one members, presided over by זוגות or "pairs" of Pharisaic masters (including Gamaliel, who in Acts 5:34 is certainly not head of the court). None of these is a high priest. They meet in the לשכת הגזית, the chamber of hewn stone. In the New Testament and Josephus the court is made up of an unspecified number of people, headed by the high priest, who officially meet in the βουλευτέριον, even though meetings could be arranged elsewhere when the council was summoned (probably not in its entirety) for an ad hoc meeting. The Gospels record that the court which tried Jesus met in the high priest's house (Matt. 26:3, 57; Mark 14:53-54; Luke 22:54; John 18:15).

Although it has been suggested that the rabbinic Sanhedrin is a later rabbinic institution, it is more likely that the Beth Din or Great Sanhedrin in Jerusalem during the first century was a Pharisaic court that dealt with matters of the school, and not a general court at all. The name "Great Sanhedrin" implies that there were lesser "sanhedrins" — local Pharisaic courts — scattered around the country. The absence of political rulings coming from this period confirms that the Pharisaic Beth Din had no authority to pass judgments on concerns not within the jurisdiction of the sect. As Neusner has argued, nearly all of the verifiably early decisions of the Pharisaic masters concern sectarian issues. The one exception is the case of Gamaliel; he initiated laws that had general influence.[83] It was surely his unusual position as a member of the high-priestly Jerusalem court as well as his status as one of the leaders of the Pharisaic Beth Din that enabled this to happen. The real power was in the court presided over by the high priest.

82. E.g., Schürer, *History of the Jewish People,* vol. 2, 199-226, esp. 211, 215, 217, 225-26.

83. Neusner, *Rabbinic Traditions about the Pharisees,* vol. 3, 301-18; cf. vol. 1, 341-76 on Gamaliel.

It was the high priest and his συνέδριον that had the sole power to manage Judean judicial affairs under the Romans, and then only with Roman approval.[84] Sometime after the destruction of the Temple, the Beth Din or Sanhedrin of the Mishnah may have become the religious court governing the land, and only then have gained the authority to pass far-reaching judgments. Some scholars have distinguished between a "lesser Sanhedrin" made up of priests that acted politically and a "great Sanhedrin" made up of scribes that issued religious rulings.[85] This is a dubious distinction; to remove religious authority from the priesthood seems ill-founded.

A comparative model for a specific self-governing Pharisaic court may be found in the Essene court. According to Philo the authorities treated the Essenes as a self-governing entity (*Every Good Man Is Free* 90–91). Josephus states that they had their own court made up of no less than one hundred men to decide verdicts. They could even pass a sentence of death in the case of blasphemy (against Moses) (*War* 2.145). In the *Damascus Document,* we find ample evidence of an Essene judicial system functioning independently (CD 9:17-23; 12:3-7; 15:12-15). If guilty of a capital offense, the culprit was to be excluded from the pure meal, which, according to Josephus, resulted in death (*War* 2.143-44).

Finally, before we come to the important issue of the identity of the Pharisees in the Fourth Gospel and their relationship with John, it is worth stressing that at no point in Josephus do we get the impression that the Pharisees and the chief priests were in league with one another, unless they were forced by circumstances and pragmatism. In general, the Pharisees' stance with the people led them to look critically at the chief priests. Josephus himself admits that chief priests were known to commit crimes (*Ant.* 20.181, 206-07). The characterization of the chief priests as corrupt is found in the Pseudepigrapha (*Adam and Eve* 29:3, interpolation; *2 Apoc. Bar.* 10:18; *Testament of Moses* 7) and in *Targum Pseudo-Jonathan* (1 Sam. 2:17, 29; Isa. 17:11; 24:5; 28:1; Jer. 7:9; 8:10; 6:13; 23:11), as Craig

84. Schürer, *History of the Jewish People,* vol. 2, 208-10.

85. A. Büchler, *Das Synedrion in Jerusalem und das Grosse Beth-Din in der Quaderkammer des Jerusalemischen Tempels* (Vienna: Hölder, 1902) 1-194; H. Mantel, *Studies in the History of the Sanhedrin* (Cambridge, MA: Harvard University Press, 1961) 61-101; E. Lohse, "συνέδριον," *TDNT* 7 (1971) 862; E. Rivkin, "Beth Din, Boule, Sanhedrin: A Tragedy of Errors," *HUCA* 17 (1975) 181-99.

Evans has pointed out.[86] More importantly, Evans notes the strongly critical tradition of rabbinic literature when it comes to the chief priests in Jerusalem. Simon the son of Gamaliel protests their gross inflation of the prices of Temple sacrifices; a pair of doves is sold for a gold dinar (*m. Ker.* 1:7). In the Tosephta, the powerful priests steal tithes (hides) from the poorer priests, leaving them to starve (*t. Menaḥ.* 13:18-19; cf. *t. Zebaḥ.* 11:16-17; *b. Pesaḥ. 57a; Ant.* 20.206-07). The chief priests use bribery and are wicked (*Pesiq. R.* 47:4). Woes are pronounced on the iniquities of the high-priestly families of the Herodian period (*t. Menaḥ.* 13:21; cf. *b. Pesaḥ.* 57a; *t. Zebaḥ.* 11:16-17; *y. Maʿaś. Š.* 5:15). These passages all reflect a highly negative attitude to the chief priestly hierarchy.

To conclude this preliminary discussion, the Pharisees at the time of John the Baptist and Jesus were influential socially, but had little judicial power unless one of their number happened, like Gamaliel, to be of a wealthy, aristocratic family in favor with the high priest. They may have been represented in the γερουσία (συνέδριον) to some degree, but their representation may not have been significant until nearer the time of the revolt. The judicial council was an institution, but the high priest could form an ad hoc συνέδριον to act in specific cases. Rabbinic traditions concerning a Pharisaic court, or Sanhedrin, are best understood as relating to a body that in the Herodian period had no political authority and no religious authority concerning matters beyond the jurisdiction of the sect. If laws were made concerning Temple matters and related concerns, these were "ideal world" laws made by a body that hoped to attain control over these spheres in due course. Pharisees may have gained more legal power after the destruction of the Temple and consolidated this religious power in the Land of Israel in the second century through the synagogues. The popular assessment of the corruption of the chief priests was preserved in traditions found in a variety of sources, including rabbinic literature. Nothing indicates that the chief priests and the Pharisees formed a united front and constituted legal authorities in Jerusalem or elsewhere. While absence of evidence does not necessarily mean evidence of absence, the diverse material from Mark, Luke-Acts, Josephus, and rabbinic sources coheres in providing the impression that Pharisees

86. C. A. Evans, "Opposition to the Temple: Jesus and the Dead Sea Scrolls," in *Jesus and the Dead Sea Scrolls,* ed. J. H. Charlesworth (New York: Doubleday, 1992) 235-53.

were neither closely associated with the chief priests nor well represented in the judicial council of Jerusalem.

The Pharisees in the Fourth Gospel

The Fourth Gospel was probably written towards the end of the first century. This general time frame corresponds to the period of Yavneh (Jamnia) in rabbinic tradition (ca. 70-130 CE). At Yavneh Yohanan ben Zakkai apparently established an academy that developed Pharisaic tradition and synthesized elements of Judaism beyond Pharisaism.[87] The relationship between this academy and those in charge of the synagogues in the Land of Israel and the Diaspora is unclear. However, if synagogues had previously been largely under the control of priests, and ultimately the high priest in Jerusalem, it would be rash to imagine that, after 70 CE, priests suddenly and completely lost all importance and power in the multifarious synagogues of the Jewish world. Unyielding generalizations should be resisted here. Josephus' continuing claims for the prerogatives of the priesthood in scriptural interpretation mitigates any simplistic notion that the Pharisees swiftly replaced priests as the sole religious authorities in the Yavneh period.[88] More likely, without the Temple and the authority of the high priest, Jewish religious leadership devolved to communities, with synagogues as central religious foci. A coalition of priestly and proto-rabbinic elements may have obtained during this period in the synagogues of the Land of Israel. At any rate, it is such a coalition of priests and Pharisees that we encounter in the Fourth Gospel as representing Jewish religious authority. Here the Pharisees are clearly in league with the chief priests or rulers. The suspicion that this relationship reflects the historical situation in the Land of Israel *after* the destruction of the Temple has been a prime reason to date this Gospel fairly late. The Gospel writer read the situation of his own age back into the age of Jesus.

87. See S. J. D. Cohen, "The Significance of Yavneh: Pharisees, Rabbis, and the End of Jewish Sectarianism," *HUCA* 55 (1984) 27-53.

88. See S. N. Mason, "Priesthood in Josephus and the 'Pharisaic Revolution,'" *JBL* 107 (1988) 657-61, who argues against Rivkin's notion of a "Pharisaic revolution" at the end of the first century (Rivkin, *A Hidden Revolution*).

Some scholars think that the writer of the Fourth Gospel uses the term Ἰουδαῖοι, "Judeans" or "Jews," in a distinctive way so that, although the label can refer to Jews in general, it can at other times refer strictly to the Judean (Jerusalem) authorities.[89] In John 1:19-27 the Ἰουδαῖοι in Jerusalem send priests and Levites to investigate John the Baptist. They are clearly the Judean authorities, or members of the Jerusalem court, who had the power to send such a deputation. Schwartz has argued convincingly that this passage reflects a usage in which a scribe could be called a Levite in some cases.[90] We may conjecture that some kind of source document or oral tradition available to the fourth evangelist mentioned an investigation of John by the Jerusalem authorities. But the reference to "Pharisees" in John 1:24 alerts us to a further distinctive use of terms in the Fourth Gospel, for the "Pharisees" are either equated with the "Jews" of 1:19 or are part of their number. The priests and the Levites are sent by "the Pharisees," that is, the Ἰουδαῖοι.

In John 3:1 Nicodemus is identified as "a man from the Pharisees" and "a ruler of the Jews." It is unclear whether the terms are synonymous, though it appears highly likely. Nicodemus appears only in the Fourth Gospel, but he may well have been a historical figure. Rabbinic sources describe a Naqdimon ben Gurion (or Bunai), a wealthy and generous man of pre-70 Jerusalem (*b. Giṭ.* 56a; *b. Taʿan.* 19b-20a; *Gen. Rab.* 41:1; 98:8; *Lam. Rab.* 1:31; *Eccl. Rab.* 7:11; *ʾAbot R. Nat.* [A] 6, [B] 13). His adult daughter is described as being in much hardship during the revolt (*t. Ketub.* 5:9-10; cf. *Sifre Deut.* 305), which, if true, may mean he was a contemporary of Jesus. Josephus mentions a certain Gorion (Gurion) the son of Nicomedes (Nicodemus?) in a list of Jewish officials who negotiated with the besieged Roman garrison (*War* 2.451).[91] The tradi-

89. See S. Zeitlin, "The Halaka in the Gospels and Its Relation to the Jewish Law in the Time of Jesus," *HUCA* 1 (1924) 357-63; U. C. von Wahlde, "The Johannine 'Jews': A Critical Survey," *NTS* 28/1 (1982) 33-60; M. Lowe, "Who Were the *Ioudaioi?*" *NovT* 18 (1976) 101-30.

90. Schwartz (1992), 94-95. The Ἰουδαῖοι here are the "Judean authorities," as von Wahlde, "The Johannine 'Jews,'" has argued. His chart (pp. 39-40) identifies where the writer of the Gospel uses Ἰουδαῖοι to refer to authorities and/or people; in general, this is plain from the context.

91. Cf. T. Ilan, "The Attraction of Aristocratic Women to Pharisaism during the Second Temple Period," *HTR* 88 (1995) 20, who equates this figure with Nicodemus himself. Transpositions of letters could happen, but this would involve a transposition of name placement as well. Josephus' reference to a certain Gurion (*War* 4.358) may

tional picture of Nicodemus has it that he was elderly at the time he met Jesus (if he did so), but nothing in the account tells us this. A man so wealthy and renowned may very well have been included in the court. It is not stated in rabbinic sources that he was a Pharisee or a "sage."

John 4:1, 3 states, "When Jesus learned that the Pharisees had heard, 'Jesus is making and baptizing more disciples than John'. . . he left Judea and went off again into Galilee." Evidently, Jesus is afraid of action against him instigated by the Pharisees and leaves the area of their apparent jurisdiction (Judea). Again, they appear to be equated with the Jerusalem or Judean authorities. We will return to this passage below.

John 7:32-52 has the chief priests and Pharisees comprising the Jerusalem council and standing in close association with one another. Together they have authority to send court officials, ὑπηρέται, to arrest Jesus, and they order them to do so, though they do not succeed. The ὑπηρέται go back to the "chief priests and Pharisees" (7:45), and the Pharisees ask them if they too have been deceived. They ask, "Has any of the rulers or the Pharisees believed in him?" (7:48). Again, there is a possible distinction between ruler and Pharisee, as in the description of Nicodemus. But both were members of the court. Nicodemus, in fact, appears in this judicial context to ask that they give Jesus a fair hearing (7:50).[92]

John 8:12-30 describes Jesus' conversation with the "Pharisees" (8:22), who claim that his testimony about himself is not valid. This is based on Deut. 19:15 (cf. 17:6), which states that the evidence of two witnesses is needed. The point is not a distinctively Pharisaic one. Moreover, the conversation takes place in the treasury, within the Temple precincts, in the priestly domain (8:20).

A blind man who has been healed by Jesus on the Sabbath by the pool of Siloam is brought to the "Pharisees" in John 9:13. The Pharisees debate whether a man from God would heal on the Sabbath (9:16). Later they react to Jesus' statement that his coming into the world was for judgment so that those who do not see may see and those who see may

---

also refer to someone of the same family. This characterization of Gurion is remarkably like the characterization of Nicodemus in the Fourth Gospel.

92. John 7:53–8:11 will not be considered here, since it is widely understood to be an insertion into the Fourth Gospel from a tradition that has more in common with the synoptic Gospels. The Pharisees who appear here are probably not to be equated with the characteristic Ἰουδαῖοι of the Fourth Gospel.

become blind, by saying: "But we are surely not blind, are we?" (9:40). Jesus responds that they retain their sin because they say "we see."

In John 11:45-46 it is clear that the "Pharisees" are in authority. After the raising of Lazarus, some people go to them. "And the chief priests and the Pharisees gathered together the court, and said, 'What are we to do?'" Later the "chief priests and the Pharisees" give orders that anyone who knows where Jesus is should let them know so they can arrest him (11:57).[93]

In John 12:10 it is stated that the "chief priests" planned to put Lazarus to death as well as Jesus. The Pharisees are curiously missing, but they appear on their own in John 12:19, when they note Jesus' entry into Jerusalem and say to one another, "You see that there is nothing you can do. Look, the whole world has gone after him." The Pharisees are here directly opposite in character to the Pharisees of Luke at precisely this instant. In Luke (19:39-40) the Pharisees are nervous about Jesus' noisy entry into the city, but as worried supporters rather than as antagonists. They address him as "teacher" and ask him to order his disciples to stop praising God "with a loud voice" for the acts of power they had seen. The Pharisees clearly fear the wrath of the authorities; they are not acting as judicial authorities themselves. In the Lucan narrative, this is the Pharisees' last appearance. They simply vanish after this warning, as if they would have nothing to do with Jesus in Jerusalem itself.

John 12:42 reads, "Nevertheless, many even from the rulers believed in him, but because of the Pharisees they did not confess it, in order that they should not be put out of the synagogue." If we believe Acts, Paul got letters from the high priest and court to punish people who professed that Jesus was the Messiah; he did not receive such authority from the Pharisaic leaders.[94] The language of the Fourth Gospel again reflects the situation

93. Raymond Brown asks whether this is a mistake, for the Pharisees had no authority to convene a court like this. But it is surely not a case of simplification, as Brown suggests, but of a deliberate attempt to remake the court in a later image; see R. E. Brown, *The Gospel According to John I–XII* (Garden City, NY: Doubleday, 1966) 439.

94. Acts 9:1-2, "Saul . . . went to the high priest and asked him for letters to the synagogues in Damascus, so that if he found any who belonged to the way, men or women, he might bring them bound to Jerusalem." Acts 22:5, ". . . as the high priest and the whole council of elders can witness concerning me. From them I received also letters to the brothers in Damascus, and I went there in order to bind those who were there and to bring them back to Jerusalem for punishment." Acts 26:12, "I was traveling to Damascus with the authority and commission of the chief priests."

of a later time, when synagogue authorities appear to have wished to expel Christians from worship. This attitude is represented in the *Birkat ha-Minim,* part of the daily *Amidah* that was purportedly approved by Gamaliel II in the last decades of the first century (*b. Ber.* 28b). The *Birkat ha-Minim* either specifically cursed מינים, the Christians, or implicitly cursed them (as נוצרים, "heretics").[95] It is probably this situation that the Gospel writer addresses.

Judas appears in Gethsemane in John 18:3 with a σπεῖρα ("maniple, cohort")[96] and ὑπηρέται from the "chief priests and Pharisees." In John 7:32-52, the ὑπηρέται are sent out by order of the court (comprised of chief priests and Pharisees). The Pharisees then completely and suddenly disappear from the Passion account, which concentrates purely on characterizing the opposition to Jesus as being 'Ιουδαῖοι in general (18:20, 21, 36; 19:7, 12, 14, 31), though when being more specific they are described simply as "chief priests and ὑπηρέται" (19:6; cf. 19:15). Presumably the abbreviation "the Jews" was used by John for "the chief priests/rulers of the Jews" (John 19:21) here as elsewhere (John 1:19; 2:18, 20; 3:25; 5:10, 15, 16, 18; 7:1, 11, 13, 15, 35; 8:22, 31, 48, 52, 57; 10:24, 31, 33; 11:8; 13:33; 18:12, 14, 31, 36, 38; 19:7, 12, 14, 31, 38; 20:19) because it served to mass the Jews into one homogeneous throng opposed to Jesus.

The writer of the Fourth Gospel was clearly not all that concerned to portray an accurate historical picture of who was responsible for the death of Jesus. In his view, the 'Ιουδαῖοι were responsible; the people were represented by their leaders. The writer of the Gospel wanted to draw a wedge between the Jews and his own group. The statements that various people "feared the Jews" (7:13; 9:22; 19:38; 20:19) may be understood to reflect some historical situation in which people feared the Judean authorities, that is, the chief priests, elders, and scribes (the Jerusalem court), but it was clearly of no interest to the writer to be specific about this. The statement that many of the rulers believed in Jesus secretly but did not say so because they were afraid of the

95. See J. E. Taylor, *Christians and the Holy Places: The Myth of Jewish-Christian Origins* (Oxford: Clarendon, 1993) 26-27, contra Reuven Kimelman, "The *Birkat Ha-Minim* and the Lack of Evidence for an Anti-Christian Jewish Prayer in Late Antiquity," in *Jewish and Christian Self-Definition. Volume Two: Aspects of Judaism in the Graeco-Roman Period,* ed. E. P. Sanders (Philadelphia: Fortress, 1981) 226-44.

96. See F. Millar, "Reflections on the Trials of Jesus," in *A Tribute to Geza Vermes: Essays on Jewish and Christian Literature and History,* ed. P. R. Davies and R. T. White (Sheffield: JSOT Press, 1990) 370.

"Pharisees" (John 12:42) shows an attempt to distinguish among the Judean authorities some (chief priests/rulers) who believed and others (Pharisees) who did not. But Nicodemus is described as being both a ruler and a Pharisee, as well as a believer in Jesus (3:1-2; cf. 7:48). The picture we get from the Fourth Gospel is therefore muddled.

There are no Sadducees in the Fourth Gospel. It is possible that the writer replaced "Sadducees" in his source material with "Pharisees," finding the references to Sadducees obsolete. Alternatively, we may look to the word ὑπηρέται and conjecture that this appeared more frequently in the source material for the Gospel and that at times the writer substituted "Pharisees" instead. As we saw above, the ὑπηρέται may be identified with the חזנים of the Mishnah: levitical scribes who served the high priest (cf. Mark 14:53-55). At the time of the Gospel writer (ca. 90-120 CE), the ὑπηρέται serving local courts may generally have been Pharisees (though we cannot know), but this was not the case at the time of Jesus and John. Whatever the case, it would be extremely unwise to read the "Pharisees" of the Fourth Gospel as being the historical Pharisees of Jesus' time. The word "Pharisee" appears to have been inserted into whatever material the Gospel writer possessed, in order to make the story more understandable to his own community in his own time. If there are authentic historical traditions contained in the Fourth Gospel, which seems very likely, it is necessary to read behind the terminology of Ἰουδαῖοι and "Pharisees" to arrive at what may have been mentioned in John's sources. However, it seems highly improbable, given the foregoing discussion, that Pharisees actually appeared in the source material.

To conclude this section, the portrayal of the Pharisees in the Fourth Gospel makes them part of the class of Ἰουδαῖοι who oppose Jesus and especially links them with the Jerusalem court. "Pharisees" can therefore at times simply be synonymous with "members of the court," who seem to hold a collective power. Again, this scenario most likely reflects a later situation, after the destruction of the Temple, which was the high priest's power base. There could be no high priest without a Temple. The real focus of the Fourth Gospel is to attack the Jewish authorities opposing the community in which the Gospel was shaped (though probably not finally redacted), possibly somewhere in the Land of Israel. Since the Gospel writer recognized that the Jewish community of his time was led by people who stood in the tradition of the Pharisees (and chief priests), "Pharisees" were read back into historical traditions in order to put them in opposition to Jesus.

John and the Pharisees in the Fourth Gospel

According to John 1:19, John the Baptist's testimony about Jesus was given "when the Jews sent priests and Levites from Jerusalem to ask him, 'Who are you?'" In John 1:24 we are then told that the members of this delegation "had been sent from the Pharisees."

What are to make of this situation? If the "Pharisees" of the Fourth Gospel are not really historical Pharisees, but indicative of either the Judean authorities in Jerusalem or the Jewish legal authorities in the Land of Israel around the turn of the first century, then we may think of two possible scenarios.

In the first scenario, we could consider this story to reflect a historical tradition in which the Judean authorities sent a deputation to ask John who he was and what he was doing. In this case, we may have in John 1:19 an allusion to what is found in the synoptic Gospels, for in the parable of the wicked tenants the chief priests, scribes, and elders are accused of not believing and even of killing John (Mark 12:1-12 = Matt. 21:33-46 = Luke 20:9-19).[97] But we are not given any details of specific action taken against John by the Jerusalem court in any of our sources. Rather, the direct responsibility for the death of John rests with the tetrarch Herod Antipas (Mark 5:17-29 = Matt. 14:3-12; cf. Luke 3:19-20; Mark 6:16; 9:9; so also Josephus, *Ant.* 18.116-19). It is only in the Fourth Gospel that we get a reference to the authorities' specific inquiries about John. In a sense, the questions put to John by the "priests and Levites from Jerusalem" in John 1:19-25 are similar to the one the chief priests, elders, and scribes ask Jesus in Mark 11:28 (= Matt. 21:23; Luke 20:2): "By what authority do you do these things?" The priests and Levites (= scribes) proceed to ask John, "Why then do you baptize if you are neither the Messiah, nor Elijah, nor the prophet?" (John 1:25). The question implies that John's immersion of people required divine authority.

Comparisons with synoptic material might make the questions appear critical and intended to trap John. However, it may be wrong to conclude that the Jerusalem delegation regarded John as a charlatan, and it may be misguided to look to the synoptics for understanding the Johannine narrative. We are not told what the Jerusalem authorities came to think about John or even that they were implicitly

97. See below, pp. 252-55.

hostile to him. In the synoptic Gospels, the narratives have the chief priests, elders, and scribes debating with each other about how to respond to Jesus' query of whether John's immersion was authorized by God or human beings. They argue among themselves, "If we say 'from Heaven,' he will say, 'Why then did you not believe him?'" (Mark 11:31 = Matt. 21:25 = Luke 20:5).[98] But here in the Fourth Gospel there is no hint that the authorities are cynical about John. John gives his response, and they are silent. They do not murmur or plot against him. Jesus certainly leaves Judea (the area of their jurisdiction) and goes to Galilee in response to the news that the "Pharisees" have heard he is making and baptizing more disciples than John (4:1, 3).[99] We can conclude from this story, then, that the authorities were understood to be hostile to *Jesus.* In the narrative, Jesus realizes that his position is unsafe. But the story does not say or even imply that *John* was unsafe. John clearly does not leave Judea, which in terms of Roman control included Samaria and therefore Aenon near Salim, where he was baptizing.

It is probably wrong to understand Ἰουδαῖοι and "Pharisees" here as a reference to the Jerusalem council of the time of Jesus and John. So here we must resort to a second scenario, which sees these references in light of the time when the Gospel was written. The writer sets up a deputation from the Jewish authorities in order to ask John who he is, eschatologically, so that John can affirm to everyone that he is not the Christ. We are told nothing in this section about whether the Jerusalem delegation was for or against John, but it is implied that he did not need to fear the authorities.

In fact, the words attributed to Jesus concerning John the Baptist in John 5:31-36 suggest that "the Ἰουδαῖοι" whom he is addressing (John 5:16-19) held John in high regard. The passage reads:

> If I bear witness concerning myself, my witness is not true. But there is another witness concerning me, and I know[100] that the witness is true which he witnessed concerning me. You sent [people] to John,

98. We will consider the possibility that John was identified with Elijah in Chapter 6.

99. John 4:2 is usually considered a scribal addition to the text. There is no reason to doubt this view.

100. Some late manuscripts have "we know," οἴδαμεν. "You [pl.] know," οἴδατε, also has some manuscript support.

> and he witnessed to the truth. I receive [authority] not by human witness, but I say these things in order that you may be saved. *He was a light, burning and shining. You were willing to rejoice for a time in his light.* But I have the greater witness than John: the works that the Father has given me in order that I should complete them, these works that I do, they witness concerning me that the Father has sent me. (John 5:31-36)

Jesus specifically states here that John — who is referred to in the past tense and is therefore already dead — was recognized by "the 'Ιουδαῖοι," who "rejoiced for a time in his light." These are evidently the same 'Ιουδαῖοι who sent the deputation to question John back in 1:19-25. The point of this passage is that John should be recognized by them as having pointed to Jesus. They do not recognize this, nor do they accept that Jesus is performing works that bear witness to the fact that he is sent by God. But Jesus uses the testimony of John as a weighty point. If the "Jews" of the Gospel did not accept John as righteous, then this would be a useless form of argument, for they could dismiss John himself as a false prophet. The testimony of John is a significant factor in proving Jesus' status only if both parties accept him as worthy of great respect. The implicit understanding is that John should be held in high regard, and his statements should be valued. Therefore, in this story Jesus stresses his witness concerning him.[101] That Jesus uses evidence he expects his hearers to recognize as important is made clear in that he finishes his argument by pointing to Scripture (5:39-47), especially the final two verses: "If you believed Moses, you would believe me, for he wrote concerning me. But if you do not believe the things he wrote, how will you believe what I say?"[102]

All this means that we should probably read the passages concerning John's interaction with the 'Ιουδαῖοι in the Fourth Gospel as re-

101. Webb notes that John the Baptist is called a witness in one way or another by means of the μαρτυρ- word group, in John 1:7 (2x), 8, 15, 32, 34; 3:26; 5:33, 34, 36 and possibly 3:32 (2x), 33. The idea is found also in 1:35-7; 3:27-30; 10:41; R. L. Webb, *John the Baptizer and Prophet: A Socio-Historical Study* (Sheffield: JSOT Press, 1991)75 n. 84.

102. Wink notes that " 'The Jews' are again the focus of indictment in this section . . . not John's disciples"; W. Wink, *John the Baptist in the Gospel Tradition* (Cambridge: Cambridge University Press, 1968) 97. It is for this reason that their accuser is Moses, not John.

flecting a positive relationship in terms of the Johannine narrative. So, despite the questions voiced by the priests and Levites at the beginning of the Gospel, their reaction to John is favorable; they accept that he is not the Messiah, Elijah, or the "prophet," but one who wishes to make straight the way of the Lord. He baptizes with water in preparation for one coming after him (John 1:19-28). They recognize him as a burning, shining light and rejoice in the time he is around. Yet, since the Ἰουδαῖοι here are really the synagogue authorities of the writer's own age — read back into the narrative as the Jerusalem authorities — we should not conclude that the Jerusalem court (chief priests, elders, and scribes) of John's time did in fact approve of him. Rather, the Jewish authorities of the writer's own time approved of John, and these stood in the Pharisaic tradition.

The Fourth Gospel does not specify who opposed John. It assumes that everyone hearing or reading the Gospel has prior knowledge concerning him, as if his story was so well-known that it was not necessary to tell. For example, in 3:24 it is stated, "John, of course, had not yet been thrown into prison." But nowhere in the Gospel does the writer describe John's arrest or death or relate who engineered it. The reader is expected to know the famous story of John already. John's job in the Fourth Gospel is to witness to Jesus; anything else about him is irrelevant.[103] John must prefigure Jesus rather than remain independent. To achieve this effect, the fourth evangelist needed to tell little of John's story beyond reference to a few small amendments of the tradition. This would not have been necessary unless the Gospel writer could say, in a manner of speaking, to the Jews of his own time and place, "Well, you accept that John was good and righteous, so look at what he said regarding Jesus."

John 3:25 states, Ἐγένετο οὖν ζήτησις ἐκ τῶν μαθητῶν Ἰωάννου μετὰ Ἰουδαίου[104] περὶ καθαρισμοῦ. "Then there arose an inquiry from

103. For the Johannine redaction of the Baptist tradition, see E. Lohmeyer, *Das Urchristentum 1: Johannes der Täufer* (Göttingen: Vandenhoeck & Ruprecht, 1932) 26-31; R. E. Brown, "John the Baptist in the Gospel of John," *CBQ* 22 (1960) 292-98; Wink, *Gospel Tradition,* 87-106; E. Bammel, "The Baptist in Early Christian Tradition," *NTS* 18 (1971-72) 95-128; J. Ernst, *Johannes der Täufer: Interpretation, Geschichte, Wirkungsgeschichte* (Berlin: de Gruyter, 1989) 186-216; and Webb, *John the Baptizer and Prophet,* 70-77.

104. Some important manuscripts have the plural here; however, with the plural we would expect a qualifying "some," which is absent here.

the disciples of John, along with a Jew, concerning purification."[105] The inquiry is specifically the question that follows, for immediately afterwards "they" — disciples and Jew together — come to John and say, "Rabbi, the one who was with you across the Jordan . . . he is immersing here and all are going to him" (3:26). It seems fairly clear in the Greek text that purification and immersion are equated and that both a Jew and the disciples of John are concerned about Jesus' doing it. It is hard to know whether the 'Ιουδαῖος is representative of the authorities. At any rate, he is acting in unison with the disciples of John to voice suspicion of Jesus' baptizing. Here again, we may have a reference to the contemporary Jewish authorities of the Gospel writer's time, who approved of the immersion of John, but not of Christian baptism.

It is also quite probable that the Pharisees of 4:1 are somehow linked with the Jew(s) of 3:25. John 3:26 reads, "he is immersing and all are going to him," and John 4:1 reads, "Jesus is making disciples and immersing more than John." The point about Jesus' popularity is driven home in 10:40-42, which narrates an incident apparently associated with a time after John's death. Jesus goes to the place beyond the Jordan where John had been baptizing, and many come to him and say, "John performed no sign, but everything he said concerning that man is true." However, in 4:1, 3 the Jews and the Pharisees are concerned about the movement's popularity, and they specifically stress the issue of Jesus' immersion. As a result, feeling their criticism, Jesus leaves Judea and goes to Galilee. John stays in the general area.

If we translate the elements of the passage concerning John with these considerations in mind, the section runs as follows:

> Then there arose an inquiry from the disciples of John, along with a *Ioudaios,* concerning purification. And they came to John and said to him, "Rabbi, the one who was with you beyond the Jordan, the one to whom you testified — he is immersing here and all are going to

105. My translation differs from the standard ones. The NRSV has: "Now a discussion about purification arose between John's disciples and a Jew"; cf. NJB. The Greek text does not seem to support this rendering; the inquiry (ζήτησις) is from (ἐκ) the disciples with (μετά) a Jew. The preposition μετά with the genitive case can mean "between," but it does not work with the syntax of the whole sentence to translate it this way, unless one alters ἐκ; "an inquiry from the disciples of John between a Jew" does not make sense. The common sense of μετά — "with, in common with" or even "with the help of" — seems preferable.

> him (3:25-26)." . . . Then when Jesus knew that the Pharisees had heard "Jesus is making disciples and immersing more than John" . . . he left Judea and went again into Galilee. (John 4:1, 3)

In view of the overall character of the Fourth Gospel, it seems likely that these passages derive from issues faced by the Johannine community. In other words, they reflect continuing debate with the Jewish community. Those who continued to cherish the traditions of John the Baptist, including disciples of John who endured after his death, must have encountered nothing of the opposition in the synagogues at the end of the century that the (Jewish-) Christians encountered. They may have been among the Jews opposed to the Christians. More than that, the Jewish authorities appear to have held John in very high esteem, while vehemently rejecting the beliefs of the Christian community of the Fourth Gospel. As Robert Webb notes, each group — the synagogue and the church — may have claimed John the Baptist in support of its own point of view.[106]

This solution seems far better than one that sets up a hypothetical Baptist movement continuing into the early second century — somehow separate from church or synagogue — that the Fourth Gospel is trying to address.[107] The main target of the statements of the Fourth Gospel is the Jewish authorities of the writer's time and place, not a "Baptist community." J. C. Thomas has recently shown how the writer of the Fourth Gospel was very well acquainted with many of the issues that were of concern to emerging rabbinic Judaism.[108] The debate with

106. Webb, *John the Baptizer and Prophet,* 77.

107. Such a solution is sometimes given in studies of the Fourth Gospel or John the Baptist. See, e.g., M. Dibelius, *Die urchristliche Überlieferung von Johannes dem Täufer* (Göttingen: Vandenhoeck & Ruprecht, 1911); R. Schnackenburg, "Das vierte Evangelium und die Johannesjünger," *HeyJ* 77 (1958) 21-38; R. E. Brown, *The Birth of the Messiah: A Commentary on the Infancy Narratives in Matthew and Luke* (London: Chapman, 1977) 46-54; cf. H. Lichtenberger, "Täufergemeinden und frühchristliche Täuferpolemik im letzten Drittel des 1. Jahrhunderts," *ZTK* 84 (1987) 36-57; idem, "Reflections on the History of John the Baptist's Communities," *FolOr* 25 (1988) 45-49; C. H. Kraeling, *John the Baptist* (New York: Scribner, 1951) 158-87; but see Wink, *Gospel Tradition,* 98-105. Wink sees the prime opponent of the Fourth Gospel as "Pharisaical Judaism," but distinguishes this from the "normative Judaism" of the Yavnean (Jamnian) scholars. He assumes that in the eyes of the Pharisees, "both Baptists and Christians belonged to the heretical sectarian baptist movement," without really making sense of John 5:3.

108. J. C. Thomas, "The Fourth Gospel and Rabbinic Judaism," *ZNW* 82 (1991) 159-82.

the synagogue is the key polemical issue reflected in the Gospel. Therefore, the passages concerning the Baptist are best understood as forming part of this polemic. John was a "good man," as Josephus himself tells us (*Ant.* 17.116), claimed by both sides.

Extrapolating from this, if both the Jewish community of the time of the Fourth Gospel and Josephus held John in high esteem, then it is very likely that Jews of the time of Jesus generally held John in high esteem. Given the close association of the Pharisees with the general populace, along with evidence of the Jewish elite's esteem of John in the Fourth Gospel and in Josephus, it seems likely that Pharisees at the time of John generally approved of him. Whatever the views of the real judicial council in Jerusalem, or the chief priestly hierarchy, the view that prevailed among Jewish authorities after the destruction of the Temple seems to have been that John was a "burning and shining light" in whom they had rejoiced. Perhaps responding to criticisms by these authorities — that Jesus was simply a wayward and misguided disciple of John — the writer of the Fourth Gospel remade John into a proto-Christian whose only function was to bear witness to Jesus.[109] If all this is on target, then the relationship between the Pharisees and John was positive.

John and the Pharisees in the Synoptic Gospels and Jewish-Christian Tradition

We need now to consider the Pharisees and John in the synoptic Gospels. There are two key passages that place the Pharisees in opposition to John: Matt. 3:7 and Luke 7:29-30. We shall deal with these briefly and conclude that they come from editorial modifications of the tradition. After this, we will consider the positive evidence of Mark 2:18-20.

Matthew 3:7

In Matt. 3:7 "many Pharisees and Sadducees" come for immersion and are singled out by John as the "offspring of vipers" who need to bear

109. So also Webb, *John the Baptizer and Prophet,* 77.

fruit worthy of repentance. It is very likely that Matthew sought to have the Pharisees and the Sadducees, representing the synagogue of his own day, roundly condemned by John. Therefore, Matthew introduced them at an early stage in his narrative when they were not found in his Q material. The Q source would otherwise be consistent with what we learn from Mark and Josephus, that crowds of people came to John for immersion; this is indeed what we have in Luke (3:7).

Matthew's purpose was to class John and Jesus together and have them opposed by the Jewish authorities, identified as "Pharisees and Sadducees."[110] Robert Webb considers the reference to Pharisees and Sadducees to be the original reading.[111] However, Matthew's employment of this reference is typical of his editorial modifications to Q and Mark (e.g., Matt. 16:1, 5-12; 21:45; 23:32-36). Furthermore, the conjunction of Pharisees and Sadducees is not historical, for both in Josephus and in rabbinic literature we find the Pharisees and Sadducees in marked opposition to one another (e.g., *m. Yad.* 4:6; *b. Yom.* 19b; *t. Ḥag.* 3:35; *b. Nid.* 33b; Josephus, *War* 2.165-66; *Ant.* 13.16-17, 292-96). We also find this opposition reflected in Paul's strategy in front of the council at Acts 23:6; he could rely upon the Pharisees and Sadducees to argue. John P. Meier notes that Matthew sees "Judaism as a united front opposing Jesus and his disciples just as Israel of old opposed and martyred the prophets sent to it."[112] Therefore, he joins the two groups — Pharisees and Sadducees — together in a solid phalanx. Such a tendency is not without parallel in early Christian literature. Justin Martyr, in his *Dialogue with Trypho* (ca. 150 CE), introduces Pharisees where they do not occur in some passages he is quoting (*Dial.* 51:2; 76:7; 100:3).

In order to assess the historicity of the Matthean version, we should note that in the Jewish-Christian Pseudo-Clementine literature, we have the view that Pharisees were baptized by John. The relevant passage reads:

> The scribes and the Pharisees . . . [while] baptized by John and holding the word of truth from the tradition of Moses as the key of the

110. Wink, *Gospel Tradition,* 34 n. 1.

111. Webb, *John the Baptizer and Prophet,* 173-78.

112. J. P. Meier, "John the Baptist in Matthew's Gospel," *JBL* 99/3 (1980) 389; idem, *A Marginal Jew: Rethinking the Historical Jesus. Volume Two: Mentor, Message, and Miracles* (New York: Doubleday, 1994) 30.

kingdom of heaven, have hidden it from the hearing of the people. (*Recognitions* 1:54; cf. 11:301; 46:3; *Homilies* 3:18; 18:15)

This passage has been identified as belonging to the oldest stratum of the Pseudo-Clementine literature,[113] but we need look no further than the Gospel of Matthew for the origin of the view that John baptized Pharisees. On this matter, the Pseudo-Clementines do not represent an independent source. Logically, Matthew does not tell us that John rejected the Pharisees. They came to him to be immersed and, one could conclude, in due course they were immersed after bearing good fruit. John did not send them away, giving them no chance of repentance; he just told them to bear fruit that befits repentance first. The Gospel of Matthew was especially associated with Jewish-Christian groups. According to the fourth-century heresiologist Epiphanius, certain Jewish-Christians used a Gospel of Matthew in Hebrew that made their particular interpretations of this Gospel plain. For example, instead of what stands in the Greek text at Matt. 3:5, their version read, "and it happened that John was baptizing, and Pharisees went out to him and were baptized, and all of Jerusalem" (Epiphanius, *Panarion* 30.13.4).[114] If this was indeed an altered version of Matt. 3:5, then the reference to the Pharisees was added to make what follows — John's specific criticism of the "Pharisees and Sadducees" — less severe. The Pharisees came out and were baptized, notwithstanding the criticism, just like everyone else.

Therefore, the fact that fourth-century Jewish-Christians, who may have traced their antecedents to the Pharisaic Christians of Acts 15:5 (cf. Gal. 2:12), believed that Pharisees were immersed by John should probably not be accorded historical weight. In wishing to vindicate their Pharisaic antecedents, certain Jewish-Christian groups using a somewhat modified Hebrew version of Matthew's Gospel probably emphasized the fact that Pharisees did come to John for baptism in this Gospel.[115] Historically, however, it seems unlikely that the Pharisees would have considered it necessary to repent and be immersed, since

113. Bammel, "The Baptist in Early Christian Tradition," 116 n. 9.

114. See W. Schneemelcher, ed., *New Testament Apocrypha I: Gospels and Related Writings,* trans. and ed. R. McL. Wilson (Cambridge: Clarke, 1991) 169.

115. That a Hebrew (or Aramaic?) version of Matthew's Gospel existed is attested in the fourth century not only by Epiphanius but also by Eusebius (*Hist. Eccl.* 3.24.6; 5.8.2; 5.10.3; 6.25.4). It is first attested by Irenaeus (*Adv. Haer.* 1.26.2) in the second century.

they were already assumed to be righteous and clean. We cannot rule out the possibility that individual Pharisees were inspired by John's message to practice inordinate self-scrutiny, resulting in a suspicion that they might have fallen short of true righteousness, and then came to John. However, we do not need to assume that Pharisees in general felt that way. Nor do we need to assume that Pharisees who did not go out to be immersed by John stood in opposition to him.

Luke 7:29-30

In Luke 7:29-30 a polemical point is made against Pharisees, based on the view that they did not go out to John for immersion:

> And all the people listening and the toll collectors accounted God righteous, having been immersed [with] John's baptism, but the Pharisees and lawyers rejected the will of God for themselves, not having been immersed by him.

In its present form, this is Luke's commentary. It has some parallels with Matt. 21:32, though these are thematic rather than linguistic. In Luke's text, the Pharisees and lawyers are pitted rather awkwardly against "all the people and the toll collectors." The reference to "all the people" seems to hark back to Mark's text, where "all the country of Judea and *all the people* of Jerusalem" go to be baptized in the Jordan (Mark 1:5). In commenting that the Pharisees and lawyers rejected the will of God for themselves, Luke tells us something of his views concerning John's baptism. In Luke's opinion, everyone should have been baptized by John in preparation for the coming of the Messiah.[116] His commentary, however, sits very badly with what follows, namely, Jesus' harsh denunciation of "this generation," which includes more people than Pharisees and lawyers (Luke 7:31-35). In this pericope, it is not the Pharisees and lawyers who fail to believe in John, but, collectively, the people of his

116. See the discussions on Luke's redaction of the Baptist tradition in Lohmeyer, *Johannes der Täufer,* 21-26; Wink, *Gospel Tradition,* 42-86; Bammel, "The Baptist in Early Christian Tradition," 105-09; E. Lupieri, *Giovanni Battista fra Storia e Leggenda* (Brescia: Paideia, 1988) 53-80; Ernst, *Johannes der Täufer,* 81-154; Webb, *John the Baptizer and Prophet,* 60-70.

time and place, whom Luke has just identified as doing the right thing in going out to be immersed by John. Indeed, historically, the Pharisees, though probably not baptized by John, were not necessarily opposed to him because of this. It is Luke who connects their lack of immersion by John with failure to comprehend his message or wholly accept the will of God.

Let us think of this further. Would John have demanded that the Pharisees, who had such a reputation for righteousness, repent (i.e., turn away from neglect of Torah to obedience)? If someone were righteous already, then repentance cannot have been required, and John's immersion was connected with repentance. Repentance was necessary only if someone was *not* righteous; it had no significance apart from this, for righteous people would have been accounted pure already both inwardly and outwardly. *Jesus* may have claimed that some Pharisees did indeed need to repent, because of their hypocrisy, but we have no evidence for a similar attitude being held by John, and it would be unwise to assume that John called all to repent. Moreover, Jesus could apparently also accept the righteousness of the Pharisees, as we have seen. We may remember, in order to emphasize the point, that Mark 2:16-17 has:

> And the scribes of the Pharisees, seeing that he ate with sinners and toll collectors, said to his disciples, "Why does he eat with toll collectors and sinners?" And hearing [this] Jesus said to them, "It is not the healthy who have need of a doctor, but those who are sick; I have not come to call the righteous, but sinners."

In other words, Jesus here accepts that there are righteous people already and that Pharisees are included in their number, but his purpose is to focus on the people who are not righteous and call them to repentance. His stories about the lost sheep and lost coin (Matt. 18:12-14; Luke 15:1-10) and the prodigal son (Luke 15:11-32) reflect the same consciousness. The Pharisees are among those who have not gotten lost or strayed from home. Likewise there is nothing in John's message that should lead us to conclude that he called everyone to come to his immersion.

If it is axiomatic that John called *sinners* to repentance, then would he have singled out Pharisees and Sadducees in particular as sinners? Would they have gone to John in the first place? Luke 7:28-30 implies that the Pharisees did not go to John, and Luke here seems to equate this lack of response to John's call with disbelief. But the Pharisees may well not have come, though still approving of what John set out to do. If the Pharisees were already considered by John to be basically righteous, then there was no point in their going out to him. Pharisees may have stood back in admiration of John's achievements, respected him, and even dealt with those coming from John who had turned from past lives of disobedience to the Law. The Pharisees' lack of baptism did not necessarily mean that they were in opposition to John; they simply did not need to repent. Like Jesus, John too had come to call sinners to repentance. When he challenged those coming to him to bear fruit worthy of repentance (Matt. 3:8 = Luke 3:8), the challenge was made to people who had previously borne no such fruit.

In the Aramaic *Targum Pseudo-Jonathan* of Isaiah, the congregation of God is made up of those who do not sin and "those who have repented from sin" (7:3; 10:21-22; 33:13; 57:19). The Targum's definition of the righteous illustrates the notion that those who repented, even if rather late, would be included with the righteous on the same terms when it came to final judgment. The wicked person who repents would also be called "my servant," as the Targum has it (42:19); but God's servants existed already. This illustrates what is only logical.

The repentant sinners he immersed would have been included on equal terms with the righteous as God's servants. This view is, in fact, reflected in Jesus' parable of the prodigal son (Luke 15:11-32) and especially in the parable of the hired workers (Matt. 20:1-6), where those who are hired to work in the vineyard in the eleventh hour get the same wages as those who were hired early in the morning. John called the disobedient to repent and follow the Law (Luke 1:17), but at no point in our sources does he consider that only those who come to him will be counted as God's servants. Nor does he insist that the righteous come to him for immersion to ensure their own salvation, as if immersion functioned like some kind of "seal." If they were righteous, then they did not need immersion.

Mark 2:18-20

In the Gospel of Mark, we have one crucial piece of positive evidence for a direct, supportive relationship between the Pharisees and John. The relevant passage reads:

> And the disciples of John and the Pharisees were fasting; and they [people] came and said to him [Jesus], "Why do the disciples of John and the disciples of the Pharisees fast, but your disciples do not fast?" And Jesus said to them, "The sons of the bridal-chamber are not able to fast when the bridegroom is among them. During the time they have the bridegroom with them, they are not able to fast, but the days will come when the bridegroom is taken away from them, and then they will fast on that day." (Mark 2:18-20)

In the story as told by Mark, the disciples of John and of the Pharisees are fasting at the same time, and people belonging to neither group expect Jesus' disciples to be doing the same. Walter Wink has proposed that the words "and the Pharisees" were added to the story, but he does not supply a reason.[117] Presumably the reasoning is that conflict stories with the Pharisees may derive from the time that church and synagogue were in bitter opposition, but this does not explain why the Pharisees should have been linked with John's disciples in Mark, a fact that had to be expunged from the versions of Matthew and Luke. At any rate, it is not a conflict story. The Pharisees themselves do not challenge Jesus. The point to be noted here is that the disciples of the Pharisees and the disciples of John are directly linked together by the statement that they kept a fast at the same time.

According to Luke 18:12, the Pharisees fasted twice a week. Luke is probably referring to an actual custom in which fasts might be called on Mondays and Thursdays (cf. *t. Ta'an.* 2:4). Only after the destruction of the Temple did certain individuals take it upon themselves to fast every Monday and Thursday (*b. Ta'an.* 12a; cf. *b. Giṭ.* 56a).[118] In the late first- or early second-century manual the *Didache,* we get a reflection of this custom of keeping fasts twice a week in a Christian milieu. We also find a deliberate separation of Christian fast days from Pharisaic fast days: "Your fasts should not coincide with those of the hypocrites. They fast on Mondays and Thursdays. You should fast on Wednesdays and Fridays" (*Didache* 8).[119] (The Pharisees are called

117. Wink, *Gospel Tradition,* 12; D. E. Nineham, *The Gospel of St Mark* (Harmondsworth: Penguin, 1963) 12.

118. *EncJud* 7, col. 1193.

119. The practice of later Christian fasting on Wednesdays and Fridays is mentioned by Tertullian (*De ieiunio* 2) and Clement of Alexandria (*Stromateis* 7.12.75).

"hypocrites" here by a conflation of Matt. 6:16 with the anti-hypocrisy woes of Matthew 23.)

Despite the prescriptions, fasting seems usually to have been a personal decision, and rules of fasting were probably not as rigid as Luke 18:12 implies. The fast referred to in Mark 2:18a could not have been the Day of Atonement, the only fast prescribed in Torah (Lev. 16:29; 23:27; Num. 29:2); otherwise, all Jews would have been fasting, and the two groups would not have been singled out; nor could it refer to the practice of personal, random fasting, for the two groups were supposed to be fasting at the same time. The point of the questioners in Mark 2:18 is not that Jesus and his disciples never fast, but only that on a specific occasion they are not keeping a fast with the disciples of the Pharisees and the disciples of John. We can only speculate about why the people expected Jesus' disciples to fast on this occasion. Their expectation might have come about because Jesus was so closely connected with the disciples of John that people thought he was one of them (as he may well have been) and would therefore do as they did. But the expectation may also have come about because Jesus and his disciples usually did keep the same fasts as the Pharisees and the disciples of John. The questioners seem to have understood that there was a close relationship between the groups: disciples of the Pharisees; disciples of John; Jesus and his disciples. Why were Jesus' disciples not fasting, when the disciples of John and the Pharisees were doing so?

In reply, Jesus rejects the necessity of being bound by either the practices of the Pharisees or the disciples of John by comparing himself with a bridegroom at a wedding. Only when the bridegroom is taken away from the "sons of the bridal chamber" — either the bridegroom's attendants or the wedding guests in general — should they fast. Fasting is out of place at a wedding feast. The usual interpretation of Jesus' response is that he is making prophetic allusions to his death and a blanket denial of the necessity of any fasting whatsoever; fasting is appropriate only in a Church that is in an interim period between Christ's physical presence on earth and his return at his second coming.[120]

John A. Ziesler has argued that the saying is directed entirely against the Pharisees,[121] who are like men who had the bridegroom

120. So Wink, *Gospel Tradition*, 12.

121. J. A. Ziesler, "The Removal of the Bridegroom," *NTS* 19 (1973) 190-94.

taken away from them and are therefore in the situation of mourners. According to Ziesler, the saying justifies not fasting at all. However, the taking away of the bridegroom at a wedding is not a cause for mourning; it simply marks the end of the festivities. Rudolf Bultmann regarded Mark 2:19a as a secular *mashal* used by the Church at a time when conflict with the Baptist was acute.[122] On this view, Jesus defends the actions of his disciples, not himself; therefore, he speaks up in defense of the practice of the Church. However, it may be argued that the questioners are using a circumlocution to avoid a direct challenge of Jesus. In asking a question about the practices of his disciples rather than directing the question at him, they avoid direct confrontation. At any rate, they are merely asking a question. They themselves are not fasting, anyway.

In the usual interpretation, Jesus is the bridegroom (Messiah), who is taken away from the party — that is, killed. But then what of the resurrection? To read the verse as entirely a post-Easter construction leaves us with only half the story. In the view of the Church Jesus was still present with Christians; they were not bereft of him. Furthermore, if the disciples of Jesus never fasted while Jesus was alive, then what do we make of Matt. 6:16-18, where Jesus tells his disciples to fast, but to do it secretly, without bragging about it for the sake of human approval? In this saying, Jesus advises:

> And when you fast, do not look dismal, like the hypocrites, for they disfigure their faces so that their fasting may be seen by people. Amen, I say to you, they have their reward. But when you fast, anoint your head and wash your face, that your fasting may not be seen by people but by your Father who is in secret, and your Father who sees in secret will reward you. (Matt. 6:16-18)

Obviously, there is the problem of authenticity here. The Matthean saying may not come from Jesus.[123] Still, it reflects a tradition known in the Matthean community that the disciples of Jesus did fast when he was alive. Moreover, it ties in quite well with what is said in the Mishnah (*m. Ta'an.* 1:4; cf. 1:5, 6; *m. Yoma* 8:1), that those fasting should bathe, anoint themselves, engage in work, and even have sex. Both the state-

122. R. Bultmann, *The History of the Synoptic Tradition,* 18-19.

123. E. P. Sanders, *Jesus and Judaism* (Philadelphia: Fortress, 1985) 402 n. 24.

ment of Matt. 6:16-18 and sayings of the later rabbis reflect a concern that fasting should not be abused to score points for good behavior in the community. The saying is directed not against fasting, or against Pharisees, but against outward shows of religious devotion that advertise the piety of the person fasting. If Matt. 6:16-18 is a genuine saying of Jesus, then either Mark 2:19-20 is not, or else the usual interpretation is incorrect. But if the bridegroom is simply an image, and not a messianic allusion, we do not have to consider either saying inauthentic or problematic. Fasting was an important part of Jewish piety, and it seems unlikely that Jesus would have dismissed it as useless. We do not need to read the saying in this way. Joachim Jeremias noted that the comparison between the Messiah and a bridegroom is unknown in Judaism before the Christian Fourth Gospel.[124] Moreover, when a bridegroom is taken away from a wedding, it is to the bridal chamber with his new bride, and no one would recognize this happy event as a reason for instant fasting. The point is that only when the wedding celebration is over should one fast. You cannot fast at a feast.

At face value, the pericope seems to indicate that Jesus has sat down to have a festive dinner with his disciples in a certain town and that they are celebrating his presence with them by means of this meal instead of keeping to a fast prescribed by Pharisees for those who wished to follow the Pharisaic way, as the disciples of John were doing. Jesus is like a bridegroom at the wedding feast among his attendants or guests. When he goes away to another town, then his disciples can go along with their usual fasts. This would make sense in terms of the logistics of Jesus' mission. He was "on the road" around the villages of rural Galilee. His disciples could not celebrate his arrival in their town by maintaining any fasts they might ordinarily maintain. He could not schedule his itinerary to take account of their usual practices. Such may be the original *Sitz im Leben* of the saying. It does not need to be post-Easter in its provenance. This is not to say that Mark intended the pericope to be this limited in its application. Mark draws general conclusions out of specific situations (e.g., Mark 7:19b), and a general conclusion may be intended here.

Some may object at this stage that the references to Pharisees in Galilee are out of place, since Josephus does not mention Pharisees

124. Jeremias, *New Testament Theology: The Proclamation of Jesus* (London: SCM, 1971) 105.

living there, and that the authenticity of this saying is therefore suspect. Morton Smith, for example, did not accept that there were Pharisees in Galilee.[125] But James Dunn has pointed out that while Josephus only describes Pharisees in Galilee who have been sent from Jerusalem (*War* 2.569; *Life* 189-98), his aim was to write a military history in which Pharisees are only mentioned in the context of his story. He was not a social historian.[126] Moreover, Rabbi Yohanan ben Zakkai apparently lived as a youthful Pharisee in Arab (Araba), a Galilean village probably situated some fifteen kilometers from Nazareth, for eighteen years, sometime between 20 and 40 CE.[127] There may have been a deliberate policy of stationing promising young Pharisees in Galilee to ensure the availability of halakhic rulings.[128] Yohanan's pupil, Hanina ben Dosa (*b. Ber.* 34b), also came from Arab. The "very strict" Eleazar of *Ant.* 20.38-48 was most likely, according to Dunn, a Pharisee,[129] and he came from Galilee. Luke has Pharisees only outside the walls of Jerusalem.

As for the phrase in Mark 2:18, "disciples of the Pharisees" (οἱ μαθηταὶ τῶν Φαρισαίων), this implies that there were people who regulated their lives according to Pharisaic *halakhot,* probably under instruction from Pharisaic teachers, while not necessarily counting themselves as Pharisees proper. These "disciples of the Pharisees" would have been distinguished from the majority of ordinary Jews of Galilee who did not follow Pharisaic *halakhot:* the people whom the rabbis later refer to rather disparagingly as עמי הארץ ("people of the land").[130]

125. Morton Smith, *Jesus the Magician* (San Francisco: Harper & Row, 1978) 157; Sanders, *Jesus and Judaism,* 198, 390 n. 90, 292.

126. Dunn, "Pharisees, Sinners, and Jesus," 280.

127. Ibid.; cf. Smith, *Jesus the Magician,* 157; Neusner, *A Life of Rabban Yohanan ben Zakkai,* 2d ed. (Leiden: Brill, 1970) 47-48, 51.

128. Dunn, "Pharisees, Sinners, and Jesus," 280; Neusner, *Yohanan ben Zakkai,* 48.

129. Dunn, "Pharisees, Sinners, and Jesus," 281.

130. On the עם הארץ, see Sanders, *Jesus and Judaism,* 180-87; A. Oppenheimer, *The ʿAm Ha-Aretz: A Study in the Social History of the Jewish People in the Hellenistic-Roman Period* (Leiden: Brill, 1977). The disciples of the Pharisees appear also in Matt. 22:16 and should probably be equated with the "sons" of the Pharisees in Matt. 12:27 (Luke 11:19). As we have already noted, Josephus uses μαθηταί for the "sons" of the prophets of 2 Kgs. 2:15, while the Aramaic targums also refer to תלמידי נביאיא, "disciples of the prophets," at the same point; see for this K. H. Rengstorf, "μαθητής" *TDNT* 4 (1967) 434, 443.

It has sometimes been assumed that the "disciples of John" referred to here in Mark 2:18 were a kind of inner circle clustered around him and were not really living in Galilean villages.[131] In fact, there is no evidence that John built up an inner circle, though some of his disciples may have aimed to stay close to him, just as some of Jesus' disciples joined him on the road. The recorded teaching of John strongly suggests that he wanted most people to go home to their usual jobs (Luke 3:10-14).[132] Disciples of John came to Jesus with a question from John about Jesus' identity (Matt. 11:2-6; Luke 7:18-21), and disciples of John buried their dead teacher after Herod Antipas had beheaded him (Mark 6:29; Matt. 14:12). But even if John did have disciples who wanted to stay particularly close to him, this does not preclude us from supposing that he had disciples at a distance as well. Just as people could consider themselves to be disciples of a deceased teacher (*m. 'Abot* 1:12; 5:19; *b. Yoma* 4a; *b. Sukka* 28a; *b. Soṭa.* 13a), so also could they be disciples of a teacher *in absentia.*[133] At any rate, the questioners in Mark 2:18 seem to be taking note of the fasting of both disciples of Pharisees and disciples of John that they have observed locally.

It seems quite possible that Mark 2:18-20 might accurately reflect history. The pericope suggests that the disciples of John were expected to follow Pharisaic *halakhot* on the matter of fasting, without actually being counted as either disciples of the Pharisees or Pharisees proper. If they were expected to do this on this matter, then it may be assumed that they were expected to follow Pharisaic *halakhot* in other ways too, without actually becoming disciples of the Pharisees. Jesus and his disciples were linked with John and were expected to behave as John's disciples did. Indeed, this expectation may well have given rise to the conflict between Jesus and the Pharisees reported in the Gospels.

In favor of the authenticity of Mark 2:18-20 is that the pericope was considered awkward by those who adapted it. Quite understandably, the pericope was deemed sufficiently problematic by Matthew and Luke to be altered in their versions. Matthew changes it so that the incident is related not to a specific occasion on which the disciples of both the

131. C. H. H. Scobie, *John the Baptist* (London: SCM, 1964) 133.

132. Scobie, *John the Baptist,* 132 does accept this.

133. W. B. Badke, "Was Jesus a Disciple of John?" *EvQ* 62 (1990) 197.

Pharisees and John were fasting together, but to the principle of fasting in general, despite the inconsistencies this alteration creates within his own Gospel (cf. Matt. 6:16-18). In Matthew, the disciples of John and the Pharisees are therefore no longer closely linked; they are simply two groups who happen to be in the habit of fasting:

> Then the disciples of John came to him, saying, "Why do we and the Pharisees fast [some manuscripts add "much"] but your disciples do not fast?" (Matt. 9:14)

In complete contrast to what Matthew has recorded in 6:16-18, Jesus' disciples are characterized as not fasting. Moreover, the questioners are no longer other people who observe a discrepancy, but the disciples of John themselves. They are not only distinguished from the Pharisees — though siding with them — but are also, in a sense, opposing the practice of Jesus and are a separate group, potentially antagonistic towards him. Luke modifies Mark in a different way:

> And they said to him, "The disciples of John fast often and offer prayers, indeed just like those [disciples] of the Pharisees, but yours eat and drink." (Luke 5:33)

Luke then also prefers to have the disciples of the Pharisees and the disciples of John frequently fasting rather than fasting on a specific day together. He links them by stating that the disciples behave ὁμοίως καὶ οἱ τῶν Φαρισαίων, "indeed, just like those [disciples] of the Pharisees." On account of Luke's positioning of the story, the people who ask Jesus about his disciples' lack of fasting are "Pharisees and their scribes" themselves (Luke 5:30), but this is probably unintentional. If Luke had expressly intended to identify them as the questioners, he would have had them use the expression "our disciples" rather than "those [disciples] of the Pharisees."

Therefore, in Matthew and Luke we see a clear attempt to disassociate the Pharisees and the disciples of John from each other, and also an attempt to disassociate Jesus and his disciples from either of these two groups. This only serves to increase the likelihood that Mark's story is basically authentic, for the early Church would not have invented a story that did not cohere with its views on the proper relationship between disciples of the Pharisees, John, and Jesus.

In conclusion, Mark seems to reflect accurately an actual situation in the life of Jesus. In that situation, the disciples of John kept the same fast as the Pharisees, meaning that they accepted at least some of the Pharisaic *halakhot,* while Jesus accepted the *halakhot* in principle but felt that he had the (prophetic) authority to overturn them if it suited him. Jesus therefore claimed to be able to announce his own rulings to suit the specific conditions of his itinerant lifestyle without recourse to Pharisaic argument or approval.

Given the evidence of Mark 2:18-20, it would be difficult to conclude that the Pharisees must have opposed John, even if they were doubtful about Jesus. We have seen that Luke 7:29-30 is anti-Pharisaic commentary, based on the assumption that the Pharisees were not immersed by John. But their lack of immersion does not indicate that they were opposed to John. In regard to the Fourth Gospel, the evidence suggests that the author believed that the Jews of his age looked favorably upon John, even though not upon Jesus. The Pharisees, as an influential religious grouping within Second Temple Judaism, may well have accepted that John was a "good man," as Josephus did at the end of the first century. Certainly, if John called for those who had strayed from the Law to repent; asked for good deeds, righteousness, and obedience to the Law in preparation for the coming end; and offered the necessary purificatory immersion, it is hard to imagine that the Pharisees could possibly have objected to him. They may not have agreed that immersions were ineffective without prior righteousness, but in turning people back to the Law, John was hardly to be sneered at. If some people speculated about his identity in the eschatological scheme of things, that is not to say that he himself claimed anything. As we find noted in the Fourth Gospel, John was probably regarded by the Jews of his time and by the generations that followed as a lamp, burning brightly. Josephus records that many people regarded the destruction of Antipas' army as a just divine punishment for his terrible crime of murdering John; God was on John's side (*Ant.* 18.118-19). That John's name has been deleted from rabbinic tradition may well derive from his appropriation by the Church. In response to the polemic from Christian circles that John always meant to point to Jesus, the rabbis might have considered it a wise move quietly to forget about him, at least in written tradition. It is some loss.

CHAPTER 5

Opposition and Death

Thus far in this study we have concentrated on examining the nature of John's baptism and his teaching. We have suggested that his prophecy was understood mainly to involve the prediction that the end was coming soon. We have argued that John had a positive relationship with the Pharisees, however one might conceive this group, and that he was also remembered positively in Jewish communities at the end of the first century. With only these factors in view, it may seem that there was nothing about John that anyone could possibly have objected to. Yet both in the New Testament and in Josephus we learn that John was executed by Herod Antipas. According to Josephus, the tetrarch, for one, found John so dangerous that he put him in chains, imprisoned him in the fortress of Machaerus, and — after a certain period of time — killed him. The New Testament attributes Antipas' action to John's criticism of Antipas' marriage to Herodias, his half-brother's ex-wife; Josephus indicates that there was more to it than mere criticism of Antipas' personal affairs. The two presentations need not be mutually exclusive. We shall review the evidence here.

The Wilderness and Revolution

John's prime choice of location, if the synoptic Gospels are to be believed, was just beyond the Jordan near Jericho. This place had important religious associations. It was in Perea, beyond the Jordan across from Jericho, that Elijah went up in a whirlwind to heaven, in a chariot of fire pulled by horses of fire (2 Kgs. 2:4-14). There may have been a belief that Elijah would descend at the place he went up to heaven (cf. Mal. 4:5). In gathering people where he did, John met them at a site of great religious and historic significance that would have increased the importance of an immersion there. Elijah's own ascent at this place ultimately derived its special significance from the fact that already in his day it was recognized as a highly meaningful zone in Israel's history. This was the point at which Joshua crossed the Jordan to enter the promised land and take it for the people of Israel (Josh. 1:2, 3). In the story of this crossing, Joshua causes the river to part, opposite Jericho, just as Moses had caused the parting of the Sea of Reeds, enabling the Israelites to flee from Egypt.

Not surprisingly, sometime after John's activities at the Jordan, another person also chose this locality in order to make religio-political statements against the Roman occupying power. In *Ant.* 20.97-98 (cf. Acts 5:36) Josephus reports that a man named Theudas, whom he calls a "magician" or "imposter" (γόης), went out to the Jordan and proclaimed that he would repeat Joshua's miracle. Theudas persuaded a "great portion" of the people that he was a prophet and that they should take their possessions with them and come with him across the Jordan, in imitation of Joshua and the Israelites. The Roman procurator, Fadus (44-46 CE), was possibly advised that this was an action in imitation of an event that had sparked the great wars that had won the land for the Israelites.[1] Whatever the case, he promptly sent cavalry out against Theudas and his followers. Many were killed, many were captured, and Theudas was executed — as John had been — by decapitation. His head was carried into Jerusalem, clearly as a warning for anyone who wished to stage revolutionary biblical reenactments.

However, it was not only the crossings of the Jordan that had religious significance. The wilderness itself had meaningful resonances

1. It is not implied in the account that they were going from Judea into Perea, contra J. D. Crossan, *The Historical Jesus: The Life of a Mediterranean Jewish Peasant* (San Francisco: HarperSanFrancisco, 1991) 162. On Theudas, see R. Gray, *Prophetic Figures in Late Second Temple Jewish Palestine: The Evidence from Josephus* (Oxford: Oxford University Press, 1993) 114-16; R. A. Horsley and J. S. Hanson, *Bandits, Prophets, and Messiahs: Popular Movements in the Time of Jesus* (Minneapolis: Winston, 1985) 141, 167.

if anyone wanted to make use of them. In the eschatological day of the Lord, it was believed, the wilderness would be turned into a fruitful place, full of water and fertility (Isa. 35:6-7; 41:18-20; 51:3). In the meantime, it carried associations of the Exodus and wandering of the Israelites before the entry into the promised land (cf. Hos. 2:14-15). There was no one, ultimate wilderness that indicated these links; those of Zin and of Judea, the Negev and the Sinai — all carried the same associations: the wilderness was the place of transition, of trusting in God, of being led towards liberation and security. It was in the wilderness that God revealed himself to Moses (Exodus 3) and that Elijah heard the "still, small voice" (1 Kings 19). The wilderness could be seen as a kind of staging post towards the final destination, which was Jerusalem.

In Josephus' writings, we find a number of "deceivers and imposters," as he calls them, who assembled people in the wilderness with a view to revolution. Apparently, Theudas was one of several. Josephus says there were many of these people during the procuratorship of Felix (52-60 CE) who led crowds out to the wilderness in the belief that God would give them "signs and wonders," or more specifically "signs of freedom," σημεῖα ἐλευθερίας (*War* 2.258-61; *Ant.* 20.167-68).[2] Such actions fueled revolutionary instincts, and Felix quickly silenced the demonstrations. Josephus himself links these men with revolutionaries, whom he dubs "brigands" (*Ant.* 20.160-61; cf. *War* 2.253) because they incited people to revolt (*War* 2.264-65; cf. *Ant.* 20.172).

Only a few years after John, Pontius Pilate (26-36/7 CE) massacred the followers of a Samaritan prophet who assembled a crowd of people at a village named Tirathana so that they would ascend Mt. Gerizim and uncover the sacred vessels supposedly buried there (*Ant.* 18.85-87).[3] The wilderness does not feature here, and such demonstrations may not have threatened Roman rule militarily, but they were in themselves anti-Roman in tenor and were therefore perceived as a threat to the

2. Josephus also uses the expression "signs of freedom" (*War* 2.259) for the plagues that Moses invoked upon Egypt prior to the Exodus (*Ant.* 2.327; cf. *War* 6.283-85). See Crossan, *Historical Jesus,* 164; Horsley, " 'Like One of the Prophets of Old': Two Types of Popular Prophets at the Time of Jesus," *CBQ* 47 (1985) 455; P. W. Barnett, "The Jewish Sign Prophets — A.D. 40-70: Their Intentions and Origin," *NTS* 27 (1980-1981) 682-83; and Gray, *Prophetic Figures,* 118-20.

3. See Crossan, *Historical Jesus,* 160-61.

established order.[4] Pilate's violent attack on the demonstration, which led to his recall to Rome in 36/7 CE, gives us a background against which the crushing of other popular movements may be understood.

Popular leaders who massed followers with a view to witnessing signs that would signal the end of Gentile control of the Land of Israel met similar untimely ends. In the procuratorship of Felix, an "Egyptian" assembled a crowd of people in the wilderness who then went on to the Mount of Olives, where they expected to see the walls of Jerusalem come tumbling down (*Ant.* 20.169-72; *War* 2.261-63; cf. Acts 21:38) just as the walls of Jericho crumbled for the army of Joshua. Again, the biblical precedent lent itself to revolutionary thinking. Felix sent out the infantry and cavalry, killed many of the Egyptian's supporters, and captured hundreds of others, though the Egyptian himself got away. Josephus calls the clash a "battle" (*Ant.* 20.172), indicating that the supporters of the Egyptian were armed.[5] Acts 21:38 refers to these people as "four thousand assassins," while the Egyptian himself is someone who "stirred up a revolt."[6] The Egyptian was followed by another unnamed man who led his followers out to the wilderness (*Ant.* 20.188), and Festus (60-62 CE) sent the usual cavalry and infantry to annihilate the leader and his followers.[7]

According to Josephus, beyond Judea in the province of Cyrene, a man named Jonathan the Weaver also convinced many Jews to follow him out to the nearby wilderness where they would see "signs and visions" (*War* 7.437-39). Some prominent citizens informed the gover-

4. See D. M. Rhoads, *Israel in Revolution 66-74 C.E.: A Political History Based on the Writings of Josephus* (Philadelphia: Fortress, 1976) 84 n. 77; cf. R. Macmullen, *Enemies of the Roman Order: Treason, Unrest, and Alienation in the Empire* (Cambridge, MA: Harvard University Press, 1966) 128-62.

5. See D. R. Schwartz, *Studies in the Jewish Background of Christianity* (Tübingen: Mohr-Siebeck, 1992) 31.

6. Interestingly, in the story of Acts (21:38), the Roman tribune in Jerusalem, noting that Paul speaks Greek, says to him, "Then you are not the Egyptian." Why this Egyptian might not know Greek is unexplained; he must have spoken the local dialect of Palestinian Aramaic in order to communicate with his supporters. A true Egyptian would have spoken some form of Coptic and/or Greek. Perhaps his nickname was מצרי (Hebrew and Aramaic), meaning "Egyptian." There may have been a popular understanding of him as being like Moses, another "Egyptian"; so Horsley, " 'Like One of the Prophets of Old,' " 458-60. See also Horsley and Hanson, *Bandits, Prophets, and Messiahs*, 170; and Gray, *Prophetic Figures*, 116-18.

7. See Gray, *Prophetic Figures*, 122-23.

nor of Jonathan's "departure and preparations," and the army was duly sent off to do its job. In *Life* 424-25 Josephus describes Jonathan as one who "roused rebellion" in Cyrene. In *War* 7.440, however, he states that Jonathan was unarmed, but this is partly to exonerate himself, since there was a suspicion that Josephus had supplied Jonathan with arms for battle and money (*War* 7.447-50). Jonathan was tortured and then burned alive (*Life* 425).

All the above figures are often classified as "sign prophets."[8] They led movements for liberation and waited for some sign from God to indicate that the moment had come. If one wanted to play with the motif, it seems that the route from wilderness to city and open revolt was clear. Interestingly, Josephus does not specify John's location in the wilderness beyond the Jordan. We may conjecture that by doing so he would perhaps have had to link John with others whom he denounces as charlatans. Quite to the contrary, as we have seen, Josephus describes John as a "good man" who was killed on account of Antipas' paranoia (*Ant.* 18.116-19).

Josephus must have been aware, however, that the wilderness was meaningful as a religious symbol in his time and that it featured in the operations of those who hoped for the overthrow of Roman occupation. The wilderness was an eschatological motif, but also a poignant political one, for eschatology was deeply connected with the hopes of those who anticipated a time when Jerusalem would be freed from Gentile (Roman) rule. This idea is found in Isaiah 35, which begins with mention of the wilderness (35:1) and the highway for God's people (35:8) and ends with their triumphal entrance into Je-

8. The term was first used by Barnett, "Jewish Sign Prophets," 679. The key discussions of the sign prophets are found in R. A. Horsley, "Popular Messianic Movements Around the Time of Jesus," *CBQ* 46 (1984) 471-95; idem, "'Like One of the Prophets of Old'"; idem, "Popular Prophetic Movements at the Time of Jesus: Their Principal Features and Social Origins," *JSNT* 26 (1986) 3-27; Barnett, "Jewish Sign Prophets"; see also R. L. Webb, *John the Baptizer and Prophet: A Socio-Historical Study* (Sheffield: JSOT Press, 1991) 333-39. Prophecy as a whole in this period is discussed by J. Barton, *Oracles of God: Perceptions of Ancient Prophecy in Israel after the Exile* (London: Darton, Longman, and Todd, 1986); cf. Gray, *Prophetic Figures,* esp. 112-13. D. E. Aune classifies these men as "eschatological" or "millenarian"; see D. E. Aune, *Prophecy in Early Christianity and the Ancient Mediterranean World* (Grand Rapids: Eerdmans, 1983) 126-29. Our literary sources, however, do not explicitly indicate that these men believed that the end would be soon, only that God would perform a sign to indicate that freedom from Gentile rule was imminent.

rusalem on the day of the Lord (35:10). Isa. 51:9-11 employs Exodus typology.[9] Throughout Isaiah 52–53 the language of liberation is clear, and it connects the wilderness with the coming of the kingdom of God, when all those who oppress Israel will be thrown off. In other words, the essence of Isa. 40:3, if it was important to John, could be interpreted as much as a call for preparation to revolt as for renewed obedience to the way of God.

We may be justified in asking, therefore, whether John really *was* like the men who led people out to the wilderness with expectation of signs and who hoped for the deliverance of Jerusalem from the hands of the Romans. Certainly, despite Josephus' scepticism, these revolutionary leaders could be defined as prophets. Is it in the context of these popular prophets or revolutionary leaders that John should be understood? Clearly, the focus of these leaders was the overthrow of Gentile rule. Yet, whatever political agenda may be found in John's teaching, he did not call upon those he assembled to witness a sign founded on an incident in the Bible. As we have seen, John's immersion itself was not a sign. If he proclaimed that the end was near, this does not mean that he expected people to do anything to hasten its coming. People were supposed to be concerned with righteousness, not rebellion. In the Fourth Gospel, moreover, John is expressly said to have done no sign (John 10:41).

The potentially revolutionary associations of the wilderness did not necessarily obtain in John's activity. John could have chosen the wilderness as the venue of his activity for reasons other than revolution. The wilderness could just be the wilderness, and there were many reasons for people to go there.[10] As we have seen, John's decision to live on what grew naturally would have meant that he had to live in the wilderness and probably wander, since he would exhaust the natural food supply in any one place. (Those who came out to him would certainly have helped that process, even with food baskets of items that might last a little while.) The placement of John's baptizing activities just where Joshua crossed into Judea is a traditional Christian focus,

9. See B. W. Anderson, "Exodus Typology in Second Isaiah," in *Israel's Prophetic Heritage: Essays in Honor of James Muilenburg*, ed. B. W. Anderson and W. Harrelson (New York: Harper, 1962) 177-95.

10. Gray, *Prophetic Figures*, 137, 141. For the symbolism of the wilderness see also P. W. Hollenbach, "John the Baptist," *ABD*, vol. 3, 892.

fueled by Christian speculation. It may have been considered appropriate for him to be at the site of Joshua's crossing. However, the Gospels do not give us one specific site. Q indicates that he "went into all the region about the Jordan" (Luke 3:3; cf. Matt. 3:5). Mark states only that he was "in the wilderness" immersing in the Jordan (Mark 1:4-5; cf. Matt. 3:6). The Fourth Gospel has John "beyond the Jordan" (10:40) but also at a certain natural spring — Aenon near Salim (3:23) — and he may have gone elsewhere. John chose Aenon for the plentiful supply of water, and he worked along the Jordan for the same reason. Clearly, then, water was more important for John's mission than wilderness. Wilderness was necessary only for his diet.

Josephus did not think of John as a deceiver and imposter who led the people astray. That Pontius Pilate acted with such ferocity in quashing the Samaritan demonstration (*Ant.* 18.85-86) probably indicates that he would have done likewise with any such demonstration among the Jews closer to Jerusalem, and John's gathering of people by the Jordan would surely have been interpreted as a demonstration if Pilate had detected any traces of political agitation. It is interesting, therefore, that it was Herod Antipas who arrested John. There was no massacre of John's followers by the Jordan or any capturing of his disciples. Pilate would have crossed the Jordan to round up the crowds if he had felt it necessary, just as Fadus must have done with Theudas. Josephus presents Antipas as carrying out a preemptive strike against John just in case things got out of hand. The rulers of the land, then, probably did not put John in the same category as they would the later revolutionary leaders. According to Josephus, Antipas killed John to avoid the possibility that John's following might develop in ways that would make him dangerous, even though it appeared at the time that he was not dangerous. But Antipas may have detected a very real possibility. Had John continued to act for much longer than he did, he very well might have come to be viewed as someone more like Theudas than Josephus would have cared for.

As we have seen, John was probably remembered positively in Jewish circles of the end of the century, just when Josephus was writing. Josephus himself avoids mentioning any eschatological message of John, clearly wishing to remove any political considerations from John's actions. He avoids most eschatological matters in his writings, but, more importantly in this case, eschatological language would have been read by the Romans as being anti-Rome, or at least anti-Gentile.

Although John did not advise anyone to take up arms, the whole thrust of his message, founded as it was on the prophetic literature (especially the book of Isaiah), included the fundamental teaching that the righteousness of people would lead God to act in history, to redeem his people from the rule and oppression of the Gentiles. Some people who came to John may easily have understood his message along political lines. It is difficult to determine precisely what John intended by what he did and said. The intent and the reception of his wilderness venue and proclamation may have been two different things. Nevertheless, it is hard to imagine that John was ignorant of the political dimensions of his activity.

It is basic to the message of Isaiah, as it is to the deuteronomistic history,[11] that God has handed over his people to the Gentiles because of their sins (e.g., Isa. 1:2-31; 9:17-21; 42:24; 50:1-2; 57:17; 59:2-15; 64:5-7). Once a faithful remnant (cf. Amos 3:12) of righteous people do what is just, obey the Law, and make effective prayers for peace, then God will lift the curse of Gentile domination, destroy the wicked, and remove the rule of the Gentiles from Jerusalem (Isa. 58:1-14). Jerusalem will be entered by the "righteous nation that keeps faith" (Isa. 26:2), namely, those who do not turn aside from the way of the Lord, for "when you turn to the right or the left, your ears shall hear a word behind you, saying, 'This is the way, walk in it'" (Isa. 30:21). Zion will be "redeemed by justice, and those in her who turn by righteousness" (Isa. 1:27). The highway through the wilderness for the remnant of the people will be like the one for Israel in the Exodus (Isa. 11:16). The path of the righteous is made smooth (Isa. 26:7; cf. 57:14) because repentance — turning to the Law — is salvation: "In returning and rest you will be saved; in quietness and trust will be your strength" (30:16). Doing justice will bring salvation, and the righteous will rest in peace (57:1-2). Salvation is this-worldly and is connected with the liberation of Jerusalem from Gentile control. The city will be renewed for the righteous to live in joyfully.

The *Targum Pseudo-Jonathan* of Isaiah makes it even more specific

11. The classic exposition of the deuteronomistic history is to be found in M. Noth, *The Deuteronomistic History* (Sheffield: JSOT Press, 1981); but see also O. H. Steck, *Israel und das gewaltsame Geschick der Propheten: Untersuchungen zur Überlieferung des deuteronomistischen Geschichtsbildes im Alten Testament, Spätjudentum und Urchristentum* (Neukirchen-Vluyn: Neukirchener Verlag, 1967) 62-64, 122-24.

that the day of the Lord will come against the kings of the Gentiles and all the "tyrants of the provinces" (2:13-16). On the day of the Lord, God will blow away the Gentiles like chaff from the threshing floor (41:15). Gentiles continue to plunder Israel only because Israelites do not repent of their sins and return to God's service (9:12-23, 17, 21; 10:4; 27:4-5). The righteous will be left alone in the midst of the kingdoms (17:6; 24:13) and will witness the punishment of the wicked in the fires of Gehenna until the righteous say that they have seen enough (66:24).

To stress the point, eschatological language and exhortations to repentance could be interpreted as highly political. The language of a return to the Law and righteousness was itself political as well as eschatological in implication. To modern minds, there are conceptual demarcations between what is religious, political, or moral that did not exist to the same degree in Second Temple Judaism. As Anthony Saldarini has noted, "In traditional society, religion was embedded in the political and social fabric of the community."[12] If the Romans could differentiate between politics and religion, secular and sacred, this was not the case with the Jewish people they hoped to control. The language of John the Baptist could itself become fuel for revolutionary instincts, which Antipas, as a Jew, must have recognized.

Therefore, what Pontius Pilate may have been slow to grasp, unless we assume that he judiciously stepped back on this occasion, Herod Antipas may not have been. What Josephus puts down to Antipas' paranoia may have been justifiable suspicion, if not of John himself then certainly of the turbulent crowds. Antipas must have known the conceptual route from wilderness to Jerusalem and sensed the potentially revolutionary meaning of John's call to righteousness and purity. John's message could be taken, though couched in the language of repentance and morality, as seriously anti-Roman, for imperial rule was one of the things that would be shaken off in the

12. A. J. Saldarini, *Pharisees, Scribes, and Sadducees in Palestinian Society: A Sociological Approach* (Wilmington, DE: Glazier, 1988) 5. For Josephus and other Jews, πολιτεία encompassed the legal aspects of Judaism; see Y. Amir, "The Term *Ioudaismos:* A Study in Jewish-Hellenistic Self-Identification," *Immanuel* 14 (1982) 34-41. The νόμοι, "laws," of the Jews are comparable to the νόμοι of the ancient Greek city-states (cf. Josephus, *Ant.* 1.5-6, 18-26; 3.223; 4.139, 193; 11.192; *Ag. Ap.* 1.7-9, 166-67, 190, 211-12; 2.151-56); they have legal and philosophical dimensions. I am grateful to Steve Mason and Ellen Birnbaum for providing this information through the IOUDAIOS discussion group.

coming day of judgment. If God listens only to the prayers of the righteous, then anyone praying to God for deliverance from Gentile domination would need to be righteous and obedient to the Law before his or her prayers were answered. A call to righteousness could, then, have been seen as a first step towards revolt. Obedience to Torah would prompt God to deliver his faithful remnant.

In the *Targum Pseudo-Jonathan* of Isaiah, there is a relationship drawn between the "prodigy of the sea" — the Sea of Reeds parted by Moses — and "the wonders of the Jordan" — the parting of the Jordan by Joshua — along with "the war of the Gentile fortresses" (*Tg. Ps.-J.* Isa. 9:1). These powerful links seem to have been known at the time of John, if Theudas' example is considered. Therefore, a gathering of people in the wilderness at the Jordan near Jericho, a call to renewed purity and obedience to the Law, together with eschatological language would collectively have been considered by some elements in society to be anti-Roman and would therefore have fueled attitudes that were part of a revolutionary *Zeitgeist*. If John was hailed as a prophet, then there would have been even more reason for Antipas to feel worried. A prophet who predicted the end was hardly someone the tetrarch wanted on his back doorstep.

We shall now consider John's reputation as a prophet in a discussion of what prophecy was understood to be at the time, but before proceeding it may be worth mentioning one further point, namely, that John was probably not completely otherworldly and naive in his outlook. Innocence may be used as a point in favor of viewing John as a nonpolitical figure who went lamb-like to his own slaughter, but it does not quite ring true. In a world where politics and religion were so closely interwoven, the wilderness was not an escape from the religious and political realities of Jerusalem. The interests of the documents found near Qumran betray a deep involvement with the politics of the past, present, and future, despite the community's quietistic and separatist lifestyle. It seems preferable to me, though this must remain a personal opinion, to think of John as very well aware of the implications of his message and of what the crowds coming to him were hoping for, and to credit him with an eye to contemporary events and figures. As we shall see, his criticism of Antipas has to be understood against the backdrop of the discontent and expectations of the crowds around him. He appears in our sources as literate and intelligent and a powerful figure able to command a huge following.

Prophets and Prophecy

As is well known, there is clear evidence in the Gospels that the early Church followed the lead of many of John's disciples, including Jesus, who considered him a prophet (Mark 1:6; 9:9-13; 11:32; Matt. 3:4; 17:10-13; 21:26 = Luke 20:6). In the Q tradition, Jesus refers to John as a prophet (Luke 7:26; Matt. 11:9), probably Elijah (Matt. 11:14), despite the fact that elsewhere in the New Testament we find reflections of the view that John denied he was such a figure (Acts 13:25; John 1:21).

In the nativity account in Luke, an angel of the Lord announces to Zechariah, John's father, that his son "will be filled with the Holy Spirit" (Luke 1:15) and go before God "with the spirit and power of Elijah" (1:17). The nativity story is itself constructed to hark back to the births of Samson (Judg. 13:2-24) and Samuel (1 Sam. 1:1-23), who were not only considered to be *nazirs,* but also seen as prophets. For Christians, John was definitely a prophet.[13]

Against this, there was probably a view that true prophecy did not exist any longer. For example, in the Tosephta it is stated that after the death of the latter prophets, "the Holy Spirit came to an end in Israel" and only "the daughter of the Voice" could be heard (*t. Soṭa* 13:2-6). This view can be traced back to at least the second century BCE, since the same view that prophecy had ceased is found in 1 Maccabees (4:45-46; 9:27; 14:41; cf., e.g., *2 Apoc. Bar.* 83:5).[14] Josephus, who by his own admission conducted himself publicly according to the Pharisees (*Life* 12), despite his reservations about them, seems highly suspicious of anyone claiming to be a prophet. The exact succession of the prophets of old was suspended (*Ag. Ap.* 1.41; cf. 1.29, 37, 40). As noted above, he characterizes the common people of his age as hopelessly gullible and prone to believe "charlatans and pretended messengers of the deity" (*War* 6.288). His negative comments seem to indicate that among ordinary people there was a tendency to consider certain people to be prophets of one kind or another. And, after all, Josephus could claim

13. For a detailed analysis of portrayals of John as prophet in the synoptic tradition and a comparison with the presentations of prophets in biblical and pseudepigraphal literature, see M. Tilly, *Johannes der Täufer und die Biographie der Propheten. Die synoptische Täuferüberlieferung und das jüdische Prophetenbild zur Zeit des Täufers,* BWANT 137 (Stuttgart: Kohlhammer, 1994).

14. See Gray, *Prophetic Figures,* 7, 169 n. 2 and Aune, *Prophecy in Early Christianity,* 103-06.

with the benefit of hindsight that such people were false; their "prophecies," that is, predictions, did not come true.

To complicate the situation, Josephus himself may have accepted that some sorts of postbiblical "prophetic" activity could take place. As Rebecca Gray has recently argued, Josephus perceived a distinction between the ancient prophets, who were in very close touch with God, and those of his own time, who did "prophetic" actions such as interpreting dreams and making true predictions.[15] But it should be noted that even when Josephus does seem to endorse by implication the validity of the true predictions — such as those made by himself (*War* 3.354; cf. 4.626) or Jesus son of Ananias (*War* 6.288) and others — he does not explicitly call these men "prophets." It is rather left to the reader to decide.

Richard Horsley has distinguished three types of prophets recognized within Second Temple Judaism: exegetical, oracular, and millennial.[16] This is useful, but modern typologies of prophecy tend to avoid the issue of what prophecy meant to different groups of people at this time. Many kinds of prophets may be distinguished.[17] But none of them would necessarily have been recognized as such by some of the more educated of society. On the other hand, all of them, and more, could have been recognized by poorly educated peasants, who stood in awe of anyone who could read,[18] let alone interpret the Scriptures and relate them to the present or the future. Since defining someone as a prophet is ultimately subjective, classifying "prophets" as a group needs to be done rather cautiously. One person's prophet is another's trickster. Empirically, there is no such thing as a prophet. "Prophet" is not a job description or even a definition of human aptitude. The interpretive task here is to clarify the criteria people used to determine

15. Gray, *Prophetic Figures,* 7-34.

16. Horsley, "Popular Prophetic Movements."

17. See, for example, not only the work of Horsley et al. (above, n. 8), but also the discussions of prophecy and its types in Crossan, *Historical Jesus,* 158-67; J. Blenkinsopp, "Prophecy and Priesthood in Josephus," *JJS* 25 (1974) 239-62; Aune, *Prophecy in Early Christianity;* and J. Becker, *Johannes der Täufer und Jesus von Nazareth* (Neukirchen-Vluyn: Neukirchener Verlag, 1972) 41-54.

18. In some traditional societies where literacy is poor, the man who can read is considered to possess spiritual or magical power. For example, the Marabouts of the Gambia and Senegal sometimes write out passages from the Koran to be eaten in certain remedies. The ability to read the Koran in itself provides the Marabout with considerable prestige, and his ability to know what passage might "fit" the requirements of the situation is tantamount to a spiritual power. This was described to me in detail during my residence in West Africa from 1990 to 1992.

whether a person was to be identified as a prophet in a given society. In regard to John the Baptist, therefore, we need to ask who considered him a prophet and by what criteria they did so.

For the later rabbis, prophecy seems to have been defined as the result of the indwelling of the Holy Spirit (the spirit of prophecy), which fills someone with heavenly power and the knowledge of the mind of God, enabling him (invariably him) to perform cures and miracles, know the past, predict the future, and give authoritative decrees on matters of law.[19] It is the capacity to give authoritative decrees that is, possibly, most important, not miracles or the power to predict the future. After all, magicians could perform miracles; healers, wonder-workers, and holy men could perform cures and exorcisms; all sorts of people could claim to see the future by various means; but authoritative legal interpretation and judgment were critical. According to the Tosephta, the present generation is not worthy of the prophetic Holy Spirit (*t. Soṭa* 13:3; *y. Soṭa* 24b; *b. Soṭa* 48b). The "men of the great assembly" had replaced the prophets as transmitters of the oral law (*m. 'Abot* 1:1). Discussion had replaced inspiration as the grounding for legal interpretation and judgment. The view of the writer of 1 Maccabees is the same: one day a prophet would make authoritative judgments about the defiled stones of the altar (1 Macc. 4:46) or the choosing of a high priest (1 Macc. 14:41). In the meantime people had to manage in other ways. If we find this view stretching from 1 Maccabees to the Talmuds, we may suppose that certain people believed this in the time of John as well. Josephus' caution itself betrays that he was aware that calling a person a "prophet" should not be done glibly. We do not need to associate this view with any one school of thought, for it seems quite likely that this was a view that distinguished the educated elite from the non-educated rather than a sectarian belief.

Josephus describes prophets as those who, with the chief priests, wrote the records of the nation (*Ag. Ap.* 1.29), namely, the Hebrew Scriptures. The prophets who wrote the records obtained their knowledge from "the inspiration that was from God" (*Ag. Ap.* 1.37). They therefore had the gift of the prophetic spirit that would give them knowledge of the distant past (as well as the future). All the Hebrew Scriptures were thought to have been written by prophets, for the writ-

19. For the importance of authoritative preaching and decrees, see M. Turner, "The Spirit of Prophecy and the Power of Authoritative Preaching in Luke-Acts: A Question of Origins," *NTS* 38 (1992) 66-68.

ing down of the Law itself was deemed a prophetic act. Moses was the greatest prophet — both as lawgiver and chronicler, the writer of the first five books. Then, as Josephus tells it, "the prophets coming after Moses wrote the history of the events in their own times in thirteen books" (*Ag. Ap.* 1.40). If the canon was to close, then prophets had to disappear, for one of the roles of a prophet was to write down new Scripture in accordance with his function as interpreter of the primary Law set by Moses and with his inspired knowledge of both the past and the future. Of course there could be no more prophets![20]

In the deuteronomistic history, prophets have the specific function of calling Israel to repentance. Since Israel was continually disobedient, and this caused God to punish the nation through various calamities, God sent prophets to exhort Israel to repent and return to the Law (Neh. 9:26, 30; 2 Kgs. 17:13). As John Kloppenborg notes, the presentation of John in Q picks up on the deuteronomistic portrayal of a prophet (Luke 3:7b; 7:24-26).[21] We may surmise that some people believed that John was a prophet because he behaved in a way consistent with this portrayal, just as in Zech. 1:3-6, where the prophet's preaching of repentance is linked with the former prophets. However, a person's preaching repentance did not necessarily indicate that the preacher was a prophet. O. H. Steck has observed that renewed preaching along these lines is usually ascribed to sages and scribes (4 Ezra 7:129-30; *Assumption of Moses* 9; *2 Apocalypse of Baruch* 31–32, 44–45, 85).[22] Therefore, one person might consider John a prophet, while another might consider him a sage or good man, on the basis of the same characteristics.

There were similar ambiguities surrounding those who made predictions. The "exegetical prophets," according to Richard Horsley's classification, or "sapiential prophets," according to David Aune's and Robert Webb's, would have partially fulfilled the criteria of prophecy, according to the educated elite, and they may have been considered prophets by many of the ordinary people, even if they did not consider themselves to be so. These prophets were men who were considered very wise and knowledgeable about Scripture, so wise and knowledge-

20. On the importance of historical writing as prophetic activity, see Gray, *Prophetic Figures*, 8-16.

21. J. S. Kloppenborg, *The Formation of Q: Trajectories in Ancient Wisdom Collections* (Philadelphia: Fortress, 1987) 104-05.

22. Steck, *Israel und das gewaltsame Geschick der Propheten*, 194.

able that they had a gift for finding in it predictions of the future. Josephus describes three Essenes — Judas (*Ant.* 13.311; *War* 1.78-80; cf. *War* 2.159), Menahem (*Ant.* 15.373-79), and Simon (*Ant.* 17.345-47) — who were classed as prophets by those who defined prophecy as true prediction. He also describes Pharisees as having this faculty of predicting on the basis of Scripture (*Ant.* 15.3-4; 14.172-76; 17.41-45). The predictions appear to have been quite specific — for example, that Herod's throne would be taken from him and his descendants.[23] If in retrospect the predictions turned out to be true, then the predictor was vindicated; to some he would be a prophet.

The Teacher of Righteousness of the Dead Sea Scrolls may be classed with these predictive prophets, though he may have been perceived as having more in common with the lawmaking prophets of old. It is likely that he defined the laws governing the community and that the sectarian community of the scrolls came to identify him with the awaited "Prophet" (like Moses) of 1QS 9:11.[24] Prophecy here seems to be the interpretation of hidden meaning in Scripture, which is precisely what the Teacher of Righteousness did (1QpHab. 2:6-10; 7:1-5a). The Holy Spirit or Wisdom was thought to empower people to interpret Scripture correctly and also to enable people to find in it the hidden meanings or mysteries that would unlock the past and future. The same spirit that enabled the prophets to write Scripture also enabled people to understand it. God taught Israel "through those anointed with his holy spirit and those who see the truth," that is, the prophets (CD 2:12-13; cf. 1QS 8:16). The interpretation of Scripture was carried on through "the Teacher of Righteousness to whom God has made known all the mysteries of the words of his servants the prophets" (1QpHab 7:4-5a).

Rebecca Gray has disputed whether *pesher* commentaries found at Qumran may be equated with what Josephus refers to in *War* 2.159 as Essene prophecy, and she is probably right to question this identification.[25] Josephus is probably focusing on predictions rather than interpretations. However, correct interpretation of Scripture to unlock the past, present, and future is the broader activity into which specific predictions (understood by some as "prophecies") should be under-

23. See Webb, *John the Baptizer and Prophet,* 322-26.

24. So G. Vermes, *The Dead Sea Scrolls in English,* 2nd ed. (Harmondsworth: Penguin, 1975) 49-50.

25. Gray, *Prohetic Figures,* 105-07.

stood. The latter takes place not separately but within the general framework of the former. The two phenomena should not be identified, as Gray notes, but the one is clearly much bigger than the other. As we find in the Habakkuk *pesher*, right (that is, inspired and multilayered) exegesis of Scripture was thought to lead both to predictions and to a proper understanding of history.

It seems from the evidence we have that many of the ordinary people did not care to make distinctions between true prophecy and intriguing predictions and that they were willing to ascribe prophetic powers equally to the sage and to the illiterate peasant if that person seemed convincing. Sages may have balked at being classed with the uneducated and at the gullibility of those who sought out such people. On the one hand, we have very learned, elite men who expounded Scripture and who, on the basis of their wisdom, piety, and scriptural knowledge, made predictions from time to time. On the other hand, just about anyone (sometimes even women; cf. Luke 2:36-38) could make predictions. The ability to foresee the future and the power of second sight were what made a prophet. This popular understanding of prophecy is reflected in Luke's narrative: the soldiers who beat Jesus ask mockingly, "Now prophet — who hit you?" (Luke 22:64), and the "Pharisee" who has Jesus to dinner doubts whether he is a real prophet because he does not appear to know, without being told, that the woman who anoints him is a sinner (Luke 7:39).[26]

This popular understanding of a prophet as someone who knows everything by the power of second sight is found also in the Fourth Gospel's tale about the Samaritan woman at the well. Jesus appears to know all about her relationships with men, and she responds, "Sir, I see that you are a prophet." The same attitude is preserved in rabbinic literature. People ask Hanina ben Dosa, "Are you a prophet?" after he knows that the daughter of Nehonia had come out of a pit she had fallen into (*b. B. Qam.* 50a; cf. *b. Yebam.* 121b, *b. Ber.* 34b).[27] In these instances, it seems unlikely that anyone placed Hanina ben Dosa on an equal footing with Moses or Isaiah; a contemporary prophet was not the same as a prophet of old. But a contemporary prophet — a predictor, a seer, a psychic — was still a prophet by a popular definition that Josephus scorns.

26. See G. Vermes, *Jesus the Jew: A Historian's Reading of the Gospels,* 2d ed. (London: SCM, 1983) 87.

27. See Crossan, *Historical Jesus,* 148.

Revolutionary leaders like Theudas or the Egyptian may have earned their popular reputation as prophets through their predictions.[28] They convinced people that signs and wonders would occur, but not necessarily that they would be instrumental in their occurrence. The signs and wonders would be effected by God and would indicate that liberation was soon to come. On the grounds of Scripture, perhaps, or second sight, they announced that Jerusalem would soon be free and that the time was ripe for successful revolt.

Only one person of the centuries preceding Josephus is credited by him with the power of true prophecy along the lines of prophets in ancient Israel: John Hyrcanus I (135-104 BCE), the Hasmonean high priest and ruler. Hyrcanus is said to have made predictions through direct inspiration from God, not through the interpretation of Scripture. He could "foresee and foretell the future" (*Ant.* 13.299-300; *War* 1.68-69; cf. *Ant.* 13.282-83).[29] Josephus states that Hyrcanus had the "gift of prophecy" (*War* 1.69; *Ant.* 13.299). He had direct revelations from God that were proved true.[30] Interestingly, Hyrcanus is remembered in rabbinic literature with almost equal esteem (e.g., *t. Soṭa* 13:5).

Josephus himself apparently predicted Vespasian's impending elevation to imperial office (*War* 3.400-402), but he never calls himself a prophet. Rabbi Yohanan ben Zakkai supposedly made the same prediction (*'Abot. R Nat.* 4:5; *b. Giṭ.* 56a-b), but rabbinic tradition likewise fails to call him a prophet.[31] Josephus makes it clear that he found his own prediction as an "oracle" within Scripture (*War* 6.312-13). In other words, it did not come from a blinding flash of insight directly from God but from his interpretation of Hebrew writings. While elsewhere Josephus describes his interest in the interpretation of dreams (*War* 3.351-54), dream interpretation seems to have been a corollary of his

28. Horsley considers them to be "millennial" prophets (" 'Like One of the Prophets of Old,' " 454 n. 42).

29. See Vermes, *Jesus the Jew,* 2d ed., 93.

30. Webb classifies John Hyrcanus I as a "clerical" prophet because he was a priest (*John the Baptizer and Prophet,* 317-19). Only two instances of Hyrcanus' prophetic activity are given: in one he heard a heavenly voice while burning incense in the Temple (Josephus, *Ant.* 13.282-83), and in the other he saw the future of his sons in a dream (*War* 1.68-69; *Ant.* 13.299-300). Josephus possibly regarded Hyrcanus as a prophet of the ancient type. He was in very close contact with God (*War* 1.69).

31. G. Vermes, *Scripture and Tradition in Judaism: Haggadic Studies* (Leiden: Brill, 1961) 34-35.

interpretation of Scripture. Steve Mason has noted that Josephus attributed his predictive faculty to the fact that he was a priest and was therefore familiar with the prophecies of sacred Scripture. It is this scriptural knowledge that gave him the key to the future.[32] Rebecca Gray has argued that Josephus did understand himself to be a prophet, even without any specific statement to that effect.[33] Her uncovering of Josephus' veiled language is intriguing; it seems that he may have hoped secretly to be identified by his readers as a prophet like Jeremiah, an identification endorsed, he hoped, by his timely prediction. But if this is so, Josephus avoids mentioning his private aspiration directly. Rather, he seems to be aware that many of those he respected would have considered this ambition laughable.[34]

There were, according to Josephus, people who claimed to have received divine oracles. While the high priest John Hyrcanus I had true revelations, Josephus, who was certainly snobbish, seems to have considered that revelations coming to the ordinary people were bogus. And even if they turned out to be true, he did not accept that the person giving the oracle was a prophet. During the siege of Jerusalem by Herod in 37 BCE certain "weaker people" around the Temple were seized by possessions and made up θειωδέστερον, "oracular utterances" (*War* 1.347). Later, during the 60's, a certain man named Jesus son of Ananias, a "simple peasant," was seized by possession while in Jerusalem during the Feast of Tabernacles and cried out an oracle: "A voice from the east, a voice from the west, a voice from the four winds, a voice against Jerusalem and the sanctuary, a voice against the bridegroom and the bride, a voice against the people!" His constant cries around the streets of Jerusalem seemed to have constituted a social disturbance. He was brought before the Roman governor and flogged, but despite this punishment he continued to utter these words all the time for seven years and five months, until, during the siege of Jerusalem, he said, "Woe once again to the city and to the people and to the temple . . . and to me also." He was then hit by a rock and died

32. S. N. Mason, *Flavius Josephus on the Pharisees: A Composition-Critical Study* (Leiden: Brill, 1991) 270-71.

33. Gray, *Prophetic Figures*, 35-79.

34. Cf. L. H. Feldman, "Prophets and Prophecy in Josephus," *JTS* 41 (1990) 405-06, who is critical of Gray's thesis; also S. N. Mason, Review of *Prophetic Figures in Late Second Temple Jewish Palestine: The Evidence from Josephus*, by Rebecca Gray, in *IOUDAIOS Review* (electronic) 4.006 (February 1994).

(*War* 6.300-309).[35] Despite his acceptance of Jesus' predictions, Josephus does not call him a prophet, and there seems to be something painfully comic about the presentation.

Josephus spares the reader any information that would locate John the Baptist's activities at the same place as Theudas' later demonstration, and he also avoids mentioning that anyone recognized John as a prophet, even though he notes that many were willing to do whatever he advised them to do. Josephus' skepticism of those popularly considered to be prophets may have made him reticent in this case. He scornfully relates how, during the burning of the Temple in 70 CE, a "false prophet" proclaimed to the people of Jerusalem that God commanded them to go to the Temple court, where they would receive "signs of freedom" (*War* 6.283-85), when in fact they were doomed. Josephus comments that the "numerous prophets" — he forgets to add that they were "false" — were suborned by the "tyrants" (Jewish revolutionary leaders) "to delude the people by exhorting them to wait for help from God" (*War* 6.286). It would have been easy for readers to class John with this group, if Josephus had mentioned eschatology or noted that John was deemed a prophet by the masses that came to him.

Furthermore, the nature of John's prophecy was predictive: the end was soon. Clearly, the end was not yet. Given Josephus' wariness, a prophet could only be considered a prophet if he made a true prediction. John's prediction had not yet come true, though it might yet. To call John a prophet would have meant believing John's prediction to be true, but Josephus would not take such a risk. Moreover, Josephus' Roman readership would only have been amused to read that John, supposedly so good, believed in the eventual termination of Roman control of Judea as an act of God's benevolence. However, to scoff at John's predictions would have been to cast John in an unfavorable light as a false prophet, whereas Josephus accepted that he was a good man who advised righteousness and piety. Josephus may have reasoned that it was better to avoid this issue completely. What the ordinary people said of John was irrelevant.

However, there is something more implied in the rather approving manner in which Josephus refers to the destruction of Antipas' army as divine vengeance for the execution of John. God would not have acted with such vengeance had not John been very much on God's side, as it were. Good men could be killed without God exacting so

35. Gray, *Prophetic Figures,* 158-63.

ferocious a retaliation; the degree of the vengeance was commensurate with God's assessment of John.

That Josephus could consider John divinely approved without calling him a prophet perhaps gives us a clue to the later Jewish position on John reflected in the Fourth Gospel. He could be a bright lamp (John 5:35) without being a prophet. As Vermes notes in regard to rabbinic Judaism, "although prophecy as such was believed to have ended, it was still possible to conceive that a favoured individual might be endowed with the gift of prediction."[36] Since this view that prophecy had ceased was current in some elite circles during the first century, this may well sum up the Pharisees' position on John. The later rabbis acknowledged that a predictive capacity could exist in the form of interpretation of Scripture or second sight (brought about through God's favor) without it being prophecy as such. They were reluctant to evoke miracles and refused to ascribe any real importance to them if they did take place. Miracles might testify to the indwelling of the prophetic spirit, but they could be tricks or even demonic acts.

The Gospels testify to the existence of this sort of skepticism in the first century (note, for example, Mark 3:22-26=Matt. 12:23-26=Luke 11:15-18 and Matt. 9:34: "He casts out demons by the prince of demons"; cf. John 7:20; 8:48, 52; 10:20). There is little doubt that some people — variously identified in the Gospels — thought that Jesus' healings and exorcisms were effected not by his possession of the Holy Spirit but through his possession by a demonic power. This may well have been a widely accepted notion; many Jews may have waited for proof. Likewise, in a saying of Jesus, it is suggested that some attributed John's "prophecy" to demon possession (Matt. 11:18; Luke 7:33). In the latter case, the context demands that the people ("this generation") who thought John possessed by a demon were those who whined like children in the marketplace, who had gone out to see John but had considered him unconvincing (Matt. 11:7-19; Luke 7:24-35). We will return to this passage in the last chapter.

That John claimed the need for a new kind of immersion seems clear from the evidence. As we argued above in Chapter 2, this claim was probably based on an exegesis of Isaiah (though others, including Jesus, may have considered this innovation to be divinely ordained, so Mark 11:27-33 and parr.). However, people may have understood John to be

36. Vermes, *Jesus the Jew,* 2d ed., 93.

defining something new in Law (that is, that immersion should follow inner cleansing) and therefore considered him to be a prophet of the old type. Others may have seen him as a prophet along the lines of the deuteronomistic history, because he was calling Israel to repentance. On the other hand, his reputation among most of the population as a prophet may have rested purely on the plausibility of his prediction that the end would soon come and on his knowledge of Scripture. People seem to have flocked to him and hoped for leadership from him.

Typologically, then, John does not belong to the general category of "Leadership Popular Prophets" proposed by Webb.[37] There is no evidence that he predicted that signs and wonders would take place and that he would lead people to a redeemed Jerusalem in just a short time. It is difficult to be precise with so little evidence, but John's type of prophecy may have been of the same type as the sapiential or interpretive prophecy of the Pharisees and the Essenes noted by Josephus. Whether called prophecy or not, the procedure of finding in Scripture the key to the future characterizes this particular type of activity. Moreover, like the Teacher of Righteousness, such prophets would also have been considered "teachers of righteousness," and therefore it is not surprising that we find disciples mentioned in regard to them (*Ant.* 13.311).

We just do not know how John arrived at the conviction that the end was near and that, because of its nearness, he should urgently proclaim an immersion of repentance for the remission of sins. However, the substance of his "prophecy" does not come across as a new oracle. He did not behave like one claiming to communicate the mind of God to the populace, as did Jesus son of Ananias. There may be a superficial similarity between the prophecy of Jesus son of Ananias and that of John, given Jesus' reference to a "voice" and John's possible use of Isa. 40:3. Webb notes that the voice of Isa. 40:3 was a "clearly recognized idiom referring to the voice of God."[38] But this is not so, for the voice of Isaiah asks that the paths of "our God" be made straight, which suggests that the voice is of an Israelite. Furthermore, this verse may have been connected with John in particular by the early Church as an appropriate vehicle for explaining him; it is very difficult to assess its

37. Webb, *John the Baptizer and Prophet,* 333-39. See also the criticism of Webb's position by J. P. Meier, "John the Baptist in Josephus: Philology and Exegesis," *JBL* 111/2 (1992) 235-36 n. 28.

38. Webb, *John the Baptizer and Prophet,* 340.

authenticity on the lips of John. Horsley's identification of John as an oracular prophet therefore seems inaccurate.[39] John's prediction of the coming one, who would be far greater than he and who would judge Israel, seems to be a straightforward prediction without the poetry of an oracular utterance such as we find on the lips of Jesus son of Ananias. The call to repentance could be made by any sage.

Did John think of himself as a prophet? An answer would depend on his particular view of the nature of prophecy, but we have no idea what that might have been. If he sought to convince people of his prophetic insight, this did not lead him to consider himself highly. According to the Fourth Gospel, he did not identify himself with any end-time prophetic figure (John 1:20-21); all these were still to come. The book of Acts independently preserves his denial that he was Elijah (Acts 13:25). His self-deprecation was so great that, in a saying preserved by all four Gospels and Acts, he states that his relationship with the coming eschatological figure of judgment put him beneath the status of a slave; he was not worthy even to untie the thong of the sandal of the coming one (Mark 1:7; Luke 3:16; John 1:27; Acts 13:25; cf. Matt. 3:11). If this self-estimation is historical, then John would have disappointed anyone asking him about his place in the eschatological scheme of things. He would likewise have disappointed anyone asking whether he was a (non-eschatological) prophet. Did John himself share the skepticism toward prophecy that was the mark of the educated few? We cannot know for certain, but he likely was educated; his possible use of Scripture and interpretation suggests as much. Despite his conviction that he carried a message in accordance with the will of God, he was in his own estimation a lowly figure.

One conclusion seems to be clear. If John had *explicitly* linked his prediction of an imminent judgment and his practice of immersion with the immediate overthrow of Roman rule in Judea, or if he had made prophetic claims, Josephus would have denounced him as a charlatan. This is our surest indication that, despite Antipas' action, John said nothing directly against the occupying power and did not incite people to revolt. That revolt was implicit in his message remains, nevertheless, quite possible. His message was, like that of every expert in prediction, an ambiguous one.

39. Horsley, "'Like One of the Prophets of Old,'" 450-54; Hollenbach, "John the Baptist," 887, 891.

Herod Antipas

If we are to understand John's significance during his own time we must explore further the reasons for his death, even though such an exercise must be speculative. We have limited resources at our disposal; none of them is entirely reliable.

It has been suggested that John was someone whom — with his call to righteousness in the wilderness — ordinary people classed with the prophets who later gathered people together in uncultivated areas of the land in order to see signs and wonders or march on Jerusalem. Antipas seems to have suspected that his message could flower into this particular form of prophecy-cum-revolution, and he had to act quickly before it did. Josephus writes:

> And when the others gathered together, because they were indeed excited to the highest degree by hearing his teaching, Herod feared that such great persuasiveness over the people might lead to some kind of conflict, for they looked as if they would do everything by his advice. [He thought it] much better to get rid [of John] before some innovation from him took place, striking first to remove [the possibility of any] change coming about, so as not to regret getting into complicated affairs. Therefore, on account of the suspicion of Herod, John was sent in chains to Machaerus . . . and there he was killed. (*Ant.* 18.118-19)

"The others" at the beginning of Josephus' description of John's arrest must refer back to people already mentioned. The most natural reading is simply to think of those Jews who came to believe after John's death that Antipas' army had been destroyed by God as vengeance for John's murder (*Ant.* 18.116).[40] These Jews are to be distinguished from "the Jews" in general whom John exhorted.

40. Contra Webb, *John the Baptizer and Prophet*, 36, who thinks that "the others" may refer to anybody, even Gentiles. However, in Acts John the Baptist does not address Gentiles, but "all the people of Israel" (Acts 13:24). Meier suggests that he may have been speaking to nonvirtuous Jews as opposed to the virtuous Jews just referred to ("John the Baptist in Josephus," 232), but since they are described as being prepared to do anything he advised, they cannot have stayed nonvirtuous for very long. Rather, this statement indicates that they were all those Jews who came to John (in a crowd), repented, did what he advised, and were immersed.

According to Josephus, Herod appears to have thought that while everything was peaceful now, some "innovation" (νεώτερον) in John's teaching could change all that. Gray notes that Josephus uses the similar word νεωτερισμός to refer to innovation in the cultic sphere (*Ant.* 5.101, 111; 9.204), but elsewhere it refers to politically revolutionary change or outright revolt (e.g., *War* 5.152).[41] It would take only a small change in emphasis and the situation might lead to rather more complicated affairs (εἰς πράγματα ἐμπεσών).[42] Antipas feared στάσις; in one manuscript this word is replaced by ἀπόστασις, revolt. But στάσις itself in Josephus refers to civil dissension.[43] He uses the word to refer to civil demonstrations against the Romans (*Ant.* 18.8) or clashes between Jewish factions (*Ant.* 18.8).[44]

Antipas, according to Josephus, reasoned that if he did not act quickly and make a preemptive strike against John, then something disastrous might happen that would lead him to regret his noninterference. The many popular prophets of the wilderness and elsewhere had yet to appear, and the massacre of Samaritans by Pontius Pilate was still a little time away, but the mood of the people may have been correctly gauged by Antipas here. If they held the same kind of expectations of John as they would later of other "prophets," and if they interpreted the book of Isaiah in the manner outlined above, then Antipas' fears may not have been completely groundless.

One should recall at this point that Josephus characterizes his "fourth philosophy" — the so-called Zealots — as being a kind of revolutionary wing of the disciples of the Pharisees. According to Josephus, the Zealots agreed in all respects with the opinions of the Pharisees, except that they were convinced that God alone was their master and therefore had a "passionate love of liberty" (*Ant.* 18.4-10, 23). They took their name "from their professed zeal for *virtue*" (*War* 7.270). One of

41. Gray, *Prophetic Figures,* 201 n. 18.

42. The word ἐμπεσών means "rushing in violently." See LSJ, 545.

43. Josephus, *Jewish Antiquities, Books XVIII–XX,* trans. L. H. Feldman, vol. 9, LCL (Cambridge, MA: Heinemann, 1965) 83 note *f.*

44. See the discussion in T. Rajak, *Josephus: The Historian and His Society* (London: Duckworth, 1983) 91-94. Josephus himself was preoccupied with the dangers of στάσις. See also R. A. Horsley, "High Priests and the Politics of Roman Palestine: A Contextual Analysis of the Evidence in Josephus," *JSJ* 17 (1986) 44-48; Webb, *John the Baptizer and Prophet,* 38. Gray rightly notes that Josephus' language in relation of John is charged with political overtones (*Prophetic Figures,* 119, 201 n. 20).

the main aims of the revolutionaries was to keep "religious rules from contaminations" (*War* 2.391) and to "preserve inviolate all the institutions of the ancestors" (*War* 2.393).[45] Josephus accuses the Zealots of defiling the Temple, largely because they allowed themselves to be killed by Roman missiles within its precincts (*War* 4.202, 215).

Interestingly, when the apostle Paul refers to his "former life in Judaism" (Gal. 1:13-14), he professes to have been extremely zealous (ζηλωτῆς) for the traditions of his ancestors. In Phil. 3:5-6 he describes himself in terms of the Law as a Pharisee and in terms of zeal (ζῆλος) as a persecutor of the Church. In other words, his zeal manifested itself in action, in his case the action of persecuting those who claimed that the Messiah had already come in the person of Jesus of Nazareth. Zealousness for the Law was presumably considered a positive attribute in Pharisaic circles, and one that might manifest itself in a variety of ways, some more political than others.[46] It is well known that only in the *Antiquities* (ca. 93/94 CE) does Josephus describe the "Zealots" separately as a fourth philosophy among the (educated male) Jews (*Ant.* 18.23-25). In the *Jewish War* (ca. 73 CE), only three philosophies are described: Essenes, Pharisees, and Sadducees (*War* 2.119-66). It is possible that Josephus decided to detach the Zealots from the ambit of the Pharisees by citing them as a different group. But his language betrays that — whatever they were — they were closely aligned with the Pharisees. It is then possible that Zealots were disciples of the Pharisees whose zeal for virtue manifested itself in ways that threatened Rome, but not a cohesive group.

With the Zealots it is apparent that religious and political ideology intertwined. Passionate feelings excited by John's teaching may have been aroused not simply on account of zeal for the Law, but also on account of fervor that was tied up with an expectation of deliverance from Roman rule. Scobie dismissed the idea that John could have had anything in common with the Zealots — understood as a sect — because "his message was not a political one and he was opposed to

45. See Rhoads, *Israel in Revolution,* 167. Horsley has challenged the old view that the Zealots were a party and has argued that there was no sustained and cohesive movement of nationalistic, violent resistance to Roman rule during the first century; see R. A. Horsley, *Jesus and the Spiral of Violence: Popular Jewish Resistance in Roman Palestine* (San Francisco: Harper & Row, 1987) 77-89.

46. See J. D. G. Dunn, *Jesus and the Spirit: A Study of the Religious and Charismatic Experience of Jesus and the First Christians as Reflected in the New Testament* (Philadelphia: Westminster, 1975) 270-71.

violence,"[47] but such a judgment seems too hasty. An apolitical John (along with an apolitical Jesus) is certainly something that the Gospel writers wished to visualize, but it is not an image appropriate to the age in which John and Jesus lived. As for John's supposed nonviolence, he appears to have been pacifist in his own particular message, but we do not know if he considered active revolt inappropriate at all times, in the present and in the future. He did not tell the men serving as Antipas' soldiers to lay down their weapons and beat them into plowshares. In John's teaching, one could be a righteous soldier by not robbing people and by being content with one's wages (Luke 3:14). John evidently did not tell these men to stop serving as soldiers, nor did he ask the toll collectors to desist from collecting revenue for the wicked oppressors of Israel. It may well be that Luke included these two items from John's body of teaching in his Gospel precisely to prove to anyone associating John with revolt that he did not endorse it.[48] But such instructions concerned the period prior to judgment. What might happen at the time of God's action to liberate a captive Jerusalem would have been a different matter.

John appears from the Gospel accounts to have said something directly damning about Herod Antipas. John may have implicitly linked Antipas with the Gentile oppressors of Israel on account of the apparent disregard for Torah shown by Antipas and his family. The association of the "princes" of Israel with Gentile oppressors is found in Isa. 1:23: "Your princes are rebels and companions of thieves" (9:16) and even more explicitly in the *Targum Pseudo-Jonathan* of Isaiah (24:1; 27:1; 28:1-4). In the new realm, "no king who does evil" would be permitted (*Tg. Ps.-J.* Isa. 35:9).

The synoptic Gospels state that John accused Antipas of disobeying the Law.[49] Specifically, and infamously, Antipas had married his living half-brother Herod's wife, Herodias.[50] In order to do this he had

47. C. H. H. Scobie, *John the Baptist* (London: SCM, 1964) 33.

48. See B. Kinman, "Luke's Exoneration of John the Baptist," *JTS* 44/2 (1993) 595-98.

49. Ibid.

50. Mark and Matthew state that Herodias was the wife of "Philip" (Mark 6:17; Matt. 14:3); Josephus says that she was married to "Herod" (*Ant.* 18.109, 136). Herod the Great had two sons named "Herod," one born of Cleopatra of Jerusalem and the full brother of Philip the tetrarch (*Ant.* 17.21; *War* 1.562) and the other, the son of Mariamne II (*War* 1.562, 573, 588; *Ant.* 17.19; 18.109, 136). Luke dropped the name "Philip,"

divorced his first wife, whose father, the Nabatean king Aretas IV, later went to war with Antipas and totally destroyed his army (*Ant.* 18.109-15). John would probably not have criticized the tetrarch for his divorce of Aretas' daughter, despite the political instability which resulted from the action. It was perfectly lawful for a man to divorce his wife (Deut. 24:1-4), and Josephus too was not against divorce and remarriage. After all, he divorced his own wife because he "was not pleased with her behavior" (*Life* 426). Josephus himself was not critical of Antipas directly but of Herodias, who "confounded the directives of the fathers" by divorcing a living husband (*Ant.* 18.136). What was permissible for a man was not permissible for a woman.

It is possible that John did not consider Herodias a free woman eligible to remarry but thought her still married to her first husband, since her initiation of divorce was unlawful. The real issue as presented in Mark, however, is that Herodias was technically Antipas' brother's wife, and as such the union was against the Law (Lev. 18:16) even if the divorce was legal. In Lev. 20:21 this kind of union is deemed impure: "If a man takes his brother's wife, it is impurity; he has uncovered his brother's nakedness; they shall be childless." As with the Marcan version of what John states, the scriptural passage does not in fact state that the brother needs to be alive, though this is implied. However, in the case of a dead brother who was childless, a man was obligated to marry his widowed sister-in-law (Deut. 25:5-10). Illicit bodily connections between people resulted in a corresponding bodily impurity that could have such consequences.[51] If Josephus was at all familiar with this accusation, he may have preferred not to discuss it since in Roman law marriage of a man to his living brother's ex-wife was acceptable. However, he did note that Herodias' divorce of her husband was contrary to Jewish custom, and since Josephus was knowledgeable in matters of

---

perhaps because he was aware that it was an error. It is also omitted in several manuscripts of Matthew and Mark; see H. W. Hoehner, *Herod Antipas* (Cambridge: Cambridge University Press, 1972) 131-36. Hoehner suggests that the reference is to Herod son of Mariamne II, called "Philip," but this seems apologetic. It is more likely that Mark's story reflects some confusion between Herodias' first husband, Herod, and Herodias' son-in-law, Philip the tetrarch, whom her daughter Salome married sometime before his death in 34 CE (*Ant.* 18.136-37); see J. P. Meier, *A Marginal Jew: Rethinking the Historical Jesus. Volume Two: Mentor, Message, and Miracles* (New York: Doubleday, 1994) 172.

51. See J. Neusner, *The Idea of Purity in Ancient Judaism. With a Critique and a Commentary by Mary Douglas* (Leiden: Brill, 1973) 14-15, 22-25, 34-38.

Scripture, he would also have known of Lev. 18:16 and 20:21. Since Antipas' marriage was contrary to Scripture, it is very likely that John was among several pious men who criticized the marriage; it would have been strange if John were the only Jew to have mentioned it. Josephus does not mention this marriage and family matter, but instead attributes Antipas' execution of John to the tetrarch's fear that John's popularity with the crowds would lead to some form of sedition.

Webb is surely right that we should not imagine a man-to-man war of words between John and Herod Antipas, despite the direct form of address in Matthew (14:4) and Mark (6:18); John's criticisms were probably made to the crowds around him, and Antipas would have received a report about them.[52] Furthermore, as Webb notes,

> when an accusation that a ruler of Jews is a Torah-breaker and impure is placed within the same context as John's proclamation of the imminent removal and destruction of the wicked (which would include Antipas, from John's point of view and those who followed him) by an expected figure of judgment and restoration . . . then his rebuke of Antipas takes on new, indeed serious, implications for Antipas' continued political control of his subjects.[53]

If this is so, then John's criticism of Antipas' marriage was all that was needed to prompt Antipas, who was already suspicious, to arrest and kill John, in case personal criticism led to incitement of those in Perea and Galilee to revolt against him. Antipas had already run into conflict with those who followed the rules of Torah carefully when he built his new capital city, Tiberias, on an old graveyard (*Ant.* 18.36-38), which was an unclean zone, but he did not immediately round up everyone

52. Webb, *John the Baptizer and Prophet,* 367.

53. Ibid., 368. See also Horsley and Hanson, *Bandits, Prophets, and Messiahs,* 177-78 and Hollenbach, "John the Baptist," 892-93, who see evidence of class conflict in John's pronouncements. Their analysis requires us to see John as an alienated, poor, rural priest, but we simply do not know whether he was or not. See Carl Kazmierski, *John the Baptist: Prophet and Evangelist* (Collegeville, MN: The Liturgical Press/Michael Glazier, 1996) 27-29, for a critique of Hollenbach's position. In challenging Antipas, he certainly took it upon himself to confront an individual member of the upper class, but whether he confronted the class itself is unknown. In regard to the general compatibility of Josephus and Mark in the story of John, see Scobie, *John the Baptist,* 178-86 and J. Ernst, *Johannes der Täufer: Interpretation, Geschichte, Wirkungsgeschichte* (Berlin: de Gruyter, 1989) 340-46.

who criticized him and throw them into prison. Criticism of Antipas alone, even in such a personal matter as his marriage, would not have been sufficient motivation for him. Just as Herodias was criticized by some regarding her marital affairs, as later reported by Josephus, so would Antipas have tolerated such criticism. It was the combination of John's criticism and the popular assembly in the wilderness — as Josephus describes it — that made John dangerous when other critics were not worth killing. Furthermore, people appear to have seen John as a prophet, and personal criticisms by someone whom people considered inspired by God were potentially more dangerous than others, in that they could induce people to act in ways that would suggest to the Romans that Antipas might not have adequate control over the population he governed. A massing of religiously excited people in the wilderness beside the Jordan and elsewhere, the hailing of someone as a prophet, and that person's criticism — all these factors together must have spelled trouble as far as Antipas was concerned.

In Mark's Gospel, while mention is made of people coming from Jerusalem and Judea,[54] nothing is stated concerning anyone coming from Perea (Mark 1:5a; cf. Matt. 3:5). This may be because it was in Perea that many of John's activities took place, as the Fourth Gospel indicates (10:40), and therefore people did not need to come *from* there. At the time of John, there were many Jewish towns and villages in Perea, despite a strong Gentile presence in the large cities.[55] Luke's reference to John going into the region around the Jordan (Luke 3:3) seems to come from a Q reference to this location (cf. Matt. 3:5b), indicating that John traveled around the region. Antipas would have known that the Jewish population of his own territory was excited by John. Like Josephus, many may have considered John to be a good man and held him in high esteem, even if they did not accept, as some did, that he was a prophet (cf. Mark 11:32, where *all* hold John to be a prophet).

54. Mark 1:5a; cf. Matt. 3:5. Mark uses the language of someone who knows the distinctions between different regions in the locality; note, e.g., Mark 3:7-8; cf. Matt. 4:25; Luke 6:17. That Jerusalem is singled out within Judea (Mark 1:5; cf. 3:7-8) also comes from a local understanding that the city "dominates all the neighborhood as a head over the body," as Josephus puts it (*War* 3.54). The entire region of the Land of Israel is referred to as "Judea" by Graeco-Roman writers; see Feldman, "Prophets and Prophecy in Josephus," 5-11.

55. E. Schürer, *The History of the Jewish People in the Age of Jesus Christ (175 B.C.–A.D. 135)*, rev. and ed. G. Vermes et al., vol. 2 (Edinburgh: Clark, 1979) 10-13.

Antipas was thought to have done an evil thing in murdering him, and therefore when Antipas' armies were utterly defeated by Aretas IV, Jews who had gone out to him considered his defeat a fitting punishment from God because of his crime in putting John to death (*Ant.* 18.117, 119).

The colorful tale of the death of John as found in Mark 6:17-29, and modified in Matt. 14:3-12,[56] runs as follows:

> For Herod himself had sent [for John] and had John arrested and had him bound and put in prison, on account of Herodias, the wife of his brother Philip, because he had married her. For John had been saying to Herod, "It is not lawful for you to have the wife of your brother Philip." And Herodias had a grudge against him and wanted to kill him, and could not, for Herod was afraid of John, knowing that he was a righteous and holy man, and he kept him safe. And when he heard him he was very perplexed; and he was hearing him gladly. And a special day came when Herod on his birthday gave a banquet for his lords and chiliarchs and the leading men of Galilee; and when his daughter [of Herodias][57] came in and danced, she

56. On the relationship of the two accounts, see Hoehner, *Herod Antipas,* 113-17; J. P. Meier, "John the Baptist in Matthew's Gospel," *JBL* 99/3 (1980) 399-400; and J. Gnilka, "Das Martyrium Johannes des Täufers (Mk 6,17-29)," in *Orientierung an Jesus: Zur Theologie der Synoptiker,* ed. P. Hoffmann et al. (Freiburg: Herder, 1973) 89-90. Meier thinks that Matthew was entirely indebted to Mark and that Matthew's alterations reflect his theological program. The extent of Matthew's modifications leads Hoehner to suggest that there were two separate traditions of the Baptist's death. For other, later versions of the Baptist's death, see Hoehner, *Herod Antipas,* 123-24.

57. The reading here is disputed, since early manuscripts vary, but it is likely that the unnamed daughter is referred to as "his" (Herod's) and that scribes altered this to "her" in order to make it clear that the daughter was Herodias' by her previous marriage. Mark 6:22 most probably read in its original form: καὶ εἰσελθούσης τῆς θυγατρὸς αὐτοῦ Ἡρῳδιάδος. To read her name as "Herodias" (so Meier, *Marginal Jew,* vol. 2, 172), however, ignores the possibility that Ἡρῳδιάδος might still be semantically genitive (as is αὐτοῦ), even if included in a genitive absolute phrase, as here. Given that the daughter asks "her mother" (Herodias) what she should ask for (6:24), it is clear that she is Herodias' daughter. Although a child could gain an adoptive father, the child's true mother remained his or her mother. Mark, in fact, seems to make plain the actual relationships: the daughter is indeed Antipas', as legal guardian or adoptive father, but Herodias is the mother, and the genitive of Herodias may be translated as indicating her maternity: she is "of Herodias." Moreover, to introduce the name of a young girl would be unusual in this cultural context; even Antipas' first wife, daughter of Aretas IV,

> pleased Herod and those who were reclining at table with him, and the king said to the girl, "Ask of me whatever you want and I will give it to you," and he swore to her, "Whatever you ask of me, I will give it to you, even up to half my kingdom." And she went out and said to her mother, "What shall I ask for?" And she said, "The head of John the Baptist." And straight away she came quickly before the king and asked, saying, "I want you to give me immediately the head of John the Baptist on a plate." And although the king was very sorry, because of his oath and because of those reclining at table, he did not want to refuse her. And straight away the king sent an executioner and commanded him to bring [John's] head. And he went and beheaded him in the prison, and brought his head on a plate and gave it to the girl, and the girl gave it to her mother. And when his [John's] disciples heard, they came and took away his body, and laid it in a tomb. (Mark 6:17-29)

It is an evocative story: the wicked queen Herodias manipulates her husband, by means of her daughter (Salome), into murdering John during Antipas' birthday banquet. So evocative are the images that Salome's dance and John's head on a platter have been popular subjects of Christian art for centuries. Interestingly, Luke omits the story in his gospel, and only briefly mentions the imprisonment and beheading of John in two places:

> Herod the tetrarch, who had been reproached by him [John] concerning Herodias, his brother's wife, and concerning all the evil things that Herod had done, added this also to them all: he shut up John in prison. (Luke 3:19-20)

> Herod the tetrarch heard about everything that had taken place, and he was perplexed because it was said by some that John had been

is unnamed in Josephus' account. If Mark did wish to give her name and believed that it was the same as her mother's, one would at least expect a note that she was "also named Herodias." Lastly, we know that she was named Salome, so if Mark were giving us her name, he would be wrong. Given that Mark confused Herodias' first husband with the first husband of Salome, anything is possible, but it seems more likely that he did not know the name of the daughter or did not think it important, and that he wished only to indicate that the daughter was both Antipas' (legally) and "of Herodias," which makes perfect sense.

> raised from the dead, by some that Elijah had appeared, and by others that one of the prophets of old had risen. Herod said, "John I beheaded. Who is this about whom I hear such things?" And he tried to see him [Jesus]. (Luke 9:7-9)

Luke may have omitted the tale out of skepticism about its historicity or else out of a wish not to give too much space to John,[58] but he mentions something new: that John reproached Herod Antipas for "all the evil things that Herod had done." If this comment derives from historical information, John's criticism of Antipas may have been for a whole host of things that rendered him disobedient to the Law and impure.

It is noteworthy that in both of Antipas' known transgressions — his building of Tiberias on a graveyard and his marriage to Herodias — the issue of impurity is foremost. According to Josephus, Jews settling in Tiberias would be unclean for seven days (cf. Num. 19:11-16), and therefore Antipas could only find as new settlers "a promiscuous bunch" forcibly brought there from Galilee and elsewhere in Antipas' territories, even possibly slaves and prisoners whom he freed and provided with houses and land, on the condition that they never leave the city (*Ant.* 18.36-38). His marriage to Herodias was not one that would be punished formally, but it was still impure and, as noted above, the punishment was thought to be childlessness. Luke's use of the word ἐλεγχόμενος, "having been reproached," in 3:19 carries the sense that John had put Antipas to shame. Declaring that Antipas, a Jewish ruler, was in a state of continual uncleanness would certainly have been considered an attempt to shame the tetrarch. Given the importance of being clean to John and to other Jews and the nature of John's immersion, John may have declared that Antipas was someone who needed to repent, bear good fruit, and then come to immersion in order to be clean. Antipas' carelessness about the site of Tiberias would only have served to stress the point.

58. Hoehner contests the thesis of Bultmann, *The History of the Synoptic Tradition* (Oxford: Blackwell, 1963) 301, that the story of John's death was not originally found in Mark (i.e., *Ur-Markus*). Hoehner notes that Luke had already included a great deal about the Baptist, and, since Luke had concluded the content of John's preaching near the beginning of his Gospel, culminating in John's imprisonment (3:19-20), it would have been unnatural for him to follow Mark in mentioning him here; see Hoehner, *Herod Antipas*, 112-13.

In portraying Antipas as actively hostile toward John rather than ambivalent, Luke preserves a tradition not only of intense antipathy between John and Antipas, but also between Jesus and Antipas. In Luke 13:31-33 Pharisees warn Jesus that Herod wants to kill him, and Jesus responds by calling the tetrarch "that fox." Only in the Lucan passion narrative is a direct confrontation between Antipas and Jesus introduced. Antipas is described as mocking Jesus by dressing him in a gorgeous robe and sending him back to Pilate (Luke 23:7-12). This is striking, because, contrary to Luke and Josephus, Mark's account (6:17-29) all but exonerates Antipas for the death of John. In Mark, Antipas is trapped by an honorable motive: that of keeping his oath in front of witnesses.[59] We could, of course, put Luke's depiction down to his redactional activity, which betrays some bias against the tetrarch. But the bias against him must have come from somewhere. Luke's antipathy toward Antipas seems hard to trace to direct conflict between him and Jesus; rather, it seems to be traceable to Antipas' action concerning John. Perhaps to amplify the characterization of Antipas as an enemy of Jesus and John, Luke includes Antipas in his passion narrative.[60]

Mark's depiction of Antipas is, by contrast, almost positive. This may derive from an awareness that many Jews in powerful positions, just like Josephus, thought of John as "a righteous and holy man." Antipas "heard him gladly," implying that he got John to come up and deliver his teaching to him, rather in the fashion of a visiting sage at court, though Antipas was greatly "perplexed."[61] This statement may reflect a Christian view that, despite the Jewish acceptance of John as a good man, the Jews had failed to understand what he was talking about. Mark indicates that Antipas did not really know what to do with John, once he had him in prison. Antipas is then manipulated by his cunning wife, Herodias, who is described as having a grudge against John, though we are told nothing about why. Therefore, the Marcan depiction of Antipas as sympathetic to John may possibly be additional evidence of a Christian awareness of the kind of attitude we find exhibited by Josephus. This attitude has made its way into the story of Antipas'

59. Hoehner, *Herod Antipas,* 165-67.

60. For a detailed discussion of the historicity of the passage, see Hoehner, *Herod Antipas,* 224-50.

61. For an alternative reading, "he did many things," see D. A. Black, "The Text of Mark 6.20," *NTS* 34 (1988) 141-45.

execution of John as a literary device, to increase the irony, and interest, of the tale.[62] Antipas *did* respect John.

Matthew and Luke shy away from such light treatment of Herod Antipas. While Luke deletes the whole story and describes Antipas as doing "evil things" (Luke 3:19-20), Matthew alters Mark's characterization slightly. In Matthew's Gospel Antipas definitely "wanted to put John to death" but "he feared the people, because they held him to be a prophet" (Matt. 14:5; cf. 23:26). He therefore delays the execution of John and keeps him in prison for a while. All the Gospels indicate that John was not immediately executed, but was held for a time in prison (cf. John 3:24). In Matthew's version nothing is said about Antipas thinking John righteous and holy or being very sorry about John's death. He is sorry about the request from Salome, but it is implied that his sorrow springs from his fear of the people, who believed that John was a prophet. He did not want an awkward public-relations situation.

The long story in Mark's Gospel should probably not be considered historical in many of its details. It has marked literary characteristics that seem rooted in biblical precedents. Some of the tale of the banquet is likely to derive from popular Jewish imagination, which sought for details of what would have been seen in some quarters as a martyrdom. Herodias' hatred of John is similar to Jezebel's hatred of Elijah (1 Kings 18; 19:2), and her cunning is the same as Jezebel's in regard to Naboth's vineyard (1 Kings 21). Antipas is like Ahab, the manipulated king: "There was no one like Ahab, who sold himself to do what was evil in the sight of YHWH, incited by his wife Jezebel" (1 Kgs. 21:25). For Mark, John was Elijah (Mark 9:11-13); it was fitting that he too should be in conflict with a cunning Jezebel and a weak Ahab. John's bold proclamation echoes Nathan before David (2 Sam. 12:1-12) and Elijah before Ahab (1 Kgs. 21:17-24).[63]

After the daughter dances so pleasingly, Antipas promises to give her anything she wants, even half his "kingdom." Antipas did not, in fact, have a kingdom; he had a tetrarchy, and this was not really his to

62. Hoehner wonders whether the positive appraisal of Antipas and the negative depiction of Herodias stem from the fact that Herodias' brother, Agrippa I, persecuted the Church and was also instrumental in Antipas' deposition; anyone who was a foe of Agrippa's could not be too bad; see Hoehner, *Herod Antipas,* 121. This seems a little stretched.

63. Hoehner, *Herod Antipas,* 118 n. 1.

give away freely to his young stepdaughter. Any such transaction would have needed the approval of Rome. The story of Esther seems to have influenced the Marcan tale. The words of Antipas to Salome are almost exactly the words of King Ahasuerus (Artaxerxes) to Esther: "What is your request? It shall be given to you, even half my kingdom" (Esth. 5:6; 7:2). A banquet follows, and bound by oath, the king has to obey Esther's wish. Esther identifies Haman, his trusted official, as an enemy and Haman is killed (Esther 7).[64]

In addition, the Herodians were well known for their birthday parties (cf. Persius, *Satura* 5.180); Josephus tells us that Antipas himself was chosen to throw a fantastic party on the Euphrates for the treaty signing between Tiberius' representative, Vitellius, and Artabanus of Parthia, and even constructed a magnificent pavilion in the middle of the river for the occasion (*Ant.* 18.102). With Antipas' reputation as "the host with the most," people could easily believe that he was engaged in a festivity at the time he decided to do away with John.

A characterization of Herodias as a manipulative woman and Antipas as a man who was pushed around by his wife may also have fueled the tale. According to Josephus, Herodias prodded Antipas into voyaging to Rome to request a better deal after her brother Agrippa achieved much success (*Ant.* 18.240-55). Gaius Caligula was not impressed. The whole plan backfired, and the pair ended up banished to Lyons. Josephus comments, "Thus did God punish Herodias for her jealousy of her brother, and Herod too for listening to the silly talk of a woman" (*Ant.* 18.255). Accordingly Antipas may have been considered a man who listened too much to what his wife said — a definite indication of male weakness in a patriarchal society.[65] Moreover, this characterization may reflect a general understanding of Antipas as a bad ruler. Susan Fischler's interesting analysis of the characteristics of imperial women in the literature shows how their presentation indicates an assessment of the emperors themselves. As Fischler writes, "By definition, 'good' emperors had wives and

64. See R. Aus, *Water into Wine and the Beheading of John the Baptist: Early Jewish-Christian Interpretation of Esther 1 in John 2:1-11 and Mark 6:17-29* (Atlanta: Scholars Press, 1988), who thinks that the core story was composed in Aramaic in Israel or Syria. For further motifs of biblical and classical literature, see Gnilka, "Das Martyrium Johannes des Täufers," 87-89.

65. Hoehner prefers to believe the Marcan tale of Antipas' vacillation and hesitation, on account of the parallels in the characterization of Herodias and Antipas found in Josephus.

mothers they could control, who never overstepped boundaries set by convention."[66] Moreover, the women themselves could be symbolic of a state in disorder. Clearly, the depiction of Herodias as wicked and cunning ultimately reflects back on Antipas.

Such elements of the Marcan account indicate that it may well derive in part from a Jewish martyrology that was redacted by a Christian author (the writer of the gospel himself perhaps).[67] It is possible that Mark combined a story widely told among Jews and Jewish-Christians, which had passed to his Gentile church, with a sympathetic presentation of Antipas stressing that he considered John holy and righteous and that he listened to his philosophy with interest, despite being unable to understand it. Luke and Matthew, on the other hand, seem to have known of another story that characterized Antipas as intensely hostile to John. Josephus records a separate story indicating Antipas' hostility, and elsewhere he tells of Antipas' apparent indifference to Jewish purity laws.

In passing, it must be said that the bringing in of John's head on a plate is an element that cannot be traced to biblical precedents, even though beheading is found in the story of Judith and Holofernes (Jdt. 13:1-10a). It is certainly *possible* that popular imagination embellished a true incident involving some inspection of John's head on the part of Antipas. There may not have been a banquet, a dance, conniving women, or a rash oath. There may have been only a few witnesses — soldiers and members of Herod's court — in the palace-fortress of Machaerus.[68] Nevertheless, John may have been beheaded on Antipas' orders[69] at

66. S. Fischler, "Social Stereotypes and Historical Analysis: The Case of the Imperial Women at Rome," in *Women in Ancient Societies: An Illusion of the Night*, ed. L. J. Archer et al. (New York: Routledge, 1994) 127.

67. Bultmann noted that the story seems to have been adapted from Hellenistic Jewish tradition (*History of the Synoptic Tradition*, 301), but Hoehner points out that the Semitisms indicate a Palestinian origin (*Herod Antipas*, 118-20). However, Hoehner's speculation that the story could be traced to Jesus' disciples Joanna (Luke 8:3; 24:10) or Manaen (Acts 13:1) seems a little too specific. Aus sees it as an "etiological haggada" of Jewish provenance *(Water into Wine)*. Schenk notes numerous Marcan redactional characteristics and thinks that Mark himself composed the story out of different legends and fables; see W. Schenk, "Gefangenschaft und Tod des Täufers: Erwägungen zur Chronologie und ihren Konsequenzen," *NTS* 29/4 (1983) 468-70.

68. On Machaerus as the location of John's execution, see Hoehner, *Herod Antipas*, 146-48.

69. As one who held the Roman *ius gladii*, Herod Antipas had the power to behead.

Machaerus, and his head may have been brought up to Antipas on a plate for inspection. Antipas may have wished to see evidence that John was really dead. This was probably a common enough proof for a ruler to seek. Tiberius instructed Vitellius that if Aretas should be slain his head was to be brought to him (*Ant.* 18.115). Proof of the execution of Theudas was the exhibition of his head to the inhabitants of Jerusalem (*Ant.* 20.97-98). If there is anything historical in all this, such an inspection may have prompted further elaboration.

We are told that John's disciples took his body and laid it in a tomb (Mark 6:29; Matt. 14:12), a statement probably indicating that the tomb of John the Baptist was known at the time the Gospels were written. If this is so, then Antipas probably did allow a few of John's disciples to come and take the body away. He thought enough of John, or was decent enough, not to throw his corpse off the walls for the wild beasts and vultures to tear to pieces. Where they buried John has been forgotten. Traditionally, Christians identify the tomb of John the Baptist in Samaria (Sebaste, modern Sebastiye), in the Cathedral of John the Baptist there. But this probably results from a confusion between Herod Antipas and Herod the Great, the tetrarch's famous father. Herod the Great was much involved in building Sebaste, after being granted the city by Octavian in 30 BCE. In the Byzantine period it was thought that Herod Antipas had a palace where the banquet took place. The tomb itself is a Roman one dating from the second to third centuries and cannot therefore be genuine.[70] It seems quite likely, however, that John was buried somewhere beyond the Jordan, close to where he proclaimed his message, and near Machaerus itself, or else in his hometown.[71]

Antipas killed John but spared his disciples, in the same way that Pilate would kill Jesus but let his disciples go free. The group of John's disciples were, it appears, largely dispersed and not considered a threat. As for the larger group of people who came to John, Antipas seems to have reasoned that the removal of the focus of the crowds' fervor would smash any militaristic hopes among those who were impressed by him

70. See J. Murphy-O'Connor, *The Holy Land: An Archaeological Guide from Earliest Times to 1700*, rev. ed. (Oxford: Oxford University Press, 1992) 403-06.

71. A *martyrion* for the remains of John the Baptist appears to have existed in the Byzantine period at the site of Er-Ramthaniyye in the Golan; see C. Dauphin, "Er-Ramthaniyye: Surveying an Early Bedouin Byzantine Pilgrimage Centre in the Golan Heights," *BAIAS* 8 (1989-90) 82-83. It is not clear where these remains originally came from. The site has not been excavated.

and that the threat of conflict or even revolt would fizzle out.[72] In doing this, he set a precedent that Pilate may have looked to when faced with deciding about what to do about Jesus of Nazareth in Jerusalem.

The Chief Priests, Elders, and Scribes

In the last chapter, we noted that the Fourth Gospel does not expressly indicate that levitical scribes sent from Jerusalem viewed John negatively. In terms of the story (John 1:19-28), we are not told one way or another, but it is possible that they assessed him fairly positively, or at least did not actively discourage what he was doing. We cannot conclude from this story alone that there was any historical persecution of John by the chief priests, elders, and scribes — the Jerusalem hierarchy.

However, in Mark's Gospel the situation is rather different. While Mark characterizes Antipas as rather pro-John, even though Antipas killed John, he preserves a tradition in which Jesus attacks the chief priests and their associates for their complicity in John's murder by not believing him:

> And he came again into Jerusalem. While he was walking around in the temple, the chief priests and scribes and elders came to him and said, "By what authority do you do these things?" or "Who gave you this authority in order to do these things?" Jesus said to them, "I will ask you a question. Answer me, and I will tell you by what authority I do these things. Was [the authority for] the immersion of John heavenly or human? Answer me." And they argued among themselves, saying: "If we say, 'Heavenly,' he will say, 'So why did you not believe him?' But shall we say, 'Human'?" They were afraid of the people, for all held that John was really a prophet. So they answered Jesus by saying, "We don't know." And Jesus said to them, "Neither will I tell you by what authority I do these things." (Mark 11:27-33)

The gospel continues with the parable of the wicked tenants (Mark 12:1-12), and the same order is retained by Luke (20:9-19). Matthew inserts the parable of the two sons at this point (Matt. 21:28-32) and then proceeds with the parable of the wicked tenants (21:33-46). In all cases,

72. So Webb, *John the Baptizer and Prophet*, 376.

the theme of the section describing Jesus' interaction with the chief priests, scribes, and elders in the Temple appears to be John the Baptist. The parable of the wicked tenants in its Marcan version is as follows:

> And he began to speak to them in parables. "A man planted a vineyard and put a hedge around it and dug a pit for the wine press, and built a tower, and let it out to tenant farmers, and went elsewhere. At the right time he sent a servant to the tenant farmers in order to take some of the fruit of the vineyard from them [as required by the contract]. But they took him and beat him up and sent him off with nothing. So again he sent another servant, and this one they wounded on the head and shamed. So he sent another, and this one they killed, and many others whom they either beat up or killed. He had still one more: a much-loved son. Finally, he sent him to them, saying, 'They will respect my son.' But those farmers said to each other, 'This is the heir. Come on, let us kill him and the inheritance will be ours.' So they took him and killed him and threw him out of the vineyard. What then will the owner of the vineyard do? He will come and destroy the tenant farmers and give the vineyard to others. Have you not read the Scripture: 'The very stone the builders rejected — this one has become the cornerstone. This was the Lord's doing, and it is wonderful in our sight'(Ps. 118:22-23)?" And they tried to seize him but feared the crowd, for they knew that he told the parable against them. So they left him and went away. (Mark12:1-12)

Following on from Jesus' implied accusation that the chief priests, elders, and scribes have not recognized that John's authority was from God, Jesus appears to be making a much more pointed accusation — that the chief priests and their associates were like those who killed the prophets, and indeed God's beloved son. There is only one son here, the heir, and it seems likely that the author of Mark's Gospel intended that the parable should be understood as a reference to Jesus' imminent death. John J. Collins has argued convincingly on the basis of Qumran documents and parallels in the Old Testament Pseudepigrapha that the Davidic Messiah could be called God's son, by virtue of the precedent that kings of Israel were called sons of God.[73] In view of Mark's repeated identi-

73. J. J. Collins, *The Scepter and the Star: The Messiahs of the Dead Sea Scrolls and Other Ancient Literature* (New York: Doubleday, 1995) 154-72.

fication of Jesus as the son of God, from the very first verse of the gospel (Mark 1:1) onward, it would be surprising if any other figure were intended as the reference. However, if the exchange here is based on an oral tradition concerning Jesus' interaction with the chief priests concerning John, we may be entitled to wonder whether Jesus himself may have used "son" with a different perspective. In the Wisdom of Solomon (2:13-16), a "son of God" is a righteous man. Clearly, there is a difference here between the prophets of this story, who are servants, and the son, who is the heir. In Mark's redaction, Jesus appears to be referring to the death of prophets in the past and adding John to their number, thereby linking the chief priests with the murder of John the prophet (servant), and intimating that his own death (as son) would soon follow. But if historical, the saying can also read not as a prediction of Jesus' own death, but entirely in relation to John. Malcolm Lowe has noted that without any initial assumption that the "son" of the parable must refer to Jesus, "one would be almost compelled to regard all this as a *continuation* of the question about the Baptist."[74] After all, it is John who has been killed, not yet Jesus.

It seems quite clear why the chief priests would have been so upset by the parable. The owner of the vineyard is God. The vineyard is Jerusalem or Israel in general or, more specifically, the Temple. The tenant farmers are those who look after the property and take their due, but they are also expected to give God his due. In Mark's narrative, the following section about taxes emphasizes precisely this: giving God his due (Mark 12:13-17; cf. *Gospel of Thomas* 100). God is owed total obedience and acceptance of his servants, the prophets. But the chief priests — the tenants — have behaved in an abominable way, mistreating and killing all the servants of the owner (the prophets) and even, in the end, *a* much-loved son (there is no definite article here).[75] But at this point the Marcan version becomes odd; the reasoning of the tenant farmers is silly, for killing the heir would not under any legal system gain them the inheritance. This seems to read very easily as Christian redaction. Christians claimed the inheritance of the ancient Hebrews, believing the Jews had missed out by their rejection of the

74. M. Lowe, "From the Parable of the Vineyard to a Pre-Synoptic Source," *NTS* 28 (1982) 258.

75. For later parallels to calling a man very close to God a "son of God," see Vermes, *Jesus the Jew*, 2d ed., 192-222.

Messiah. In Mark's story the tenants may be understood to refer to Jews as a whole, represented by their ostensible leaders, who have lost the inheritance of God. However, the conclusion of the story does indicate that it was the Jerusalem hierarchy that felt threatened, not all Jews. Moreover, in the version of the parable in the *Gospel of Thomas* (logion 65), the tenant farmers simply note that the son is the heir *of the vineyard* and seize him and kill him not because they hope for the inheritance, but apparently in a fit of jealousy. Moreover, in *Thomas'* version, the previous servants are not killed, only the son. If only the son was killed in the original version of the parable, then this would argue even more strongly in favor of identifying the son as John. Mark would then have altered the parable so that the tenants kill a number of prophets, among whom John may be classed. If only one person is killed, then the audience would very naturally have thought of John.

At any rate, God will punish the tenant farmers by removing them from caring for his vineyard and giving it to others. If we take it that the tenant farmers are the chief priests currently in control of the Temple, then the "others" need not refer to Gentiles; all that is stated is that the present chief priests will lose power. The statement about the cornerstone fits with an image of a building, as if the son were to be the cornerstone of a new Temple comprising Jews who had been obedient to God and who accepted God's prophets. If Jesus quoted Ps. 118:22-23 in Hebrew, the equation of son, בן, and stone, אבן, would have been readily apparent, and would have echoed John's wordplay as found in Q (Matt. 3:9; Luke 3:8).[76] A connection between the parable and the statement about the cornerstone is also found in the *Gospel of Thomas* 65 and 66, which possibly shows that the association between these component parts was known early on.

The accusation against the chief priests reflects the accusation Jesus makes following the disturbance in the Temple (Mark 11:15-16 = Matt. 21:12-13 = Luke 19:45-48). The Temple has been made into a "cave of thieves" (Mark 11:17), just as the wicked tenants are essentially thieves, rapists (cf. "shamed," 12:4), and murderers. In response to this also, "the chief priests and the scribes heard it and sought a way to destroy him, for they feared him, because all the crowds were

76. Meier suggests that the wordplay in John's message might have been *'abnayyā'* ("stones") and *bĕnayyā'* ("sons"), but as he himself notes, such Aramaic reconstructions are conjectural; see Meier, *Marginal Jew*, vol. 2, 75 n. 51.

impressed by his teaching" (Mark 11:18). Jerusalem as the locus of opposition to God's prophets is found also in Q: "O Jerusalem, Jerusalem, killing the prophets and stoning those who are sent to you!" (Luke 13:34; Matt. 23:37). Elsewhere, Jesus puts the guilt of all the prophets' deaths on "this generation" (Luke 20:49-51; Matt. 23:32-36). The context of the narrative demands a Jerusalem setting, though the reference is not simply to the chief priests.

What comes out most strongly in the story about Jesus' question concerning John's authority is that the chief priests and their associates simply will not say either way whether the authority for John's immersion of repentance is divine or human. Infuriatingly, they remain cautious and circumspect. Jesus' question is pointed: Did John decide to immerse following repentance out of his own human decision, interpreting Scripture, or was it something he was authorized to do by God? If authorized by God, then he was a prophet, as "all the people" in this story believe. If he was a prophet, then the chief priests might be expected to condemn Antipas for his action and to believe John's prediction of an imminent end. Indeed, people may have wanted the chief priests to come out strongly for John's divine authorization, but this story reflects an understanding that they did not. In the Fourth Gospel also there is a curious silence concerning the chief-priestly attitude to John. We may read between the lines and find evidence of a positive attitude in Jewish communities at the end of the century, but it is only implied.

Certainly, it would be difficult to argue that the chief priests strongly condemned Antipas for his murder of John. They may not have approved of Antipas' action, but if they failed to challenge it then this may explain why we find Jesus presented as vehemently denouncing the chief priests in Jerusalem as prophet-killers at worst, or prophet-abusers at best. There may well have been circles who were profoundly disappointed in the chief priests' apparently placid acceptance of John's murder. In Mark, the chief priests are characterized as not "believing" John. This seems to mean that they did not believe he was a prophet; they did not believe in the accuracy of his prediction of the coming one or of the end, or in the necessity of immersion following repentance. Nevertheless, we do not know how many of them might, with Josephus, have considered John a "good man," even still. If so, how much could they have done to stop Antipas? What would have happened if they had criticized the action of someone who ruled a large part of the country at the behest of Rome? Whether cowardly or astute, the chief priests, in remaining silent, appear to have alienated those who thought of John as a prophet, a group that included Jesus.

Chronology

Finally, a word needs to be said about the date of John's death. It is common to assume that John was murdered around the year 30 CE,[77] close to the presumed time of the beginning of Jesus' own prophetic activities. This results from an initial dating of John's appearance to 27-29 using Luke 3:1-3, which has John begin his activities in the fifteenth year of Tiberius Caesar, though a variety of calculations have been used for pinpointing which year was the emperor's "fifteenth."[78] Generally, John is dated according to the normal Roman method, so that Tiberius' reign is understood to have begun after the death of Augustus on 19 August 14. Using this convention, Josephus describes the battle between Aretas and Antipas as being around the time that Antipas' brother Philip died, which he dates to the twentieth year of Tiberius, that is, 34 (*Ant.* 18.106-09). The story of a key reason for the battle — Antipas' divorce of Aretas' daughter — and the description of Antipas' murder of John then follow. In fact, the battle must have taken place after Lucius Vitellius became governor of Syria in 35 CE, since he is linked with the events.[79]

77. So Crossan, *Historical Jesus,* 230; Schwartz, *Jewish Background of Christianity,* 190-91 n. 39. The war with Aretas is often dated to 34 C.E., and the reference to Antipas' trouble with John is then regarded as a flashback. Schenk, on the other hand, believes that there is no reason to assume that the reference is a flashback and accordingly argues that John's death should be placed much closer to 34 ("Gefangenschaft und Tod des Täufers"). Saulnier, however, pushes all the dating back and argues that Antipas and Herodias married in 23 at the latest; John was executed 27/28; Aretas vanquished Antipas' army around 29; Antipas is then found in Jerusalem with Vitellius in the spring of 37, after the recalling of Pilate, and he negotiated with the Parthians there; in 39 Agrippa accused Antipas of plotting with the Parthians; see C. Saulnier, "Herode Antipas et Jean le Baptiste," *RB* 91 (1984) 362-76. See also E. M. Smallwood, *The Jews under Roman Rule: From Pompey to Diocletian* (Leiden: Brill, 1976) 183-87, who suggests that Aretas' victory over Antipas was in 27. Hoehner, however, places the war with Aretas in 36/7 and the death of John in 31/2 (*Herod Antipas,* 110-71, 254-57).

78. See Hoehner, *Herod Antipas,* 313-66.

79. Ibid., 251 n. 7.

The battle need not have followed precisely after the insult to Aretas' daughter. It was, according to Josephus, a quarrel that began with this incident, but it was also occasioned by a dispute about territorial boundaries (*Ant.* 18.113).[80] Such quarrels could brew for some time before breaking out into hostility. Josephus notes that the immediate cause of Antipas' defeat was that some men from the tetrarchy of Philip who had joined his army played him false (*Ant.* 18.114). Such language does not mean that Philip still administered his tetrarchy (that is, that the battle took place before Philip's death), for Josephus seems to have found it useful to refer to "the tetrarchy of Philip" rather than to the technically correct designation "former territory of Philip now annexed to Syria." For example, later, when he discusses how this area passed over to Agrippa, Josephus still refers to it as "the tetrarchy of Philip" (*Ant.* 18.237). Rather, there are good reasons to date the battle with Aretas to very late in 36 or more likely 37. In particular, the aftermath of the battle with Aretas is linked to the death of Tiberius. After the destruction of his army, Antipas wrote immediately to Tiberius in Capri to ask for retaliation against Aretas (*Ant.* 18.115). Tiberius agreed and asked his commander in Syria, Vitellius, to wage war on Aretas. This order was sent just before the death of Tiberius on 16 March 37. Vitellius received the order after he had just been south to Judea to recall Pilate for poor management of Judean affairs and depose Caiaphas from the high priesthood (*Ant.* 15.405; 18.90-95). Vitellius had also apparently just signed the treaty with the Parthian king Artabanus on the order of Tiberius (*Ant.* 18.96-105), and he would presumably have been wearied of long journeys on the orders of the emperor.[81] According to Josephus, Vitellius disliked Antipas intensely since the tetrarch, in his desire to impress the emperor, had beaten Vitellius to Tiberius with detailed news of the treaty signing (18.104-05), but Vitellius may also have been un-

80. Identifying a certain Gamalike as the source of the dispute seems preferable to altering the strong manuscript evidence of the name from Gamalike or Gamalitis to either Galaaditidi or Gabalitidi in southern Idumea; cf. Josephus, *Ant.* 2.6. The Latin equivalent, Gamalica (or Gamalitica, in Ambrosianus), is also found; see Hoehner, *Herod Antipas,* 254 n. 4. There seems to be a simple confusion between the name of the town and the name of Gamala, also known as Gamalitis, which was a well-known city in the Golan. The fact that we do not know of a place called Gamalica should not be a problem, since our knowledge of sites in the Roman period is incomplete.

81. For the dating of the treaty with Artabanus see Hoehner, *Herod Antipas,* 251-54.

happy about waging a war so soon after the signing of the treaty. Thus Vitellius seems to have made a quick and easy decision when, hearing of the death of Tiberius, he no longer felt it necessary to complete the reprisal (18.124). Pilate did not reach Rome before Tiberius was dead (18.89), and Vitellius did not complete the purpose of his second visit before the same news reached him. It seems likely, therefore, that the battle between Aretas and Antipas took place in early 37, after Vitellius had been south once to depose Pilate and Caiaphas, not long before the death of Tiberius.[82]

The latest date for John's death is therefore not the battle with Aretas but the eviction of Pontius Pilate and Caiaphas, who were Judean prefect and high priest respectively when Jesus was killed. Obviously, Jesus was killed after John. John must have been executed, therefore, before 37. However, if Mark's story is correct in dating the death of John to a time when Herodias' daughter Salome was still living with her mother, then we must push back his execution to sometime before 34, when Philip died; Salome became the wife of Philip at some stage before this. In Mark's story, she is described as a κοράσιον, a girl, possibly around twelve years old.[83] This does not create a problem, if we remember that a girl might be married from this age onwards.

The chronology of John, then, seems fairly clear from our historical sources: he appeared sometime around 28/29 and was dead sometime before 34. The difficulty for scholars has been how to fit this together with a traditional dating of Jesus' one- to three-year mission, according to which Jesus was executed around the year 33. There is no reason to assume that Jesus came to John immediately after John's first appearance proclaiming his immersion and making his predictions. There is also no reason to assume that John must have been active for

82. Hoehner distinguishes three visits by Vitellius: (1) he deposed Pilate in autumn 36 (*Ant.* 15.405); (2) he deposed Caiaphas and appointed Jonathan (*Ant.* 18.90-95); (3) he deposed Jonathan and appointed Theophilus (*Ant.* 18.123). The first is dated autumn 36; the second, Passover 37; and the third, Pentecost 37; see Hoehner, *Herod Antipas*, 313-16.

83. The word κοράσιον (Mark 6:22) is also used in the Gospel of Mark at 5:41, 42 (cf. Matt. 9:24, 25; Luke 8:42) for a girl aged twelve. Salome may have married Philip the tetrarch at age thirteen or fourteen; so Hoehner, *Herod Antipas*, 151-57. The marriage produced no children, possibly because it was very short, or he was ill, or else she was too young to conceive. Salome later went on to marry her uncle Aristobulus (Herodias' brother), with whom she had three children (*Ant.* 18.106, 137).

a very short time only. The reference in Mark 6:20 to Herodias having a grudge against John may indicate that he was known to have been active for some time, a period in which something might have taken place that resulted in Herodias' grudge. In an age before mass media, if John appeared and made his announcements in various places in late 28, he may have waited another year before he really became well known. John may also have been in prison for some time before his execution.[84] Although we cannot trust our sources absolutely, they do agree in pointing to this approximate chronology. John may have been killed as late as 33 or early in 34. For all we know, Jesus' death may have followed quite soon after, or as late as 36. In the sequence of Pilate's atrocities and offenses outlined by Josephus, the execution of Jesus is the third of four major items he mentions, the last being the massacre at Tirathana (*Ant.* 18.55-64; 85-89),[85] which may indicate that the death of Jesus occurred late in the period of Pilate's prefecture. At any rate, these dates will probably never be fixed with absolute precision.

Jesus continued with his own mission and was executed sometime between the death of John and the recalling of Pilate in early 37. In the wake of some instability in Judea, Aretas, deeply offended by Antipas' rejection of his daughter and determined to settle a border dispute by military means, mustered an army, waged war, and destroyed Antipas' army in 37, shortly before the death of Tiberius, but close enough to the time of John's execution for many to consider the destruction of his army directly linked to his murder of a prophet.

In conclusion, John attracted many people of Judea who believed he was a prophet on the basis of his prediction of a coming figure of

84. Hoehner, *Herod Antipas,* 171, and see p. 170.

85. Although it is generally considered quite likely that Josephus made mention of Jesus as one "called the Christ" (cf. *Ant.* 20.200-201), in the passage included in the section concerning Pilate's offenses (*Ant.* 18.63-64), the extant version of this passage about Jesus — the so-called *Testimonium Flavianum* — is usually thought to have been heavily altered by Christians, probably in the late third century, to ensure that Josephus' history cohered with the traditional Christian view of Jesus' death and resurrection. For discussion see C. A. Evans, "Jesus in Non-Christian Sources," in *Studying the Historical Jesus: Evaluations of the State of Research,* ed. B. D. Chilton and C. A. Evans (Leiden: Brill, 1994) 466-77. Very probably, Josephus' text is preserved far more accurately in an Arabic version, which makes it explicit that Pilate "condemned him to be crucified and to die"; see S. Pines, *An Arabic Version of the Testimonium Flavianum and Its Implications* (Jerusalem: Israel Academy of Sciences and Humanities, 1971) 16.

judgment and his innovative immersion. Galileans may have been more skeptical. Many of the more educated people in society may have refrained from calling John a prophet, though they may have considered his prediction true and may have endorsed his employment of an immersion that could be accepted on the basis of scriptural precedents (that is, on the basis of human authority). Perhaps for this reason Josephus could consider John a "good man" even though remaining careful about ascribing prophetic identity to him. The substance of John's prophecy had yet to take place, so Josephus could not say that John's prediction was accurate. Josephus preferred to concentrate on John's distinctive type of immersion and on his exhortations to repentance and righteousness. The view that educated men with power and influence thought of John as a "righteous and holy man" may also lie behind the characterization of Antipas in Mark's story. Although the chief-priestly hierarchy of Jerusalem was possibly criticized by Jesus for lack of belief in John and accused of complicity in John's murder, this does not indicate that the chief priests were against John, only that they may have kept silent on the matter, much to the disappointment of those who considered John a prophet. Both the crowds who flocked to him and the educated elite could recognize John as a "burning and shining lamp" (John 5:35) snuffed out prematurely by a lawless, and foolish, vassal of Rome.

CHAPTER 6

John and Jesus

It has been argued thus far that John called those Jews who were not righteous, by his definition, to walk along the way of righteousness in accordance with his teaching. Following this turning to righteousness, their bodies would be effectively purified, and as righteous and purified people they would become faithful children of Abraham who performed the will of God, thus acquiring the merit necessary for a favorable judgment at the eschatological trial. While John accepted that righteous people existed already in society, he aimed his exhortations at the unrighteous and defined a very high moral standard that went beyond what was actually required by the Law. The end was coming soon, and if they did not turn it would be too late; their fate would be the fire of Gehenna. A coming figure, possibly Elijah, was about to arrive.

In seeking an immersion of repentance in the Jordan River, Jesus therefore placed himself with the lawless and unrighteous who had recently turned back to God and had come to be purified, confessing their sins publicly to indicate their acknowledgment of their transgressions. In the Gospel of Mark and the Fourth Gospel, we first meet Jesus with John at the Jordan. Whatever he was before is irrelevant to the writers of the Gospels and is simply omitted. While Matthew and Luke have nativity accounts that define Jesus as the Son of God from conception, they too are almost completely silent about the years before Jesus was baptized. As time passed, the silence was filled by apocryphal stories about Jesus' "wondrous childhood,"[1] but it is fairly safe to say that such stories of his youthful exploits and miracles have no grounding in history. Although Luke does include a curious story of how Jesus was left at the Temple by his "parents" (both Mary and Joseph) — who seem to have forgotten that he was the Son of God (Luke 2:49-52) — and was later found as a student listening to the teachers there, this is not enough upon which to build a biography of his early life.

That Jesus was baptized by John has been a problem almost from the beginning of Christianity, and not only because his being baptized indicated that he might have been subordinate to John. Jesus apparently turned away from sin and, as Michael Grant notes, this "set the theologians of subsequent centuries a conundrum. For how could Jesus have been baptized for the forgiveness of his own sins, when according to the Christology which developed after his death, he was divine and therefore sinless?"[2] Often the solution is given that he wished to humble himself by participating with the sinful in this important ritual. As A. M. Hunter has stated: "He [Jesus] discerned the hand of God in John's mission, and by His acceptance of John's baptism identified Himself with the people whom He came to save."[3] Some scholars have sought to deny that John ever baptized Jesus.[4]

As I outlined in the Introduction to this book, discomfort about the baptism of Jesus is found already in the Gospel of Matthew (3:14-15). Jesus comes forward to be immersed, but John tries to prevent him and says, "I need to be immersed by you, and you come to me?" Jesus calmly reassures him, "Let it be so for now, for it is right for us in this way to fulfill all righteousness." Jesus therefore does the decent thing, but he does not really need to do it. Luke and the writer of the Fourth Gospel both modify the tradition of Jesus' baptism. Luke relativizes John by means of the

1. See D. R. Cartlidge and D. L. Dungan, eds., *Documents for the Study of the Gospels* (Philadelphia: Fortress, 1980) 92-103.

2. M. Grant, *Jesus* (London: Weidenfeld and Nicolson, 1977) 49. In early Christian tradition, Jesus came to be regarded not only as sinless (2 Cor. 5:21; Heb. 4:15; John 8:46; 1 Pet. 1:19; 2:22) but also as the forgiver of sins (e.g., 1 Cor. 15:3; Rom. 3:23-26).

3. A. M. Hunter, *The Work and Words of Jesus* (Philadelphia: Westminster, 1950) 36.

4. E.g., R. H. Fuller, *The Mission and Achievement of Jesus: An Examination of the Presuppositions of New Testament Theology* (London: SCM, 1954) 52; M. S. Enslin, "John and Jesus," *ZNW* 66 (1975) 1-18; E. Haenchen, *Der Weg Jesu: Eine Erklärung des Markus-Evangeliums und der kanonischen Parallelen* (Berlin: de Gruyter, 1968) 60-63. For a critique of Enslin, see R. L. Webb, "John the Baptist and His Relationship to Jesus," in *Studying the Historical Jesus: Evaluations of the State of Current Research*, ed. B. D. Chilton and C. A. Evans (Leiden: Brill, 1994) 216-18.

Nativity story (Luke 1–2), and in the Fourth Gospel, John points to Jesus as one who will supersede him (John 1:29-34).[5] At the beginning of the second century, Ignatius of Antioch stated that Jesus was immersed, not so that the water would purify him, but so that he might "purify the water" (Ign. *Eph.* 18:2; cf. Ign. *Smyrn.* 1:1, where Ignatius takes the Matthean view). Justin Martyr, some decades later, explained that Jesus was baptized "solely for the sake of humanity" (*Dialogue* 88). This endeavor to deny that Jesus was immersed for repentance is also found in noncanonical Christian Gospels. In the *Gospel of the Ebionites*, immediately after Jesus' baptism, John asks Jesus to baptize him (Epiphanius, *Haer.* 30.13.7-8).[6] In the *Gospel of the Hebrews* quoted by Jerome (*Contra Pelagium* 3.2), Jesus' mother and brothers urge him to go to John for baptism, but Jesus says there is no need because he is sinless. Later Christian tradition linked Jesus' baptism with the descent into Hades, where the dead awaited liberation.[7] As Joachim Jeremias noted, Jesus' baptism by John was such a "scandalizing piece of information" that it simply cannot have been invented by the early Church.[8] In one way or another, all the traditions aim at damage control, to cope with this problematic but incontrovertible fact.

At face value, the circumstances seem quite clear: Jesus accepted the veracity of John's predictions of the imminent end and counted himself as one who had not fulfilled the Law adequately. With a repentant heart, he turned from his past ways and committed himself to walking along the way of righteousness in accordance with John's teaching. He may have given away his possessions to the poor. He then came to John for the purification of his body, which completed the process of turning around to become one of God's obedient people. How far off the tracks Jesus may have been can only be the subject of fruitless speculation. He may well not have been particularly lax or sinful in regard to Torah. Sensitive people can imagine that they have behaved far worse than they actually have. We just cannot know.[9]

5. See above, 2-5.

6. W. Schneemelcher, ed., *New Testament Apocrypha I: Gospels and Related Writings*, rev. ed., English trans. ed. R. McL. Wilson (Cambridge: Clarke, 1991) 169.

7. See K. McDonnell, "The Baptism of Jesus in the Jordan and the Descent into Hell," *Worship* 69 (1995) 98-109; "Jesus' Baptism in the Jordan," *TS* 56 (1995) 209-36.

8. J. Jeremias, *New Testament Theology: The Proclamation of Jesus* (London: SCM, 1971) 45.

9. Meier describes Jesus' baptism as a "watershed" or "conversion" and states, "As far as our meager sources allow us to know, before his baptism by John, Jesus was a

In this final chapter, we will consider further some of the implications of our conclusions concerning John and his immersion, in order to determine what we can know about Jesus and his relationship with John. There is a substantial body of material in the Jesus tradition concerning John that we will explore. It must be said, though, that this subject is so vast and complex that it deserves its own thick monograph rather than a final chapter in a book about John. The present study is exploratory rather than conclusive and does not aim to be exhaustive. We will simply touch the surface of some issues that relate to scholarly discussions of the historical Jesus.

Jesus' Baptism and Vision

As we saw in the Introduction, the Gospel accounts of the actual immersion of Jesus differ. All of them pass over details of the procedure. In Chapter 2, we explored what the act of immersion entailed and considered the possibility that immersions took place *en masse,* with John presiding. It certainly would not have been necessary for John to baptize people singly or hold on to each person in a close embrace. People were immersed "confessing their sins" in public.[10] The possibility that John's immersion involved a group of people under his direction, at one time, has a bearing on how we understand Jesus' baptismal vision and on the question of whether John was aware of it.

The primary text for Jesus' baptismal vision is Mark 1:9-11:

> And it happened in those days that Jesus came from Nazareth of Galilee
> and was immersed in the Jordan by John.
> And immediately when he came up from the water

respectable, unexceptional, and unnoticed woodworker in Nazareth"; see J. P. Meier, *A Marginal Jew: Rethinking the Historical Jesus. Volume Two: Mentor, Message, and Miracles* (New York: Doubleday, 1994) 108-09. Hollenbach thinks that Jesus must have considered himself to be a sinner in somehow participating in the oppression of the weaker members of society; see P. W. Hollenbach, "The Conversion of Jesus: From Jesus the Baptizer to Jesus the Healer," *ANRW* II.25.1 (1982) 196-219.

10. See also Meier, *Marginal Jew,* vol. 2, 111.

he saw the heavens splitting apart
and the Spirit like a dove coming down onto him,
and there was a voice from the heavens:
"You are my beloved son,
in whom I am satisfied."

In Mark 1:9-11, there is an indication that this account derives from a report of Jesus' own mystical experience. The reference to heavens opening is a way of indicating such experience, as in Stephen's vision of Acts 7:56 or Peter's vision of Acts 10:11 (cf. Rev. 4:1; John 1:51). The experience is described as being something personal to Jesus: "he saw" the Spirit descending, and the voice addresses him alone in the second person singular. Moreover, the voice (of God) also seems to refer to some action Jesus has done that has given God satisfaction, for εὐδόκησα is aorist. The aorist is used most often in narrative for a single completed action, rather than a habitual or continuous action, which would require the imperfect indicative.[11] God has been well pleased or satisfied by something that has taken place. There seems to be in Mark a direct correspondence between Jesus' immersion of repentance in the Jordan and God's satisfaction. His vision takes place "immediately" as he comes up out of the water, and the voice seems to refer back to some action just completed. We have concluded that John's immersion completed a process of becoming "holy," in that one became both pure inwardly through repentance, obedience to God, and acts of loving-kindness, and then pure outwardly because the purity of one's body was only possible after attaining inner purity. It is at this final stage that the voice approves of Jesus.

This scenario caused some discomfort in the early Church. There was a growing tendency to remove the awareness of the descent of the Spirit from the personal experience of Jesus to something that other people could recognize, so that the scene could function as a theophany. In Luke's version, Mark's description of a personal experience is still retained, though Luke detaches it from the baptism and places it at a time when Jesus is in prayer afterwards (Luke 3:21-22). For Luke, Jesus was baptized "when all the people were baptized," but nothing extraordinary happened. Then, during his prayer, "heaven was opened and he saw the Holy Spirit come down upon him in bodily form like a dove, and there was a voice from heaven: 'You are my beloved son, in whom

11. This use of the aorist is widely documented.

I am satisfied.'" God does not so obviously approve of the baptism of Jesus, then, but is responding to his prayer. The motif of Jesus in prayer is one especially dear to Luke (cf. 5:16; 6:12; 9:18, 28; 11:1; 22:41-46). Luke also adds that the Spirit was "in bodily form" like a dove, as if he were trying to make sense of the image.[12]

In Matt. 3:16-17, while Jesus still sees this descent of the Spirit, the voice is public and makes a general announcement:

> And when he was immersed, Jesus immediately went up from the
> water
> and behold, the heavens were opened[13]
> and he saw the Spirit of God descending like a dove
> and coming onto him (ἐπ' αὐτόν).
> And behold a voice out of the heavens was saying,
> "This is my beloved son, in whom I am well pleased."

In the Fourth Gospel, the whole experience belongs to John the Baptist, who claims that *he* has seen the Spirit descending as a dove out of heaven and remaining on Jesus (John 1:32-33).[14] In John 1:34 the manuscripts have two main variants; in one the voice states, "This is the son of God," and in the other, "This is the chosen of God." The words of the voice recall Ps. 2:7, "You are my son. Today I have begotten you," and also Isa. 42:1, "Behold my servant, whom I uphold; my chosen one, in whom I delight." The awareness of these parallels found its way into certain

12. Jeremias puts this Lucan form into an entirely separate tradition (*New Testament Theology*, 50), but in view of Luke's interest in the motif of Jesus in prayer, this is surely his own invention, used to modify Mark's story. For the view that there was a Q version of Jesus' baptism, including some kind of vision story, see Meier, *Marginal Jew*, vol. 2, 103-04, 183-84; H. Schürmann, *Das Lukasevangelium*, vol. 1 (Freiburg: Herder, 1969) 197, 218. If a Q version existed, it may have indicated that when Jesus was immersed (Luke and Matthew use an aorist passive participle), the heavens "were opened" (Matthew; Luke) and the Holy Spirit (Luke) or God's Spirit (Matthew) came down "upon him" (Luke; Matthew) and a voice said: "*This is* my beloved son" (Matthew). In other words, it is possible that the Q version was more public and less subjective and experiential in its presentation than the Marcan version. As Meier points out, the Q version of the temptation in the wilderness presupposes that Jesus has been identified as son of God; he is also there the possessor of prophetic power.

13. Some manuscripts add "to him" here.

14. See R. E. Brown, *The Gospel According to John I–XII* (Garden City, NY: Doubleday, 1966) 55-72.

versions of the story, so that in the Western text of Luke 3:22 we have at times, "You are my son. I have begotten you today." In the *Gospel of the Hebrews* the Spirit states that Jesus is "my first-begotten son who reigns for ever."[15] These textual modifications seem to have arisen as attempts to correlate the voice at Jesus' baptism with scriptural verses, so that the voice was made to fit more completely with the Hebrew precedents. With the modifications, it is much easier to link the statement with dogmatic assertions about Jesus, so Jesus can be identified as the new king of Israel and/or the servant of Isaiah.[16]

Some commentators have cast doubt on the authenticity of the vision as an actual experience of Jesus, despite the fact that we have a considerable range of early material all linking some kind of vision with Jesus' baptism. We also have definite apologetic formulations that try to deal with this problem.[17] Various Hebrew texts have been cited by scholars who would understand the baptismal vision-report as a kind of "Christian midrash" designed to explain the meaning and character of Jesus' mission.[18] In fact, there is no clear biblical parallel for the

15. Schneemelcher, ed., *New Testament Apocrypha I,* 177.

16. For further possible parallels, see Meier, *Marginal Jew,* vol. 2, 106-07.

17. Those who doubt the historicity of the vision include Meier, *Marginal Jew,* vol. 2, 106-08, following A. Vögtle, *Die sogenannte Taufperikope Mk 1,9-11. Zur Problematik der Herkunft und des ursprünglichen Sinns* (EKKNT/Vorarbeiten 4; Zürich: Benzinger, 1972) 105-39, but against C. H. H. Scobie, *John the Baptist* (London: SCM, 1964) and J. Ernst, *Johannes der Täufer: Interpretation, Geschichte, Wirkungsgeschichte* (Berlin: de Gruyter, 1989) 337. The Jesus Seminar voted against the notion that Jesus saw the heavens open and the spirit descend on him like a dove; none of its members considered the event's historicity certain; 12% thought it probable; 44% thought it possible; and 44% thought it unlikely. As for the heavenly voice, no scholars thought it certain; 8% thought it probable; 36% thought it possible; and 56% thought it unlikely. However, scholars were more positive about Jesus experiencing some kind of "vision" (possible) or "visionary experience" (possible) or "powerful religious experience" (probable) at his baptism. See W. B. Tatum, *John the Baptist and Jesus: A Report of the Jesus Seminar* (Sonoma, CA: Polebridge, 1994) 148-151. The main objection to the historicity of the dove simile and the voice appears to be that scholars believe these reflect the christological interest of the early Church. As I hope to show, the vision itself need not be interpreted as messianic.

18. See Meier, *Marginal Jew,* vol. 2, 106-08. For Meier, Mark 1:10-11 reflects numerous scriptural echoes. He notes that the spirit's descent indicates that Jesus is the one who will immerse with the spirit (Mark 1:8) and that it has royal and prophetic associations; cf. Isa. 11:2; 61:1. That the descent of the spirit makes a prophet is correct, but immersion in spirit does not necessarily follow from this. Meier thinks that Ps. 2:7

Marcan version,[19] and the Johannine and other modifications fit better with a theory that sees Christians trying to make sense of the tradition by imposing scriptural parallels upon it, rather than making it up from scratch out of Greek biblical precedents. Hesitation in ascribing a vision to Jesus here seems to derive from a worry that we might end up with a subjective psychologizing of Jesus, similar to what we find in the old "lives of Jesus" of the last century.[20] But to suppose that Jesus just gradually realized, in a rather rational manner, that he should go out to teach and heal as a prophet seems much more to reflect scholarly "psychologizing" in its basic conceptualization than to suppose that Jesus did have a visionary experience of some kind that set him on his radical, "inspired" path. Without some direct apprehension on the part of Jesus that the Spirit was upon or in him, we have a spiritless Jesus, unless we concur with Matthew and Luke that he was endowed with the Spirit from birth.

As we have noted, the early Church found Jesus' immersion by John a problem. They would have left it out if they could. The reason that they could not entirely dispense with it was that Jesus' mission *began* with his immersion by John in the Jordan. Many people were baptized by John without their being led to a mission of teaching and healing; something else must have led to Jesus' specific prophetic activity. The Gospels indicate

---

provides the words of the voice, but the Marcan text is not a quotation of Ps. 2:7 (LXX). Meier asserts that "[the] beloved," ὁ ἀγαπητός, refers to an only son and reflects the sacrifice of Isaac. He suggests that "in you I am satisfied" reflects Isa. 42:1, where the servant (prophet) is one "with whom I am well pleased"; but the words are not the same as the LXX version. He notes that Ezekiel was by the river Chebar in Babylon when he saw a vision (Ezek. 1:1), which is an interesting prophetic parallel, but only that. Lastly, he considers the rending of the heavens to be a motif from Isa. 63:19, whereas it is simply a way of referring to a visionary experience. For more on visionary experiences in this period, see C. Rowland, *The Open Heaven: A Study of Apocalyptic in Judaism and Early Christianity* (New York: Crossroad, 1982); A. F. Segal, *Paul the Convert: The Apostolate and Apostasy of Saul the Pharisee* (New Haven: Yale University Press, 1990) 34-71.

19. The correspondences between Mark 1:10-11 and Ps. 2:7 and Isa. 42:1 are exceedingly slight. Behind Mark 1:11 (Σὺ εἶ ὁ υἱός μου ὁ ἀγαπητός) we are supposed to find LXX Ps. 2:7 (υἱός μου εἶ σύ), but the order of the words is different, and there is no mention of ὁ ἀγαπητός in the Psalm. Where Mark continues with ἐν σοὶ εὐδόκησα, we are supposed to see LXX Isa. 42:1, προσεδέξατο αὐτὸν ἡ ψυχή μου, which is even more baffling as a supposedly obvious parallel. Moreover, in the LXX the chosen one, ὁ ἐκλεκτός, clearly refers to Israel as a nation.

20. Meier, *Marginal Jew,* vol. 2, 108.

that this factor was linked with John's immersion. Therefore, it is here that we have "the beginning of the good news" (Mark 1:1).

We cannot know precisely what Jesus experienced, but what we have in Mark's narrative may still reflect how Jesus articulated this experience to his disciples. This is not to say that we have in Mark precisely (translated into Greek) what Jesus told his disciples concerning the vision. Mark may well have modified the received tradition. But if the entire story were invented by the early Greek-speaking Church, the voice would likely repeat obvious messianic scriptural verses, in their Septuagint form. What we have here, though, is not necessarily messianic identification or overt quotation. Clearly, for Mark, Jesus was the Son of God, the royal Messiah (so Mark 1:1). However, as many have pointed out, in the Scriptures a "son of God" could be an angel, an Israelite king, or an Israelite in general.[21] A "son of God" could be a righteous man, one close to God, like Honi the Circle-Drawer, who is called by Josephus a "righteous man and dear to God" (*Ant.* 14.22-24) and who in the Mishnah prays "I am like a son of the House before you" (*m. Ta'an.* 3:8).[22] This does not mean that Honi considered himself to be like the King-Messiah. The statement in Mark 15:39 (= Matt. 27:54), "Truly this man was a son of God," is "translated" by Luke as "Certainly this man was righteous (δίκαιος)" (Luke 23:47). Therefore, the statement "You are my beloved son in whom I am satisfied" may mean that at the moment of his baptism Jesus heard a heavenly voice accounting him righteous, like a parent acknowledging the good behavior of a child. The statement does not necessarily imply that he was the King-Messiah. The statement may be wholly appropriate to the experience of someone who had repented and undertaken to be righteous. At this point, after becoming pure in body as well as in heart, Jesus experienced complete acceptance by God — confirmation of God's forgiveness and endless loving-kindness. This confirmation is itself reflected in Jesus' insistence upon the image of God as a loving Father.[23]

21. See, e.g., G. Vermes, *Jesus the Jew: A Historian's Reading of the Gospels,* 2d ed. (London: SCM, 1983) 194-97.

22. See J. D. Crossan, *The Historical Jesus: The Life of a Mediterranean Jewish Peasant* (San Francisco: HarperSanFrancisco, 1991) 142-56.

23. J. D. G. Dunn, *Jesus and the Spirit: A Study of the Religious and Charismatic Experience of Jesus and the First Christians as Reflected in the New Testament* (Philadelphia: Westminster, 1975) 63; cf. Jeremias, *New Testament Theology,* 55-56.

The reference to Jesus as "beloved," ἀγαπητός, has been taken to mean that Jesus was somehow unique and also destined for death. John Meier suggests that behind this Greek word lies the Hebrew יחיד, "only" or "only beloved," which is the word that is applied to Isaac (Gen. 22:2, 12, 16). Meier states that "in every instance" where יחיד is translated by ἀγαπητός in the LXX, it is used of a beloved child who is dead or destined for death.[24] This is not quite the case, for the participial form of the word is used in Prov. 4:3, where a beloved only child of a mother is instructed to acquire wisdom. Moreover, while יחיד can be translated by ἀγαπητός, this does not mean that ἀγαπητός must be translated with reference to יחיד; it can be, if we understand ἀγαπητός in terms of one sense of the verb ἀγαπάω, that relating to something or someone with which one must be content.[25] Otherwise ἀγαπητός is an extremely common word, used to refer to someone who is "beloved" in any sense. It is used widely in the letters of Paul and other New Testament writings: "beloved of God" (so Rom. 1:7; cf. 1 Thess. 1:4); "beloved brothers/sisters" (Eph. 6:21; Col. 4:9; Phlm. 16; 2 Pet. 3:15; James 1:16); beloved "sons/children" of a "teacher/father" (1 Cor. 4:4, 17; cf. 2 Tim. 1:2). In 1 John 3:2, the author writes, "beloved, now we are children of God"; frequently, we find people addressed or referred to as "beloved" (Rom. 11:28; 16:8, 12; Col. 3:12; 4:4; Heb. 6:9; 2 Pet. 3:8; 1 John 3:21; 4:1, 7, 11; 3 John 11; Jude 20). Thus ἀγαπητός as an isolated word need not carry associations with Isaac or with doomed children in general. In the Scriptures, there is indeed a frequently repeated motif of the ultimate tragedy being the death of an only beloved son (e.g., Amos 8:10; Jer. 6:26; Zech. 12:10), but this does not mean that everyone referred to as a "beloved" or "only beloved" son is destined to suffer a tragic death.

It is worthwhile to look behind the Greek form of the text. Since first-century Aramaic reconstructions are often conjectural, we may do better to consider other Hebrew equivalents of ἀγαπητός. The word יחיד is not the only term in Hebrew for "beloved"; יחיד refers specifically to a specially loved child or an only child. More commonly, we find דוד. For example, the LXX of Isa. 5:1 has τοῦ ἀγαπητοῦ μου for דודי, "my beloved." In Hebrew "beloved" may also be expressed by אהוב (cf. Neh. 13:26) or, in a special case, by חמודות (Dan. 9:23; cf. 10:11, 19). These

24. Meier, *Marginal Jew,* vol. 2, 188-89.

25. LSJ, 6.

latter two alternatives are not translated in the LXX by ἀγαπητός, but this does not mean that neither of them could have been used by Jesus in his description of God's words. If this story of Jesus' baptism derives ultimately from Jesus' own description of his experience, then God's words must have been passed on to his disciples in Hebrew or Aramaic, then later translated into Greek, and finally adapted to the concerns of each Gospel writer. The Greek text of Mark may therefore point to any one of several alternative words in Hebrew or Aramaic for "beloved."

A lengthy analysis of all the possibilities would be out of place here. However, it may be helpful to look further at Daniel 9–10 for an understanding of "beloved" both in the context of Jesus' baptismal vision and in the reworking of that vision in the story of the transfiguration (Mark 9:7 and parr.), where Jesus is presented as a prophet like Elijah and Moses (Mark 7:4-5), as well as in the parable of the wicked tenants, where the owner sends "a beloved son," υἱὸν ἀγαπητόν (Mark 12:6). In Daniel 9, the prophet is described as having prayed to God confessing the sins of Israel and having pleaded for forgiveness (9:4-19). While he was still at prayer "confessing my own sins and the sins of my people Israel" (9:20), the angel Gabriel (like a bird) "swooped on me in full flight" and told Daniel that he had come to teach him to understand, "for you are beloved (חמודות), so understand the word and comprehend the vision" (9:23b). There follows an eschatological prediction.

In Daniel 10, it is said that another vision was given to Daniel, during a three-week penance in which he abstained from wine and meat. As he stood on the bank of the Tigris River, he saw a shining man (10:5-8). A voice was heard, saying, "Daniel, you are a beloved man (איש חמדות); comprehend the words that I will tell you" (10:11; cf. 10:19). In this context, the underlying concept is that Daniel as a prophet is especially beloved, treasured, or desired by God. The root חמד means in Qal form "desire" or "take pleasure in."[26] Therefore, someone who is חמוד is "desired" or "beloved." The (feminine) noun means "loveliness, attractiveness, preciousness" (cf. Cant. 5:16), and the plural is therefore "desired, precious things/ones" (cf. Gen. 27:15; Ezra 8:27; 2 Chr. 20:25; Dan. 11:38, 43). Daniel is therefore one of God's treasures or desired ones. The LXX has for Dan. 10:11 and 19 ἀνὴρ ἐπιθυμιῶν; Daniel is "a man of desired ones," which renders the Hebrew idiom.

26. BDB, 326.

The notion of a special prophet being "beloved" or "desired" by God is found also in one possible reading of Jer. 11:14-15, where it is the prophet (not Israel) who is beloved and prays to God for his people. This reading is confirmed by the *Targum Pseudo-Jonathan* of Jeremiah.[27] In the Targum, the Hebrew דודי, "my beloved," is rendered as חביב קדמי, "a beloved one before me"; the word חביב continues in Arabic and modern Hebrew and is a common designation of affection. It is in this regard that Isa. 42:1 is interesting, for here again the prophet is considered somehow special to God; in this case he is "chosen," בחיר. The "servant" here is not the only one who is so chosen, for other prophets are also described in this way: Moses (Ps. 106:23) is "his chosen one," as is David (Ps. 89:4), who is also his "servant."[28] In *1 Enoch* we find Enoch referred to as "the chosen one," "the elect one," and "the anointed one" (49:2-4; 51:3-5; 52:4-9; 55:4; 61:4-9; 62:2-16). There seems to be a good case, then, for understanding the term "beloved" in Jesus' baptismal vision in light of the notion that prophets are especially beloved, chosen, treasured, or desired by God.

In conclusion, there is nothing to suggest that the account of Jesus' baptism as found in Mark is a literary construction modeled on Daniel 9–10, Jer. 11:14-15, Isa. 42:1, or Ps. 89:4, 106:23. The linguistic correlations are too slight. However, there are curious points of correlation between Daniel's narrative and the sequence of events we find in Mark. Jesus is in, rather than by, a river. He has, by implication, confessed his sins. The flurry of Gabriel's wings may be paralleled in the swooping down of the dove. Now, with the voice, Jesus is addressed not only as a righteous son but a beloved one, as Daniel was. In other words, God acknowledges here by this address that Jesus is chosen as a prophet. In Daniel, the angel Gabriel refers to vision and word; in Jesus' experience, we have both a vision and a word.

27. See A. Sperber, ed., *The Bible in Aramaic: Based on Old Manuscripts and Printed Texts,* vol. 4.B: *The Targum and the Hebrew Bible* (Leiden: Brill, 1992) 15-16.

28. "Servant" correlates with the notion that David was not only a king but also a prophet; see 11QPs[a]. The characterization of the prophets as God's servants is widely attested in the Qumran documents: 1QpHab 7:4-5; 4Q504 3:12; 5:14 (Moses); 4Q390 frag. 2; 4Q166-67 2:5-6. In the *Hodayoth,* the author (probably the Teacher of Righteousness) speaks of himself as one on whom God has shed his Holy Spirit and Wisdom (1QH 7:6; 9:33; 12:11-14; 14:12; 16:12-13; 17:25-26) and, repeatedly, as one who is God's servant (7:16-18; 10:30; etc.); cf. 1QS 11:16, 1QpHab 2:2-3, even though the Teacher is never explicitly called a prophet.

The Spirit itself is the spirit of prophecy. The Targums regularly replace the "spirit of YHWH" with the "spirit of prophecy."[29] The Holy Spirit is also the spirit of prophecy in rabbinic literature.[30] The Holy Spirit could be identified with the personified divine Wisdom, חכמה. Since the terminology is feminine in gender, both Wisdom and the Holy Spirit could be personified as a kind of feminine hypostasis of God. So, in the *Gospel of the Hebrews,* Jesus claims that his "mother, the Holy Spirit" carried him off to Mount Tabor in Galilee.[31] In the Wisdom of Solomon, Wisdom is described as the "breath and power of God" (Wis. 7:25) who, in every generation, "passes into holy souls and makes them friends of God and prophets" (7:27). The notion that the Spirit of YHWH comes upon or in a person, and that this is in a sense an "anointing" or commission, is found in Isa. 61:1-2, used in Luke 4:18-19 to sum up the essential character of Jesus' work: "The Spirit of the Lord YHWH is upon me, for he has anointed me to bring good news to the poor . . ." (cf. Luke 3:22; 4:1, 16; Acts 10:38) and 1 Kgs. 19:6, where Elijah is told to anoint Elisha as a prophet after him. The notion that prophets were "anointed ones" is also found in Qumran documents (CD 2:12; 6:1; 1QM 11:7; 4Q521 frag. 8: "all her [the Holy Spirit's/Wisdom's] anointed ones"; cf. 11QMelch 2:15-16).[32] In the Targum of Isaiah, the basic understanding that this is the role of a prophet is emphasized: "The prophet said, '*A spirit of prophecy* before the Lord God is upon me, because the Lord has exalted me to announce good tidings to the poor. . . .' "[33] In being "anointed" with the spirit of prophecy, the prophet could be understood as an "anointed one" or "messiah."

Therefore, the descent of the Spirit, which comes in or upon Jesus, makes him a prophet; upon his immersion, the voice itself accompanies

29. M. Turner, "The Spirit of Prophecy and the Power of Authoritative Preaching in Luke-Acts: A Question of Origins," *NTS* 38/1 (1992) 76-77.

30. Ibid., 77-82.

31. Schneemelcher, ed., *New Testament Apocrypha I,* 177.

32. See J. J. Collins, *The Scepter and the Star: The Messiahs of the Dead Sea Scrolls and Other Ancient Literature* (New York: Doubleday, 1995) 118-19, and his Chapter 5 as a whole.

33. B. D. Chilton, *The Isaiah Targum: Introduction, Translation, Apparatus, and Notes* (Wilmington, DE: Glazier, 1987) 118. See also Ps. 105:15; 1 Kgs. 19:16; Neh. 9:30; cf. CD 2:12-13; 1QS 8:16 and, for other parallels, see Str-B, vol. 2, 127-38.

the descent by accounting him righteous, beloved, and chosen by God and therefore worthy of the Spirit.

The image of the dove may have been difficult to understand even in the first generations of the Church. In the description of the baptismal vision in the *Gospel of Hebrews* it is omitted.[34] It is not found as a symbol of the Holy Spirit in the Hebrew Scriptures.[35] It could be the symbol of Israel (Ps. 74:19; 56:1 [LXX]), but this does not seem to fit here. As Joachim Jeremias noted, the "strangest parallels from the history of religion have been adduced in attempts at explanation" of the dove motif.[36] The fact that the dove does not easily fit with scriptural precedents would in itself seem to suggest that it too may have come from Jesus' description; it cannot be seen as a Christian construct if Christians did not understand its significance. This is not a symbolic story, constructed so that everyone hearing it would immediately recognize the motifs. Luke tries to explain that the Spirit was in bodily form like a dove, clearly trying to make something of a simile that has no meaning for him.

At this point, it might be worth recalling an experience of my own. In 1986, I was walking across Jaffa Road in Jerusalem when a dove came flying out of the sky and brushed the top of my head before disappearing again over the rooftops. Perhaps it was a mother bird whose nest was nearby and she was protecting her young. At any rate, it seems to me that the experience of being hit by a dove might have made a good parallel to being hit by the Spirit of God, if the Spirit was understood to have been like a rushing wind. Indeed, in Aramaic and Hebrew, the same word is used for both wind and spirit, and it is considered a forceful phenomenon. In Acts 2:2 the Spirit comes down on a large group of Jesus' disciples with "a sound like the rush of a violent wind." I can verify that a dove coming down on someone with wings flapping is something like a very powerful rush of wind striking one's head, with a noise of windy flurry and flapping. It is quite a shock and is certainly not a gentle experience. At any rate, the description of the Spirit coming down upon Jesus like a dove coming

34. Schneemelcher, ed., *New Testament Apocrypha I,* 177.

35. See Str-B, vol. 1, 123-25.

36. Jeremias, *New Testament Theology,* 52. For a negative response to the search for mythological parallels, see L. E. Keck, "The Spirit and the Dove," *NTS* 17/1 (1970) 41-67.

out of the sky seems to me a particularly apt one to explain a rushing power of God that had singled out one person to strike.[37]

When Jesus describes another vision — that of seeing Satan falling from heaven (Luke 10:18) — he describes his fall as being "like lightning." It would be pointless here to try to find a symbol of Satan as lightning in the Scriptures. The simile is intended to describe a mystical apprehension in terms drawn from the material world. Satan's falling was therefore fast, bright, and powerful like lightning is, and as lightning shoots from the sky to the earth, so Satan fell from the sky to the earth.[38] Therefore, it seems possible that Jesus used similes to illuminate his experience of the spiritual, but not symbols.

If Jesus had some awareness of the descent of the Spirit, he must from that time on have understood himself to be a prophet. His earliest disciples also thought so. As noted above, in the story of the transfiguration (Mark 9:2-8 = Matt. 17:1-8 = Luke 9:28-36), this is how Jesus is presented; he is a prophet of such high status that he stands with Moses and Elijah. As at the baptism, a voice from heaven also declares at the transfiguration: "This is my beloved son." But the voice addresses the disciples and adds, "Listen to him" (Mark 9:7). The easiest reading of this story is that the earliest disciples of Jesus recognized him as a prophet like Moses or Elijah who should be listened to. He was a beloved son of God. If he was considered by the nascent Church to have been the eschatological royal Messiah, or the only Son of God, then the tradition of the transfiguration would have involved Moses and Elijah bowing down to him, but in this story they are simply "talking with him"; the impression is that Moses, Elijah, and Jesus were perceived as equals by Jesus' earliest disciples.

It has long been recognized by scholars that Jesus was seen pri-

37. Jeremias, *New Testament Theology,* 52, suggests that the descent of the Spirit was probably accompanied by a "gentle sound like a dove" (so also Keck, "The Spirit and the Dove," 63-67). I do not find this point convincing, in view of my own noisy and rather alarming encounter with a dove!

38. Cf. J. V. Hills, "Luke 10:18 — Who Saw Satan Fall?" *JSNT* 46 (1992) 25-40, who thinks the demons saw Satan fall. J. Marcus suggests that it was the vision of Satan falling that Jesus experienced at the Jordan, rather than the one described by Mark; see J. Marcus, "Jesus' Baptismal Vision," *NTS* 41 (1995) 512-21. However, in this case, we are still left without a "beginning" for Jesus' prophetic awareness. We might do better to suggest that he had several visionary experiences: one at the Jordan, one of Satan falling, and possibly others that went unrecorded.

marily as a prophet by his earliest followers. As Cleopas says in Luke 24:19, Jesus was "a prophet mighty in action and word before God and all the people." Often the scholarly issue concerns what kind of prophet he was. For example, Martin Hengel sees him as an "eschatological charismatic."[39] Geza Vermes defines him in terms of the charismatic *ḥasidim* of Galilee.[40] James Dunn sees him as a prophet and charismatic, making a distinction between the two,[41] while E. P. Sanders considers Jesus a "charismatic prophet."[42] As Vermes has noted, by using "prophet" with "charismatic," we are making a distinction between Hebrew and Greek concepts: "In Palestinian Jewish parlance — *charisma* being a Greek concept absent from the Gospels and used only by Paul in the New Testament — a person wielding such authority is known as a prophet."[43] The Galilean *ḥasidim* described by Vermes would then have been considered, popularly, as prophets.[44] In the view of Paul, every Christian possesses a gift *(charisma)* as a result of the indwelling of the Spirit, but it might manifest itself in different ways, only one of which is called "prophecy." The varieties of gifts of the Spirit are given as: the utterance of wisdom, the utterance of knowledge, faith, gifts of healing, working of miracles, prophecy, discernment of spirits, speaking in tongues, interpretation of tongues (1 Cor. 12:4-11). Here Paul appears to be using the word "prophecy" in the sense of prediction, for strictly speaking the exercise of any of these gifts would make one a prophet. They are all evidence of a person possessing the prophetic spirit.

Jesus' working of miracles itself appears to have bolstered his reputation as a prophet, as did his wise and knowledgeable utterances, discernment of spirits, exorcisms, and healings. In the early Christian community, one could be a charismatic without necessarily being a "prophet" (maker of predictions), but one could not be a "prophet," so defined, without being also a charismatic. Since in Pauline theology the Christian community is thought to constitute the body of Christ on earth, it was right that it should possess the powers attributed to Jesus

39. M. Hengel, *The Charismatic Leader and His Followers* (Edinburgh: Clark, 1981).

40. Vermes, *Jesus the Jew,* 2d ed.

41. Dunn, *Jesus and the Spirit.*

42. E. P. Sanders, *Jewish Law from Jesus to the Mishnah: Five Studies* (London: SCM, 1990).

43. G. Vermes, *The Religion of Jesus the Jew* (London: SCM, 1993) 73.

44. Vermes, *Jesus the Jew,* 2d ed., 89-90.

(plus the new power of tongues), only spread out among all the people of the Church. Its seems doubtful that exactly the same distinctions between components of prophecy were made in Second Temple Judaism, and they may owe much to Greek concepts. While it may be useful to distinguish between prophets as prediction-makers and charismatics as possessors of the Holy Spirit to varying degrees, we should tread carefully in regard to such definitions.

As we return to the question of Jesus' relationship with John, we find Jesus upon his immersion experiencing some kind of visionary awareness of his own prophetic empowerment. As we shall see, John himself may have had no idea that this had taken place, for later on, from prison, he asked Jesus whether he was the "coming one." If Jesus' immersion was part of a mass immersion, with numerous people immersing themselves in the Jordan under the general direction of John, John may not have been fully cognizant of what people were experiencing. Such ritual events can be highly charged and can evoke profound feelings and strong emotions; extreme reactions may not have been uncommon. If Jesus seemed to onlookers to be in a trance or altered state, it may not have been apparent to John what this involved. Jesus himself need not have told anyone immediately about his experience. Of course, all this must remain speculative, but there seems no reason to assume that John knew about the vision at the time of Jesus' immersion.

Two Prophets?

If Jesus understood himself to have become a prophet at his baptism by John, we need to consider the subsequent relationship between Jesus and John. In Mark's Gospel, Jesus is "immediately" propelled by the Spirit out into the wilderness (Mark 1:12-13). He has no chance to tell anyone, least of all John, about what has taken place. We are also given the impression that Jesus was not at the Jordan for very long before his immersion, for he comes from Nazareth and is immersed without any preparation. However, all through our discussion we have seen how aspects of John's teaching and lifestyle might be further explained by looking to the Jesus tradition. In Chapter 3 it was suggested that Jesus may even have given to his disciples the prayer taught by John. In other words, Jesus appears to have taken over many of John's ideas and continued them in his own life and teaching. If this is so, then we may presume that Jesus studied under John for some period. If he did indeed go out to the wilderness after his immersion, the time he spent absorbing John's teaching would have been prior to this. In fact, Q and Luke both present John as teaching people prior to their immersion rather than after it. This would mean that people placed themselves in the position of disciples of John in order to learn how to be purified effectively both inwardly and outwardly. Once they felt fairly confident of their righteousness, by John's definition, they then came for immersion. The immersion itself did not make them disciples; their acceptance of John's teaching did. Many people may have come out to listen to John without actually accepting the necessity of his immersion or putting themselves under his instruction. Not all of the people became his disciples. Once people were immersed, however, they would already have accepted John's teaching and therefore become his disciples prior to this.

Shortly after his sojourn with John by the Jordan, Jesus seems to have followed in John's footsteps by going out into the wilderness for some period of time to live as John lived, trusting in God to provide the necessities of life. Jesus may not have headed out into the desert just to copy John, however. He may have considered this wilderness experience and the overcoming of temptation to be essential as proof of his God-given power. Although nothing is ever said of John defeating temptation in the wilderness, the assumption that he, as a holy man, was able to resist the evil powers resident there may be implied in the descriptions we have concerning him. The spirits of the sins of the people, which on the Day of Atonement entered the scapegoat (Leviticus 16), later known as a demon Azazel, were supposed to live in the wilderness. In 4 Macc. 18:8 this demon is the "seducer of the desert." In Matt. 12:43 Jesus describes an unclean spirit going out of a person and wandering through waterless regions looking for a resting place.[45] Therefore, evil spirits were thought to live in the wilderness, and temptation of any kind may have been interpreted as temptation by the Devil.

In Mark's very brief account of Jesus' temptation (Mark 1:12-13), it is simply stated that he was tempted by Satan. It would not be surprising if temptation to abandon his desert lifestyle soon came upon him. In the Q version, the temptations by Satan are much more specific and are concerned with the issue of whether or not he really is the "son

45. See Scobie, *John the Baptist,* 47.

of God," in particular, whether he as possessor of the Holy Spirit is able to evict demons. In the synoptic Gospels demons in general recognize this ability in "the son of God" (see Mark 3:11; Luke 4:41; Mark 5:7; cf. Luke 8:28; Matt. 8:29) and do not wish to be evicted.[46] The title "the son of God" here may refer to a prophet who is able to exorcise, but the temptations by Satan are generally directed at someone who is particularly righteous before God, as Jesus and others who had been immersed by John would have been expected to be. In the Wisdom of Solomon the ungodly plot against the righteous man and note, sneeringly, that he calls himself "a child of the Lord" (2:13) and that "he avoids our ways as unclean; he calls the last end of the righteous happy and boasts that God is his father" (2:16). The ungodly wish to test him, "for if the righteous man is God's son, he will help him, and will deliver him from the hands of his adversaries" (2:18).

Satan accordingly tempts Jesus to misuse his prophetic powers, but none of the temptations has anything to do with his being the royal Messiah as such. For example, the temptation to command the stones to becomes loaves of bread (Matt. 4:3-4; Luke 4:3-4) is designed to try to get Jesus, as prophet, to use the indwelling power of God to effect a miracle to assuage his hunger. The temptation to throw himself down from the Temple (Matt. 4:5-7; Luke 4:9-12) draws on Psalm 91, which is addressed to those who "have made the LORD your refuge, the Most High your dwelling place" (Ps. 91:9); the temptation has nothing to do with messiahship but may be interpreted as a trial faced by all who put their absolute trust in God. The temptation to worship Satan for the sake of worldly power (Matt. 4:8-9; Luke 4:5-8) again would fit anyone who determined to worship God alone. Significantly, Jesus responds each time by recourse to the book of Deuteronomy, which encapsulates the Mosaic Law (Deut. 6:13, 16; 8:2-3). Whereas the Israelites as a whole failed to pass certain tests in the wilderness, Jesus stands firm,[47] but the temptations are aimed at a righteous person who has been invested with prophetic power by God, and not at a Christian royal Messiah, the new king of a new Israel.

Jesus, after his stay in the wilderness, goes on to Galilee and begins a mission very different from that of John. Most importantly, he heals,

46. Vermes, *Jesus the Jew,* 2d ed., 202-03.

47. See C. H. Dodd, *The Founder of Christianity* (New York: Macmillan, 1970) 116.

exorcises, and raises people from the dead; he also teaches and proclaims the good news. In the synoptic Gospels Jesus amazes people by rewarding the faithful with acts — δυνάμεις, "miracles" — of prophetic authority, ἐξουσία (e.g., Mark 1:21, 27; 6:2; cf. Luke 4:32; 7:29; Matt. 13:54). As we saw, the same authority is attributed to John by Jesus, in regard to his baptism (Mark 11:27-33 = Matt. 21:23-7 = Luke 20:1-8), though John does not perform miracles. Nevertheless, it seems that for Jesus, John's immersion of repentance was not something John decided upon after a thorough exegesis of Scripture, but was divinely decreed; people needed immersion following repentance, for no one was clean unless the inner being was pure in accordance with the high standards John defined.

As for miracles, we noticed in the last chapter that John's possession of the Holy Spirit may have been seen as his ability to understand the Scriptures correctly, thereby finding the clues of the future. John himself did not attempt to show that this gift involved being so inhabited by the Holy Spirit that he had the authority to make new laws, raise the dead, perform signs and wonders, or inspire a following that would claim his spirit still lived on beyond his death.

Jesus, by contrast, appears to have gone about fulfilling his role as prophet in an entirely different way. For Jesus, the possession of the Holy Spirit appears to have meant that he did have the full range of powers attributed to the prophets of old. In particular, his healings and exorcisms were considered to be a manifestation of the power of the Holy Spirit, the finger of God (Luke 8:20; cf. Matt. 12:28). When some people (possibly Pharisees) claim that Jesus possesses not the Holy Spirit but a demon or "unclean spirit" (Matt. 9:34; Mark 3:28-19; Luke 12:10; Matt. 12:31-32), Jesus hotly reacts that these critics have insulted the Holy Spirit and decrees that they are guilty of eternal sin.

What, then, of the relationship between John and Jesus as prophets? Were they opposed or supportive of one another? We have noted that in the parable of the wicked tenants (Matt. 21:28-32), Jesus may have referred to John as "a beloved son." The discussion above would indicate that the expression "a beloved son" designates a special prophet, distinguished from other prophets by his closer relationship with God. If Jesus did describe his visionary experience in the Jordan in the manner outlined above, then he would also have considered himself "a beloved son." If both John and Jesus were so close to God, what was their relationship?

Elijah and John

When considering Jesus' relationship to John, one thinks of Elisha's relationship to Elijah. Elisha was a disciple of Elijah, his "master" or "lord" (2 Kgs. 2:3). Elisha was made Elijah's successor beyond the Jordan. Elisha received a double portion of the Holy Spirit that had been in Elijah's possession (2 Kgs. 2:9-15). He could part the Jordan River like Elijah (2 Kgs. 2:8) and Joshua (Josh. 3:14-17; 2 Kgs. 2:14-15). Whereas Elijah was a solitary figure, Elisha was surrounded by followers and moved among people, performing miraculous healings wherever he went. The story of Elijah and Elisha (1 Kings 16–2 Kings 13) may itself have been constructed to echo traditions of the Exodus and the entry into the promised land.[48]

The very early disciples of Jesus may have thought that the pattern of the relationship between Elijah and Elisha was being repeated in John and Jesus, for certain miracles of Jesus appear to be deliberately designed to recall Elisha's miracles, in particular, the cure of a leper (2 Kgs. 5:1-14; cf. Mark 1:40-55 and parr.) and the raising of a dead child (2 Kgs. 4:32-37; cf. Mark 5:21-43 and parr.).

For much of the early Church, John was Elijah *redivivus* (see, e.g., Mark 9:11-13; Matt. 11:14; 17:10-12; Luke 1:17). It seems quite possible that Jesus thought so too. For example, in a passage following the transfiguration, Jesus identifies John as Elijah (Mark 9:9-13 = Matt. 17:9-13). Interestingly, in the same passage Jesus refers to John/Elijah by using the Aramaic circumlocution for "human being" or "man," preserved in Greek as ὁ υἱὸς τοῦ ἀνθρώπου.[49]

48. Crossan, *Historical Jesus,* 138-41.

49. The usual translation of ὁ υἱὸς τοῦ ἀνθρώπου is the androcentric expression "son of man," even though ἄνθρωπος is "human being, person," and an absolutely literal translation would be "the son of the human being." In the underlying Hebrew and Aramaic expressions, בן אדם and בר (א)נש(א), respectively, אדם/(א)נש(א) refers both to the individual first human being (Adam) and to humankind in general; the reference is, therefore, to an individual human being, a person, or (if male) a man (cf. Dan. 2:38; 7:13; 8:17; Ps. 80:17[18], and 93 times in the book of Ezekiel). The scholarly literature on the meaning of the term is vast, but see for important discussions G. Vermes, "The Use of בר נשא/בר נש in Jewish Aramaic," in *An Aramaic Approach to the Gospels and Acts,* by M. Black, 3d ed. (Oxford: Clarendon, 1967) 310-28; idem, "The Son of Man Debate," *JSNT* 1 (1978) 19-32; idem, *Jesus the Jew,* 2d ed., 160-91; J. A. Fitzmyer, "Another View of the Son of Man Debate," *JSNT* 4 (1979) 58-68; J. R. Donahue, "Recent Studies in the Origin of 'Son of Man' in the Gospels," *CBQ* 48 (1986) 484-98; M. Casey, *Son of*

> And as they were coming down from the mountain, he ordered them not to relate what they had seen, except when the Son of man (ὁ υἱός τοῦ ἀνθρώπου) had risen from the dead. And they kept the saying to themselves, questioning, "What is it to rise from the dead?" And they asked him, saying, "Why do the scribes say that Elijah must come first?" And he said to them, "Elijah comes first to restore everything, and how is it written about the Son of man (ὁ υἱὸς τοῦ ἀνθρώπου) that he would suffer many things and be despised? But I say to you that indeed Elijah has come, and they did to him what they wanted, just as it is written about him." (Mark 9:9-13)

In the first use of the expression "the man" (Mark 9:9), it seems likely that Mark understands the reference to apply to Jesus himself. No one else is referred to. It was, after all, Jesus who would rise from the dead (cf. Mark 9:30-32). This is what makes the present passage incoherent.[50] In Mark 9:10 the disciples are characterized as being ignorant

---

Man: The Interpretation and Influence of Daniel 7 (London: SPCK, 1979); idem, "General, Generic, and Indefinite: The Use of the Term 'Son of Man' in Aramaic Sources and in the Teaching of Jesus," *JSNT* 29 (1987) 21-56; idem, "The Use of the Term בר (א)נש(א) in the Aramaic Translation of the Hebrew Bible," *JSNT* 54 (1994) 87-118; J. J. Collins, "The Son of Man in First Century Judaism," *NTS* 38 (1992) 448-66; B. Lindars, *Jesus, Son of Man: A Fresh Examination of the Son of Man Sayings in the Gospels in the Light of Recent Research* (Grand Rapids: Eerdmans, 1983).

50. See Ernst, *Johannes der Täufer*, 30, who thinks that the argumentation is illogical. Meier, *Marginal Jew*, vol. 2, 226, thinks the saying is a Christian construction because prior to Christianity there was no expectation that Elijah would prepare the way for the Messiah as such. Actually, in the core pericope, there is no mention of the royal Messiah. For the debate concerning Elijah's preparatory role, see M. Faierstein, "Why do the Scribes say that Elijah Must Come First?" *JBL* 100 (1981) 75-86, who argues that Elijah was not expected to prepare the way for the Messiah; D. C. Allison, "Elijah Must Come First," *JBL* 103 (1984) 256-58, who argues that he was; and J. A. Fitzmyer, "More about Elijah Coming First," *JBL* 104 (1985) 295-96, who agrees with Faierstein. Some scholars would prefer to see the reference to "the son of humankind" as an interpolation; see, e.g., R. L. Webb, *John the Baptizer and Prophet: A Socio-Historical Study* (Sheffield: JSOT Press, 1991) 53; W. Wink, *John the Baptist in the Gospel Tradition* (Cambridge: Cambridge University Press, 1968) 13-17; Ernst, *Johannes der Täufer*, 30-34, though Wink does accept that it must refer to Elijah in this context. Bultmann thought that verse 12b was a post-Marcan interpolation from Matt. 17:12 (*The History of the Synoptic Tradition* [Oxford: Blackwell, 1963] 125). For a judicious examination of the passage, see Justin Taylor, "The Coming of Elijah, Mt. 17,10-13 and Mk. 9,11-13: The Development of the Texts," *RB* 98/1 (1991) 107-19.

of the Pharisaic belief in bodily resurrection at the end of days; but only the Gentile audience of Mark's Gospel could really have been expected to ask the question "What is it to rise from the dead?" From them we might expect a question like: "Who is 'the man' who is to rise from the dead?"

It may be erroneous to see Mark 9:9-13 as a cohesive unit. Verses 9-10 form a kind of appendix to the story of the transfiguration and explain why this visionary event on the part of Jesus' closest disciples was known only after Jesus' resurrection. The question concerning rising from the dead is left unanswered, curiously hanging in the air and remaining unexplained; it is a question that will only be answered as the story of Jesus' death and resurrection unfolds. The unanswered question closes the story of the transfiguration in a rather strange way. The pericope about John in verses 11-13 is self-standing and need not originally have had any connection with the transfiguration. While the first instance of "the man" who will rise from the dead (9:9) is most likely a reference to Jesus, the second use of "the man" (9:12) must refer to Elijah/John. As an independent unit, then, the pericope in verses 11-13 is perfectly intelligible. It derives from a time after John was imprisoned and executed. Jesus appears to say that Elijah/John will suffer and die in accordance with the Scriptures.

We have little information about expectations concerning Elijah in Jewish literature from the Second Temple period, but those we do know about are clearly founded on the prophecies of Mal. 3:1-5 and 4:5-6. Elijah was expected to "prepare the way" before YHWH (Mal. 3:1) and to have a purificatory role:

> He will sit as a refiner and purifier of silver. He will purify the descendants of Levi and refine them like gold and silver, until they present offerings to YHWH in righteousness. Then the offering of Judah and Jerusalem will be pleasing to YHWH as in ancient days and as in former years. (Mal. 3:3-4)

Since John's immersion was intended for purification and repentance, it is easy to see how these verses from Malachi could be seen to apply to John. With cleansing and the presentation of offerings "in righteousness," God would be pleased at last. Without righteousness, God could not be pleased. Following his pleasure, God would judge Israel (Mal. 3:5). Elijah would not only cleanse but also restore everything to rightness:

> Look, I will send you the prophet Elijah before the great and terrible Day of YHWH comes. He will turn the hearts of parents towards their children and the hearts of children towards their parents, so that I will not come and strike the land with a curse. (Mal. 4:5-6)

In Mark 9:11 the disciples report that the scribes say that Elijah will come to "restore all things." This expectation seems to derive not only from Malachi but also from Sirach:

> At the appointed time, it is written, you [Elijah] are destined to calm the wrath of God before it breaks out in fury; to turn the hearts of parents to their children, and to restore the tribes of Israel. (Sir. 48:10)

The comments in Mark 9:11-13 suggest that Jesus and his early disciples may have understood John to be fulfilling the functions of Elijah as one who would restore the tribes of Israel. They may have understood John's mission to be that of urging the lost people of Israel to return to the Law and be cleansed inside and outside. These actions would amount to a restoration of the tribes, for the people could not properly constitute the true children of Israel as long as their unrighteousness remained. This perspective fits well with John's statement that calling Abraham one's father meant nothing without righteous deeds (Matt. 3:8-9 = Luke 3:8).

Aside from Malachi and Sirach, there are a few other texts that inform us about expectations centered on Elijah. A papyrus fragment from Qumran cave 4 (4Q558) has the words "therefore I will send Elijah be[fore]."[51] A more substantial text from Qumran is 4Q521, a Hebrew text whose script dates to the Hasmonean period. John J. Collins has argued that in the longest fragment of 4Q521 (fragment 2 ii), the words "heaven and earth will obey his messiah" refer to an anointed eschatological prophet, either Elijah or an Elijah-like prophet. The text goes on to say that God will (apparently through the agency of this anointed prophet) "release captives, giving sight to the blind and raising up those who are bo[wed down]. . . . heal the wounded, give life to the dead and preach good news to the poor. . . ." (Another fragment of 4Q521, fragment 2 iii, has the words "the fathers will return to sons the sons," which certainly seems to reflect the Elijah tradition, but this may not be associated with

51. J. J. Collins, *The Scepter and the Star,* 116; see also J. Starcky, "Les quatres étapes du messianisme à Qumrân," *RB* 70 (1963) 481-505.

the figure previously mentioned, since we have no idea how the parts of this document fit together.) Collins supports the identification of this figure with Elijah or an Elijah-like prophet by noting that Elijah was credited with raising the dead in his historical career (1 Kings 17). He also notes that the association of Elijah with eschatological resurrection may be attested in the Hebrew text of Sirach from the Cairo Genizah (Sir. 48:11). The notion that the resurrection of the dead will come through Elijah is also found in rabbinic literature (*m. Soṭa* 9; *y. Šeqal.* 3:3).[52]

In the *Sibylline Oracles* 2.187-89 it is said that Elijah will return, but since the passage is known only in a Christianized form, it is generally not considered relevant in discussions of first-century Elijah traditions.[53] In *1 Enoch* 90:31, 37 Elijah is symbolized as a ram who, with three angels, prepares the final scene in which the Messiah appears as a white bull with large horns.[54] Certainly, if hope for a royal Messiah was prominent in the first century, people would have expected Elijah to come before this figure. Yet the first clear attestation of the notion that Elijah will precede the Messiah is found in a Christian, not a Jewish, source (Justin Martyr, *Dial.* 8:4; 49:1). In some sectors of early Judaism, Elijah may have been identified with the zealous figure of Phineas, since *Tg. Ps.-J.* Exod. 4:13 seems to identify the two. In *Tg. Num.* 25:12 Phineas is the messenger of the covenant who lives forever to proclaim the good news of the redemption at the end of days.[55]

The main point to be derived from this brief survey of texts is that Elijah was expected by some Jews to come before the end, but how one imagined the end depended on many factors. There was no one, fully supported scenario among Jews of this time.

There is little evidence in the extant literature to endorse Jesus' view, as recorded in Mark 9:12, that the eschatological Elijah would have to suffer. Conceivably such a view could have been based on an interpretation of Isaiah 53 that identified the suffering servant with Elijah. Early Jewish evidence for a suffering Elijah cannot be sought with con-

52. Collins, *The Scepter and the Star,* 119.

53. Ibid., 116.

54. See G. Vermes, *Jesus the Jew,* 2d ed., 94-95. There are problems with dating the section of *1 Enoch* known as *The Parables of Enoch* (*1 Enoch* 37–71), since no fragments from this section were found among the Qumran documents. Overall, however, most of *1 Enoch* does seem to predate the mid-first century.

55. R. Hayward, "Phinehas — The Same as Elijah: The Origins of a Rabbinic Tradition," *JJS* 29 (1978) 22-34.

fidence in the Coptic *Apocalypse of Elijah* since it is a third-century CE Christian (or at least Christianized) work.[56] Nevertheless it is possible that it utilized a Jewish notion of a suffering Elijah that was then adapted to fit with Christian theology. Even if the notion of a suffering Elijah was not widespread, the evidence of Mark 9:11-13 certainly indicates that it was the view of Jesus and/or the early Church. How could this have come about? The documents from Qumran may provide a clue.

John J. Collins has recently made interesting links between Qumran documents that may illuminate our understanding of expectations surrounding Elijah. The biblical basis for the expectation of "he who will teach righteousness at the end of days" in CD 6:11 is Hos. 10:12, "until he comes and teaches righteousness for you," a passage that is associated with Elijah in later Jewish tradition.[57] There may be some reason to connect Elijah with the expected priestly "messiah of Aaron." The Targumim also refer to Elijah as a "high priest," a view that may derive from 1 Kgs. 18:30-39, where Elijah builds an altar and offers sacrifice. In Christian tradition John is identified with Elijah and is also a priest (Luke 1:5). There is evidence from Qumran that a priestly teacher was expected who would "atone for all the sons of his generation" (4Q541, fragment 9 i). The messiahs of Aaron and Israel both atone for sin in CD 14:19.[58] In 4Q541 it is said of the atoning figure that he will suffer at the hands of people who spread lies about him. This fragment is especially reminiscent of Elijah, since it says that "his fire will spring forth to all the ends of the earth"; one of the remarkable acts of Elijah was that he called down fire or lightning from heaven (1 Kgs. 18:38; 2 Kgs. 1:9-14). Also, Elijah ascended to heaven in "a chariot of fire" with "horses of fire" (2 Kgs. 2:11; cf. 2 Kgs. 6:17). Carl Kazmierski observes that Elijah is rejected by the rulers of Israel in 1 Kings

56. See J. A. T. Robinson, "Elijah, John and Jesus: An Essay in Detection," in his *Twelve New Testament Studies* (London: SCM, 1962) 45 n. 39; Wink, *Gospel Tradition,* 14 n. 2.

57. J. J. Collins, *The Scepter and the Star,* 113. A. S. Van der Woude, *Die Messianischen Vorstellungen der Gemeinde von Qumrân* (Assen: Van Gorcum, 1957) 55, argued that the eschatological interpreter of the Law in CD 6 should be identified with Elijah, since CD 7:18 identifies Balaam's star with this figure "who will come to Damascus," which may be a reference to 1 Kgs. 19:15, where Elijah is told by God, "Go, return on your way to the wilderness of Damascus. And you must come and anoint Hazael to be king over Aram." Collins links the interpreter of the Law with the Messiah of Aaron, the eschatological high priest.

58. Collins, *The Scepter and the Star,* 115, though on pp. 124-26 Collins argues against the view that atoning for sins indicates martyrdom.

19.[59] This may well have provided a paradigm for an Elijah rejected and persecuted by those in power.

If, then, some of the Qumran texts give the eschatological teacher and high priest, who was expected to suffer and atone for sin, Elijah-like characteristics, perhaps this qualifies as evidence for belief in a suffering Elijah. Other texts might provide corroborating evidence. Justin's presentation of Trypho's views (*Dialogue* 89–90) may indicate that there was a (Jewish) view in the second century that an "anointed one" would suffer (though not be crucified). In Sir. 4:15-17 he who obeys Wisdom will judge the nations, but only after being tormented. In the Wisdom of Solomon (2:12-20) the righteous man who calls God his father is tested, tormented, and condemned to a shameful death. In addition, there is the Jewish-Christian apocalyptic presentation of two prophets in Revelation 11, both of whom are killed. They prophecy for 1260 days clothed in sackcloth (as John was). Fire (an Elijah motif) proceeds from their mouths and devours their enemies (Rev. 11:5). The prophets, who seem identical, are killed by the beast from the abyss but are revived and ascend into heaven after a voice from heaven says, "Come up here!" It certainly seems possible that this story may derive from some expectation of Elijah's return; here we have twin prophets, for "Elijah" was, in some early Christian circles, both Elijah and John the Baptist.

If Jesus and his early disciples believed that John was Elijah, what then of Jesus' own prophetic role? Did Jesus expect (or consider himself to be) an end-time *Elisha* figure — the successor of Elijah? An end-time role for Elisha is not attested in the literature, and this silence tends to rule out the possibility that Jesus expected an Elisha figure to follow the Elijah figure. Sir. 48:12 says, "When Elijah was enveloped in the whirlwind, Elisha was filled with his Spirit. He performed twice as many signs and wonders with every saying of his mouth. Never in his life did he tremble before any ruler, and no one could intimidate him at all." But while Elijah was taken up into heaven with chariots of fire (2 Kings 2), Elisha died a natural death (2 Kgs. 13:14-21). Despite his double portion of the Spirit, he did not dwell in heaven; nor did he exercise such a hold on the imaginations of Jews during the Second Temple period as Elijah did. Since Elisha apparently did not dwell in heaven like Elijah, he was passed over in eschatological expectations.

59. Carl Kazmierski, *John the Baptist: Prophet and Evangelist* (Collegeville, MN: The Liturgical Press/Michael Glazier, 1996) 82-83; see also 96-103.

It should be remembered that John himself apparently denied that he was Elijah (John 1:21; cf. Acts 13:25). The early Church seems to have had a dogged determination to identify him as Elijah, even while preserving faithfully John's own denial. If it is right that John himself was expecting Elijah, as "the coming one," it seems strange that Jesus would invert this expectation and transfer it to John. John points forward and Jesus points backward. During the time they were both alive, how did they relate? For this, we have to consider the evidence of Q.

Elijah and Jesus

Most important in our discussion of the relationship between John and Jesus is the Q passage in which John sends disciples to Jesus to ask him if he is "the coming one" (Matt. 11:2-6; Luke 7:18-23):

> John, having heard from prison of the works of the Messiah, sent [word] through his disciples and said to him [Jesus], "Are you the coming one or should we expect another?" And Jesus answered and said to them, "Go tell John what you see and hear; the blind see again and the cripples walk, lepers are cleansed and the deaf hear, and the dead are raised and the poor are brought good news. And blessed is anyone who is not offended by me." (Matt. 11:2-6)

> And John's disciples reported concerning all these things. And having summoned two of his disciples, John sent [them] to the Lord, saying, "Are you the coming one or should we expect another?" Having come to him, the men said, "John the Baptist has sent us to you, saying, 'Are you the coming one or should we expect another?' " In that hour Jesus had healed many people of diseases, plagues, and evil spirits, and to many blind people he had granted sight. And he answered and said to them, "Go tell John what you see and hear; the blind see, the cripples walk, the lepers are cleansed and the poor are brought good news; and blessed is anyone who is not offended by me." (Luke 7:18-23)

John is told about what Jesus has been doing, and, if our identification is correct, he wonders if Elijah has in fact come. At the very least, John's question serves to show that Matthew's addition to the baptism, where

John tries to prevent Jesus from being immersed (Matt. 3:14-15), cannot be historically accurate if the question of the Baptist is also to be considered as such. They cannot both be true. Walter Wink has recently argued a case for the historicity of this section on the grounds of the generally accepted criteria of authenticity.[60] As Wink notes, "The early church would scarcely have ascribed uncertainty to John and then answered his uncertainty with baffling ambiguity."[61]

Upon hearing news of what Jesus was doing and saying, John wonders if Jesus is Elijah. The early Church seems to have been rather embarrassed about this. After all, in the Christian redaction of the material relating to him, John expects the coming of the royal Messiah, which he knows — at least according to Matthew and John — to be Jesus. The Lucan nativity story serves to ensure that John is recognized as subordinate and that he is cognizant of the fact. In Matthew's version John asks his question after he has heard of the "works of the Messiah" (11:2). But Luke's version does not have this reference to the Messiah. The question in Luke's Gospel follows the raising of the widow's son in Nain, after which people say, "A great prophet has risen up among us," and "God has visited his people" (Luke 7:16). In Luke, John hears about "all these things" (7:18) having to do with Jesus' prophetic actions. In other words, in the Lucan version, John's question seems to concern whether Jesus is the expected prophet of the last days, that is, Elijah.

According to Matthew and Luke, Jesus' response to the question is, "Go and tell John what you hear and see; blind people have sight restored and the lame walk, lepers are cleansed and deaf people hear, and the dead are raised and the poor hear the good news, and blessed is the one who is not offended by me" (Matt. 11:4-6; cf. Luke 7:22-23). Despite the fact that in the Q version of John's sayings preserved in Matthew (3:11-12) and Luke (3:16-18) the prediction of the "one coming" indicates an eschatological judge, Jesus does not respond to John by saying that the winnowing fork is in his hand, or that he is about to separate the good from the bad and burn the chaff with unquenchable

60. W. Wink, "Jesus' Reply to John: Matt. 11:2-6/Luke 7:18-23," *Forum* 5 (1989) 121-28; cf. E. M. Boring, "The Criteria of Authenticity," *Forum* 1/4 (1985) 3-38. See also M. Dibelius, *Die urchristliche Überlieferung von Johannes dem Täufer* (Göttingen: Vandenhoeck & Ruprecht, 1911) 33-37. For the original form of the pericope, see the discussion in Ernst, *Johannes der Täufer,* 56-58. There seems to be an addition in the Lucan form, with Jesus doing dramatic healings at the time the disciples come to see him.

61. Wink, "Jesus' Reply to John," 125.

fire. Clearly there is no claim to be divine in Jesus' reply, and it is equally difficult to see him claiming to be the royal Messiah.[62] As with Luke's prelude to the question, so with the answer here: it affirms that Jesus has the prophetic power to heal and raise the dead, as Elijah or Elisha had. In addition, Jesus affirms that he is proclaiming the good news of the kingdom of God to the poor. There are echoes of Isaiah in Jesus' response that set his activities in an eschatological framework (Isa. 29:18-19; 35:5-6; 61:1). Jesus seems to link his mission with John's; they both belong to the era of the end, and the final day is drawing near.[63]

John may be excused for wondering if Jesus was Elijah, since if Jesus was indeed continuing John's immersion, he too would have been fulfilling the purifying function of the prophet. Jesus' healing of people is also described as making people clean.[64] The good news of the kingdom of God and the swift arrival of God as judge were also part of Jesus' message. In addition, Jesus performed "miracles," as did the historical Elijah. Elijah raised the dead, the only son of a widow (1 Kgs. 17:17-24), and in the Lucan version it is after Jesus raises the child of the widow in Nain and is acclaimed as a prophet that John asks his question (Luke 7:11-17). Moreover, the synoptic Gospels confirm that people were saying that Jesus was Elijah (Mark 8:28 = Matt. 16:14 = Luke 9:19; Mark 6:15 = Luke 9:8).

As mentioned above, we now have among the Qumran documents an interesting fragment that seems to link similar prophetic activities together, 4Q521. Fragment 2 ii begins by saying, "... heaven and earth will listen to his messiah and [everyone th]at is in them will not turn away from the commandments of holy ones." Further along the text continues, "the Lord ... will liberate the captives, restore sight to the blind, and raise up the b[owed down] ... for he will heal the wounded, give life to the dead

62. So Bultmann, *History of the Synoptic Tradition,* 23, 110, 128, 151; cf. Wink, *Gospel Tradition,* 124-26.

63. Wink, *Gospel Tradition,* 125-26; Meier, *Marginal Jews,* vol. 2, 130-37. Meier's idea that this is not what John envisioned, however, seems unconvincing, for we do not know exactly what John imagined would take place. Jesus' reply seems to be drawing on motifs that John may well have expected, for all we know, in order to convince John that he was all right.

64. Mark 1:40-45 = Matt. 8:1-4 = Luke 5:12-16; cf. Matt. 11:5 = Luke 7:22; 17:11-19; Mark 1:21-28 = Luke 4:33-37; Matt. 12:43-45 = Luke 11:24-26; Mark 5:1-8 = Luke 8:26-29; Mark 6:7 = Matt. 10:1; cf. Luke 9:1; Mark 7:25; cf. Matt. 15:22; Mark 9:25 = Luke 9:42; cf. Matt. 17:18.

and bring good news to the poor."[65] Here two passages from Scripture (Ps. 146:8 and Isa. 61:1) are conflated. Ps. 146:8 reads:

> YHWH liberates the captives
> YHWH opens [the eyes] of the blind
> YHWH raises up those who are bowed down

while Isa. 61:1 has:

> The Spirit of the Lord YHWH is upon me
> because YHWH has anointed me
> to bring good news to the afflicted
> to proclaim liberty to captives
> and freedom to prisoners.

If we separate out the elements of our passages, we can see that in both Q 7:22 (= Luke 7:22) and in 4Q521 there are elements of Ps. 146:8 and Isa. 61:1, but the correlation is not particularly strong. Notably, a prime feature of both Ps. 146:8 and Isa. 61:1 — the liberation of captives — is altogether absent in Q 7:22

liberates captives	Ps. 146:8	4Q521		Isa. 61:1 (x2)
restores sight	Ps. 146:8	4Q521	Q7:22	
straightens bent/lame	Ps. 146:8	4Q521	Q7:22	
tells good news to afflicted/poor		4Q521	Q7:22	Isa. 61:1
raises dead		4Q521	Q7:22	
cleanses lepers			Q7:22	
makes deaf hear			Q7:22	

Where both 4Q521 and Q7:22 do agree, over against Scripture, is in the linking of raising the dead with the other activities. Another fragment of 4Q521 (fragment 7) refers to "the one who gives life to the dead of his people."[66] 4Q521 does not in its readable fragments

65. See Collins, *The Scepter and the Star,* 117; G. Vermes, *The Dead Sea Scrolls in English,* 4th ed. (Harmondsworth: Penguin, 1995) 244-45; E. Puech, "Une apocalypse messianique (4Q521)," *RevQ* 15 (1992) 475-519.

66. Collins, *The Scepter and the Star,* 119.

contain references to the lepers being cleansed or the deaf hearing. For the latter motif, we need to look to Isa. 29:18 and Isa. 35:5-6. The cleansing of the lepers may go back to Elisha in 2 Kings 5. Both 4Q521 and Q7:22, then, draw upon eschatological motifs from the Psalms and Isaiah. In replying to John with the use of these motifs, Jesus sets his own activities in an eschatological framework. In eschatological texts, God is usually the prime actor, though sometimes he is said to act through an agent. This seems to be the case in 4Q521, where through the agency of an anointed end-time prophet (Elijah or an Elijah-like figure) the Lord releases captives, gives sight to the blind, etc. In the narrative of Luke and Matthew, it is Jesus who acts as an agent of God.

If John's question from prison and Jesus' reply are read in the light of 4Q521, then Jesus would seem to be telling John that he, Jesus, is indeed the anointed end-time prophet. It is perhaps better to see here the general expectation that an anointed prophet of God would raise the dead, rather than to think that the motif of the raising of the dead must point exclusively to Elijah. Elijah does seem to be referred to elsewhere in 4Q521 (frag. 2 iii), but not specifically in the passage in question. Whatever the case, in 4Q521 we have some agent of God functioning as a channel for God's power in the eschatological age, even though it is God who ultimately acts through this person.

Robert Miller has pointed out how Luke's Gospel in particular contains numerous associations between Jesus and Elijah, but while Luke wished to maintain that Jesus was in many ways like Elijah, he wanted to stress that he was in fact the royal Messiah.[67] In Q, John is Elijah, and Jesus denies such a role for himself.[68] Indeed, if Jesus saw John as Elijah, he cannot have supposed himself to have been this figure as well. If the identification of Jesus as Elijah had been made in Q, this would not cohere with the identification of John elsewhere.

If historical, then, Jesus' elusive answer to John's question seems to indicate that he did not wish to disappoint John, but neither did he

67. R. J. Miller, "Elijah, John, and Jesus in the Gospel of Luke," *NTS* 34/4 (1988) 611-22.

68. Matt. 10:34-36 = Luke 12:51-53. Whereas Elijah was to restore the hearts of parents to their children and vice versa, Jesus says that he sets parents and children against each other.

wish to propose outright that he himself was Elijah.[69] John evidently denied that he was Elijah (Acts 13:25; John 1:21), and it is possible that Jesus knew of these denials but still insisted, despite the Baptist's denials, that John was indeed Elijah.

To understand Jesus' reply, we may again think of Elisha. Elisha worked more cures than Elijah did; he raised the dead (2 Kgs. 4:18-37); he cleansed a leper (2 Kgs. 5:1-14); he healed the blind (2 Kgs. 6:15-23; cf. Josephus, *Ant.* 9.182). Jesus may not have wanted to define himself precisely in the eschatological scheme of things, and he may have left it up to others to arrive at a definition. But he must have believed himself to possess the Holy Spirit as a prophet of some kind, and, given his reference to the wonders that were taking place through him, it is reasonable to think that he, as well as his followers, "saw his miracles as testifying to his being a true messenger from or agent of God," in the words of E. P. Sanders.[70] As a prophet and (possibly) a descendant of David, he may have considered himself to be a royal "anointed one" or "messiah," for all we know. At any rate, God was accomplishing through him what John implicitly anticipated: the kingdom of God coming upon the world. Jesus, then, appears to have believed that he and John were acting in unison as agents of God.

We need not doubt the historicity of the Q tradition that John sent disciples to Jesus from prison. On the other hand, we need not go so far as to imagine "a rather enlightened jail administration under Herod Antipas, visiting hours, and an open line of communication with the outside world," as Vermes humorously conjectures.[71] Prisoners at this time were expected to be fed by their family and friends, and therefore outside contact was inevitable. The New Testament refers many times to visiting prisoners.[72] Rabbi Akiba had a disciple attend him in prison (*b. 'Erub.* 21b). There

69. J. A. Fitzmyer, *The Gospel According to Luke I–IX: Introduction, Translation, and Notes* (Garden City, NY: Doubleday, 1981) 664. The blessing on those who are not offended by Jesus relates to the blessing in Matt. 13:16-17; Luke 10:23-4; so Meier, *Marginal Jew,* vol. 2, 202 n. 104. The blessing does not specifically mean that John should not be offended by him.

70. E. P. Sanders, *Jesus and Judaism* (Philadelphia: Fortress, 1985) 173.

71. G. Vermes, *Jesus the Jew,* 2d ed., 32.

72. Matt. 25:36, 39, 44; Acts 24:23; Eph. 3:1; 4:1; 6:21-22; Phil. 1:12-14; 4:18; Col. 4:7-14. On Matthew's use of δεσμωτήριον, not a typical Matthean word, see Meier, *Marginal Jew,* vol. 2, 198-99 n. 89. Luke has already stated that John was arrested; to restate it would be redundant in his narrative.

would have been a period when John was in prison, before his execution, during which he could communicate with the outside world.

But the overlap between John's imprisonment and Jesus' activities in Galilee cannot have been very long. By the time Jesus was well known John was dead, since there were apparently rumors that Jesus was John resurrected. Some people said, "John the Baptist has been raised from the dead" (Mark 6:14; cf. Matt. 14:2; Luke 9:7). Herod Antipas is also said to have believed this (Mark 6:16; Luke 9:9), though this might have been popular speculation designed to characterize the tetrarch as continuing in his paranoia about John, a paranoia now enhanced by a guilty horror of John's coming back to haunt him in a different form. Jesus' disciples inform him of what people are saying: that he is John the Baptist, or Elijah, or one of the prophets, brought back to life. Peter thinks Jesus is the royal Messiah, but he is ordered sternly not to tell anyone (Mark 8:27-30; cf. Matt. 16:13-20; Luke 9:18-21). Certainly, Jesus and John could not have had contemporaneous missions if this tradition of considering Jesus a resurrected John is to be given credence; it could only have arisen if people knew that Jesus did not appear on the scene until John had been taken away. If they had been baptizing at the same time in opposition to one another, then no one could have supposed that Jesus was John in resurrected form.

These considerations, then, would suggest that Jesus began to go about in Galilee only after John was arrested and that, soon after John was arrested, he was killed. The precise time of John's execution may not have been accurately known; it was close enough to the time that Jesus came into Galilee as a prophet to suggest to some that Jesus was John. People may have believed that John had been killed at a time when, in fact, he was still alive in prison. However, the passage concerning John's question seems to indicate that as Jesus became known, John was still alive. His death may have followed shortly afterwards.

Jesus the Baptist?

At this point we may consider the Fourth Gospel's presentation of Jesus and John having two simultaneous immersing missions. In the Gospel of Mark, there is no conflict between John and Jesus. Jesus appears to have been prompted to leave the wilderness by the news (from whom?) that John had been arrested by Herod Antipas: "After John had been arrested,

Jesus came into Galilee proclaiming the good news of God and saying, 'The time is fulfilled, and the kingdom of God is at hand. Repent, and believe in the good news" (Mark 1:14-15). Matthew's version is similar (4:12-17), with the inclusion of a scriptural quotation to prove that Isa. 9:1-2 was fulfilled by Jesus' going to Galilee (cf. Luke 4:14). In other words, Jesus is described as repeating more or less what John had been saying, after John's own voice had been silenced by his arrest.

The much later Fourth Gospel tells an entirely different story. John and Jesus are both active in different places at the same time, and Jesus is making more disciples than John (John 3:25–4:3). Although John is a witness to Jesus, they are distinct and different and may even be viewed as baptizing in competition with one another. But John in the Fourth Gospel is quite at ease with this situation, for Jesus "must increase, but I must decrease" (John 3:30).

There has been a tendency among scholars to consider the Johannine picture as more accurate, so that Jesus and John did in fact have separate activities, teachings, and baptisms.[73] This scenario is perceived as being more awkward for the early Church to explain, because, if this was so, Jesus might be considered John's rival. The idea, then, is that Mark invented the notion that John was out of action when Jesus arrived on the scene. John was therefore most effectively accommodated chronologically in the position of precursor. Jeremias suggested that the Johannine editorial qualification that it was not Jesus but his disciples who baptized (John 4:2) is intended to free Jesus from being John's competitor.[74] But the verse does not free the disciples from being John's competitors, and Jesus still presumably sanctions their activities.

73. J. Jeremias, *New Testament Theology,* 45-46; C. H. Dodd, *Historical Tradition in the Fourth Gospel* (Cambridge: Cambridge University Press, 1963) 279-87; R. E. Brown, *The Gospel According to John I–XII* (Garden City, NY: Doubleday, 1966) 153-55; W. Schenk, "Gefangenschaft und Tod des Täufers: Erwägungen zur Chronologie und ihren Konsequenzen," *NTS* 29/4 (1983) 458-59. For an examination of this, see Ernst, *Johannes der Täufer,* 206-10; and Meier, *Marginal Jew,* vol. 2, 120-23. E. Linnemann thinks that Jesus gave up baptizing when he heard that the Pharisees were aware of his success, because John was in conflict with the Pharisees and Jesus did not want to embarrass him; see E. Linnemann, "Jesus und der Täufer," in *Festschrift für Ernst Fuchs,* ed. G. Ebeling et al. (Tübingen: Mohr-Siebeck, 1973) 219-36.

74. Jeremias, *New Testament Theology,* 46. Meier conjectures that the editorial comment was designed to avoid having Jesus' appear as a mere subordinate imitating the master's baptism (*Marginal Jew,* vol. 2, 196 n. 75).

The issue that resulted in the editorial comment of John 4:2 does not seem to have been the competition implied in the story, but the fact that Jesus baptized at all. As Raymond Brown notes, "There is no plausible theological reason why anyone would have invented the tradition that Jesus and his disciples once baptized."[75] In other words, it is simply something that the author of the Fourth Gospel accepted as a given, well-known fact that could not be disputed. If Jesus baptized, it may have been as John baptized, and as Philip later did in the name of Jesus. As noted in Chapter 2, the distinctive Christian baptism, which involved water and Spirit, did not develop until after the Pentecost experience.

The issue for the writer of the Fourth Gospel — as opposed to the editor who added the comment in 4:2 about Jesus not baptizing — was *when* Jesus baptized, not whether he did so or not. He presents the view that Jesus and his disciples were baptizing at the same time as John. As we have seen in regard to the Fourth Gospel, the presentation is aimed at neutralizing criticism from Jews at the end of the century in regard to Jesus and Christian baptism. The presentation of John and Jesus indicates that John was always happy about Jesus; John says that Jesus will increase while he, John, will decrease. Their missions, side by side, indicate a happy harmony. In this way, the criticism that John would not have approved of Jesus was offset entirely.

The Marcan tradition is chronologically earlier than the Johannine one. Why would Mark have invented a story that has no recognition of Jesus as Messiah by John and that has Jesus seeming so closely aligned with John that he feels no compulsion to perform as a prophet until John is unable to do so, as if he were a replacement? It is more likely that the Fourth Gospel's account is the invented one. We have already argued that the Fourth Gospel's characterization of John was designed to snatch him away from Judaism to make him the witness to Jesus, when the Jews of the time recognized John as a good man worthy of much respect. If this is so, then the reasons for inventing a story in which John and Jesus work separately and yet John completely accepts Jesus' superiority become quite evident. It should be noted that the story is itself illogical. If John really recognized that Jesus was so much his superior, why did he not stop immersing people and become Jesus' disciple? The writer of the Fourth Gospel could not, presumably, argue that John became Jesus' disciple; this was plainly not so. But he could

75. Brown, *John I–XII,* 155.

present John as approving of Jesus, if people were not altogether clear about when Jesus precisely started his own mission.

John is therefore presented in the Fourth Gospel as witnessing to Jesus, the lamb of God who takes away the sin of the world. Presupposing that his audience already has a basic knowledge about John, the writer of the Fourth Gospel retells the story with a particular slant. John is happy about Jesus' activities and his success. In terms of what this presentation wished to achieve, it is effective, despite its logical flaw in not recognizing that John should have stopped his own activities completely and joined the disciples of Jesus. If the writer of the Fourth Gospel knew the Marcan version of things, he rejected it as a suitable vehicle for his debate with the synagogue.

What then of the baptism administered by Jesus? The Fourth Gospel's report that Jesus conducted a mission of immersion may be historical. If Jesus accepted John's teaching, so focused on the idea that inner purity had to precede outer purity, we might expect that he too asked repentant and newly righteous people to immerse, in order to be outwardly pure. That this is not stated in the Gospels need not be a problem for the historian, for it would have been something with which the Gentile Church felt little sympathy, and we therefore have an excellent reason to account for its omission. Moreover, with Pauline concepts of baptism as an immersion into the death and resurrection of Jesus coming to precedence in the nascent Church, the fact that Jesus himself promoted an immersion of repentance would have been hopelessly complicated to explain. However, as we saw in Chapter 2, the deacon Philip may have immersed in accordance with Jesus' practice, derived from John. In Acts 19, the "immersion of John" practiced by Apollos was most likely the same kind of immersion; Apollos was not a disciple of John, but of Jesus.

With the development of a new Christian baptism involving the imparting of the Holy Spirit, this kind of water-only immersion of repentance was to be replaced. In the redaction of the tradition of immersion in Luke-Acts, John baptizes with water for repentance (though it is not explicitly stated that this was for ritual uncleanness), then after Jesus' death we find Philip and Apollos doing a similar or identical water immersion, but we also have another true Christian immersion involving the Holy Spirit. Baptism was extremely important in the early Church, but we have a curious hiatus of the procedure when it comes to Jesus. While baptism appears to have started with John, it is as if it began, then stopped, then began again only after Jesus died and was raised from the dead. This presentation seems to be apologetic, designed to pass over in silence the awkward problem of what Jesus' immersions really meant.[76]

In Acts 1:21-22 it is stated that the one who is to replace Judas as one of the twelve apostles must be "one of the men who have accompanied us during all the time that the Lord Jesus went in and out among us, beginning with the immersion of John until the day when he was taken up from us." This statement would not be problematic were it not for the fact that Luke's Gospel does not indicate that Jesus' twelve apostles were present at the time of his own immersion, nor does the Gospel even so much as hint that any of them was ever involved with John. For this, we have to look to the account of the Fourth Gospel (chaps. 1–2). However, taken as a separate entity, Luke-Acts should be comprehensible on its own terms. In Luke's Gospel, Jesus does not really start "going in and out" among people until after his own sojourn in the wilderness (see Luke 4:14-15). Simon, James, and John do not leave everything to follow Jesus as disciples until Luke 5:1-11, and the physical context is the Sea of Galilee, not the Jordan. Moreover, "the immersion [sing.] of John" (τοῦ βαπτίσματος 'Ιωάννου, Acts 1:22) is a very ambiguous way of referring to *Jesus'* immersion, which Luke passes over rather cursorily anyway, or even to the immersions of "all of the people" by John in the Jordan; instead, it seems to refer to the type of immersion that John performed. Luke's Gospel begins with the institution of this type of immersion — the immersion of repentance for the remission of sins, which John proclaimed. Luke never states that Jesus practiced this kind of immersion; neither does he state that Jesus' closest disciples were involved with John and immersed by him. We just do not have a clear reference.

In the story of Pentecost in Acts 2, it is assumed that all those gathered in the upper room *have already been immersed in water.* The twofold Christian baptism of water and Spirit is here established; Christians traced the origin of this distinctive type of baptism to the story of Pentecost, where only the Spirit is given (Acts 2:38, 41). If Jesus did not immerse people with "the immersion of John," then all of these disciples of Jesus (about 120 people; cf. Acts 1:15) would have to have been immersed by John; otherwise, the components of Christian baptism

76. The final editor of the Fourth Gospel modified the text in order to avoid this problem, for as Meier notes, it would have seemed impious to claim that Jesus did not confer the Spirit when he baptized (*Marginal Jew,* vol. 2, 196 n. 75).

(water and spirit) would not be complete. Only later in the story of Acts do we find that people could receive the Spirit prior to immersion in water, but even so immersion in water was still necessary (10:44-48). In Acts, the apostles (and others) seem quite comfortable immersing people, without having been given any instruction in the text to do this. Peter announces that everyone hearing them after Pentecost must "repent . . . and be immersed in the name of Anointed Jesus for the remission of your sins," and they would receive the gift of the Holy Spirit (Acts 2:38). It is hard to imagine how Peter could have immersed in water "in the name of Jesus" had Jesus himself not immersed people; Peter's exorcisms and healings "in the name of Jesus" follow from being given authority by Jesus to do these things, as we find indicated in the job description of the apostles in Luke's Gospel (9:1-2). There seems to be a glaring lacuna here.

All in all, then, it seems likely that Jesus continued John's immersion of repentance. Jesus himself need not have called people together for group immersions in large bodies of water like the Jordan or in springs. Effective immersion could have taken place in any public *miqveh* or in Lake Gennesaret, from which Jesus rarely strays far. It was noted in Chapter 2 that there is some evidence of Jesus holding the belief that inner purity was necessary prior to outer purity (Matt. 23:25-26). While Mark wished to invalidate the entire purity system of Judaism for Christian communities (Mark 7:1-23), this does not fit well with what we know of conflicts between Jewish and Gentile Christians in the first century (Galatians 2; Acts 15).[77] Jesus may well have endorsed the fundamental conceptual framework of the immersion of repentance. It would be strange to conclude that Jesus could think of John as a prophet, whose authority for immersion of repentance came from God, and yet disregard in his own mission the necessity of immersion following repentance.

Jesus, John, and the Kingdom of Heaven

Directly after John's question via his disciples in Q (Matt. 11:2-6; Luke 7:18-23), we have a block of material relating to John, spoken by Jesus in the context of his Galilean mission. Matthew and Luke have broken up

77. See above, 84 n. 62.

this Baptist block of Q in different ways, but it appears largely intact in Matt. 11:7-19 and Luke 7:24-35. The Q material in full comprises Matt. 11:7-19; 21:28-32; Luke 7:24-35; 16:16. The material in Matt. 11:12-13 is paralleled in Luke 16:16; scholars are divided on which evangelist preserves the order of Q here; if Luke is closer to Q then the material was not part of Q's main Baptist block.[78] Matt. 21:28-32 is paralleled in Luke 7:29-30; Matthew may have moved his version of this material from its original position in Q; he places it with Marcan Baptist material in the context of Jesus' debate with the chief priests, elders, and scribes (cf. Mark 11:27-33). It is possible that in Luke 7:29-30 Luke has abbreviated and paraphrased Q but left the material in its original position in the Baptist block. Both Matthew and Luke may have felt that the Q Baptist block was a little long and too enthusiastic about John. Abbreviations and relocations of material lessened its force without necessarily lessening its tone. But the shape of the Baptist block in Q need not concern us further.

The main Q block on John is prefaced by the passage concerning his question to Jesus from prison (Matt. 11:2-6; Luke 7:18-23). Jesus then addresses the Galilean crowds. In the following discussion, the material will be divided up into several sections, the first being Matt. 11:7-11; Luke 7:24-28.

Matt. 11:7-11= Luke 7:24-28

The text given here follows Matthew, with significant Lucan variants given in brackets.[79]

> After they [Luke: the messengers of John] went away, Jesus began to speak to the crowds concerning John: "What did you go out into the wilderness to look at? A reed shaken by the wind? [No!] But what did you go out to see? A man clothed in soft material? [No!] Look, those

78. See P. S. Cameron, *Violence and the Kingdom: The Interpretation of Matthew 11:12* (Frankfurt: Lang, 1984) 214-26; J. S. Kloppenborg, *The Formation of Q: Trajectories in Ancient Wisdom Collections* (Philadelphia: Fortress, 1987) 112-13; Wink favors neither context (*Gospel Traditions,* 20).

79. The precise form of Jesus' original saying need not concern us here. In general, this section is considered mostly authentic by commentators; see Meier, *Marginal Jew,* vol. 2, 139, 205 nn. 114-16; C. H. Kraeling, *John the Baptist* (New York: Scribner, 1951) 138.

> who wear soft clothing [Luke: who are beautifully clad and who live in luxury] are in the houses of kings. But what did you go out to see? A Prophet? Yes, I tell you, and more than a prophet. This is the one about whom it is written: 'Behold, I send my messenger before your face who shall prepare your way before you.' Amen I tell you, among those born of women there has arisen no one greater than John the Immerser [Luke: none is greater than John], but one who is least in the kingdom of heaven [Luke: of God] is greater than he.

Jesus asks the Galilean crowds, who are not otherwise noted as being among those who have gone out to John, why they went out to see him. In phrasing his questions, he uses ridiculous images that may have been designed to make people laugh. A reed blowing in the wind is exactly what one would see along the southern Jordan River; reeds form a thick covering around the riverbanks. The reference to soft clothing reflects an awareness that John was dressed in anything but nice clothes.[80] There may be implicit criticism here in Jesus' use of the verb "to see"; Jesus may be implying that they did not understand (recall the words "he who has ears to hear, then hear" [Matt. 11:15]). The crowds are spectators rather than participants in John's cause. We will return to this point in due course. The main interest of the present section, however, lies in John as a prophet. The scriptural quotations (LXX Exod. 23:20; Mal. 3:1) end with an alteration of the Elijah tradition: he comes "before you" as opposed to "before me." This might be an appropriate alteration if Jesus were addressing God, but here he is addressing the crowds. Some scholars have accordingly seen the scriptural quotations as later additions to the original saying.[81]

Of key interest here is the saying of Luke 7:28 = Matthew 11:11.

> I tell you, among those born of women no one is greater than John, but one who is least in the kingdom of God is greater than he. (Luke 7:28)

80. G. Theissen detects historical allusions here to Herod Antipas: Antipas' coins showed a reed, and the tetrarch would have been dressed beautifully, living in royal houses. John is therefore contrasted with his foe. See G. Theissen, *Lokalkolorit und Zeitgeschichte in den Evangelien. Ein Beitrag zur Geschichte der synoptischen Tradition* (Freiburg: 26-44.

81. See Meier, *Marginal Jew,* vol. 2, 141, 206 nn. 120, 121; Ernst, *Johannes der Täufer,* 61 n. 94; J. H. Hughes, "John the Baptist: The Forerunner of God Himself," *NovT* 14 (1972) 211; Kloppenborg, *Formation of Q,* 108 n. 29.

> Amen, I tell you, among those born of women there has arisen no one greater than John the Immerser, but one who is least in the kingdom of heaven is greater than he. (Matt. 11:11)

John is both the greatest person ever, and yet the smallest or least (μικρότερος) in the kingdom of God is greater than he is. Some have seen this statement as a product of the early Church.[82] Others find in μικρότερος a reference to Jesus, who is greater than John.[83] This logion is found in the *Gospel of Thomas* as

> From Adam until John the Baptist there is among those born of women no one superior to John the Baptist, in that his eyes will not be lowered/broken (?). But I have said that whoever among you becomes as a child shall know the kingdom, and shall become superior to John. (Logion 46)

Thomas' version may be a development from the Q tradition, combined with Mark 10:15 (= Matt. 18:3 = Luke 18:17).[84] The saying may suggest that John was of the material, human order ("born of woman"), whereas those in the kingdom of God are born of the Holy Spirit and belong to another, superior order. However, this does not fit with the presuppositions of Matt. 11:12-13 = Luke 16:16, or Matt. 21:28-32, where people are entering the kingdom of God by means of John. If all these statements were put together, Jesus would be saying that John enabled people to enter the kingdom of God, but they then became greater than he.

In favor of the originality of the Q saying is the fact that "born of woman" is, in the singular, a Semitic phrase simply meaning a human being.[85] It is never used to contrast a material with a spiritual order.

82. See Ernst, *Johannes der Täufer*, 62-63. Dibelius, *Die urchristliche Überlieferung*, 8-15, 121 n. 1; J. Becker, *Johannes der Täufer und Jesus von Nazareth* (Neukirchen-Vluyn: Neukirchener Verlag, 1972) 75. Catchpole thinks it was inserted into the material by the Q editor; see D. R. Catchpole, "The Beginning of Q: A Proposal," *NTS* 38 (1992) 210-13; see also J. P. Meier, "John the Baptist in Matthew's Gospel," *JBL* 99/3 (1980) 394-95.

83. P. Hoffman, *Studien zur Theologie der Logienquelle*, 2d ed. (Münster: Aschendorff, 1975) 220-24, though see Meier's refutation of this position (*Marginal Jew*, vol. 2, 208 n. 132).

84. See Webb, *John the Baptizer and Prophet*, 79.

85. It is found this way in rabbinic literature (ילוד אישה); *b. Šabb.* 88b; *Num. Rab.* 4; *'Abot R. Nat.* 2, etc.; see S. T. Lachs, *A Rabbinic Commentary on the New Testa-*

Later Christian interpretation may have been brought to bear upon this saying. Paul himself uses "born of woman" to contrast the earthly with the spiritual: "But when the fullness of time came God sent out his son, born of woman, born under the Law, in order to redeem those under the Law in order that we might receive adoption as sons" (Gal. 4:4-6). But a material-spiritual dichotomy may not have been apparent in the original intent of the Q saying.

Meier's classification of the saying as "dialectical negation" is, I think, very helpful here; Jesus need not be undermining John, whom he so intends to praise. Rather, he is extolling the significance of the "least" in the kingdom of God.[86] Moreover, if we lay aside a later consciousness, which would have us find John and Jesus in contrast, what comes across in the saying is a paradox that fits with other paradoxical sayings of Jesus in regard to those who are "first" (superior) and "last" (inferior) in the kingdom of God, for in the kingdom of God everything is inverted. In terms of Matthew's narrative, Jesus has just referred to his disciples as "these little ones" (τῶν μικρῶν τούτων, Matt. 10:42). The model of perfection in Jesus' schema is the little child or baby; God has revealed his wisdom to babies (Matt. 11:25-26; Luke 10:21). The kingdom of God belongs to little children (Mark 10:13-16 and parr.). There are a number of sayings in which opposite categories are inverted: "Whoever exalts himself will be humbled, and whoever humbles himself will be exalted" (Matt. 13:12 = Luke 14:11; 18:14); or "whoever would be great among you must be the servant, and whoever would be first among you must be a slave of all" (Matt. 20:26-27; 23:11 = Luke 22:26; also Mark 9:33-35 and parr.; Mark 10:15 = Luke 18:17).

With the motif of the first and greatest being last and least we get some clue, perhaps, to the conundrum of Jesus' statement on John. The point does not really concern John at all, who remains "more than a prophet"; there is still no one greater than him. The point is about the radical inversions of the kingdom of heaven, in which someone as insignificant as an innocent little baby may be considered "greater" than John (who is still part of the kingdom, and no doubt the greatest one in it); the innocent little baby is the paradigm of excellence. This is hyperbole, designed to confound (cf. *Acts of Philip* 34). It does not

---

ment: The Gospels of Matthew, Mark, and Luke (Hoboken, NJ: KTAV, 1987) 192-93. It is also found in Qumran literature: 1QS 9:21; 1QH 13:14; 18:13, 23-24.

86. See Meier, *Marginal Jew,* vol. 2, 142-43.

relativize John; it dramatically promotes the small, humble, and lowly. The swap from greatest to least is found also in a saying from Matthew's special material, where whoever relaxes one of the least of the commandments of the Law is "the least (ἐλάχιστος) in the kingdom of heaven." Antithetically, the one who performs the commandments is "great in the kingdom of heaven" (Matt. 5:19).

Luke 7:28 may be paraphrased as "no one alive is greater than John the Baptist." It is not really evident whether John the Baptist is alive or dead. David Catchpole has noted that the verb used in Matt. 11:11 is ἐγήγερται, "has arisen," which is a biblicism rarely used in the synoptic Gospels. It refers to the divine appointment of someone to some function.[87] That it appears in Luke 7:16 ("a great prophet has risen among us") may indicate that it was the Q reading, preserved by Matthew, and echoed by Luke at another place. As Catchpole notes, "Jesus surveys the whole of human history and declares that at no time has anyone been appointed by God to a more significant mission than that of John."[88]

Luke 7:31-35 = Matt. 11:16-19

Following Luke here, the text reads:

> But to what shall I compare the people of this generation, and what are they like? They are like children sitting in the marketplace and calling out to the others, saying, "We piped for you, and you did not dance. We wailed, and you did not weep." For John the Immerser has come neither eating bread nor drinking wine, and you say, "He has a demon." The man [lit., son of humankind] has come eating and drinking, and you say, "Look, a glutton and a drunkard, a friend of toll collectors and sinners." Yet Wisdom is accounted righteous by all her children.[89]

In Mark 11:32 (= Matt. 21:36; cf. Mark 14:5), the chief priests note that "all" the people hold John to be a prophet. However, it is curious that in Mark 1:5-6 (cf. Matt. 3:5; Luke 3:3) John immerses people from *Judea,* including

87. Catchpole, "The Beginning of Q," 209.

88. Ibid.

89. For the differences between the versions, see Ernst, *Johannes der Täufer,* 72-73; for general discussion, see Meier, *Marginal Jew,* vol. 2, 144-54.

Jerusalem, but no mention is made of *Galilee.* Jesus is implying in this saying that those he addresses are skeptical about John and himself. He links John and himself together as failing to impress these people. In the context of the Q narrative, Jesus is addressing the Galilean crowds. It has just been said that these (or, perhaps, some of these) went out "to see" John. It has not been stated that they were immersed by him for their repentance. Moreover, in Matthew directly after these comments about people's unbelief, Jesus goes on to condemn angrily certain Galilean towns close to the northeast part of Lake Gennesaret for not believing in the divine authority of his own work or repenting (Matt. 11:20-24; cf. Luke 10:13-15):

> Then he began to chastise the cities in which most of his acts of power had been done, because they did not repent. "Woe to you, Chorazin. Woe to you, Bethsaida. Because, if the acts of power done in you had been done in Tyre and Sidon, they would have repented ages ago in sackcloth and ashes. But I tell you, it will be more tolerable for Tyre and Sidon on judgment day than for you. And you, Capernaum, will you be exalted to heaven? You will be brought down to Hades. For if the acts of power done in you had been done in Sodom, it would have remained standing to this day. But I tell you that it will be more tolerable for Sodom on judgment day than for you.

Jesus' scornful words concerning people who are never satisfied conclude, then, with this denunciation of Galilean towns that were full of people who did not believe Jesus was a true prophet. The Galilean people are like whining children in a marketplace,[90] who see John and scoff that he is mad or "has a demon" or see Jesus and scoff that he is a glutton, a drunkard, and a friend of sinners. Both are prophets, and both are rejected. Jesus then denounces the unbelieving towns.

Luke 7:29-30 = Matt. 21:28-32

In Luke's narrative, this last section is preceded by a redactional comment:

90. The precise meaning of the children's complaint is not important for our present purpose. They are characterized as whining and dissatisfied. For different interpretations, see Meier, *Marginal Jew,* vol. 2, 147, 210 nn. 142-45.

> And all the people who heard (ἀκούσας), and the toll collectors, accounted God just, having been immersed with the immersion of John. But the Pharisees and the lawyers rejected the will of God for themselves, not being immersed by him. (Luke 7:29-30)

This seems to be an attempt to characterize the Pharisees as not really understanding or believing John and Jesus, but, as we have seen, the overall movement of Q seems to suggest that it was precisely "all the people"(of Galilee) who are unbelieving. A key word may be ἀκούσας, given the contrast in the material between those who "see" and those who "hear." However, numerous scholars have suggested that Luke is cognizant of a Q saying preserved in Matthew in a completely different place. Matt. 21:28-32 contains the parable of the two sons, which is placed in the context of Jesus' dialogue with the chief priests, elders, and scribes found in Mark 11:27-33 (cf. Luke 20:1-8). It reads as follows:

> But what do you think? A man had two children; and he went to the first and said, "Child, go and work in the vineyard today." But he answered and said, "I don't want to." But afterwards he changed his mind and went. So he [the man] went to the second and said the same; and he answered and said, "I go, sir," but he did not go. Which one of the two did the will of the father?" They said, "The first one." Jesus said to them, "Amen, I tell you that the toll collectors and the prostitutes go into the kingdom of God ahead of you. For John came to you in the way of righteousness, and you did not believe him, but the toll collectors and prostitutes believed him. And when you saw, you still did not afterward change your minds (μετεμελήθητε) and believe him." (Matt. 21:28-32)

If this material was originally in the Q block on John, the parable would fit with the theme of the unbelieving Galileans who complain to Jesus that he spends his time with "toll collectors and sinners." In the Q block, those Galileans who whine and do not believe either John or Jesus are characterized as illegitimately claiming a moral higher ground; they pronounce that John "has a demon," and complain that Jesus consorts with "toll collectors and sinners" and that he eats and drinks. Interestingly, it is the Pharisees who appear most often in the later Christian characterization of people who claim higher moral ground. In Matt. 11:16-19 = Luke 7:31-35, the Pharisees are not mentioned — which may indicate that the section is fairly early source material. However, Matthew inserted the Pharisees as addressees in his Marcan source material in 21:45, and therefore they are implied by the context as the addressees of the parable of the two sons. On its own, the parable does not require us to presume that the addressees are Pharisees, or chief priests, scribes, and elders in Jerusalem. The identity of the addressees depends on the context of the story. With Matthew's placement, the parable appears in the context of Jesus' debate with the Jerusalem authorities about John. If we place the parable in the Q block concerning John, the addressees are the unbelieving, critical, and whining Galileans, whose towns will shortly be utterly destroyed.

It would be difficult to imagine Galileans claiming higher moral ground, if we were to accept the later rabbinic caricature of Galileans as being careless in matters of the Law (and included among the "people of the land").[91] Caution is warranted, however, in accepting that caricature as an accurate depiction of first-century Galilean Jews. The characterization of the "stupid Galilean" must surely be put down to Judean prejudice. Whatever grains of truth may be contained in these later stories, we need not assume that Galilean Jews were incapable of claiming higher moral ground or of discerning a true prophet from a false one.

In fact, the internal meaning of the parable is broad and not specifically concerned with those who administer the Temple or Israel, as we find in the Marcan parable of the wicked tenants, or with those who claim legal authority. Here, those who say they will do the will of God but do not are contrasted with those who say they will not but do. If the parable did appear in the Q Baptist block, then those who say they will do the will of God but do not are the Galileans who went out "to see" John but scoffed at him and who now scoff at Jesus. Meanwhile, those who do the will of God are those toll collectors and sinners who, though saying they would not do the will of God, turn around, change their minds, and do it. These are the very people whom the scoffers complain about in Matt. 11:19 and Luke 7:35. Their doing the will of God is presumably accomplished by repenting and being immersed by John, and/or by believing that Jesus is a true prophet (and repenting and being immersed by him). John's advice to toll

91. See S. J. D. Cohen, review of *The 'Am Ha-Aretz: A Study in the Social History of the Jewish People in the Hellenistic-Roman Period*, by Aharon Oppenheimer, *JBL* 97 (1987) 596-97.

collectors in Luke 3:12 indicates that these people did come to John seeking a prescription for righteousness; on returning to their home towns they need not have abandoned toll collecting, and the stigma of that profession in the minds of other townsfolk may have remained. We have already seen that the word "prostitute" was a derisive term for women who, at any time in the past, had engaged in unlawful sexual intercourse. With their immersion by John and their prior acceptance of his teaching about righteousness and repentance, these people were "entering the kingdom of God" before those who claimed to be doing the will of God and yet did not.

In Luke 7:29-30 we find the expression τὴν βουλὴν τοῦ θεοῦ, "the will of God," which may pick up on the parable, though Matthew has τὸ θέλημα, a different Greek word for "will." Matthew Black thinks that the clause "they rejected the will of God for themselves" in Luke goes back to an Aramaic original.[92] If this is so, it is tempting to suggest that it goes back to Q, which contained numerous Aramaicisms. Luke seems to have decided not to use the parable and yet has echoed its lesson.[93] However, his decision not to use the parable may have come from a sense that Pharisees should have been addressed by it, and his insertion of the Pharisees in his editorial comment may also be designed to ensure that "all the people who heard" and "the Pharisees" are seen in contrast here. Luke hardly felt bound to include everything in his source material. In regard to the Gospel of Mark, for example, there are numerous passages used by Matthew but omitted by Luke.[94] Much less often, Matthew omits a small section of Mark used by Luke alone.[95] In particular, Luke appears to abbreviate mention of John. For example, despite having the nativity story of John included with that of Jesus (Luke 1:5-80) — which, in fact,

92. M. Black, *An Aramaic Approach to the Gospels and Acts. With an Appendix on The Son of Man, by Geza Vermes,* 3d ed. (Oxford: Clarendon, 1967) 103.

93. See E. Bammel, "The Baptist in Early Christian Tradition," *NTS* 18 (1971-72) 103, who suggests that, for this reason, it cannot have been in Q.

94. E.g., Mark 9:43-48 = Matt. 18:8-9; Mark 4:33-34 = Matt. 13:34-35; Mark 6:17-19 = Matt. 14:3-12; Mark 11:20-25 = Matt. 21:20-22 and 6:14; Mark 9:9-13 = Matt. 17:9-13; Mark 6:45–8:21 = Matt. 14:22–15:39 and 16:7-12; Mark 10:1-12 = Matt. 19:1-12; Mark 11:12-14 = Matt. 21:18-19; Mark 14:3-9 = Matt. 26:6-13 (cf. Luke 7:36-50); Mark 15:16-20 = Matt. 27:27-31. Some small sections of Mark (e.g., Mark 4:26-29; 11:12-14) are found neither in Matthew nor in Luke.

95. E.g., Mark 12:41-44 = Luke 21:1-4.

radically relativizes John — and also having more material about John's chronology and teaching (Luke 3:1-10) than Mark or Matthew, Luke omits any precise mention of Jesus' immersion by John. He chooses not to relate the long story of John's arrest and beheading (Mark 6:17-29 = Matt. 14:3-12) but instead summarizes it in a few lines (Luke 3:19-20). He also omits an important reference to John as Elijah (Mark 9:9-13 = Matt. 17:9-13). And he probably has tampered with a passage concerning John (16:16) that is also found abbreviated and altered in Matt. 11:12-13.

The original wording of the passage in Matt. 21:32 is disputed. Some of the fifth-century Syriac versions, the Curetonian and the Peshitta, have for verse 32 "even when you did not see it, you afterward repented," while the Sinaitic Syriac and the Greek Bezae Cantabrigensis have "when you saw it you afterward repented." In other words, some manuscripts have "For John came to you in the way of righteousness, and you did not believe him, but the toll collectors and prostitutes believed him, and when you saw it you afterwards repented." As noted above, this may derive from a Jewish-Christian textual tradition, which had it that the Sadducees and Pharisees were immersed by John. Extrapolating from this, the chief priests, scribes, and elders — identified as Sadducees and Pharisees — were then characterized as having been immersed. Moreover, as we have also seen, Matthew makes the innovation of including Pharisees in the group of chief priests and elders Jesus is addressing in Matt. 21:45. If Pharisees were included, then, Jewish-Christian redaction would have ensured that they were immersed as well.

Luke 16:16 = Matt. 11:12-13

> The Law and the prophets [missing verb] until (μέχρι) John; since then (ἀπὸ τότε) the good news of the kingdom of God is told, and everyone breaks into it violently (καὶ πᾶς εἰς αὐτὴν βιάζεται). (Luke 16:16)

> From the days of John the Baptist until (ἕως) now the kingdom of heaven has suffered violence (βιάζεται), and violent people are attacking it (βιασταὶ ἁρπάζουσιν αὐτήν). For all the prophets and the Law prophesied until (ἕως) John. (Matt. 11:12-13)

Luke 16:16 is extremely difficult to interpret, and the same may be said of Matt. 11:12-13. The first part of Luke 16:16 simply does not make sense, since it does not have a verb: "the Law and the prophets [verb] until John." On account of its garbled state, scholarly opinion favors the originality (for Q) of Luke over the smoother version of Matthew.[96] Matthew supplies the word "prophesied," ἐπροφήτευσαν, and turns around a well-known reference to Scripture with the words "all the prophets and the Law." This idiosyncratic Matthean construction is generally not considered original.[97] Luke's version, however, is incomplete, and we can only speculate on the missing verb. With no good reason at all, some modern translators supply the verb "to be" in Luke 16:16, so that Jesus is then forced to imply that John somehow annulled the Law and the prophets. The NRSV, for example, translates: "the Law and the prophets *were in effect* until John came" (italics mine).[98] Such a Pauline or even Marcionite insertion is completely contradicted by the very next verse in Luke, which says "it is easier for heaven and earth to disappear than for one stroke [of a letter] of the Law to fail" (Luke 16:17).

It is possible that Q linked Jesus and John together as belonging to the era of the kingdom of God, though it is not quite clear. Luke and Matthew use different words for "until," μέχρι and ἕως respectively. Both could be understood as either inclusive or exclusive of John. For Luke, the eschatological age really begins after John is imprisoned or dead (cf. Acts 1:5; 10:37; 13:24-25; 19:4). But Matthew's use of the second "until" reflects a notion that the eschatological age is "from the days of John the Baptist until now." Thus Meier notes that in Matthew "the prophetic figure of the Baptist stands in the time of fulfillment alongside of Jesus."[99]

It is fairly likely that Q is not preserved accurately either by Luke or by Matthew. No simple solution suffices. Both may have abbreviated

96. See Meier, "John the Baptist in Matthew's Gospel," 395-97. Matthew is favored by Wink, *Gospel Tradition,* 20; cf. Hoffman, *Studien zur Theologie der Logienquelle,* 2d ed., 51-60. Kloppenborg supports the Matthean order of the saying (*Formation of Q,* 114). For careful discussion of the two versions, see Meier, "John the Baptist in Matthew's Gospel"; idem, *Marginal Jew,* vol. 2, 157-63.

97. "All the prophets and the Law" is a unique expression; the common phrase is "the Law and the prophets"; see Meier, *Marginal Jew,* vol. 2, 158, 217 nn. 181-82.

98. Meier adopts a similar approach in suggesting that the missing word is "lasted" (*Marginal Jew,* vol. 2, 160).

99. Meier, "John the Baptist in Matthew's Gospel," 396.

and adapted something more lengthy and awkward in terms of developing Christian theology. That Luke's version is incomplete and terse need not indicate its authenticity. Q may have contained a verb that Luke found unacceptable or strange. Actually, Matthew's "prophesied" gives us just such a word. If it were found in Q, Luke (just like many modern scholars) may have thought that it could not be right. Matthew himself seems to have changed the Q text in order to accommodate this verb; he inverts the common phrase "the Law and the prophets" to ensure that "all the prophets" are the ones who prophesy. "The prophets" of the usual expression are not people, but books; "the Law and the prophets" is a shorthand way of referring to written Scripture. But written Scripture, being what the prophets wrote, might yet prophesy or foretell what was to come. Any part of Scripture could be identified as a prophecy, given the right interpretation. In other words, it is possible to conceive that a text recording prophecy could itself be understood to foretell or prophesy. Moreover, in Rev. 10:7 it is clear that Christians found evidence of the good news of the kingdom of God foretold in Scripture: "in the days of the voice of the seventh angel, when he is about to blow his trumpet, the mystery of God is completed, as he told in the good news (εὐηγγέλισεν) to his servants, the prophets."

Luke states in 3:18 that it was John the Baptist who "told the good news" (εὐηγγελίζετο), and here in 16:16 this verb (εὐαγγελίζεται) is also found in relation to John's proclamation; the good news is told in John's message, which picks up on the Law and the prophets in a way that is not spelled out. Luke may have added this reference, but this would be surprising, for as noted above the kingdom of God did not really begin for Luke until John was imprisoned. It is hard to see why Luke felt it necessary to state (twice) that John told the good news, an action otherwise associated with Jesus and the eschatological age, unless he found this mentioned in his source material.

Scholarly opinion is divided also in regard to how the verbs βιάζεται and ἁρπάζουσιν should be translated, some favoring the negative, destructive translation given here, and others preferring a more positive meaning for these words, particularly βιάζεται in Luke 16:16.[100] Let us go back to the missing verb. While we have a gap in the Lucan version, we have an alternate verb in Matthew. But we also have in Matthew a semantically

100. For arguments in favor of negative translations of βιάζεται, see Meier, "John the Baptist in Matthew's Gospel," n. 44; idem, *Marginal Jew*, vol. 2, 158-59.

redundant verb in the sentence, "the kingdom of heaven suffers violence (βιάζεται), and violent people are attacking it (βιασταὶ ἁρπάζουσιν αὐτήν)." Matthew need only have stated once that the kingdom of heaven suffers violence; he states it twice, once directly and then again by saying that violent people are attacking it. It seems possible that Matthew has pulled one of these components from the sentence about the Law and the prophets and placed together two parts of a parallel construction.

Both Luke and Matthew contain the pronoun αὐτήν, "it," for the kingdom that suffers violence, which means it was referred to previously. We may wonder about Luke's possible softening of βιάζεται and prefer Matthew's blunt comment that the "kingdom of heaven suffers violence." Nevertheless, it is still possible that Luke does not really imagine that everyone is pressing into the kingdom in order to live in it, but rather that people are like violent burglars who are pressing or breaking into it in order to do harm. The image here is of the kingdom as a house under threat of violence. If so, then the supposed differences in meaning between Luke and Matthew are not so significant.

Luke refers to πᾶς, "everyone," attacking or pressing into the kingdom. Who are these people? Without an identification, we are left with the impression that everyone in general is attacking or pressing into the kingdom, which seems a rather dramatic overstatement. If Q did contain a reference to βιασταί in the first part of our passage, then it is possible that πᾶς here at the end refers to all these violent men, who now attack the kingdom of God. It may be also that Luke's εἰς is an addition to emphasize his understanding of βιάζεται as "press into."

The temporal phrases ἀπὸ τότε, "since then" (Luke) and "from the days of John the Baptist until (ἕως) now" (Matthew) are also pitted against one another in terms of originality. It is probable that ἀπὸ τότε was in Q, since it is otherwise not found in Luke-Acts, and therefore these words would not have been made up by Luke, though Matthew does use this expression, and it is then significant that he leaves it out. Actually, it seems likely that in inverting what was found in Q, Matthew could not include this reference back to what had gone before. In favor of Matthew's expression, however, is its Semitic construction.[101] While Luke has elsewhere noted that John told the good news, this does not quite fit with his view of John evidenced in Acts. Here too, Luke may

101. See Jeremias, *New Testament Theology,* 46-47; Hoffman, *Studien zur Theologie der Logienquelle,* 2d ed., 52.

have blurred the situation, so that the temporal phrase may include or exclude John. In this case, he may have omitted the phrase "from the days of John the Baptist until now" because it included John so clearly in the eschatological age. If we stand by Luke in accepting "since then the good news of kingdom of God has been told," we may still include Matthew's phrase if we expand the logion.

In Matthew's version, there is a dividing line between the "old" (the Law and the prophets) and the "new" (John and Jesus). In Luke's, John stands either at the end of the "the Law and the prophets" or at the beginning of the kingdom of God. The two, indeed, need not be mutually exclusive; the kingdom of God may be seen to complete the Law and the prophets. It was Christianity that would separate these domains into exclusive, antipathetic constructs. In our saying, the two may yet be linked together as being of God. Let us then try to reassemble the saying of Q, bearing in mind that such a reassembly must remain highly speculative. We may also include in the pericope what follows in Luke 16:17 (cf. Matt. 5:18), for this completes the meaning.

The Law and the prophets prophesied [the kingdom] until John;	(Luke/Matthew)
from then the good news of the kingdom of God has been told	(Luke)
and violent people are attacking it.	(Matthew)
From the days of John the Baptist until now	(Matthew)
everyone breaks into it violently.	(Luke)
But it is easier for heaven and earth to pass away	(Luke; cf. Matthew)
than for one stroke [of a letter] of the Law to fail.	(Luke; cf. Matthew)

This reconstruction, which incorporates nearly all of the elements of the two extant versions, gives us the sense that Scripture prophesied something in the written word until John came to fulfill the prophecy by announcing it in person. I have placed in brackets the "something" that Scripture foretold as being the coming of the kingdom. It cannot be that prophecy as such ceases with John's arrival, for clearly the early Christians believed that Scripture contained innumerable prophecies that were valid in interpretations of past, present, and future events and that prophecy continued within the Christian movement. Rather, the specific prophecy of the kingdom is now fulfilled with John's announcing the good news. Moreover, the good news continues to be announced up until the present with Jesus, and violence is done to it, just as violence was done to John. The saying may fittingly have concluded with what we have in Luke 16:17 (cf. Matt. 5:18), which gives God's assurance of the endurance of the kingdom despite attacks upon it, for what was foretold in Scripture (here, referred to as "the Law") will not fail.[102]

Although in general I am skeptical about efforts to redesign the Gospel text, it does seem here that what we have in Matthew and Luke are abbreviations and adaptations of something larger. In this reconstruction, we have a cohesive, comprehensible unit that would certainly have caused some discomfort in the early Gentile (Pauline) churches, which would have found the affirmation of the permanence of the Law and the prophets in view of the kingdom itself rather doubtful. This saying would then fit very well with the sentiment expressed in Mark 9:12-13 (cf. Matt. 17:11-12), where Elijah/John is said to "suffer many things and be treated with contempt," as it was written concerning him in the Law and the prophets. Violence was done to John, as was foretold, but the kingdom will still come in fullness.[103] The perceived attacks on the kingdom may also be reflected in a saying found in Matt. 5:10, "Blessed are those who are persecuted for the sake of righteousness, for theirs is the kingdom of heaven." Indeed, John may have been seen as one who was persecuted for the sake of righteousness by his speaking out against Antipas' marriage and gathering people together for an immersion of repentance. Given these considerations, it seems that this saying derives from a time after John's death, and it would therefore not follow well after the Baptist's question from prison in the Q narrative.

In conclusion, Jesus' statements concerning John seem to suggest that he linked himself with John. Both of them were prophets, preaching the kingdom of God and enabling people to enter into this kingdom. In placing John at the very beginning of the gospel, the early Christians retained this link between John and Jesus, but they wished to subordi-

102. Matthew's version of the saying reads: "For amen I tell you, until heaven and earth pass away, not one iota or stroke [of a letter] shall pass away from the Law, until all is accomplished" (5:18). So in the new age the Law will pass away since everyone will readily do the will of God by virtue of the indwelling Spirit (see Ezek. 36:27; Jer. 31:31-34, esp. vv. 33-34). The Law is certainly not to be forsaken; the initiative rests entirely with God. The Law's predictions will therefore stand until everything is accomplished in accordance with Scripture.

103. See Cameron, *Violence and the Kingdom*, 226-46.

nate John to the role of precursor to the Messiah. Jesus himself, though, seems to have had the utmost respect for John: John's immersion was authorized by God (Mark 11:30 and parr.); he came in the way of righteousness (Matt. 21:32); he was "more than a prophet" (Matt. 11:9; Luke 7:26); no one was greater than he (Matt. 11:11; Luke 7:18); he was in fact Elijah, who had to suffer according to the Scriptures (Mark 9:11-13). In other words, Jesus may have asserted of John precisely what John denied — that he, John, was Elijah. Certainly, John's denial seems to be evidence that there were people around him who believed he was Elijah. His death at the hands of Herod Antipas may have knocked this notion considerably. But Jesus asserted that his — John's — suffering and death were foretold in the Scriptures. After Jesus' own suffering and death, his disciples would do exactly the same thing in regard to him and develop the radical image of the suffering Messiah, basing their interpretation on Isaiah 53.[104]

It seems likely that Jesus came to John at the Jordan River as a repentant sinner, though historically whether he was or not is impossible to ascertain; decisions about this will rest on people's fundamental beliefs. It does appear that Jesus undertook to hear John's teaching and resolved to walk in the way of righteousness, as John defined it, in complete obedience to God; he therefore joined with John's disciples prior to his immersion. He learned John's teaching (and would later use it in his own body of teaching, as we saw in Chapter 3). At the moment of his immersion, as he came up out of the water, he experienced something unexpected — a vision of the Holy Spirit descending upon him and the apprehension that he was counted as a beloved son of God, in whom God was well pleased. This indicated to him that he was to be a prophet, and he recounted this experience to his own disciples in order to indicate the beginning of his prophetic mission. He seems to have copied John by going out to the wilderness in order to exist there on what he could find provided naturally by God. When he heard of John's imprisonment by Antipas, however, he went to his own home area, Galilee, and undertook to continue John's teaching and immersion, but as a prophet in his own right. He called people back from unrighteousness, defining like John a very high standard of perfection, and he

104. Citations of and allusions to Isaiah 53, equating Jesus as Messiah with the suffering servant, are frequent in the NT; note, e.g., Matt. 8:17; Luke 22:37; Acts 8:32-33; Rom. 4:25; 1 Cor. 15:3; Heb. 9:28; 1 Pet. 2:22-25.

extolled John as Elijah — "more than a prophet." He hailed John's immersion of repentance as a practice authorized by God. He proclaimed that the kingdom of God was breaking through. These were the last days, and the end was nigh; it was necessary for those not counted among the righteous to repent. In addition, he did something that John did not; he demonstrated that he was in possession of the prophetic spirit and that the end was here by rewarding the faithful with healings, exorcisms, and works of wonder. In Galilee, some believed Jesus and John, but many did not. Jesus denounced those who came to see John but who did not repent when they needed to — those who dismissed John as being possessed by a demon. These same people did not believe him, Jesus suggested. Their fate would be grim. Like John, Jesus could anticipate a happy future for the repentant and righteous but a miserable fate for those who rejected the will of God for themselves.

Conclusion

In this study I have argued that John was very much a Jew of his time who aimed to live a life of total obedience to God and who sought to retrieve other Jews from lives that were far less obedient. John was an extraordinary figure, and much admired. But he is to be understood within the context of Second Temple Judaism, not formative Christianity. He was not a proto-Christian.

We know nothing for sure about John's early life. He may have come from a priestly family, if the evidence of Luke 1:5 is historical. Certainly, he was educated in the Scriptures, but we do not know how he acquired his learning. John went out into the wilderness to exist solely on what God might provide for him there. Dressed in sackcloth to demonstrate his humility before God and his repentance, he lived a life of utmost faith. He may have taken a vow as a *nazir;* at any rate, people saw him as someone who looked like a *nazir.* We can imagine him, then, with his hair long and matted; a slim figure with sun-hardened skin, an old camel's hair sackcloth tied around his waist with a strip of leather. No evidence suggests that he was an Essene or that he had any contact with the (possibly Essene) sectarians responsible for the collection of the Dead Sea Scrolls.

John may have attracted disciples even before he started his mission to call the wayward to repentance. Bannus certainly had at least one disciple with him in the wilderness: the young Josephus, who hoped to learn something from a man of such exceptional faith and purity. But around 28-29 CE John turned his attention to people who would not otherwise have sought him out — people who fell short of fulfilling the Law.

Probably by means of his disciples, John sent out a call for those who considered themselves unrighteous to repent — to turn from the path of iniquity and to walk along the way of righteousness as he defined it. This was urgent, for the end would come soon, and God would burn up those who did not obey his will in the fire of Gehenna. Calling oneself a child of Abraham, and appealing to the inherited *zekhut* of the *aqedah*, would not help in the eschatological court. Those who would live in the new Jerusalem, saturated with Holy Spirit, would be those who obeyed Torah — cultically, morally, spiritually, and legally. The Scriptures enshrined the laws and recommendations of a just and righteous God; no one could be just and righteous who walked idly in his or her own way, neglecting to perform the duties of one obedient to the prescriptions set out by God's messengers, the prophets. After turning back to God and proving repentance by meritorious acts of *zekhut*, such as giving away possessions and food to the begging poor, then people could be purified, for without someone's true righteousness, God did not accept immersions, prayers, fasts, or sacrifices. Without God's acceptance of a person's immersion, that person remained unclean. One was clean outwardly only after one had been cleansed inwardly; inner cleansing preceded outer cleansing. Righteousness and obedience to the Law enabled one to be clean inwardly. John taught his "way of righteousness" to those who wished to be immersed. Blessed indeed were the pure in heart.

John's baptism was wholly in keeping with Jewish immersions of the time in that it was not symbolic, or an initiation rite, but for purification of the body from ritual uncleanness. It was nevertheless perceived as unique in that it specifically followed repentance. The understanding was that one was unclean outwardly until clean inwardly. Then one could come to be immersed. John's clothing of camel hair sackcloth was probably appropriate for someone who underwent repeated immersions himself, since hair sackcloth was woven so loosely that water would come through and reach every part of the body. For those who came to John as repentant sinners for immersion, sackcloth would also have been the most appropriate clothing. Now cleansed, people could pray and be heard, which in turn would hasten the full arrival of the kingdom of God. But the kingdom was already breaking through, as more Jews joined the numbers of the righteous on earth.

John seems to have based his teaching on the ethical prescriptions and eschatological expectations of the prophets, especially the book of

Isaiah. He may have taught his disciples a short prayer, rather like the so-called Lord's Prayer. Surprisingly, he accepted that toll collectors and soldiers could live a righteous life in obedience to the Law, and he gave them special advice about how they should go about their jobs. He may have given similar advice to women who had the reputation of being disreputable, though it is highly unlikely that he accepted prostitution as an acceptable way for women to make money. He sent people back home to continue their own vocations, with the expectation that they would not have to wait long before the end. In the meantime, they might have been expected to abide by the rulings given by Pharisees to those who wished to live righteously. The Pharisees had the greatest reputation for righteousness among the people of the time, and John seems to have accepted that their ways would best lead people forward on the path of obedience to God. Whereas there is nothing that would link John with the Essenes, his disciples are associated with the Pharisees. It cannot be assumed that John was a Pharisee himself, but he may have pointed people to them as examples that should be followed. In the same way, Jesus would also tell his disciples to do as the Pharisees advised.

The Pharisees in turn seem to have supported John. The New Testament material that includes them as part of John's opposition is a result of the evangelists' redaction of authentic traditions. By the end of the first century, John's reputation as a good and holy man lived on among Jews who were highly influenced by Pharisaic traditions, particularly the educated elite. Herod Antipas was thought to have done an evil thing in murdering him.

To some people of his own time, John was a prophet. Whether he believed himself to be such is not clear. For all we know, he may have felt that God had spoken to him and authorized him to immerse people who came to the Jordan after repentance, and that he was to be identified with the person calling in the wilderness in Isa. 40:3. Alternatively, he may have considered himself someone who was acting on a reading of the book of Isaiah — a sage, perhaps, but nothing more. Either way, his call for repentance and his insistence on immersion following the bearing of fruit worthy of that repentance were justification enough for many people to consider him a prophet. He does not seem to have claimed to have been possessed by the Holy Spirit, nor did he perform any healings or exorcisms. If John thought of himself as a prophet, it was as a very minor one, for in relation to the coming one — the agent of God — he considered himself less than a slave in status.

No one seems to have established a religious movement upon John. There evidently was no experience among his disciples that gave them an awareness of his prophetic spirit living on. Many of his disciples may have joined Jesus and ended up in the early Church. Others would have continued within the Pharisaic tradition to influence the Synagogue, remembering him as a shining light during their age. If communities of John's disciples existed, they did not endure as a cohesive group for long.

If these conclusions adequately reflect the historical situation, then it is easy to see why the early Church sought to modify the picture of John the Baptist. As the Church began to move away from the idea that Christians should follow the Jewish Law, the call to repentance had to be detached from its links with following Torah. In Christian understanding, John was not predicting the imminent coming of the agent of God, who would separate out the good and the bad and judge them; he was predicting the coming of the King-Messiah, namely Jesus. In the Christian outlook, John really knew that Jesus was the one he had expected. John's baptism was not for the purification of the body, following inward cleansing of the heart; it was a prelude for Christian baptism in water and Spirit. Everything about John pointed to fulfillment in Jesus and the Church. John always knew he was subordinate to Jesus. Jesus acted out a role with John when he came to him for immersion, a role that may have made him seem subordinate, but he never was, and he never really needed the immersion in the first place. He did not actually learn anything from John, for he knew all things from the beginning. John may have been the greatest person to arise in the old Israel, but the least person in the Christian kingdom of God is greater than he was. John's predictions concerned the end; nothing about him was the least bit political, and he was not a threat to Rome (indeed, neither was Jesus). He was put to death because Antipas was tricked into it by his conniving wife. Antipas only arrested him because John was critical of his marriage. Such a defensive, apologetic tone in the New Testament writings concerning John is obvious; this study has only just begun to unpack some of the reasons why such a tone was adopted.

A full examination of the material specifically concerning the relationship between John and Jesus, one based on these conclusions about John and the statements concerning John in the Jesus tradition, would be very complex; in the final chapter we were able only to begin exploring this subject. However, an immediate reaction among readers may be that, in coming to John for immersion, Jesus must have counted himself among those in need of repentance, acts of *zekhut,* and righteousness in order for inner cleansing to take place; John did not baptize the righteous. Jesus seems to have counted himself among those who were not pure inwardly or outwardly — those who were not accepted by God and who might expect to be hurled on the fire at the time of judgment. If he went through the processes indicative of repentance demanded by John, did he, too, give away his possessions and food to the poor? Certainly, he appears to have had none during his own mission. Whether Jesus came to immersion as an unnecessary statement of humility or not, his baptism by John remains an interesting problem.

I have argued that Jesus probably did have a spiritual experience in the Jordan River at the time of his immersion. His experience was one of the rushing power of God (descending like a dove), in which he heard a voice announcing his prophetic commission. His immersion may have taken place in a group, so John need not have been aware of Jesus' experience. Jesus' discipleship of John was very likely considered necessary prior to immersion, though immersion did not initiate him into a group of John's disciples. Immediately after his immersion and experience he seems to have gone away to live in the wilderness, like John.

Jesus seems to have thought that John was Elijah, and when John was killed, Jesus interpreted this as being foretold in Scripture. He may have blamed the chief priests, scribes, and elders — the religious authorities of Jerusalem — for the death of John, even though it was Antipas who acted alone in killing him. For Jesus, John was "more than a prophet," the greatest person who had ever lived; his immersion of repentance was authorized by God. It seems likely, then, that in continuing John's message, Jesus also continued his immersion. After Jesus' own death, Jesus' disciples would find this same immersion supplemented by the imparting of the Spirit, which they understood in the light of their experience of Jesus' resurrection.

The New Testament is a remarkable collection of documents. Not only does it include redactions that seek to convince us of a particular understanding of history, but the men who wrote the Gospels faithfully included sayings and stories that could themselves invalidate their interpretation of history. So great was their determination to reproduce traditional material that they included pieces that do not tally with their overall purposes or that contradict other statements they endorsed. We are fortunate to have four Gospels, and other, noncanonical works, so that these purposes may be compared and made plainer. Clearly the conclusions reached in this study will be controversial. I hope, however, that in formulating a picture of John as a Jew within the context of his time, I have contributed to our understanding of the figure of Jesus himself. The Gospel writers may have considered John's centrality at the origin of the Church a threat, but we do not need to continue to think so.

Bibliography

Abrahams, I. *Studies in Pharisaism and the Gospel.* Cambridge: Cambridge University Press, 1917.

Aland, Kurt, Matthew Black et al., eds. *The Greek New Testament.* 3d ed. New York: United Bible Societies, 1966.

Allison, Dale C. "The Baptism of Jesus and a New Dead Sea Scroll." *BAR* 18 (1992) 58-60.

———. "Elijah Must Come First." *JBL* 103 (1984) 256-58.

Alon, Gedalia. *Jews, Judaism and the Classical World: Studies in Jewish History in the Times of the Second Temple and Talmud.* Translated by Israel Abrahams. Jerusalem: Magnes, 1977.

Amir, Y. "The Term *Ioudaismos:* A Study in Jewish-Hellenistic Self-Identification." *Immanuel* 14 (1982) 34-41.

Anderson, Bernhard W. "Exodus Typology in Second Isaiah." In *Israel's Prophetic Heritage: Essays in Honor of James Muilenburg,* edited by Bernhard W. Anderson and Walter Harrelson, 177-95. New York: Harper, 1962.

Aune, David E. *Prophecy in Early Christianity and the Ancient Mediterranean World.* Grand Rapids: Eerdmans, 1983.

———. "The Use of προφήτης in Josephus." *JBL* 101 (1982) 419-21.

Aus, Roger. *Water into Wine and the Beheading of John the Baptist: Early Jewish-Christian Interpretation of Esther 1 in John 2:1-11 and Mark 6:17-29.* BJS 150. Atlanta: Scholars Press, 1988.

Avigad, Nahman. *Discovering Jerusalem.* Oxford: Blackwell, 1984.

Avi-Yonah, Michael. *Gazetteer of Roman Palestine.* Qedem 5. Jerusalem: Institute of Archaeology, Hebrew University of Jerusalem, 1976.

Badke, W. B. "Was Jesus a Disciple of John?" *EvQ* 62 (1990) 195-204.

Bahat, Dan with Chaim T. Rubinstein. *The Illustrated Atlas of Jerusalem.* Translated by Shlomo Ketko. New York: Simon & Schuster, 1990.

Bammel, Ernst. "The Baptist in Early Christian Tradition." *NTS* 18 (1971-72) 95-128.

Barnett, P. W. "The Jewish Sign Prophets — A.D. 40-70: Their Intentions and Origin." *NTS* 27 (1980-81) 679-97.

Barrett, C. K. "Apollos and the Twelve Disciples of Ephesus." In *The New Testament Age: Essays in Honor of Bo Reicke,* edited by William C. Weinrich, 29-39. Macon, GA: Mercer University Press, 1984.

Barton, John. *Oracles of God: Perceptions of Ancient Prophecy in Israel after the Exile.* London: Darton, Longman, and Todd, 1986.

Baumgarten, Albert I. "The Name of the Pharisees." *JBL* 102 (1983) 411-23.

Baumgarten, Joseph M. "The Pharisaic-Sadducean Controversies about Purity and the Qumran Texts." *JJS* 31 (1980) 157-70.

Beall, Todd S. *Josephus' Description of the Essenes Illustrated by the Dead Sea Scrolls.* SNTSMS 58. Cambridge: Cambridge University Press, 1988.

Beasley-Murray, G. R. *Baptism in the New Testament.* London: St. Martin's, 1962.

Becker, Jürgen. *Johannes der Täufer und Jesus von Nazareth.* BibS(N) 63. Neukirchen-Vluyn: Neukirchener Verlag, 1972.

Betz, Otto. "Was John the Baptist an Essene?" In *Understanding the Dead Sea Scrolls: A Reader from the Biblical Archaeology Review,* edited by Hershel Shanks, 205-14. New York: Random House, 1992. First published in *BR* (December 1990) 18-25.

Black, David Alan. "The Text of Mark 6.20." *NTS* 34 (1988) 141-45.

Black, Matthew. *An Aramaic Approach to the Gospels and Acts. With an Appendix on The Son of Man, by Geza Vermes.* 3d ed. Oxford: Clarendon, 1967.

———. *"Patristic Accounts of Jewish Sects." In The Scrolls and Christian Origins: Studies in the Jewish Background of the New Testament,* by Matthew Black, 48-74. London: Nelson, 1961.

Blenkinsopp, Joseph. "Prophecy and Priesthood in Josephus." *JJS* 25 (1974) 239-62.

Booth, Roger P. *Jesus and the Laws of Purity: Tradition History and Legal History in Mark 7.* JSNTSup 13. Sheffield: JSOT Press, 1986.

Boring, Eugene M. "The Criteria of Authenticity." *Forum* 1/4 (1985) 3-38.

Bornkamm, Gunther. *Jesus of Nazareth.* Translated by Irene and Fraser McLuskey with James M. Robinson. London: Hodder and Stoughton, 1960.

Bowker, John. *Jesus and the Pharisees.* Cambridge: Cambridge University Press, 1973.

Brandt, Wilhelm. *Die jüdischen Baptismen oder das Religiose Waschen und Baden im Judentum mit Einschluss des Judenchristentums.* BZAW 18. Giessen: Töpelmann, 1910.

Brawley, Robert L. *Luke-Acts and the Jews: Conflict, Apology, and Conciliation.* SBLMS 33. Atlanta: Scholars Press, 1987.

Bregman, M. "Another Reference to the Teacher of Righteousness in Midrashic Literature." *RevQ* 37 (1979) 97-100.

Bretscher, P. G. "Whose Sandals? (Matt. 3:11)." *JBL* 86 (1967) 81-87.

Broshi, Magen. "The Diet of Palestine in the Roman Period — Introductory Notes." *IMJ* 5 (1986) 41-56.

Brown, Francis, S. R. Driver, and C. A. Briggs. *A Hebrew and English Lexicon of the Old Testament.* Oxford: Clarendon, 1975.

Brown, Raymond E. *The Birth of the Messiah: A Commentary on the Infancy Narratives in Matthew and Luke.* London: Chapman, 1977.

———. *The Gospel According to John I–XII.* AB 29. Garden City, NY: Doubleday, 1966.

———. *The Gospel According to John XIII–XXI.* AB 29A. Garden City, NY: Doubleday, 1970.

———. "John the Baptist in the Gospel of John." *CBQ* 22 (1960) 292-98.

Brownlee, W. H. "John the Baptist in the New Light of Ancient Scrolls." In *The Scrolls and the New Testament,* edited by Krister Stendahl, 33-53. New York: Harper, 1957. First published in *Int* 9 (1955) 71-90.

Bruce, F. F. *The Acts of the Apostles: Greek Text with Introduction and Commentary.* 3d rev. ed. Grand Rapids: Eerdmans, 1990.

———. *Jesus and Christian Origins Outside the New Testament.* London: Hodder & Stoughton, 1974.

Büchler, Adolf. "The Levitical Impurity of the Gentile before the Year 70." *JQR* 17 (1926-27) 1-81.

———. *Das Synedrion in Jerusalem und das Grosse Beth-Din in der Quaderkammer des Jerusalemischen Tempels.* Vienna: Alfred Hölder, 1902.

Bullough, Vern L. *The History of Prostitution.* New Hyde Park, NY: University Books, 1964.

Bultmann, Rudolf. *The History of the Synoptic Tradition.* Translated by John Marsh. Oxford: Blackwell, 1963.

Bussmann, W. *Synoptische Studien.* Halle: Buchhandlung des Waisenhaures, 1925.

Cameron, Peter Scott. *Violence and the Kingdom: The Interpretation of Matthew 11:12.* ANTJ 5. Frankfurt: Lang, 1984.

Cartlidge, David R. and David L. Dungan, eds. *Documents for the Study of the Gospels.* Philadelphia: Fortress, 1980.

Casey, P. M. "General, Generic, and Indefinite: The Use of the Term 'Son of Man' in Aramaic Sources and in the Teaching of Jesus." *JSNT* 29 (1987) 21-56.

———. *Son of Man: The Interpretation and Influence of Daniel 7.* London: SPCK, 1979.

———. "The Use of the Term בר (א)נש(א) in the Aramaic Translation of the Hebrew Bible." *JSNT* 54 (1994) 87-118.

Catchpole, David R. "The Beginning of Q: A Proposal." *NTS* 38 (1992) 205-21.

Charlesworth, James H. *Jesus within Judaism: New Light from Exciting Archaeological Discoveries.* ABRL. New York: Doubleday, 1988.

———, ed. *The Old Testament Pseudepigrapha.* 2 vols. Garden City, NY: Doubleday, 1983-85.

———, ed. with Mark Harding and Mark Kiley. *The Lord's Prayer and Other Prayer Texts from the Greco-Roman Era.* Valley Forge, PA: Trinity Press International, 1994.

Chilton, Bruce D. *A Galilean Rabbi and His Bible: Jesus' Use of the Interpreted Scripture of His Time.* GNS 8. Wilmington, DE: Glazier, 1984.

———. *The Isaiah Targum: Introduction, Translation, Apparatus, and Notes.* ArBib 11. Wilmington, DE: Glazier, 1987.

———. "Jesus *ben David:* Reflections on the *Davidssohnfrage.*" *JSNT* 14 (1982) 88-112.

———. *Judaic Approaches to the Gospels.* Atlanta: Scholars Press, 1994.

——— and Craig A. Evans, eds. *Studying the Historical Jesus: Evaluations of the State of Current Research.* NTTS 19. Leiden: Brill, 1994.

Christiansen, Ellen Juhl. *The Covenant in Judaism and Paul.* Leiden: Brill, 1995.

———. "Women and Baptism." *StudTheo* 35/1 (1981) 1-8.

Cohen, Shaye J. D. *From the Maccabees to the Mishnah.* LEC 7. Philadelphia: Westminster Press, 1987.

———. "The Rabbinic Conversion Ceremony." *JJS* 41 (1990) 177-203.

———. Review of *The ʿAm Ha-Aretz: A Study in the Social History of the Jewish People in the Hellenistic-Roman Period,* by Aharon Oppenheimer. *JBL* 97 (1987) 596-97.

———. "The Significance of Yavneh: Pharisees, Rabbis, and the End of Jewish Sectarianism." *HUCA* 55 (1984) 27-53.

Collins, John J. *The Scepter and the Star: The Messiahs of the Dead Sea Scrolls and Other Ancient Literature.* ABRL. New York: Doubleday, 1995.

———. "The Son of Man in First Century Judaism." *NTS* 38 (1992) 448-66.

Collins, John N. *Diakonia: Re-Interpreting the Ancient Sources.* New York: Oxford University Press, 1990.

Connolly, R. Hugh. *Didascalia Apostolorum: The Syriac Version Translated and Accompanied by the Verona Latin fragments, with an Introduction and Notes.* Oxford: Clarendon, 1929.

Crossan, John Dominic. *The Historical Jesus: The Life of a Mediterranean Jewish Peasant.* San Francisco: HarperSan Francisco, 1991.

———. *Jesus: A Revolutionary Biography.* San Francisco: HarperSan Francisco, 1994.

Crown, A. D. and L. Cansdale. "Qumran: Was it an Essene Settlement?" *BAR* 20/5 (1994) 24-35, 73-78.

Dauphin, C. "Er-Ramthaniyye: Surveying an Early Bedouin Byzantine Pilgrimage Centre in the Golan Heights." *BAIAS* 8 (1989-90) 82-85.

Davies, S. L. "John the Baptist and Essene Kashruth." *NTS* 29 (1983) 569-71.

Dibelius, Martin. *Die urchristliche Überlieferung von Johannes dem Täufer.* FRLANT 15. Göttingen: Vandenhoeck & Ruprecht, 1911.

Dodd, C. H. *The Founder of Christianity.* New York: Macmillan, 1970.

———. *Historical Tradition in the Fourth Gospel.* Cambridge: Cambridge University Press, 1963.

Donahue, John R. "Recent Studies in the Origin of 'Son of Man' in the Gospels." *CBQ* 48 (1986) 484-98.

Dunn, James D. G. *Jesus and the Spirit: A Study of the Religious and Charismatic Experience of Jesus and the First Christians as Reflected in the New Testament.* Philadelphia: Westminster, 1975.

———. "Pharisees, Sinners, and Jesus." In *The Social World of Formative Christianity and Judaism: Essays in Tribute to Howard Clark Kee,* edited by Jacob Neusner et al., 263-69. Philadelphia: Fortress, 1988.

Dupont, J. "L'ambassade de Jean-Baptiste (Matthieu 11,2-6; Luc 7,18-23)." *NRT* 83 (1961) 805-21, 943-59.

Dupont-Sommer, Andre. *The Jewish Sect of Qumran and the Essenes: New Studies on the Dead Sea Scrolls.* Translated by R. D. Barnett. London: Vallentine, 1954.

Eisler, Robert. *The Messiah Jesus and John the Baptist according to Flavius Josephus' Recently Rediscovered 'Capture of Jerusalem' and the Other Jewish and Christian Sources.* London: Methuen, 1931.

Enslin, Morton S. "John and Jesus." *ZNW* 66 (1975) 1-18.

Epstein, I., ed. *The Babylonian Talmud.* Translated into English with Notes, Glossary, and Indices. 30 vols. London: Soncino, 1972-84.

Ernst, Josef. *Johannes der Täufer: Interpretation, Geschichte, Wirkungsgeschichte.* BZNW 53. Berlin: de Gruyter, 1989.

Evans, Craig A. "Jesus in Non-Christian Sources." In *Studying the Historical Jesus: Evaluations of the State of Research,* edited by Bruce D. Chilton and Craig A. Evans, 443-78. NTTS 19. Leiden: Brill, 1994.

———. "Opposition to the Temple: Jesus and the Dead Sea Scrolls." In *Jesus and the Dead Sea Scrolls,* edited by James H. Charlesworth, 235-53. ABRL. New York: Doubleday, 1992.

Faierstein, M. "Why do the Scribes say that Elijah Must Come First?" *JBL* 100 (1981) 75-86.

Feldman, Louis H. "Prophets and Prophecy in Josephus." *JTS* 41 (1990) 386-422.

———. "Some Observations on the Name of Palestine." *HUCA* 61 (1990) 1-23.

Ferguson, John. *Greek and Roman Religion: A Source Book.* Park Ridge, NJ: Noyes, 1980.

Ferris, Stephen. *The Hymns of Luke's Infancy Narratives: Their Origin, Meaning and Significance.* JSNTSup 9. Sheffield: JSOT Press, 1985.

Finkel, Asher. *The Pharisees and the Teacher of Nazareth: A Study of Their Background, Their Halachic and Midrashic Teachings, Their Similarities and Differences.* Leiden: Brill, 1964.

Finkelstein, Louis. *The Pharisees: The Sociological Background of their Faith.* 2d rev. ed. Philadelphia: Jewish Publication Society of America, 1940.

Fischler, S. "Social Stereotypes and Historical Analysis: The Case of the Imperial Women at Rome." In *Women in Ancient Societies: An Illusion of the Night,* edited by Leonie J. Archer, Susan Fischler, and Maria Wyke, 115-33. New York: Routledge, 1994.

Fitzmyer, Joseph A. "Another View of the Son of Man Debate." *JSNT* 4 (1979) 58-68.

———. *The Gospel according to Luke I–IX: Introduction, Translation, and Notes.* AB 28. Garden City, NY: Doubleday, 1981.

———. "More about Elijah Coming First." *JBL* 104 (1985) 295-96.

Flemington, W. F. *The New Testament Doctrine of Baptism.* London: SPCK, 1948.

Flusser, David. "The Baptism of John and the Dead Sea Sect." In *Essays on the Dead Sea Scrolls: In Memory of E. L. Sukenik,* edited by C. Rabin and Y. Yadin, 209-38. Jerusalem: Hekhal Ha-Sefer, 1961. (Hebrew)

———. *Judaism and the Origins of Christianity.* Jerusalem: Magnes, 1988.

———. "Two Anti-Jewish Montages in Matthew." *Immanuel* 5 (1975) 37-45.

Ford, J. Massynberde, *Revelation: Introduction, Translation, Commentary.* AB 38. Garden City, NY: Doubleday, 1975.

Fraade, Steven D. "Ascetical Aspects of Ancient Judaism." In *Jewish Spirituality from the Bible through the Middle Ages,* edited by Arthur Green, 253-88. World Spirituality 13. New York: Crossroad, 1986.

Fuller, Reginald H. *The Mission and Achievement of Jesus: An Examination of the Presuppositions of New Testament Theology.* London: SCM, 1954.

Geyser, A. S. "The Youth of John the Baptist: A Deduction from the Break in the Parallel Account of the Lucan Infancy Story." *NovT* 1 (1956) 70-75.

Gibson, J. "Hoi Telōnai kai hai Pornai." *JTS* 32 (1981) 429-33.

Gnilka, J. "Das Martyrium Johannes des Täufers (Mk 6,17-29)." In *Orientierung an Jesus: Zur Theologie der Synoptiker,* edited by Paul Hoffmann with Norbert Brox and Wilhelm Pesch, 78-93. Freiburg: Herder, 1973.

Goguel, Maurice. *Au seuil de l'évangile: Jean-Baptiste.* Paris: Payot, 1928.

Golb, Norman. "Khirbet Qumran and the Manuscripts of the Judaean Wilderness: Observations on the Logic of Their Investigation." *JNES* 49 (1990) 103-114.

———. "The Problem of Origin and Identification of the Dead Sea Scrolls." *PAPS* 124 (1980) 1-24.

———. "Who Hid the Dead Sea Scrolls?" *BA* 48 (1985) 68-82.

———. *Who Wrote the Dead Sea Scrolls? The Search for the Secret of Qumran.* New York: Scribner, 1995.

Goodblatt, David. "The Place of the Pharisees in First Century Judaism: The State of the Debate." *JSJ* 20 (1989) 12-30.

Goodman, Martin. *The Ruling Class of Judaea: The Origins of the Jewish Revolt Against Rome, A.D. 66-70.* Cambridge: Cambridge University Press, 1987.

Grabbe, Lester. *Judaism from Cyrus to Hadrian.* 2 vols. Minneapolis: Fortress, 1992.

Grant, Michael. *Jesus.* London: Weidenfeld and Nicolson, 1977.

Gray, Rebecca. *Prophetic Figures in Late Second Temple Jewish Palestine: The Evidence from Josephus.* Oxford: Oxford University Press, 1993.

Guillaumont, A., H.-Ch. Puech et al., eds. and trans. *The Gospel according to Thomas: Coptic Text Established and Translated.* Leiden: Brill, 1959.

Haenchen, Ernst. *The Acts of the Apostles: A Commentary.* Philadelphia: Westminster, 1971.

———. *Der Weg Jesu: Eine Erklärung des Markus-Evangeliums und der kanonischen Parallelen.* Berlin: de Gruyter, 1968.

Hamm, D. "Luke 19:8 Once Again: Does Zacchaeus Defend or Resolve?" *JBL* 107 (1988) 431-37.

———. "Zacchaeus Revisited Once More: A Story of Vindication or Conversion?" *Bib* 72 (1991) 249-52.

Harrington, Hannah K. *The Impurity Systems of Qumran and the Rabbis: Biblical Foundations.* SBLDS 143. Atlanta: Scholars Press, 1993.

Hayward, R. "Phinehas — The Same as Elijah: The Origins of a Rabbinic Tradition." *JJS* 29 (1978) 22-34.

Hengel, Martin. *The Charismatic Leader and His Followers.* Edinburgh: Clark, 1981.

———. *Judaism and Hellenism: Studies in Their Encounter in Palestine during the Early Hellenistic Period.* 2 vols. London: SCM, 1973-74.

———. *Die Zeloten.* 2d ed. Leiden: Brill, 1976.

——— and R. Deines. "E. P. Sanders' 'Common Judaism,' Jesus and the Pharisees." JTS 46 (1995) 1-70.

Herrenbrück, Fritz. *Jesus und die Zöllner: Historische und Neutestamentlich-exegetische Untersuchungen.* WUNT 2/41. Tübingen: Mohr-Siebeck, 1990.

Hill, D. "'Our Daily Bread' (Mt. 6.11) in the History of Exegesis." *IBS* 5 (1983) 2-10.

Hills, J. V. "Luke 10:18 — Who Saw Satan Fall?" *JSNT* 46 (1992) 25-40.

Hoehner, Harold W. *Herod Antipas.* SNTSMS 17. Cambridge: Cambridge University Press, 1972.

Hoffman, Paul. *Studien zur Theologie der Logienquelle.* 2d ed. NTAbh 8. Münster: Aschendorff, 1975.

Holladay, William L. *A Concise Hebrew and Aramaic Lexicon of the Old Testament.* Grand Rapids: Eerdmans, 1971.

Hollenbach, Paul W. "The Conversion of Jesus: From Jesus the Baptizer to Jesus the Healer." In *ANRW.* Volume II.25.1. Edited by H. Temporini and W. Haase, 196-219. Berlin: de Gruyter, 1982.

———. "John the Baptist." In *The Anchor Bible Dictionary.* Volume 3, H–J. Edited by David Noel Freedman, 887-99. New York: Doubleday, 1992.

———. "Social Aspects of John the Baptist's Preaching Mission in the Context of Palestinian Judaism." In *ANRW.* Volume II.19.1. Edited by H. Temporini and W. Haase, 850-75. Berlin: de Gruyter, 1979.

Hooker, Morna D. "On Using the Wrong Tool." *Theo* 75 (1972) 570-81.

Horsley, Richard A. "High Priests and the Politics of Roman Palestine: A Contextual Analysis of the Evidence in Josephus." *JSJ* 17 (1986) 23-55.

———. *Jesus and the Spiral of Violence: Popular Jewish Resistance in Roman Palestine.* San Francisco: Harper & Row, 1987.

———. "'Like One of the Prophets of Old': Two Types of Popular Prophets at the Time of Jesus." *CBQ* 47 (1985) 435-63.

———. "Popular Messianic Movements around the Time of Jesus." *CBQ* 46 (1984) 471-95.

———. "Popular Prophetic Movements at the Time of Jesus, Their Principal Features and Social Origins." *JSNT* 26 (1986) 3-27.

——— and John S. Hanson. *Bandits, Prophets, and Messiahs: Popular Movements in the Time of Jesus.* Minneapolis: Winston, 1985.

Hughes, John H. "John the Baptist: The Forerunner of God Himself." *NovT* 14 (1972) 191-218.

Hunter, A. M. *The Work and Words of Jesus.* Philadelphia: Westminster, 1950.

Ilan, T. "The Attraction of Aristocratic Women to Pharisaism during the Second Temple Period." *HTR* 88 (1995) 1-33.

Janowski, B. and Lichtenberger, H. "Enderwartung und Reinheitsidee: Zur eschatologischen Deutung von Reinheit und Sühne in der Qumrangemeinde." *JJS* 34/1 (1983) 31-62.

Jastrow, Marcus. *A Dictionary of the Targumim, the Talmud Bavli and Yerushalmi, and the Midrashic Literature.* 2 vols. New York: Pardes, 1950.

Jenkins, I. and D. Williams. "Sprung Hair Nets: Their Manufacture and Use in Ancient Greece." *AJA* 89 (1985) 411-18.

Jeremias, Joachim. *Infant Baptism in the First Four Centuries.* Translated by David Cairns. London: SCM, 1960.

———. *New Testament Theology: The Proclamation of Jesus.* Translated by John Bowden. London: SCM, 1971.

———. *The Prayers of Jesus.* SBT 2/6. London: SCM, 1967.

Josephus. *Against Apion.* With an English translation by H. St. J. Thackeray. Josephus in Nine Volumes. Volume 1. LCL. Cambridge, MA: Heinemann, 1926.

———. *Jewish Antiquities.* With an English translation by H. St. J. Thackeray, Ralph Marcus, Allen Wikgren, and Louis H. Feldman. Josephus in Nine Volumes. Volumes 4–9. LCL. Cambridge, MA: Heinemann, 1930-65.

———. *The Jewish War.* With an English translation by H. St. J. Thackeray. Josephus in Nine Volumes. Volumes 2–3. LCL. Cambridge, MA: Heinemann, 1927-28.

———. *The Life [and] Against Apion.* With an English translation by H. St. J. Thackeray. Josephus in Nine Volumes. Volume 1. LCL. Cambridge, MA: Heinemann, 1926.

Käsemann, Ernst. "The Disciples of John the Baptist in Ephesus." In *Essays on New Testament Themes,* 136-48. Translated by W. J. Montague. SBT 41. London: SCM, 1964.

Kazmierski, Carl R. *John the Baptist: Prophet and Evangelist.* Collegeville, MN: The Liturgical Press/Michael Glazier, 1996.

———. "The Stones of Abraham: John the Baptist and the End of Torah (Matt. 3,7-10 par. Luke 3,7-9)." *Bib* 68/1 (1987) 22-40.

Keck, Leander E. "The Spirit and the Dove." *NTS* 17/1 (1970) 41-67.

Kilgallen, John J. "John the Baptist, the Sinful Woman, and the Pharisee." *JBL* 104 (1985) 675-79.

Kimelman, Reuven, "The *Birkat Ha-Minim* and the Lack of Evidence for an Anti-Christian Jewish Prayer in Late Antiquity." In *Jewish and Christian Self-Definition. Volume Two: Aspects of Judaism in the Graeco-Roman Period,* edited by E. P. Sanders (Philadelphia: Fortress, 1981) 226-44.

Kinman, Brent. "Luke's Exoneration of John the Baptist." *JTS* 44/2 (1993) 595-98.

Kirchhevel, G. D. "He that Cometh in Mark 1:7 and Matt. 24:30." *BBR* 4 (1994) 105-12.

Kittel, Gerhard and Gerhard Friedrich, eds. *Theological Dictionary of the New Testament.* 10 vols. Translated and edited by Geoffrey W. Bromiley. Grand Rapids: Eerdmans, 1964-76.

Klausner, Joseph. *The Messianic Idea in Israel, from Its Beginning to the Completion of the Mishnah.* Translated from the 3d Hebrew edition by W. F. Stinespring. London: Allen and Unwin, 1956.

Kloppenborg, John S. *The Formation of Q: Trajectories in Ancient Wisdom Collections.* Philadelphia: Fortress, 1987.

Knibb, Michael A. *The Qumran Community.* Cambridge Commentaries on Writings of the Jewish and Christian World, 200 BC to AD 200. Cambridge: Cambridge University Press, 1987.

Kraeling, Carl H. *John the Baptist.* New York: Scribner, 1951.

de Lacey, D. R. "In Search of a Pharisee." *TynBul* 43 (1992) 353-72.

Lachs, Samuel T. *A Rabbinic Commentary on the New Testament: The Gospels of Matthew, Mark, and Luke.* Hoboken, NJ: KTAV, 1987.

Lambrecht, Jan. "John the Baptist and Jesus in Mark 1.1-15: Markan Redaction of Q?" *NTS* 38/3 (1992) 357-84.

Lampe, G. W. H. *The Seal of the Spirit: A Study in the Doctrine of Baptism and Confirmation in the New Testament and the Fathers.* London: Longmans, 1951.

Laufen, Rudolf. *Die Doppelüberlieferungen der Logienquelle und des Markusevangeliums.* BBB 54. Bonn: Hanstein, 1980.

Lichtenberger, Hermann. "The Dead Sea Scrolls and John the Baptist: Reflections on Josephus' Account of John the Baptist." In *The Dead Sea Scrolls: Forty Years of Research,* edited by Devorah Dimant and Uriel Rappaport, 340-46. STDJ 10. Leiden: Brill, 1992.

———. "Johannes der Täufer und die Texte von Qumran." In *Mogilany 1989: Papers on the Dead Sea Scrolls Offered in Memory of Jean Carmignac,* edited by Zdzislaw J. Kapera, 139-52. Qumranica Mogilanensia 2. Krakow: Enigma, 1991, vol 1.

———. "Reflections on the History of John the Baptist's Communities." *FolOr* 25 (1988) 45-49.

———. "Täufergemeinden und frühchristliche Täuferpolemik im letzten Drittel des 1. Jahrhunderts." *ZTK* 84 (1987) 36-57.

———. "Die Texte von Qumran und das Urchristentum." *Jud* 50 (1994) 68-82.

Liddell, Henry George and Robert Scott. *A Greek-English Lexicon with a Supplement.* Revised and edited by H. Stuart Jones and R. McKenzie. 9th ed. Oxford: Clarendon, 1968.

Lim, Timothy H. "The Qumran Scrolls: Two Hypotheses." *SR* 21/4 (1992) 455-66.

Lindars, Barnabas. *Jesus, Son of Man: A Fresh Examination of the Son of Man Sayings in the Gospels in the Light of Recent Research.* Grand Rapids: Eerdmans, 1983.

Linnemann, Eta. "Jesus und der Täufer." In *Festschrift für Ernst Fuchs,* edited by Gerhard Ebeling, Eberhard Jüngel, and Gerd Schunack, 219-36. Tübingen: Mohr-Siebeck, 1973.

Lohmeyer, Ernst. *Das Urchristentum 1: Johannes der Täufer.* Göttingen: Vandenhoeck & Ruprecht, 1932.

Lohse, Ernst. "συνέδριον." In *Theological Dictionary of the New Testament.* Vol. 7, Σ, 860-71. Edited by Gerhard Friedrich. Translated and edited by Geoffrey W. Bromiley. Grand Rapids: Eerdmans, 1971.

Lowe, M. "From the Parable of the Vineyard to a Pre-Synoptic Source." *NTS* 28 (1982) 257-63.

———. "Who Were the *Ioudaioi*?" *NovT* 18 (1976) 101-30.

Lupieri, E. *Giovanni Battista fra Storia e Leggenda.* BCR 53. Brescia: Paideia, 1988.

Macmullen, Ramsay. *Enemies of the Roman Order: Treason, Unrest, and Alienation in the Empire.* Cambridge, MA: Harvard University Press, 1966.

Maimonides. *The Book of Cleanness.* Translated by Herbert Danby. New Haven: Yale University Press, 1954.

Manson, T. W. *The Teaching of Jesus: Studies of Its Form and Content.* 2d ed. Cambridge: Cambridge University Press, 1943.

Mantel, Hugo. *Studies in the History of the Sanhedrin.* Cambridge, MA: Harvard University Press, 1961.

Marcus, Joel. "Jesus' Baptismal Vision." *NTS* 41 (1995) 512-21.

Marshall, I. H. *The Gospel of Luke.* NIGTC. Grand Rapids: Eerdmans, 1978.

Mason, Steve N. "Chief Priests, Sadducees, Pharisees and Sanhedrin in Acts." In *The Book of Acts in Its Palestinian Setting,* edited by Richard Bauckham, 115-77. BAFCS 4. Grand Rapids: Eerdmans, 1995.

———. "Fire, Water and Spirit: John the Baptist and the Tyranny of Canon." *SR* 21/2 (1992) 163-80.

———. *Flavius Josephus on the Pharisees: A Composition-Critical Study.* StudPost-Bib 39. Leiden: Brill, 1991.

———. "Josephus on the Pharisees Reconsidered: A Critique of Smith/Neusner." *SR* 17/4 (1988) 455-469.

———. "Pharisaic Dominance before 70 CE and the Gospels' Hypocrisy Charge (Matt. 23:2-3)." *HTR* 83/4 (1990) 363-81.

———. "Priesthood in Josephus and the 'Pharisaic Revolution.'" *JBL* 107 (1988) 657-61.

———. Review of *Prophetic Figures in Late Second Temple Jewish Palestine: The Evidence from Josephus,* by Rebecca Gray. *IOUDAIOS Review* (electronic) 4.006 (February 1994).

McDonnell, K. "The Baptism of Jesus in the Jordan and the Descent into Hell." *Worship* 69 (1995) 98-109.

———. "Jesus' Baptism in the Jordan." *TS* 56 (1995) 209-36.

McLaren, James S. *Power and Politics in Palestine: The Jews and the Governing of Their Land 100 BC–AD 70.* JSNTSup 63. Sheffield: JSOT Press, 1991.

Meier, John P. "John the Baptist in Josephus: Philology and Exegesis." *JBL* 111/2 (1992) 225-37.

———. "John the Baptist in Matthew's Gospel." *JBL* 99/3 (1980) 383-405.

———. *A Marginal Jew: Rethinking the Historical Jesus.* 2 vols. ABRL. New York: Doubleday, 1991-94.

Menken, M. J. J. "The Quotation from Isa. 40, 3 in John 1, 23." *Bib* 66/2 (1985) 190-205.

Merklein, Helmut. "Die Umkehrpredigt bei Johannes dem Täufer und Jesus von Nazaret." *BZ* 25/1 (1981) 29-46.

Michaels, J. Ramsey. "Paul and John the Baptist: An Odd Couple?" *TynBul* 42/2 (1991) 245-60.

Milgrom, Jacob. *Leviticus 1–16: A New Translation with Introduction and Commentary.* AB 3. New York: Doubleday, 1991.

Millar, Fergus. "Hagar, Ishmael, Josephus and the Origins of Islam." *JJS* 45 (1993) 23-45.

———. "Reflections on the Trials of Jesus." In *A Tribute to Geza Vermes: Essays on Jewish and Christian Literature and History,* edited by Philip R. Davies and Richard T. White, 355-81. JSOTSup 100. Sheffield: JSOT Press, 1990.

Miller, Robert J. "Elijah, John, and Jesus in the Gospel of Luke." *NTS* 34/4 (1988) 611-22.

Mitchell, Alan C. "Zacchaeus Revisited: Luke 19,8 as a Defense." *Bib* 71/2 (1990) 153-76.

Montefiore, C. G. *Rabbinic Literature and Gospel Teachings.* London: Macmillan, 1930.

Mowery, Robert L. "Pharisees and Scribes, Galilee and Jerusalem." *ZNW* 80 (1989) 266-68.

Murphy-O'Connor, Jerome. *The Holy Land: An Archaeological Guide from Earliest Times to 1700.* Rev. ed. Oxford: Oxford University Press, 1992.

———."John the Baptist and Jesus: History and Hypothesis." *NTS* 36 (1990) 359-74.

Neusner, Jacob. "The Feminization of Judaism: Systemic Reversals and Their Meaning in the Formation of the Rabbinic System." *ConJud* 45 (1994) 37-52.

———. "First Cleanse the Inside: The Halakhic Background of a Controversy Saying." *NTS* 22 (1976) 486-95.

———. "From Exegesis to Fable in Rabbinic Traditions about the Pharisees." *JJS* 25 (1974) 263-69.

———. *A History of the Mishnaic Law of Purities.* 14 vols. SJLA. Leiden: Brill, 1974-77.

———. *The Idea of Purity in Ancient Judaism. With a Critique and a Commentary by Mary Douglas.* SJLA 1. Leiden: Brill, 1973.

———. "Josephus' Pharisees — A Complete Repertoire." In *Josephus, Judaism, and Christianity,* edited by Louis H. Feldman and Gohei Hata, 274-92. Detroit: Wayne State University Press, 1987.

———. *The Judaic Law of Baptism: Tractate Miqva'ot in the Mishnah and the Tosephta. A Form-Analytical Translation and Commentary, and a Legal and Religious History.* First published as *A History of the Mishnaic Law of Purities,* vols. 13 and 14. Atlanta: Scholars Press, 1995.

———. *A Life of Rabban Yohanan ben Zakkai.* 2d ed. Leiden: Brill, 1970.

———. *The Mishnah: A New Translation.* New Haven: Yale University Press, 1988.

———. "Mr Maccoby's Red Cow, Mr Sanders' Pharisees, and Mine." *JSJ* 23 (1992) 81-98.

———. "Mr Sanders' Pharisees and Mine." *BBR* 2 (1992) 143-69.

———. "Mr Sanders' Pharisees and Mine: A Response to E. P. Sanders, *Jewish Law from Jesus to the Mishnah.*" *SJT* 44 (1991) 73-95.

———. "Pharisaic Law in New Testament Times." *USQR* 26 (1971) 331-40.
———. "'Pharisaic-Rabbinic' Judaism: A Clarification." *HR* 12/3 (1972) 250-70.
———. *The Rabbinic Traditions about the Pharisees before 70.* 3 vols. Leiden: Brill, 1971.
———. *Reading and Believing: Ancient Judaism and Contemporary Gullibility.* BJS 13. Atlanta: Scholars Press, 1986.
———. *The Transformation of Judaism: From Philosophy to Religion.* Urbana: University of Illinois Press,1992.
——— and Bruce D. Chilton. "Uncleanness: A Moral or an Ontological Category in the Early Centuries A.D.?" *BBR* 1 (1991) 63-88.
———, Peder Borgen et al., eds. *The Social World of Formative Christianity: Essays in Tribute to Howard Clark Kee.* Philadelphia: Fortress, 1988.
Newport, K. G. C. "The Pharisees in Judaism Prior to A.D. 70." *AUSS* 29 (1991) 127-37.
Nineham, Dennis E. *The Gospel of St Mark.* Harmondsworth: Penguin, 1963.
Noth, Martin. *The Deuteronomistic History.* JSOTSup 15. Sheffield: JSOT Press, 1981.
Oepke, A. "βάπτω, etc." In *Theological Dictionary of the New Testament.* Vol. 1, A–Γ, 529-46. Edited by Gerhard Friedrich. Translated and edited by Geoffrey W. Bromiley. Grand Rapids: Eerdmans, 1974.
Oppenheimer, Aharon. *The 'Am Ha-Aretz: A Study in the Social History of the Jewish People in the Hellenistic-Roman Period.* Translated by I. H. Levine. ALGHJ 8. Leiden: Brill, 1977.
Pines, Shlomo. *An Arabic Version of the Testimonium Flavianum and Its Implications.* Jerusalem: Israel Academy of Sciences and Humanities, 1971.
Pocknee, C. E. "The Archaeology of Christian Baptism." *Theo* 74 (1971) 309-11.
Puech, E. "Une apocalypse messianique (4Q521)." *RevQ* 15 (1992) 475-519.
Pusey, Karen. "Jewish Proselyte Baptism." *ExpTim* 95 (1984) 141-45.
Rajak, Tessa. *Josephus: The Historian and His Society.* London: Duckworth, 1983.
Reicke, Bo. "The Historical Setting of John's Baptism." In *Jesus, the Gospels, and the Church: Essays in Honor of William R. Farmer,* edited by E. P. Sanders, 209-24. Macon, GA: Mercer University Press, 1987.
Rengstorf, K. H. "μαθητής." In *Theological Dictionary of the New Testament.* Vol. 4, Λ–N, 415-61. Edited by Gerhard Friedrich. Translated and edited by Geoffrey W. Bromiley. Grand Rapids: Eerdmans, 1967.
Reumann, John. "The Quest for the Historical Baptist." In *Understanding the Sacred Text: Essays in Honor of Morton S. Enslin on the Hebrew Bible and Christian Beginnings,* edited by John Reumann, 181-99. Valley Forge, PA: Judson, 1972.
Rhoads, David M. *Israel in Revolution 66-74 C.E.: A Political History Based on the Writings of Josephus.* Philadelphia: Fortress, 1976.
Rivkin, Ellis. "Beth Din, Boule, Sanhedrin: A Tragedy of Errors." *HUCA* 17 (1975) 181-99.
———. "Defining the Pharisees: The Tannaitic Sources." *HUCA* 40-41 (1969-70) 205-49.

———. *A Hidden Revolution: The Pharisees' Search for the Kingdom Within.* Nashville: Abingdon, 1978.

———. "Josephus and Jesus." In *Jesus in History and Myth,* edited by R. Joseph Hoffman and Gerald A. Larue, 103-18. Buffalo: Prometheus, 1986.

———. "Locating John the Baptizer in Palestinian Judaism: Political Dimensions." SBLSP 22 (1983) 79-85.

———. "Scribes, Pharisees, Lawyers, Hypocrites: A Study in Symmetry." *HUCA* 49 (1978) 135-42.

Robinson, John A. T. "The Baptism of John and the Qumran Community: Testing a Hypothesis." In *Twelve New Testament Studies,* by John A. T. Robinson, 11-27. London: SCM, 1962.

———. "Elijah, John and Jesus: An Essay in Detection." In *Twelve New Testament Studies,* by John A. T. Robinson, 28-52. London: SCM, 1962.

Robinson, James M., ed. *The Nag Hammadi Library in English.* San Francisco: Harper & Row, 1977.

Rowland, Christopher. *The Open Heaven: A Study of Apocalyptic in Judaism and Early Christianity.* New York: Crossroad, 1982.

Rowley, H. H. "The Baptism of John and the Qumran Sect." In *New Testament Essays: Studies in Memory of Thomas Walter Manson, 1893-1958,* edited by A. J. B. Higgins, 218-29. Manchester: Manchester University Press, 1959.

———. "Jewish Proselyte Baptism and the Baptism of John." *HUCA* 15 (1940) 313-34.

Saldarini, Anthony J. *Pharisees, Scribes, and Sadducees in Palestinian Society: A Sociological Approach.* Wilmington, DE: Glazier, 1988.

Sanders, E. P. *The Historical Figure of Jesus.* London: Penguin, 1993.

———. *Jesus and Judaism.* Philadelphia: Fortress, 1985.

———. *Jewish Law from Jesus to the Mishnah: Five Studies.* London: SCM, 1990.

———. *Judaism: Practice and Belief 63 BCE–66 CE.* London: SCM, 1992.

———. *Paul.* Past Masters. Oxford: Oxford University Press, 1991.

Sandmel, Samuel. "Parallelomania." *JBL* 81 (1962) 1-13.

Saulnier, C. "Herode Antipas et Jean le Baptiste." *RB* 91 (1984) 362-76.

Scheffler, E. H. "The Social Ethics of the Lucan Baptist (Lk. 3:10-14)." *Neot* 24 (1990) 21-36.

Schenk, W. "Gefangenschaft und Tod des Täufers: Erwägungen zur Chronologie und ihren Konsequenzen." *NTS* 29/4 (1983) 453-83.

Schiffman, Lawrence H. *Reclaiming the Dead Sea Scrolls: The History of Judaism, the Background of Christianity, the Lost Library of Qumran.* Philadelphia/ Jerusalem: The Jewish Publication Society, 1994.

———. *Who was a Jew? Rabbinic and Halakhic Perspectives on the Jewish-Christian Schism.* Hoboken, NJ: KTAV, 1985.

Schillebeeckx, Edward. *Jesus: An Experiment in Christology.* Translated by Hubert Hoskins. New York: Seabury, 1979.

Schnackenburg, Rudolf. "Das vierte Evangelium und die Johannesjünger." *HJ* 77 (1958) 21-38.

———. *Baptism in the Thought of St. Paul: A Study in Pauline Theology.* Translated by G. R. Beasley-Murray. Oxford: Blackwell, 1964.

Schneemelcher, Wilhelm, ed. *New Testament Apocrypha.* 2 vols. Rev. ed. English translation edited by Robin McL. Wilson. Cambridge: Clarke, 1991-92.

Schürer, Emil. *The History of the Jewish People in the Age of Jesus Christ (175 B.C.–A.D. 135).* 3 vols.; vol. 3 in two parts. Revised and edited by Geza Vermes, Fergas Millar, Matthew Black, and Martin Goodman. Edinburgh: Clark, 1973-87.

Schürmann, Heinz. *Das Lukasevangelium.* 2 vols. HTKNT 3.1-2; Freiburg: Herder, 1969.

Schütz, Roland. *Johannes der Täufer.* ATANT 50. Zürich: Zwingli, 1967.

Schwartz, Daniel R. "Josephus and Nicolaus on the Pharisees." *JSJ* 14 (1983) 157-71.

———. *Studies in the Jewish Background of Christianity.* WUNT 60. Tübingen: Mohr-Siebeck, 1992.

Schweitzer, Albert. *The Quest of the Historical Jesus: A Critical Study of Its Progress from Reimarus to Wrede.* With a preface by F. C. Burkitt. Translated by W. Montgomery. 2d ed. London: Black, 1952.

Scobie, Charles H. H. *John the Baptist.* London: SCM, 1964.

Segal, Alan F. *Paul the Convert: The Apostolate and Apostasy of Saul the Pharisee.* New Haven: Yale University Press, 1990.

Shanks, Hershel, ed. *Understanding the Dead Sea Scrolls: A Reader from the Biblical Archaeology Review.* New York: Random House, 1992.

Skehan, Patrick W., Eugene Ulrich, and Judith E. Sanderson. *Qumran Cave 4: Palaeo-Hebrew and Greek Biblical Manuscripts.* DJD 9. Oxford: Oxford University Press, 1992.

Smallwood, E. Mary. *The Jews under Roman Rule: From Pompey to Diocletian.* SJLA 20. Leiden: Brill, 1976.

Smith, Morton. *Jesus the Magician.* San Francisco: Harper & Row, 1978.

———. "Palestinian Judaism in the First Century." In *Israel: Its Role and Civilization,* edited by Moshe Davis, 67-81. New York: Jewish Theological Seminary of America, 1956.

Sodini, J. P. "Les baptisteres byzantins: un éclairage sur les rites." *MB* 65 (1990) 45-47.

Sperber, Alexander, ed. *The Bible in Aramaic: Based on Old Manuscripts and Printed Texts.* vol. 4.B: *The Targum and the Hebrew Bible.* Leiden: Brill, 1992.

Stählin, G. "σάκκος." In *Theological Dictionary of the New Testament.* Vol. 7, Σ, 56-64. Edited by Gerhard Friedrich. Translated and edited by Geoffrey W. Bromiley. Grand Rapids: Eerdmans, 1971.

Stanton, Graham. *The Gospels and Jesus.* OxBib. Oxford: Oxford University Press, 1989.

Starcky, Jean. "Les quatres étapes du messianisme à Qumrân." *RB* 70 (1963) 481-505.

Steck, Odil Hannes. *Israel und das gewaltsame Geschick der Propheten: Untersuchungen zur Überlieferung des deuteronomistischen Geschichtsbildes im Alten Testa-*

ment, Spätjudentum und Urchristentum. WMANT 23. Neukirchen-Vluyn: Neukirchener Verlag, 1967.

Stegemann, Hartmut. "The 'Teacher of Righteousness' and Jesus: Two Types of Religious Leadership in Judaism at the Turn of the Era." In *Jewish Civilization in the Hellenistic-Roman Period,* edited by Shemaryahu Talmon. JSPSup 10. Sheffield: JSOT Press, 1991.

Steinmann, Jean. *Saint John the Baptist and the Desert Tradition.* Translated by Michael Boyes. New York: Harper, 1958.

Strack, Hermann L. and Paul Billerbeck. *Kommentar zum Neuen Testament aus Talmud und Midrasch.* 6 vols. Munich: Beck, 1922-61.

Streeter, B. H. *The Four Gospels: A Study of Origins.* London: Macmillan, 1924.

Sutcliffe, E. F. "Baptism and Baptismal Rites at Qumran." *HeyJ* 1 (1960) 179-88.

Tatum, W. Barnes. *John the Baptist and Jesus: A Report of the Jesus Seminar.* Sonoma, CA: Polebridge, 1994.

Taylor, Justin. "The Coming of Elijah, Mt. 17,10-13 and Mk. 9,11-13: The Development of the Texts." *RB* 98/1 (1991) 107-19.

Taylor, Joan E. *Christians and the Holy Places: The Myth of Jewish-Christian Origins.* Oxford: Clarendon, 1993.

———. "A Graffito Depicting John the Baptist at Nazareth?" *PEQ* 119 (1987) 142-48.

———. "The Phenomenon of Early Jewish-Christianity: Reality or Scholarly Invention?" *VC* 44 (1990) 313-34.

Tcherikover, Victor. "Was Jerusalem a Polis?" *IEJ* 14 (1964) 61-78.

———. *Hellenistic Civilization and the Jews.* Translated by S. Applebaum. New York: Atheneum, 1982.

Telford, William R. "Major Trends and Interpretative Issues in the Study of Jesus." In *Studying the Historical Jesus: Evaluations of the State of Current Research,* edited by Bruce D. Chilton and Craig A. Evans, 33-74. NTTS 19. Leiden: Brill, 1994.

Theissen, Gerd. *Lokalkolorit und Zeitgeschichte in den Evangelien. Ein Beitrag zur Geschichte der synoptischen Tradition.* NTOA 8. Freiburg: Universitäts Verlag; Göttingen: Vandenhoeck & Ruprecht, 1989.

Thiering, Barbara. *Jesus the Man.* Sydney: Theological Explorations, 1992.

———. *Re-dating the Teacher of Righteousness.* Sydney: Theological Explorations, 1979.

———. *The Teacher of Righteousness, the Gospels and Qumran.* Sydney: Theological Explorations, 1981.

Thomas, Joseph. *Le mouvement baptiste en Palestine et Syrie (150 av.J.C.–300 ap.J.C.).* Gembloux: Duculot, 1935.

Thomas, J. C. "The Fourth Gospel and Rabbinic Judaism." *ZNW* 82 (1991) 159-82.

Tilly, Michael. *Johannes der Täufer und die Biographie der Propheten. Die synoptische Täuferüberlieferung und das jüdische Prophetenbild zur Zeit des Täufers.* BWANT 137. Stuttgart: Kohlhammer, 1994.

Torrance, T. F. "Proselyte Baptism." *NTS* 1 (1954) 150-54.

Tov, Emanuel. "Proto-Samaritan Texts and the Samaritan Pentateuch." In *The Samaritans,* edited by Alan D. Crown. Tübingen: Mohr-Siebeck, 1989.

Trilling, W. "Die Täufertradition bei Matthäus." *BZ* 3 (1959) 271-89.

Turner, M. "The Spirit of Prophecy and the Power of Authoritative Preaching in Luke-Acts: A Question of Origins." *NTS* 38/1 (1992) 66-88.

VanderKam, James C. "The Dead Sea Scrolls and Christianity." In *Understanding the Dead Sea Scrolls: A Reader from the Biblical Archaeology Review,* edited by Hershel Shanks, 181-202. New York: Random House, 1992.

———. "The People of the Dead Sea Scrolls: Essenes or Sadducees." In *Understanding the Dead Sea Scrolls: A Reader from the Biblical Archaeology Review,* edited by Hershel Shanks, 50-62. New York: Random House, 1992.

Vermes, Geza. *The Dead Sea Scrolls in English.* 2d ed. Harmondsworth: Penguin, 1975.

———. *The Dead Sea Scrolls in English,* 4th ed. Harmondsworth: Penguin, 1995.

———. *The Gospel of Jesus the Jew.* London: SCM, 1981.

———. *Jesus the Jew: A Historian's Reading of the Gospels.* 2d ed. London: SCM, 1983.

———. *Jesus and the World of Judaism.* London: SCM, 1983.

———. *The Religion of Jesus the Jew.* London: SCM, 1993.

———. *Scripture and Tradition in Judaism: Haggadic Studies.* StudPost-Bib 4. Leiden: Brill, 1961.

———. "The Son of Man Debate." *JSNT* 1 (1978) 19-32.

———. "The Use of בר נשא/בר נש in Jewish Aramaic." In *An Aramaic Approach to the Gospels and Acts,* edited by Matthew Black, 310-28. 3d ed. Oxford: Clarendon, 1967.

——— and Martin Goodman. *The Essenes according to the Classical Sources.* OCT 1. Sheffield: JSOT Press, 1989.

Vögtle, Anton. *Die sogenannte Taufperikope Mk 1,9-11. Zur Problematik der Herkunft und des ursprünglichen Sinns.* EKKNT/Vorarbeiten 4, 105-39. Zürich: Benzinger, 1972.

von Wahlde, Urban C. "The Johannine 'Jews': A Critical Survey." *NTS* 28/1 (1982) 33-60.

Webb, Robert L. "The Activity of John the Baptist's Expected Figure at the Threshing Floor (Matthew 3.12 = Luke 3.17)." *JSNT* 43 (1991) 103-11.

———. "John the Baptist and His Relationship to Jesus." In *Studying the Historical Jesus: Evaluations of the State of Current Research,* edited by Bruce D. Chilton and Craig A. Evans, 179-229. NTTS 19. Leiden: Brill, 1994.

———. *John the Baptizer and Prophet: A Socio-Historical Study.* JSNTSup 62. Sheffield: JSOT Press, 1991.

Weiss, H. F. "Φαρισαῖος B-C." In *Theological Dictionary of the New Testament.* Vol. 9, Φ–Ω, 35-48. Edited by Gerhard Friedrich. Translated and edited by Geoffrey W. Bromiley. Grand Rapids: Eerdmans, 1974.

Wellhausen, Julius. *Das Evangelium Lucae.* Berlin: Reimer, 1904.

Wilkinson, John, trans. *Jerusalem Pilgrims Before the Crusades.* Warminster: Aris & Phillips, 1977.

Wilson, A. N. *Jesus.* London: Sinclair-Stevenson, 1992.

Wink, Walter. "Jesus' Reply to John: Matt. 11:2-6/Luke: 18-23." *Forum* 5 (1989) 121-28.

———. *John the Baptist in the Gospel Tradition.* SNTSMS 7. Cambridge: Cambridge University Press, 1968.

Winston, David. "Philo and the Contemplative Life." In *Jewish Spirituality from the Bible through the Middle Ages,* edited by Arthur Green, 198-231. World Spirituality 13. New York: Crossroad, 1986.

Winter, Paul. "The Cultural Background for the Narratives in Luke I–II." *JQR* 45 (1954) 159-67, 230-42, 287.

———. "The Proto-Source of Luke 1." *NovT* 1 (1956) 184-99.

Wise, Michael O. and James D. Tabor. "The Messiah at Qumran." *BAR* 18/6 (1992) 60-63.

van der Woude, A. S. *Die Messianischen Vorstellungen der Gemeinde von Qumrân.* SSN 3. Assen: Van Gorcum, 1957.

Yarbro Collins, Adela. "The Origin of Christian Baptism." *StudLit* 19 (1989) 28-46.

Zeitlin, Solomon. "The Halaka in the Gospels and Its Relation to the Jewish Law in the Time of Jesus." *HUCA* 1 (1924) 357-63.

———. "A Note on Baptism for Proselytes." *JBL* 52 (1933) 78-79.

———. "The Pharisees and the Gospels." In *Solomon Zeitlin's Studies in the Early History of Judaism,* vol. 2, 292-343. New York: KTAV, 1974.

Ziesler, J. A. "Luke and the Pharisees." *NTS* 25 (1978-79) 146-57.

———. "The Removal of the Bridegroom." *NTS* 19 (1973) 190-94.

Index of Names

Index of Subjects

Index of Scripture and Other Ancient Writings

JEWISH WRITINGS

Rabbinic Writings

Qumran Scrolls

OTHER WRITINGS